BLOOD AND IRON

BLOOD AND IRON

From Bismarck to Hitler
the von Moltke Family's
Impact on German History

OTTO FRIEDRICH

HarperCollinsPublishers

HarperCollins books may be purchased for educational, business, or sales promotional use. For information please write: Special Markets Department, HarperCollins Publishers, Inc., 10 East 53rd Street, New York, NY 10022.

FIRST EDITION

Designed by Alma Hochhauser Orenstein

Maps by Paul Pugliese

Library of Cataloging-in-Publication Data

Friedrich, Otto.
    Blood and iron : from Bismarck to Hitler the von Moltke family's impact on German history / by Otto Friedrich.
    — 1st ed.
        p.   cm.
    Includes index.
    ISBN 0-06-016866-8
    1. Moltke family.   2. Moltke, Helmuth, Graf von, 1800–1891.   3. Moltke, Helmuth James, Graf von, 1907–1945.   4. Germany—History—1918–1945.
    5. Germany—History, Military—19th century.
    I. Title.
    DD219.M7F75   1995
    943.08'092'2—dc20   30.00   95-38436

96 97 98 99 ❖/RRD 10 9 8 7 6 5 4 3 2

To my grandchildren:
Julia, Anna, Lucy,
Joseph Martin, Charlie, and Benjamin

The great questions of the time are not decided by speeches and majority decisions . . . but by iron and blood.

—CHANCELLOR OTTO VON BISMARCK

Denk ich an Deutschland in der Nacht,
So hat's mich um den Schlaf gebracht. *
—HEINRICH HEINE

What is your objection to the style of my guide? Surely it can be well and carefully and interestingly done in that form. Often when I have come upon a heap of ruins I have thought, What may not have happened here! What events are connected with these remains! The guide-book form has just that advantage over a scientific inquiry, that the latter drags the reader mercilessly through dreary wastes of minute dissertation, while the former strolls pleasantly with him through the country, remarking only what is grand, attractive, and noteworthy. . . .

As I have remarked in my introduction, legends will not be excluded. . . .

—FIELD MARSHAL HELMUTH VON MOLTKE

---

* Louis Untermeyer translated this as "Nights when I think of Germany, /Sleep is impossible for me."

Contents

List of Illustrations

Preface

IN WRITING ABOUT THE VON MOLTKE FAMILY, I HAVE TRIED TO PORTRAY one of those Teutonic clans that have played such a significant part in German history, so I might as well report that I also have connections to one of these clans, not the von Moltkes but the von Bülows.

When I was eighteen years old and quite penniless, I spent the summer of 1947 working on the Chopin études in the Copenhagen home of a cousin of my father's, a professional violinist who called herself Gerda von Bülow. Even though she was married to a Danish schoolteacher whose name was not von Bülow, she clung to her maiden name, not, I think, out of feminist principle but out of inordinate pride in having been born a von Bülow.

This pride seems to be common among the von Bülows, and even more common among those who live on the fringes of the family, not quite entitled to use the aristocratic name. My father never actually called himself von Bülow, but he, too, took inordinate pride in the fact that his mother had been born Baroness Charlotte von Bülow, daughter of a judge on the German Supreme Court, and so he hung in his study a picture of the Bülow family coat of arms, fourteen golden balls arrayed in an inverted pyramid on a shield. He also took pride in the most "Prussian" aspects of a distinctly "Prussian" upbringing. When he had to have his tonsils out as a boy, he said, the doctor simply held up the gleaming scissors and said, "Now are you a brave German boy or are you somebody who cries and has to be put to sleep?" "What did you say?" I inquired, unable to imagine submitting willingly to a pair of scissors being thrust down one's throat. "I said I was a brave German boy," my father said, rather surprised at my squeamishness, "and that was that."

My father's pride encompassed the whole Bülow family, though perhaps concentrated on Prince Bernhard von Bülow, who served as the rather unsuccessful and unpopular imperial chancellor from 1900 to 1909. There were also several Generals von Bülow, all remembered mainly for failures and defeats. In musical circles, however, the most celebrated Bülows were Hans and Cosima. Hans was the eminent pianist and conductor who championed the music of Richard Wagner; Cosima, his wife, had the distinction of being the illegitimate daughter of Franz Liszt. She duly became the mistress and then the wife of Wagner. So the Bülows' admiration for Cosima honors a woman whose main accomplishment was to adorn one of their ancestors with the horns of a cuckold. Nonetheless . . .

"When Cosima was very old, she used to give musical salons in Berlin, and I went there," Gerda von Bülow told me with a pride almost beyond pride.

"How did you manage to get in?" I asked.

"I just went," she said, "and I said at the door, 'I am Gerda von Bülow.' So they let me in. And I said 'du' to Cosima." That use of the intimate pronoun to a grande dame in her eighties may seem a rather crude breach of Berlin etiquette, but Gerda had her reasons. "All Bülows call each other 'du,'" she said.

In retrospect, it seems a little odd for the Bülows to cling to Cosima, the haughty dowager of Bayreuth who so scandalously repudiated their family. (There lives in New York at this moment a Cosima von Bülow, so named by the Claus von Bülow, né Claus Borberg, who is celebrated mainly for being prosecuted for attempting to murder his wife.) It seems a little odd, in fact, for anyone to take great pride in the Bülow name. Apart from the inept chancellor, various inept generals, and the famous cuckold, what have the Bülows actually accomplished?

I was surprised to learn not long ago that there is a Bülow, Florida, about twenty miles north of Daytona Beach. An inquiry to the South Florida Historical Association brought me a clipping from an article reporting that nothing remains of the Bülow presence in Florida but "the extensive coquino ruins of the great sugar mill, several well preserved wells, a unique spring-house and the crumbling foundations of the formerly hospitable mansion." The first Bülow on these shores, according to the article by one E. H. Butts, was a Baron Joachim von Bülow, who had apparently been sent West by the elector of Württemberg "to establish the Lutheran Church in the Carolinas." His success in establishing the Lutheran church remains problematical, but Baron von Bülow established himself very comfortably in a mansion called Savannah on Meeting Street in Charleston, and there he prospered mightily. When his grandson, Major Charles

William Bülow, had a chance to buy Florida land in 1820, he acquired a tract of nearly 6,000 acres. Bringing 300 slaves from Charleston, the major cleared 1,500 acres for sugar cane, 1,000 acres for cotton, and smaller areas for rice and indigo. On his death at age forty-four, the estate passed to his son, John Joachim, who was studying in Paris when he learned of his inheritance. Returning to Florida, John Joachim built a fine library on his estate in the wilderness and played host to such notables as John James Audubon.

This idyllic existence ended in the Seminole War of 1835. Bülow had good commercial relations with the Seminoles and opposed government plans to ship the Indians west of the Mississippi. This prompted the arrival of a Major Putman at the head of a militia known as the Mosquito Roarers. Bülow welcomed the Mosquito Roarers with several rounds from a four-pounder cannon. The Mosquito Roarers outnumbered Bülow's defenders, however. They overran the plantation and took Bülow prisoner. Making the plantation their headquarters, Camp Bülow, they pursued an unsuccessful guerrilla campaign against the Seminoles. Major Putman soon fell wounded, and his ranks were depleted by dysentery and yellow fever. He finally withdrew to St. Augustine, forty miles away, abandoning the area around the Bülow plantation to the Seminoles' revenge. The plantation went up in flames in January 1836, a fire that could be seen all the way to St. Augustine.

Bülow returned heartsick to Paris, where he soon died, at only age twenty-six, and quite unaware that the great Franz Liszt had just acquired an infant daughter who would someday marry the ruined plantation owner's distant cousin Hans von Bülow.

While eminent German families like to claim at least some of the fame that belongs to distinguished musicians, they are less likely to boast of their connections to that more paradigmatic figure, the Nazi war criminal. Unlike too many of his colleagues, Friedrich von Bülow was actually arrested and put on trial for his role in the use of concentration-camp slave-laborers by the Krupp industrial empire. Bülow was sentenced to twelve years in prison, but he served only a fraction of that term. He later described his incarceration in Landsberg, the same prison where Adolf Hitler had been confined after the Munich putsch of 1923, as "one long sunlit holiday."

Perhaps, on reflection, Cosima wasn't so bad after all.

I

Prologue: Kreisau

Schloss Moltke at Kreisau

UNINHABITED FOR LONGER THAN MANY A LIFETIME, FIELD MARSHAL Helmuth von Moltke's country estate at Kreisau now stands in a sorry state of dilapidation and decay. The roof leaks, as it has for several decades, and so the elaborately painted ceilings of the ground-floor reception rooms have fallen in. The rows of windows lining the brown stucco facade are mostly broken or boarded up. The two captured French cannon that once stood by the front door are gone. The field marshal's so-called *Schloss* (castle) is surrounded by a high wire fence, for the nearby barns have served a Polish collective farm ever since the long-disputed province of Silesia was stripped from Germany in the upheavals at the end of World War II. From the circle of red-tiled white farm buildings, two chickens now emerge and strut across the dusty barnyard, their maneuvers over their terrain contested only by a pair of towheaded little boys belaboring a small yellow soccer ball. At the edge of the barns, the lilacs bloom.

I saw battle-corpses, myriads of them. Some other lilacs inspired Walt Whitman to write of the American Civil War at about the same time that Count Moltke acquired his estate as a reward for Prussia's shattering victory over the Austrians at Königgrätz (1866). Whitman perhaps saw more than the Prussians.

> And the white skeletons of young men, I saw them.
> I saw the debris and debris of all the slain soldiers of the war,
> But I saw they were not as was thought,
> They themselves were fully at rest, they suffer'd not,
> The living remain'd and suffer'd. . . .

Repairs are finally under way at the derelict *Schloss*, for the name of Moltke resounds proudly through two centuries of German history, and the heirs to that legacy are determined to honor it. But German history is divided against itself, and so is the legacy of Kreisau. If the name of Moltke represents the field marshal's successive triumphs over the Danes, the Austrians, and the French, victories that made possible the Prussian creation of the German empire of 1871, it also represents almost the exact opposite. The last Moltke to own this estate at Kreisau was the field marshal's great-great nephew, Count[1] Helmuth James von Moltke, who was destined to witness the terrible perversion of Prussian traditions under Adolf Hitler's Third Reich and who hated what he saw. In an age when honorable men lived in fear of the concentration camps, Helmuth James von Moltke began reaching out to form alliances with like-minded patriots who would work for the replacement of the Nazi dictatorship. Three times, they gathered here in Kreisau to chart the outlines of a post-Hitler Germany. In his efforts to maintain contact with Western diplomats, Moltke met several times with George F. Kennan, who was then chargé d'affaires at the U.S. Embassy in Berlin. Kennan was deeply impressed. "I consider him . . ." he wrote in his memoirs, "to have been the greatest person, morally, and the largest and most enlightened in his concepts, that I met on either side of the battle lines in the Second World War." Nazi Germany was no place for such a man. Almost inevitably, Moltke was arrested, prosecuted, and executed. He died just as Allied armies were pushing across the Rhine to liberate Germany from its Nazi masters.

So Kreisau, a village of about 500 souls, is now a shrine both to Germany's military past and to the rejection of that past. Is it not fitting, then, that this symbol of Germany's violent history should be located in what is now Poland, a nation that did not officially exist when Field Marshal Moltke acquired his estate? Kreisau is now called Kryzowa, and at a small fork in the road from Breslau (now Wroclaw, about thirty-five miles to the northeast), a drooping branch hides much of the only sign to Kreisau; the only visible evidence of the winding back road to the Moltke estate consists of a few letters: "zowa."

But at the boarded-up windows where the aged field marshal once looked out at his green park, the spring sunshine streams so brightly through the protective wooden slats that a visitor in April 1992 can see the skeletal framework of the empty interior. Six-inch-thick wooden beams and braces reach out in all directions, both horizontally and vertically. Any movement raises clouds of dust.

---

[1]Although he is often described as Graf or Count von Moltke, the title is technically not accurate. His widow, Freya von Moltke, explains: "In the German 'revolution' after World War I titles were canceled and became 'part of the name.'" In other words, people who had a title could continue to use it socially and in business, but it was not passed on to children. "In 'society,' this change was not accepted," Freya von Moltke continues, "and people tended to continue to call my husband 'Graf,' but legally we are only 'von Moltke,' and I personally tend not to use the title."

"This was the field marshal's private room," says Freya von Moltke, the widow of the executed Helmuth James, who abandoned the estate to the triumphant Soviet army in 1945 and took her two young sons to make a new home abroad, first in South Africa, then in Vermont. "He had his bed there, and his desk. And in that pretty alcove over there, he kept a perfectly round piece of porcelain for his wig. He had no hair, the field marshal, so he wore a wig."

A white-haired octogenarian, Freya von Moltke is making one of her periodic visits to Kreisau. She has emphatically renounced all family claims to the estate, but there are symbolic duties that call her here. The previous night, at the brown brick church of St. Nicholas in the nearby town of Brieg (now Brzeg), she attended the world premiere of a solemn oratorio by two Poles, Miroslaw Gasieniec and Janusz Telejko, drawn partly from her husband's political writings and entitled *Helmuth James von Moltke, Witness to Christ.* Now she is visiting Kreisau to consult with officials of the German-Polish foundation that has acquired the estate and begun the rebuilding. The German government has provided much of the money, and bare-chested young volunteers from places like Holland are providing much of the labor. The foundation is creating "a center for international peace and understanding," here amid the potato fields of Silesia, and Freya von Moltke wants to make sure that no angry ghosts of German nationalism make an unwelcome appearance in the rebuilt shrine.

And what of the elaborate military murals that once covered these walls—one showing the soldiers of Napoleon burning down the field marshal's childhood home in Lübeck, the other showing Moltke triumphant over Napoleon III on the battlefield of Sedan? "Those are covered with boards for now," says Freya von Moltke.

"Here! Here!" cries her sister-in-law, Veronica Jochum von Moltke, from the second floor, where she has just found a memento of the departed family. It used to be a custom for all the children in a household to take turns standing in a doorway once a year while the father measured their various heights at that particular moment. "Here is Helmuth James," says Veronica, a gifted pianist who married Helmuth James's younger brother Wilhelm after the war, in 1961. "He must have been one meter ninety," she goes on, stretching out one arm but barely able to reach the ancient pencil mark, "even when they left here in 1927." Height is another one of the Moltke traditions, and Helmuth James did indeed stand well over six feet tall.

"Nineteen twenty-eight," Freya von Moltke corrects her sister-in-law from the hallway. As the widow of the executed Helmuth James, she often plays the role of guardian of family traditions. It is an integral part of the Moltke family saga that the economic crises of the 1920s, which led to the rise of Adolf Hitler, impoverished the descendants of Germany's great military hero. Helmuth James's father frugally moved out of the field marshal's *Schloss* and into a nearby cottage known as the *Berghaus,* meaning mountain house. ("Mountain" is a rather relative term in Europe, but a few modest hills do rise from the richly green meadows and the golden fields of rape around Kreisau; the long terrace that used to extend along one side of the *Berghaus* provided a splendid view of the *Eulengebirge,* or Owl Mountains, along the nearby Czech frontier.)

"And here is Willo," says Veronica, pointing out the pencil mark that represents her late husband. "And Jowo," meaning Joachim Wolfgang, the second son and the only surviving one, an art historian now living in Switzerland. "And down here are the von Hülsens, who were younger." This is an intricate familial relationship. Helmuth James's aunt Lenore married a von Hülsen, and so did his brother Jowo. "But here was a swastika that somebody painted—" Among the pencil marks representing the young von Hülsens, there are signs of angry, vehement scraping, white scars that gleam in the surrounding shadows.

"Who did that?"

"Some Poles painted the swastika, I think," says Veronica. "They thought that all Germans were Nazis, and so since Germans lived here—but Freya had it all scratched out."

"I couldn't allow the *Hackenkreuz* in this house," Freya says from the hallway.

"And who lived in this other room here?" Veronica inquires, changing the subject.

"Aunts," says Freya. "There were always several aunts here."

The Moltkes were multitudinous—the field marshal was one of eight children, his father one of thirteen—and correspondingly impecunious. So the Reichstag honored Moltke's smashing victory over the Habsburg empire in 1866 by voting him the handsome sum of 200,000 thalers[2] to buy an estate worthy of his accomplishment. After

---

[2]Translating the nineteenth-century Prussian thaler into modern currency is not easy. The Federal Reserve Bank in New York and the International Monetary Fund in Washington both profess ignorance. At the founding of the German empire in 1871, the new mark was assigned a value of three to a thaler, and the mark long had a value of four to an American dollar, which derived from the same word. A survivor of those times estimates the purchasing power of the thaler and the dollar as about the same. Both the mark and the dollar have undergone upheavals since then, of course, and $200,000 today would not buy a very substantial estate.

searching in vain for a suitable place in his native Mecklenburg, where the Moltkes had owned land for some 500 years until the field marshal's grandfather lost it in the eighteenth century, Moltke also wandered in vain through his mother's neighboring homeland of Holstein, which he had captured from Denmark in the war of 1864. Finally, Moltke ventured back to Silesia, which he remembered fondly from his surveying expeditions as a young lieutenant, and also from his studies of the military campaigns of Frederick the Great. In 1867, he finally bought from a widow named von Dresky the rather remote establishment at Kreisau, just south of the fortress that King Frederick had besieged and captured at Schweidnitz. The Kreisau property, called Crisona in documents dating back to the year 1250, included the neighboring villages of Nieder-Gräditz and Wierischau, encompassing about 1,000 acres, which the field marshal promptly started cultivating and embellishing. "I shall have to build in spring," he wrote to his brother Adolf in January 1868. "The buildings are entirely of stone, but the house has only a shingle roof, and the roof-tree is rotting. Besides, I am going to lay out a park, in which bridges must be built, roads made, and 10,000 trees planted. I shall not live to walk in their shade, but there are some fine old oaks already. . . ." In that mood—the field marshal was already nearly seventy—he made it one of his first tasks to plan a mausoleum for himself and his wife. "I hope in the spring to finish a little vault for Marie and myself . . ." he wrote to Adolf at the end of 1868. "The mausoleum will be erected on the top of a small wooded hill near the house, from whence there is a wide and beautiful view of the estate and mountains. I hope to make the spot so attractive that everyone may be tempted to linger there."

If it was ironic that the old man still had more than twenty years to live, that he had not yet even conceived his greatest triumph, the destruction of the French imperial army at Sedan, it was no less so that he had lost his wife after their first summer in Kreisau. "I had always thought that Marie would do this for me," he wrote in the same letter to his brother about the building of a mausoleum, but now he described her lying in a nearby Catholic chapel. "Nothing more beautiful can be imagined than she looked after all was over, and the sweet and tranquil look on her face. . . ." And he did soon build a mausoleum on a nearby hill, for Marie and for himself. "Every time he went to the country his first walk was to her resting place, and he gathered flowers on the way to place on her coffin," one old friend recalled. "He never missed a day when at Kreisau without going there, and even in his old age he was never deterred by the worst weather." "There lies my wife," he said on one such visit, "there my sister, and here in the middle—is my place."

The field marshal was a man of habit. Every day he fed his pigeons; every day he read his Bible. And so he continued working on his plans for Kreisau. "At your next visit you will find that great progress has been made . . ." he wrote to Adolf the following summer. "The first-floor rooms are now very pretty and ready for the reception of guests. The entrance-room on the ground-floor, which is hung with granite-marble paper, forms a tastefully arranged hall. . . . In the autumn we must proceed again with the bridges and road-making. The landscape gardener was here yesterday. He has reserved for me, at Breslau, a number of conifers, which are to be planted out around the chapel and in front of the future burial-place. . . . The harvest is almost in, except the second crop of hay and the potatoes. . . . Grapes and greengages have also come in, but the greater part of the vines will, I fear, not ripen. We only had about a dozen peaches . . ."

One July afternoon in 1870, Moltke was driving through his fields in an open carriage with Adolf, Adolf's wife, Auguste, and their two young daughters, when a telegraph boy hailed him and handed him a telegram that summoned him to the greatest challenge of his life. Moltke read the telegram, silently put it in his pocket, and drove on. The relatives showed no surprise at this, for the laconic old soldier was celebrated as *"Der Grosse Schweiger"* ("The Great Mute") and—since he did know German, Danish, English, French, Italian, Russian, and Turkish—"a man who can be silent in seven languages." All he said to his brother when the carriage returned to the mansion an hour later was "It is a stupid thing; I have to go to Berlin tonight." He then went to his study and stayed there until teatime. At tea, he still said nothing until he suddenly rose to his feet, put his hand firmly on the table, and cried out, "Well, let them come . . . We are ready." He then retired to his study again, and it was only after his departure that his family learned that the telegram had been a royal summons to Berlin to oversee a mobilization against the threat of a French invasion.

Once Moltke had won that last campaign in France, he returned to Kreisau and wrote glowingly to another brother, Ludwig, about his progress: "The pine-apple house is ready, and the plants bought. . . . When you come next year, you will find the orchard house finished and 100 plants bearing fruit, and two fountains splashing in front of the veranda and the elm trees. The water has been conducted into the kitchen garden and the hot-houses, so that it is no longer necessary to drag every watering-can full up from the Peile [river]. In the garden round the little house on the hill, into which Aunt Auguste is going to remove presently, we have planted a nursery of more than 5,000 little oaks, besides which, a road will be made this autumn through the orchard . . ."

Nearly a decade later, he was complaining only of the lack of an audience. "If you wish to see Kreisau in full beauty, you ought to come soon," he wrote to Ludwig in May 1884. "The foliage is magnificent; not a cockchafer or a caterpillar has touched it. The meadows are covered with a first cutting of hay, and it is to be carried tomorrow. The hawthorn is in full blossom, and a thousand buds are opening on the rose-trees by the chapel. And none of you are here to whom to show all this splendor! My wine-cellar is well filled, and four carriage horses are there for driving out. . . ."

Here the old soldier lived to see his ninetieth birthday (his nephew, a middle-aged army officer also named Helmuth, served him as aide-de-camp and companion, though other relatives also spent protracted periods at Kreisau). He had, of course, been remarkably old when he achieved his great victories—seventy on the day the French surrendered at Sedan. His monarch, William I, had been even older, sixty-four when he first succeeded his mentally unbalanced brother to the Prussian throne in 1861, and seventy-three when the French empire collapsed (Chancellor Bismarck was a mere fifty-five when he negotiated Napoleon's surrender at Sedan). Moltke continued to serve as chief of staff (and member of the Reichstag) for almost another two decades, retiring only when the nonagenarian kaiser died in 1888. Bismarck, believing himself indispensable, tried to remain chancellor indefinitely, first under Frederick III, who was already dying of throat cancer, and then under young William II. Bismarck could hardly believe that a fledgling monarch of twenty-nine would dare to dismiss the statesman who had united Germany and ruled it for decades. In that, he lacked the perspicacity of the kaiser's maternal grandmother, Queen Victoria of England, who described him as "such a hot-headed, conceited, and wrong-headed young man." The willful new kaiser seems to have enjoyed outwitting his venerable chancellor. To an aide, he observed: "I shall let the old man snuffle on for six months, then I shall rule myself." Bismarck actually snuffled on for a year and a half, taking months-long vacations on his country estate, largely ignoring both the kaiser and the rest of the government. When it came to the final quarrel in March 1890, the kaiser had it said that the seventy-five-year-old chancellor was resigning because of poor health. Bismarck promptly went out riding through the streets of Berlin and said of his health: "I am better than I have been for years."

It is hard not to suspect that Moltke, tending his doves and watching his plum trees grow in Kreisau, did not feel a twinge of *Schadenfreude* at the dismissal of his old rival, but perhaps not. He was a genuinely virtuous man, and besides, old age does sometimes bring the serenity of indifference. "One must have seen him walking under his beloved trees," according to one contemporary chronicle, "a slim figure in a simple coat, bent a little forward, with a step which remained light and elastic up to his latest years. His clean-shaven face, of a delicate pallor, showed scant traces of advancing age. . . . His whole appearance was full of dignity and refinement, and his whole countenance illuminated by the purity of a long life, which nothing base had ever marred."

The field marshal's ninetieth birthday was a national holiday. Schools and offices closed; dozens of official delegations came to render homage. Moltke himself attended the official celebration in Berlin, watched the torchlit parades, and listened to endless speeches. There was even a telegram of congratulations from the Habsburg emperor Franz Joseph, whose defeat by Moltke at Königgrätz in 1866 had excluded Austria from the future German Reich.

When it came planting time at Kreisau the following spring, Moltke was still at work in Berlin, at his handsome apartment in the General Staff headquarters building on the Königsplatz, just across from the Reichstag. He was finishing a report on the fortification of the North Sea island of Helgoland, and as soon as he turned that in to the kaiser, he said to Chancellor Georg Caprivi, he planned to take the waters at Bad Schlangenbad to cure an irritation of his skin. On Friday, April 24, 1891, he woke up at his customary hour of 7:30 A.M. His nephew recalled that he "was lively and seemed well." After breakfast, the nephew added: "His mind was very active, as it usually was, and he . . . told me that it would be necessary for him to go today to the Upper House to vote on the industrial measures." After walking home in mid-afternoon, the field marshal had dinner with his nephew and the nephew's wife, Liza, and some Swedish houseguests named Marcher. Also present was an old friend and musician named Friedrich Dressler, who said he had suddenly felt a strong impulse to visit Moltke. He asked the nephew, who was an ardent cellist, if they could play some duets, and so they decided to make their first attempt at Chopin's rather challenging Sonata in G minor. After dinner, the nephew recalled, the field marshal "was in excellent humor, and said playfully to Herr Dressler that he had listened to us without our knowing it, and that we had made horrible work of the music." At about nine o'clock, they adjourned to the whist table, where the field marshal was delighted to make a grand slam.

"As we were playing the last rubber," the nephew later wrote, "Uncle Helmuth, who was dealing, suddenly stopped. He laid his cards on the table, leaned back in his chair, and seemed to have difficulty in breathing. Liza asked him: 'Have you asthma, Uncle Helmuth?' Upon which he answered: 'Yes, I have a little asthma.' I said to him: 'Please, Uncle Helmuth, let me deal for you.' He pushed the cards to me and I dealt . . . We then continued the game, and Liza and I were well beaten; he thus won in grand style the last rubber he played. He drummed with his fingers on the table. . . .

"Liza asked him now, if he was well again, which he answered in the negative. We knew these attacks of asthma from which he had suffered from time to time during the last ten years. We had witnessed them a hundred times, and they had always passed over after he had sat still for a few minutes. But as he looked very pale, Liza was anxious and said to him: 'Uncle Helmuth, don't you think we had better stop?'"

The field marshal immediately agreed. At the settling of accounts, the old man found he had lost two pfennigs to his nephew and wife. The wife offered him a glass of wine, but he declined. Lamps were lit on the grand piano in an adjoining room for Dressler to provide some more music. Liza urged Moltke to remain seated at the card table, but he objected: "No, that won't do. If he is going to play for me, I must be there." With that, he rose and went to the music room. "Uncle Helmuth sat down on a chair which stood close to the door . . ." the nephew recalled, "his folded hands clasping his red handkerchief. He was dressed in a military coat which he wore unbuttoned, a white waistcoat, old gray trousers, and leather slippers; round his neck he had tied a gray silk handkerchief. This was the only relaxation in his dress that he ever allowed himself, and that only in his family circle. I asked Herr Dressler what music I should give him, but he said that he would play without music, and began a composition of his own, which, however, was of such a melancholy character that I was quite concerned. . . ."

Dressler had somewhat different memories of this moment. "I cannot play from any [music] tonight; I will try to improvise," he said, according to his memoir, *Moltke in His Home,* which also includes a printed page of his improvisation, a rather lugubrious threnody in G minor entitled *Die Letzte Melodie (The Last Melody).* "I glanced again at the dear old gentleman, and then began with a few soft chords, and from this a melody unfolded itself. My heart was heavy within me at this moment, little as I dreamed that this would be the last time he would ever listen to me. I was just about to stop playing when I noticed that the Field-Marshal slowly got up and with bent carriage left the room. . . ."

"He had left the door half open, the room itself was dark," Helmuth von Moltke recalled. "I stopped for a moment at the door and listened. I knew that Uncle Helmuth did not like us to attach too much importance to these asthmatical attacks and weary him with attentions, and I was hesitating whether to go to him or not, when I heard a faint groaning. . . . [Liza] said: 'Do go in and see if anything is the matter with Uncle Helmuth.' At the same moment we heard a deep sigh, and I went quickly into the room, which was almost dark. However, I could see Uncle Helmuth on a chair, his elbows supported on his knees, his body bent forward. I stepped to him and asked him: 'Uncle Helmuth, are you ill?' whereupon he raised his head and said: 'What?' in a voice so gentle that I shall never forget it. I became alarmed; I felt his forehead; it was cold; his hands the same. Again I cried out: 'Uncle Helmuth, are you ill?' But this time he did not answer. I cried out to Liza to bring a light, and supported Uncle Helmuth's head. It lay heavily in my hand, and at the same time it appeared to me that his whole body relaxed its tension and suddenly collapsed . . . as if it were no longer necessary for him to hold himself up; it was as if he thought: 'Now I can give way, as the others are there to help me.'"

They carried the old field marshal to his military camp bed, got his clothes off, and covered him with a blanket. He lay quietly, breathing deeply, his hands folded, but he never spoke another word. "Once it seemed as if consciousness was returning," the nephew recorded. "He made a movement as if to raise his head, then he turned it gently to the left towards the wall where the portrait of his beloved wife hung surrounded by palms. And as his eyes, already dimmed by the shadow of death, seemed to search for the features of her who had been his companion in days gone by, his spirit passed away gently and peacefully, to rest at last." It was about 9:45 P.M., barely ten minutes after the whist playing ended, when the nephew bent over and closed his uncle's eyes. By the time a Dr. Beuster arrived, he could only confirm that Moltke had died of a "lesion of the heart."

It was inevitably an occasion for imperial commemoration. The kaiser broke off a state visit to the Duke of Saxe-Weimar and summoned all the kings and princes of Germany to join him in Berlin for a great state funeral. Crowds began gathering outside the Moltke residence on the Königsplatz, where the field marshal's body lay in state, surrounded by battle flags from the imperial palace. The Empress Augusta had already sent a wreath of white roses. The kaiser, who had been visiting the Wartburg Castle, where the fugitive Martin Luther had hidden while he translated the Bible into German, hurried back to Berlin and drove directly from the railroad station to the Moltke residence. He asked to be left alone with Moltke, who lay shrouded in a white cloth, his hands folded on his chest.

The next day, lesser visitors began shuffling through. The body now lay in a coffin of polished oak, supported by gilded lions' feet. The walls were hung with black draperies; tall tapers glowed over palms and wreaths of roses. At each corner of the catafalque stood a tall officer of the General Staff, with drawn sword. And so everything remained until the morning of Tuesday, April 28, when princes and generals crowded around the kaiser to hear the funeral sermon delivered by the imperial army's Field-Provost D. Richter. He took as his point of departure the fact that Moltke read in his Bible every day, and so he had a recitation from the field marshal's Bible of the 90th Psalm, which reflects on the transience of all things mortal: "For all our days are passed away in thy wrath: we spend our years as a tale that is told. The days of our years are threescore years and ten; and if by reason of strength they be fourscore years, yet is their strength labour and sorrow; for it is soon cut off, and we fly away. Who knoweth the power of thine anger? Even according to thy fear, so is thy wrath. So teach us to number our days, that we may apply our hearts unto wisdom. . . ."

This psalm was traditionally considered a prayer by the aged Moses, and Richter insisted that Moltke was a comparable figure. "We too stand by the bier of a patriarch of his people, a prophet of modern times, a leader in times of trouble to the glory of a new kingdom," said Richter. "Next to his own people who mourn the departed, the venerable head of their family, stands our Emperor, as chief mourner . . . who has not only lost a most faithful servant but in him an Army. And with the Emperor mourn the German princes, the German army, the German nation. . . . All are united by one great grief and one desire to honour this great son of the Fatherland, 'our Moltke,' and to thank God Almighty with all our hearts for having given him to us."

In trying to assess the field marshal's character, the speaker offered a number of possibilities. "What was the secret of this blessed life, what was the secret of the wonderful strength which did not leave him though he was in his ninety-first year? Was it nature or was it the grace of God? Was it his rich deep mind or the iron energy of his will? The great work of his success in life? Was it the self-command or the unselfishness of his character? His many-sidedness or his reserved nature?" In answering that, Richter quoted Hamlet's tribute to his slain father: "He was a man, take him for all in all,/I shall not look upon his like again."

"He was a man, and let us add a Christian," Richter said to the kaiser and his retinue of officers, to the friends and relatives standing with bowed heads. "There lay the secret of his strength. To be temperate even in overwhelming success, to remain modest and simple at the zenith of glory, to triumph and yet—to be silent, that is possible only to him whose strength is not of this earth. . . . Even on his death-bed, [he] is triumphant for the last time over the last enemy, whom he never feared because he could say, 'Thanks be to God, who giveth us the victory through our Lord Jesus Christ.'

"He lives amongst us, even in us, though he is gone away," the preacher concluded, referring not to Christ but to Moltke. "He will live in the Army and in the Nation as the embodied spirit of truth and strength, discipline and temperance." The final display of those virtues, though, was left to the kaiser and his generals, and so they proceeded to stage one of the most spectacular military parades in many years. It did not cover a great deal of ground—the distance from the Königsplatz to the Lehrter Railroad Station was only a few blocks—but into that ground, they packed all the symbolic power they could summon. As soon as the benediction had been pronounced, an honor guard of officers carried Moltke's coffin down the stairs to the waiting hearse, drawn by six black-draped horses from the royal stables. As Moltke's body was loaded aboard, together with his plumed helmet, sword, baton, and various insignia, the regimental flags lining the street were lowered, bands began playing a mournful march, and troops started filing past, four squadrons of cavalry with banners fluttering on their lances, a battalion of Foot Guards, three batteries of artillery, twenty General Staff officers bearing cushions holding the dead man's medals and decorations.

It was a beautiful day, fresh and clear and breezy. On the balcony over the main entrance to the general staff headquarters, the empress and several of her young sons stood watching the vast procession take shape and get under way. Troops lined every step of the route; behind them stood the silent crowds. Everywhere there were emblems of Moltke's victories. The procession started out into the center of the Königsplatz, winding its way around the immense *Sieges Säule*, or victory column, a 200-foot tower of dark red granite, ornamented on its base by bronze bas reliefs of the battles against the Danes, the Austrians, and the French; here, too, stood three rows of cannon captured from the three defeated armies.

Behind the troops with their plumes and pennants came a dense regiment of official mourners, starting with the kaiser and the king of Saxony, with Moltke's nephew walking between them. Then, all arrayed three abreast, came the grand dukes of Baden, Hesse, and Saxe-Weimar, a long column of Germanic princelings, foreign ambassadors, Reichstag and Prussian legislators, generals, admirals, Knights of the Black Eagle, student representatives. The only important figure missing, it was widely noted, was Bismarck, who remained sulking on his country estate, contributing only a wreath and a message of condolences to the Moltke family. Up the crowded Alsen Strasse (commemorating one of the victories over the Danes), the mourners marched, all to the accompaniment of muffled drums and brass, then left onto the Kronprinzen Ufer along the banks of the Spree, then across the flower-bedecked Moltke Bridge to the Lehrter Railroad Station. While the troops drew up and presented arms before the black-draped station, a battery of artillery fired a thunderous final salute.

II

The Field Marshal

Helmuth Carl Bernhard von Moltke
(1800-1891)

Otto von Bismarck
(1815-1898)

1

"No Education but Thrashing"

FIGURES LIKE COUNT HELMUTH CARL BERNHARD VON MOLTKE DO NOT just appear out of nowhere. The Moltkes thread back through centuries of German history to a time when Germany hardly existed. "In the year 1164," according to the field marshal's own account of his origins, "Henry the Lion, Duke of Bavaria [and Saxony], conquered the Obotrites, a tribe which lived in the region now known as the Grand Duchy of Mecklenburg. He founded there the Bishopric of Schwerin, and instituted judges and knights—who, of course, were not chosen from the conquered heathens, but from his own victorious men. As early as the year 1246 we find the name of Mattheus Moltke mentioned in the records, which are still in existence, as one of the 'knights.' . . . Not much later than this, however, we hear of the Moltkes in Sweden. . . ."

The mid-thirteenth century, when Mattheus Moltke's name first appeared on a knightly register, was scarcely a time for neat national boundaries. The Mongols were invading Poland under the leadership of Genghis Khan's grandson, Batu; the Council of Lyons deposed Frederick II as emperor, and work was just beginning on the Cologne cathedral and the Alhambra in Granada. As for the wilds of Mecklenburg, the son of Henry the Lion married a granddaughter of the slain Obotrite chieftain Niklot, and so Mecklenburg duly became the only German territory ruled by a family of Slavic origin.

At least some of the Moltke knights pressed northward into Scandinavia. "We hear of the Moltkes in Sweden, and again in Denmark," the field marshal's survey continues, "where . . . they held high and influential positions in State and Church." These are not places and times that figure largely in the Anglo-American sense of history. Knut the Great, who ruled over Denmark, England, and Norway, is remembered chiefly as the unhappy King Canute who could not command the incoming tide to halt. How much less do we know of the protracted wars between King Waldemar IV and the encroaching fleets of the North German Hansa?

The Moltkes achieved an eminence in the north long before the field marshal imposed his name on the history of Prussia. One of them, Margaretha Moltke, married Christiern Nils Vasa in 1412 and thus became an ancestor of the Vasas who rose to the throne of Sweden in 1523. In Denmark, the most famous of the tribe was Count Adam Gottlob Moltke (1710–1792), who became what the *Encyclopedia Britannica* calls "the inseparable companion" of King Frederick V, who "overwhelmed him with marks of favor." Adam Gottlob became both the unofficial prime minister and one of the largest landowners in Denmark, but when Frederick died in his arms in 1766, he was banished from court by the new King Christian VII, who denounced the lanky courtier as "stork below and fox above." Adam Gottlob was understandably a conservative, but when Denmark's absolute monarchy finally lurched toward representative government, it was Adam Wilhelm Moltke, Adam Gottlob's grandson, who presided over the cabinet that introduced the constitution of 1849.

Are the Moltkes then a basically German family that migrated into Scandinavia or a Danish family with some branches in Germany?

Alexandra Isles, an extremely pretty young actress who got a lot of unwanted publicity when Rhode Island prosecutors portrayed her as the motive for Claus von Bülow's attempts to murder his wife, hesitates over the answer. Her father, Count Carl Adam Moltke, worked for more than twenty years at the Danish Mission to the United Nations, and his father, also Carl Moltke, had been Danish foreign minister. She has named her own son Adam.

"All the men in the family are called Adam," she observes, pouring out a Coca-Cola. "Adam Gottlob was kind of a hero, and the founding father. There was something I wanted to find you that once appeared in Ripley's Believe it or Not. It said Adam Gottlob Moltke was the father of twenty-two sons, and five became cabinet ministers, four were ambassadors, two were generals—they all went into public service. I think that element of public service is a very interesting thing about the Danish Moltke family. And it came back in Helmuth James, who is one of my heroes. There is no higher sense of public service than he chose. . . ."

Pressed for the exact connection between the German and Danish families, Mrs. Isles offers a small red volume that she calls "the family tree." Published by Louis Bobé in Copenhagen in 1921, *Stamtavle over Slaegten Moltke* starts with handsome pictures of the Moltke coat of arms, a shield showing three male black grouse and a helmet surmounted by six peacock feathers. *"Slaegten Moltke føres af den fremragende meklenborgske Historiker G.C.F. Lisch lidet overbevisende tilbage . . ."* it begins, reporting that Moltke has been reported to be the Wendic name for the black grouse on the family crest. Bobé rejects this theory because, he says, the Wendic language has no such name for such a bird. Besides, says Bobé, the first Moltkes also called themselves Moltiko, Moltike, and Møltike. He suggests that these were all nicknames "for the old Germanic personal name Molt or Malte."

He identifies the first known Moltke as Fredericus Moltiko, who was apparently either the uncle or the nephew of the rival claimant, Mattheus. This Fredericus first appeared in 1254 as a witness confirming the grant of certain privileges to the town of Lübeck by Jarmora, prince of Mecklenburg (or Meklenborg, as this Danish account has it). His name appears in the next few years on several similar grants by Prince Johan of Mecklenburg, and then, in 1260, on the grant of *"Silderetten,"* or herring rights, by Prince Johan and his son Henrik to the town of Wismar. Such is our knowledge of Baltic history in the thirteenth century.

Bobé traces all the intertwining branches of the Danish Moltkes as far as an Ingeborg Margrethe, who died at the age of three months in Australia in 1895, but the field marshal's chronicle rather brusquely sweeps them all aside. "The male line of all these Swedish and Danish branches died out between 1440 and 1550 . . ." he wrote. The family seat, he declared, was an estate called Stridfeld, which belonged to a knight, Eberhard Moltke, as early as 1260. "Stridfeld, near Tessin in Mecklenburg, is the ancestral home of the whole race," he wrote; "it remained in the family for 500 years, and for sixteen generations up to the year 1781 . . . This love for a home, which was not situated in a beautiful country, is very remarkable, and affords a proof of their fidelity." The field marshal's account does not say what happened to Stridfeld in 1781, only that "the German Moltkes lost by degrees all their family estates, while the Danish had large possessions in Denmark."

The Danish Moltkes also lost at least some of their possessions. Alexandra Isles recalls that her descent passed through the eldest son of Adam Gottlob Moltke, "a scruffy-looking fellow who ran off to join Voltaire and dance on the Bastille, or whatever, and he got disinherited. So everybody had to work for a living after that. I remember we used to drive by one of the family estates, and my father would always moan and groan because there was this mile-long *allée* of beautifully clipped trees. But I think he would have had to drive the tractor, which I don't think he would have enjoyed." It was apparently to re-create such a palace, to regain the lost ancestral home at Stridfeld, that the field marshal acquired Kreisau and began planting trees. As early as 1848, long before he had ever seen Kreisau, he wrote to his brother Adolf: "My favorite thought is still, that by and by we may have a family gathering on an estate—I should prefer one in our dear German land."

The future German national hero was almost destined not to be a German at all. Before Prussia became a major military power under King Frederick the Great (1712–1786), an ambitious young man in northern Germany felt a magnetic attraction toward the Scandinavian powers. When Germany was tearing itself apart in the Thirty Years War, for example, Joachim Christoff von Moltke, the great-great-great grandfather of the future field marshal, joined the invading army of Denmark's King Christian IV. After the Danes withdrew in 1629, this particularly warlike Moltke went to Poland to join the forces of Sweden's King Gustavus Adolphus in continuing the ruinous war. Moltke showed exemplary courage at the Battle of Lützen, where Gustavus Adolphus was killed in 1632, and he retired only in 1646 as a war-weary colonel.

It was the ruthless brilliance of Frederick the Great that imposed a new kind of order—Prussian military order—on central Europe. Frederick began his troublesome career by simply stealing the wealthy province of Silesia from the Habsburgs, then defending his theft through seven years of warfare against the Austrians, Russians, and French. When exhaustion finally forced him to retire from the battle-field to a life of benevolent despotism, playing his flute and debating with Voltaire, little Prussia was generally conceded an upstart's place among the great powers of Europe.

Of the ten sons born to the future field marshal's grandfather, Friedrich Casimir Siegfried von Moltke, six served as officers in the Prussian army (two others joined the Mecklenburg army and two died in childhood). One of these young Prussian officers, Friedrich Philipp Victor von Moltke, was a second lieutenant when he fell in love with

Sophie Henriette Paschen, the daughter of a prosperous merchant in the German free city of Lübeck. He duly proposed and was accepted by the girl, but not by her father. Moltke immediately departed and went to stay with an older brother, Helmuth, who was the commanding officer in the nearby town of Parchim. "Soon after," the young lieutenant later wrote in a memoir for his children, "a messenger on horseback brought a letter from Frau Paschen to my brother, telling him that soon after my departure her daughter had fallen seriously ill and had declared she would marry no one but me. Her loving father was in great trouble and ready to give his consent if I were willing to return to them. I left . . . the following day, and the same evening we were betrothed. The Privy Councillor [Herr Paschen] made one condition, that I should leave the army and look after the estate. . . ." Moltke described his thirteen years in the Prussian army as "very happy ones," but he abandoned his military career in September 1796 and married Henriette the following May.

By then, under his father-in-law's orders, he had already begun an erratic new career as a gentleman farmer. "I had bought the fee-farm of Liebenthal near Wittstock, and we went there some days after our wedding," he wrote. "Here was born my eldest son Wilhelm, March 23, 1798, and on May 22, 1799, my second son Friedrich. Then I sold Liebenthal and we went to live at Parchim, a town in Mecklenburg-Schwerin, where my brother Helmuth was commander. A third son was born to me the same year, and I called him Helmuth after my brother. I did not think then that this son forty years later was destined to be my joy, my pride, and my benefactor."

New births kept alternating with new moves. Moltke bought the estate of Gnewitz in 1801, sold it in 1803 and moved to Lübeck, where his fourth son, Adolf, was born in 1804, and his fifth, Ludwig, in 1805. In that same year, he bought the estate of Augustenhof, in the neighboring province of Holstein. The run-down condition of this estate required him to build a new house there, so Henriette and her five young sons remained in her native Lübeck while Moltke supervised the progress of the building. Though Lübeck was a German free city, the province of Holstein was ruled by the king of Denmark, and Moltke's acquisition of the estate at Augustenhof required him to become a Danish subject. As with his abandonment of his army career, he acquiesced.

In this series of moves by the handsome young ex-officer, one can sense either weakness and indecisiveness or the simple incompetence of a professional soldier attempting to pursue a new career for which he had neither experience nor vocation. And in the ensuing difficulties, one can guess the reasons for a gradual estrangement between Moltke and his wife. She was a strong-willed and educated woman, proficient in music and foreign languages, and now she found herself caring for five young sons, largely by herself, while her husband struggled to master his third farm in less than ten years.

Of this increasingly unhappy relationship, we find just a few traces in the future field marshal's correspondence. "If only my father could rent and manage a farm," he wrote his mother many years later, in 1828. "But the worst of it is that the mischief is not so much in his ill-luck as in himself. . . ." Perhaps that is relevant to another letter of the same year, in which he tells his mother: "The thought of home is to me always mingled with fears and regrets." His mother's character, as well as her influence on her sons, can best be inferred from a letter she wrote in 1830: "May you ever more and more acknowledge the hand of God, even if He lay it on you in trial. A pure faith and firm confidence give courage and strength in every situation in life. What if we lack honors and temporal blessings? They are all perishable, and there is no permanent good but the consciousness of duty fulfilled. This may God grant you!"

It was Lübeck, the medieval capital of the Hanseatic League, that provided the young Moltke with his first strong sense of place. A nation in itself, its communal rights long ago guaranteed by Henry the Lion, Lübeck had waged war against both Denmark and Sweden in the sixteenth century, and all that maritime splendor echoed through its Gothic cathedral and the ramparts surrounding its city hall. When Frau von Moltke lived there with her five sons, so did Consul Johann Buddenbrook, so Thomas Mann's description of their house on Meng Street may give us some idea of the *bürgerlich* life in nineteenth-century Lübeck:

"The 'landscape-room' on the first floor of the rambling old house in Meng Street . . . was hung with heavy resilient tapestries put up in such a way that they stood well out from the walls. They were woven in soft tones to harmonize with the carpet, and they depicted idyllic landscapes in the style of the eighteenth century, with merry vinedressers, busy husbandmen, and gaily beribboned shepherdesses who sat beside crystal streams with spotless lambs in their laps. . . . For the size of the room, the furniture was rather scant. A round table, its slender legs decorated with fine lines of gilding, stood . . . by the wall opposite the little harmonium, on which lay a flute-case; some stiff arm-chairs were ranged in a row round the walls; there was a sewing table by the window, and a flimsy ornamental writing-desk laden with knick-knacks. . . . Cold weather had set in early. The leaves of the little lime-trees around the churchyard of St. Mary's, across the way, had turned yellow, though it was but mid-October. The wind whistled around the corners of the massive Gothic pile, and a cold thin rain was falling. . . ."

Overshadowing Lübeck, as he overshadowed all of Europe in those days, stood the terrifying (or inspiring) figure of Napoleon Bonaparte. The peace of Amiens (1802) seemed to impose an end to the great struggle between France and Britain, but Britain soon drew Austria, Russia, and Sweden into its third anti-French coalition (1805). Napoleon led his army across the Rhine and crushed the Austrians, first at Ulm, then at Austerlitz. He organized most of the Germanic princelings into the Confederation of the Rhine, though Prussia did its best to remain neutral, as did the free city of Lübeck. A series of French affronts, real and imagined, finally led Prussia's King Frederick William III to blunder into the conflict, and his blunder ended in the disastrous defeat at Jena in 1806. France now dominated all of Germany.

It is difficult to imagine today the fear and revulsion that French militarism aroused throughout much of Europe less than two centuries ago. To get a sense of it, listen for a moment to a sermon preached in Boston in 1810 by William Ellery Channing: "We live in times which have no parallel in past ages; in times when the human character has almost assumed a new form; in times of peculiar calamity, of thick darkness, and almost of despair. . . . In the very heart of Europe, in the centre of the civilized world, a new order has arisen, on the ruins of old institutions, peculiar in its character, and most ruinous in its influence. We here see a nation, which, from its situation, its fertility, and population, has always held a commanding rank in Europe, suddenly casting off the form of government, the laws, the habits, the spirit by which it was assimilated to surrounding nations, and by which it gave to surrounding nations the power of restraining it; and all at once assuming a new form, and erecting a new government, free in name and profession, but holding at its absolute disposal the property and life of every subject, and directing all its energies to the subjugation of foreign countries."[1]

[1]This splendid example of national stereotyping deserves attribution. It comes from the essay on General Jomini by Crane Brinton, Gordon Craig, and Felix Gilbert in *Makers of Modern Strategy, Military Thought from Machiavelli to Hitler*, edited by Edward Mead Earle, with Craig and Gilbert, 1943. They, in turn, found it reprinted in the *Christian Register* of August 1941, whose editors felt some need to emphasize their point by substituting "Hitler" and "Germany" for Channing's thoughts on Napoleon and France.

One of the few Prussian generals who fought creditably in the defeat at Jena was Gebhard von Blücher, who ended by leading his troops on a retreat northward. Lübeck still proclaimed its neutrality, but Blücher vowed to defend it, at whatever cost, against the advancing French. Three French columns totaling 60,000 men attacked the city and battled the Prussians from street to street until Blücher finally surrendered his last 4,000 infantrymen. Whatever remained intact after the battle, the French troops plundered.

Thomas Mann treated this all somewhat comically in *Buddenbrooks,* when Pastor Wunderlich recounts the French pillage of the city. "Well, imagine a November afternoon, cold and rainy, a wretched day. . . . Prince Blücher had gone, and the French were in the town. There was little outward sign of the excitement that reigned everywhere: the streets were quiet, and people stopped close in their houses. Prahl the master butcher had been shot through the head, just for standing at the door of his shop with his hands in his pockets and making a menacing remark about its being hard to bear. . . . At that very moment, whom should I see coming towards me but our honored Madame Buddenbrook herself? What a state she was in! Hurrying through the rain hatless, stumbling rather than walking, with a shawl flung over her shoulders, and her hair falling down. . . . 'What has happened?' [I asked.] 'What has happened!' she cried, all trembling. 'They've got at the silver, Wunderlich! That's what has happened! . . . They are stealing my spoons, Wunderlich, and I am going into the river!'"

The damage to the Moltke household was somewhat more serious than that. "For three days they pillaged the town," the field marshal's father later wrote. "My house was looted, which was a great loss to me. It was still worse at Augustenhof. . . . A fire broke out . . . and in half an hour the whole farm was the scene of a conflagration which raged for two days. Nothing was insured except the poor buildings. . . ."

What effect the French sack of Lübeck had on the young Helmuth von Moltke, who had just celebrated his sixth birthday, can be inferred from his lifelong animosity toward all things French. It is customary to belittle the effect of such personal feelings on the course of history, but the boarded-over murals on the walls of Kreisau suggest rather clearly the connection between the burning of Lübeck and the retribution that Moltke later exacted from the French on the battlefield of Sedan.

The loyalties of the Napoleonic era were more complicated than that, though. The elder Moltke's assumption of Danish citizenship in June 1806 not only extended that citizenship to his sons but made him subject to a Danish call to arms. Under French pressure, but also for reasons of their own, the Danes joined Napoleon's forces in warring against Britain, which responded by sending a fleet to cannonade the burghers of Copenhagen. Moltke, who was steadily going bankrupt as a gentleman farmer, now became a major in the Danish militia, taking command of a unit that he had organized himself. It seemed to him a kind of salvation from his life as an unsuccessful son-in-law. "As I could not expect to get on by farming my estate," he later wrote, "I had to hope for better luck in the army."

Moltke was ordered to unite his battalion with some Dutch units and pursue a retreating Prussian division across Mecklenburg to the Baltic port of Stralsund. To his dismay, his men refused to march beyond the Danish border, on the ground that they had only enlisted to defend their homeland. Moltke immediately demonstrated how marriage into the Lübeck bourgeoisie had deprived him of his true vocation as a Prussian officer. He ordered his mutinous troops drawn up in formation and then ordered his artillery to take aim at them with grapeshot. "Soldiers," Moltke declared, according to his own account, "I hear that some of you are disinclined to march across the frontier. . . . A soldier's disobedience to his king is punished by death; he who is disobedient out of cowardice loses what is of more value than his life—his honor. If you retreat, it will be over my corpse, for I at least have no mind to lose my honor. Loyalty then and obedience to our most gracious king! One, two, three, Hurrah!"

Under threat of execution, all dissenters gave way, Moltke said, and "I still thank God . . . that I was not placed under the dreadful necessity of shedding blood." His troops marched on to Stralsund, dispersed the fugitive Prussians, and earned from the king of Denmark a declaration that "your behavior has been a matter of rejoicing to me." The Danish army had no glorious role to play in the closing years of the Napoleonic campaigns, however, and Moltke spent most of his time at a series of garrison posts. By 1811, he was commandant at Kiel. "In the same year I took Fritz and Helmuth to the Military Academy at Copenhagen. . . ."

There is no indication that young Helmuth had any choice in the matter, for the military had obviously been his destiny since infancy. As a boy among brothers in a family of soldiers, he had grown up with games of combat, games played with little mercy and no acceptance of defeat. One of his Danish schoolmates, who later grew to be Lieutenant General von Hegermann-Lindencrone, recalled that his older brother Fritz spent hours in pseudo-combat with the Moltke brothers. "During the Christmas season in 1815, they constructed . . .

a temple-like building, surrounded by a battlemented wall in the shape of a bulwark. A path led up to the fortress, and up it the assailant had to go to take the castle, which was defended by the others. Both parties were equipped like real soldiers. Whether the assailant should go on or be compelled to retreat was decided by throwing dice; the game was called 'The road to the Temple of Honour.'"

More realistically belligerent was a game called "Pulsog," in which one team of players tried to knock a ball into a hole in the ground with their sticks while the other players used their sticks to stop them. "Once when Helmuth was trying to put his ball into the hole and my brother Fritz was trying to prevent it," the Danish general recalled, "the fight grew very violent, all the more so as both of them were very quick and nimble. The players were using some heavy sticks that day, which at one time had been used to defend solitary houses exposed to violence from wandering vagabonds. Just at the moment Helmuth was going to hit his ball into the hole . . . [my brother] hit Helmuth's head with such a powerful blow that the latter fell down unconscious. Our endeavors to bring him to were without success. We therefore carried him up to my room and sent out someone . . . to stop our doctor. . . . When he arrived, about three quarters of an hour after Helmuth had received the blow, he found him to be in a very dangerous condition, for Helmuth had given no sign of life and looked like a dead person. At last after some treatment he began to breathe, and after an hour's time he was able to speak again. . . ."

Moltke and his brother had been installed by their father as boarders in the home of a General Lorenz, who lodged them in an unheated attic room and left them in the charge of a bad-tempered old housekeeper. This housekeeper kept a goat, which got loose one day, wandered into the general's rooms, and broke a mirror. The general angrily ordered the goat killed and fed to the Moltke boys, a rare treat for them. In later years, when somebody remarked on the field marshal's indifference to mealtimes, he said, "I was so often hungry in my youth that I became accustomed to it, and do not notice it now."

Wandering around Copenhagen on a subsequent visit with his nephew and aide, Major Henry von Burt, Moltke strolled onto the parade ground of his youth and recalled how he had once stretched his neck while standing at attention in a row of cadets. An officer strode up to him and hit him in the nose with his elbow. Young Moltke's nose began to bleed, and he started to snuffle. The officer shouted: "*Hvorfor holder Du Snuden for?* [Why do you stick out your snout?]" Major von Burt deferentially asked his uncle why he hadn't complained to his parents about such treatment, and Moltke's answer was pure stoicism. "The mail only went very seldom then," he said, "and we did not come home for years on end, and also we imagined that everything was as it should be."

Reminiscing with some friends in Berlin many years later, Moltke was still rather bitter about his Copenhagen years. "The cadets received a truly Spartan education," he said, "being treated much too strictly. The tone in which we were spoken to was very harsh, there was no trace of love or sympathy in it. In moral training the institution was not a success; there was a visible mistrust which was extremely injurious in its effects. . . . But it must be admitted that this Spartan education has produced able and in every sense soldierly men."

Moltke was more candid in a letter to his brother Ludwig. "I had no education but thrashing," he wrote. Despite the supposed benefits of being hardened and toughened, Moltke wisely saw that such Spartan education can deprive a boy of all initiative, of all willingness to experiment and take risks. "This want of self-reliance and constant reference to the opinions of others, even the preponderance of reason over inclination, often give me moral depressions, such as others feel from opposite causes. They were in such a hurry to efface every prominent characteristic, every peculiarity, as they would have nipped every shoot of a yew-hedge, that the result was weakness of character. . . ."

Moltke was a splendid-looking youth, though, the very model of a Danish cadet. Comparing him to his brother, a schoolmate later wrote: "Fairer and taller, he had a slim figure, finely-cut features and an aristocratic bearing. His beautiful blue eyes, speaking eyes that awakened confidence at once, never lost this lovable expression even in his old age."

The Danish military authorities naturally thought they had done a splendid job in educating and training the young cadet. His grades on leaving the academy after nearly eight years were rated "good" in virtually everything: conduct, fortification, artillery, history of war, tactics, mathematics, physics, military law, French, freehand drawing, gymnastics, riding, dancing. Overall, he was ranked fourth in his class. Even before his graduation, he was made a page to the king. In 1819, after placing first in the examinations to become an officer, he left Copenhagen to serve as a lieutenant in the Oldenburg infantry regiment; the following year, he was put in the rifle brigade, which was considered a distinction.

But what is the real distinction of serving in a rifle brigade of an army that had no great destiny on its horizon? Various relatives saw better opportunities elsewhere—starting with his father. The older Moltke had by now lost hope of making his own fortune as a landowner. "After negotiations with my creditors," he wrote in the memoir he composed for his children at the age of seventy-two, "I sold Augustenhof, losing thereby the whole of my own and the greater part of my wife's property. I was now once more entirely dependent on the king's service for my subsistence." Looking back on his misspent life, Moltke thought he could do worse than introduce his gifted son to the army in which he had happily served for the thirteen years before his marriage. "In 1821," the father wrote about the future commander, "he went with his father on leave to Berlin, where for the first time in his life he saw part of the Prussian army; he was so impressed with it that he had no greater wish than to join it. A letter on this subject was sent to the chief of his regiment, the Duke of Holstein-Beck. . . ."

Other accounts of this important change in direction make it more gradual and more complex. The future General Hegermann-Lindencrone, whose father was also a Danish general, recalled that young Moltke approached the older Hegermann-Lindencrone for advice. He brought "a letter that he had received from an old relation in Prussia, who . . . wrote as follows: 'I have been told that you have good capabilities and that you are in earnest with anything you undertake. If this is so . . . I should advise you to enter a larger army instead of the small Danish one. I think you would find greater satisfaction and have better prospects for the future. . . .' My father discussed the matter thoroughly with Moltke and advised him decidedly to follow this suggestion."

Whatever the origin of the idea, Lieutenant Moltke formally asked permission to resign from the Danish army that had trained him and to join the army of neighboring Prussia. His commander, the Duke of Holstein-Beck, proved surprisingly acquiescent. "I regret to lose in you an officer of whom I had great expectations," he wrote to Moltke. At the same time, he sent the necessary document from the king: "We, Frederick the Sixth, by God's Grace King of Denmark, of the Goths and Wends, Duke of Schleswig, Holstein, Stormarn, Dithmarschen, Lauenberg, Oldenburg, etc., make known that the nobleman Helmuth Carl Bernhard v. Moltke, our near and dear friend . . . has humbly requested our gracious permission to retire from our service; we herewith grant him our most gracious discharge in acknowledgment of faithful and devoted services."

2

"Always to Be Very Strong"

IN GRANTING PERMISSION FOR YOUNG LIEUTENANT MOLTKE TO TRANSFER from the Danish to the Prussian army, the Duke of Holstein-Beck expressed some doubts whether the Prussians would agree. "I am surprised that the entry into the Prussian service does not present more difficulties," he wrote to the lieutenant's father, "as all Prussian subjects have to serve, and as the promotion to officer's rank can only take place after an examination and a particular recommendation." One of Moltke's biographers, F. E. Whitton, has suggested that "the Intelligence Branch of the Prussian War Office was probably not at all averse from securing the services of the son of a Prussian officer who had necessarily a good knowledge of the Danish Army, and who spoke and wrote Danish fluently." This probably credits the Prussian Intelligence Branch with too much intelligence. All well-run organizations know, however, that it is in their interests to take in talented youths from other organizations. Moltke confronted the Prussian officer's exam in the spring of 1822 and passed with flying colors.

He was promptly assigned as a second lieutenant in the Eighth Infantry Regiment, garrisoned at Frankfurt-on-the-Oder. Perhaps not entirely by coincidence, he found that the commander of the Fourth Cavalry Brigade there was a General von der Marmitz, "whose wife," as he dryly noted, "was a Countess von Moltke." Though "a frequent visitor at their house," Moltke recorded only two aspects of this formidable commander. One was that the general spent much of his time writing, and "if anybody entered, he used to get up, covering his writing with his velvet skull-cap." The other was that "the stern general" once caught him in a breach of etiquette and delivered "a rebuke . . . which I shall not easily forget." On entering the general's study and being invited to remove his things, Moltke "was just going to put my sword into a corner of the room, when he corrected me with 'In the ante-room, please.'" From such lessons, apparently, come field marshals.

If the laborious transfer from Danish to Prussian service was supposed to provide great challenges, though, there was little sign of them in garrison duty in Frankfurt-on-the-Oder. And if the town provided any amusements, a second lieutenant could not indulge in much entertainment on his pay of a few pennies a day. A year after entering the Prussian army, Moltke applied and was accepted at its chief military academy, the *Kriegsschule* in Berlin. And there he encountered, at least in spirit, a man who would subsequently exert a large influence on his life and thought. The new director of the military academy was Major General Carl von Clausewitz, then thirty-eight, a reserved and bookish veteran of defeat and captivity in the Napoleonic wars. His post in the military academy was largely administrative, and there is no documentary evidence that Moltke ever attended any of his lectures, or ever even met him. Only a few of the general's closest friends knew that he was compiling a series of observations on the military profession, and only those few knew that he spent the next decade revising and refining those observations, condensing and elaborating them into a kind of *Summa Theologica* on war. His work was still unfinished when he was called back into active service in 1830 as chief of staff to old Field Marshal August von Gneisenau, on guard at the Polish frontier. Assigned to devise a *cordon sanitaire* against an onrushing epidemic of cholera, Clausewitz failed; the disease struck him down and killed him in Breslau, and killed Gneisenau as well.

Nobody paid a great deal of attention when Clausewitz's widow assembled and published, between 1832 and 1837, ten posthumous volumes of his *Hinterlassene Werke,* including the large and unfinished analysis that he called simply *Vom Kriege (On War)*. But whether the young Lieutenant Moltke did actually listen to Clausewitz or simply read his posthumous thoughts, or perhaps soaked up those thoughts by a kind of social osmosis at the military academy, his triumphant campaigns against Austria and France a half century later were so closely modeled on Clausewitz's concepts of military strategy that the dead man might have drawn up the plans himself and bequeathed them to his heir. And when the aged Moltke, by now the hero of his country, was asked what books had most influenced him, his first answer was the Bible, and then that epic of strategic guile, *The Iliad,* and then that elaborate study by the still relatively obscure Clausewitz, *On War.*

Clausewitz had always been something of an outsider, born in 1780 to a middle-class family of Polish origins. His father had served as an officer under Frederick the Great during the Seven Years War (1756–1763) but only because Frederick was so desperate for reinforcements in his dangerously outnumbered army that he relaxed his rule restricting officers' commissions to the Prussian aristocrats known as Junkers.

Young Carl first went to war at the age of thirteen, serving as a *Fahnenjunker,* or lance corporal, with the Prussian 34th Infantry Regiment in the First Coalition forces that pushed the French revolutionary army back from the Rhine and into the Vosges. "Advancing across that broad valley, trudging up and down those steep, wooded mountain tracks," writes one of Clausewitz's biographers, Michael Howard, "he acquired that infantryman's familiarity with terrain that was to inspire so many of the pages of *On War.*"

That campaign ended in a stalemate, though, and Clausewitz was happy to be assigned in 1801 to the new *Kriegsschule* in Berlin. There he became an admiring protégé of the founder and director, Gerhard von Scharnhorst. A Hannoverian peasant's son and a tested veteran of the fighting against the French, Scharnhorst was already grappling with the most fundamental question puzzling strategists of that era: How could a relatively untrained French rabble, recruited by the *levées en masse* that began in 1793, stand up to and even defeat the professional soldiery of Germany? Scharnhorst's answer—that the French forces represented a political commitment between the soldiers and the revolutionary state—was to be proven in blood on the battlefield of Jena, where Napoleon smashed the complacent Prussians and their mercenaries in 1806. (And it was in the nearby Battle of Auerstädt that Clausewitz, serving as an aide-de-camp to Prince August, was wounded, then captured. So was Prince August. The two of them spent a year in French captivity before peace returned. This captivity left Clausewitz with what one commentator called "a lifelong dislike for all things French, a prejudice willingly shared by Moltke.")

Prussia's feckless King Frederick William III, who had neither spirit nor talent for combat but still ruled the Prussian monarchy by divine right, had drifted into war as a junior partner to Tsar Alexander I of Russia, and now he was to be elaborately punished for having dared to oppose the mighty Napoleon. Indeed, the French emperor let it be known that he was considering the complete abolition of the Kingdom of Prussia. That would probably have been an appropriate reward (inflicted one hundred years early) for the ignorant arrogance of the House of Hohenzollern, which had brought on Prussia the curse of history.

"The Brandenburg Countries, till they became related to the Hohenzollern Family . . . have no history that has proved memorable to mankind," according to the sweeping judgment and sweeping prose of Thomas Carlyle in his *Frederick the Great.* "There has, indeed, been a good deal written under that title, but . . . there is alarmingly little that is worth knowing or remembering." Carlyle began his narrative in about 300 B.C., when the land that would become known as Prussia was "a Country of lakes and woods, of marshy jungles, sandy wildernesses; inhabited by bears, otters, bisons, wolves, wild swine, and certain shaggy Germans of the Suevic type, as good as inarticulate. . . . These latter, tall, Suevi Semnones, men of blond, stern aspect (*oculi truces coerulei*), and great strength of bone, were known to possess a formidable talent for fighting."

This legend of the Germanic talent for fighting derives partly from the celebrated account by Tacitus, *On the Origin, Geography, Institutions, and Tribes of the Germans.* "They appear as a distinct, unmixed race, like none but themselves. . . ." Tacitus wrote, with that oxlike certitude that seems to infect all foreigners trying to portray this mysterious people. "All have fierce blue eyes, red hair, huge frames, fit only for a sudden exertion. They are less able to bear laborious work. . . . Nay, they actually think it tame and stupid to acquire by the sweat of toil what they might win by their blood." Though generations of Germans have thrilled with furtive pride at Tacitus's praises, which he clearly intended partly as a rebuke to his fellow Romans ("No one in Germany laughs at vice, nor do they call it the fashion to corrupt and to be corrupted. . . ."). But despite his pose of the meticulous observer, Tacitus finally admits that many of his observations are "fabulous." Of the reports that two tribes have the faces of men on the bodies of wild beasts, for example, he concedes that "all this is unauthenticated, and I shall leave it open."

The second basis for the legends of Germanic belligerence comes from the battle of the Teutoberg Forest in A.D. 9. Jealous of the renown that Julius Caesar had won by conquering Gaul, the Emperor Augustus vowed to match him by subduing the tribes of Germany. To this end, he sent three legions, a total of some 27,000 troops, into the wilderness along the Elbe under the command of Quintilius Varus, an incompetent official corrupted by years of service in the Middle East. Unknown to Quintilius Varus, the local Cherusci tribesmen were led by a young warrior named Arminius (or Herman, according to Germanic legends). Trained at Rome in the politics of deception, Arminius led Varus's legions into an ambush in the Teutoberg Forest, near the modern city of Paderborn, where they were treated with the same mercy that the Romans themselves customarily showed on their slave-hunting expeditions into the German wilderness. Suetonius tells a pretty story of Augustus's torment at the news of the slaughter of his soldiers. "For several months in succession he cut neither his beard nor his hair, and sometimes he would dash his head against a door, crying: 'Quintilius Varus, give me back my legions!'"

The major effect of this battle was to halt the Roman effort to colonize the Germans, and so the Rhine became the permanent frontier between the "barbarians" of the north and that mixture of slavery, laws, poetry, highways, commerce, public buildings, and human sacrifices that the Romans called civilization. Later historians in Germany, like those in the conquered lands of Britain and France, have made more of this distinction than it probably deserves. Prussia, in any case, was not conquered by any form of civilization until the twelfth century, when the Polish Duke Conrad of Masovia invited the Teutonic Knights to bring the blessings of Christianity to his heathen subjects in the east. The Teutonic Order had been founded during the waning days of the Third Crusade.

During the siege of Acre, when the German crusaders were beginning to lose heart, some pious merchants from Bremen and Lübeck decided to encourage them in the winter of 1190–1191 by founding in the hulk of a beached vessel a hospice for German pilgrims. This institution soon became attached to the German Church of St. Mary the Virgin in Jerusalem, and the brethren of the hospice were given the rank of knights. Like the two earlier knightly orders of the Templars and the Hospitallers, the Teutonic Order quickly began acquiring land and riches, hence power and envy. The Holy Land was too narrow a battlefield for the Teutons' ambitions, so they willingly accepted the Duke of Masovia's invitation to convert the heathen Prussians along the coast of the Baltic, and in 1229 they began building a chain of fortresses across the sandy wastes of Prussia. The conversion of the Prussian tribesmen took the better part of four centuries, ending with the extermination of most of the Prussians, one of the first cases of genocide in this unhappy region.

What most people think of as Prussia had little to do with the exterminated heathens of the East, however, but was centered in

Berlin and surrounding Brandenburg; this territory was originally regarded as the northernmost of the marks or marches that the successors of Charlemagne organized as frontier defenses against the Slavs venturing westward from Poland and Hungary. King Otto I managed to conquer the Bohemians in 950 and the Hungarians in 955, thus acquiring the title of Emperor Otto the Great.

The Hohenzollerns were still living quietly in Swabia, on lands not far from the Lake of Constance, but one of them, Frederick by name, brought himself to history's attention by saving the life of the Emperor Sigmund on the battlefield. The emperor gratefully appointed his rescuer as hereditary margraf of Brandenburg in 1415. His new subjects lacked the emperor's gratitude, however, and opposed Frederick so vigorously that he returned to the friendlier regions of the south. His son, Frederick II, eventually marched north again with 600 horsemen and stormed the rebellious town of Berlin, whose citizens were required to swear an oath of loyalty to their new Hohenzollern rulers. So while the Prussians in the east were succumbing to genocide, the people of Brandenburg were bowing to military aggression. The ghost of Quintilius Varus might have laughed at that of the brave Arminius.

If there is one constant in German history, it is the recurrence of fratricide and civil war, and never was this more violently fulfilled than in the religious revolt led by Martin Luther. In the reformer's first attack on the sale of indulgences, that scandalous commerce in which the priests of the Roman Catholic Church preyed on Germans' guilty fear of Purgatory to raise the funds needed to build and ornament the basilica of St. Peter's, Luther's original target was Prince Albert of Brandenburg, who needed the money from indulgences not only to contribute to Michelangelo's labors in Rome but also to pay the bribes required for his own designation as archbishop and elector of Mainz.

What seemed to Luther theological arguments of high moral principle were settled all over Germany by gunpowder and the sword, and the Hohenzollern leaders could scarcely avoid playing their role in these settlements. Margraf Joachim I (1499–1535) strongly opposed Luther, dabbled in astrology, and demonstrated his Christian orthodoxy by having thirty-eight Jews publicly burned in the center of Berlin. His son, Joachim II, devoted large sums to the building of Catholic churches, but this second Joachim's own son, Johann Siegmund, became an Evangelical Protestant, and so the banners of Lutheranism came to fly high over Brandenburg.

If religious intrigue appealed to the Hohenzollerns, they paid no less attention to the great royal sport of acquiring territory by mar-

riage. Through a wedding arranged by his grandfather, Johann Siegmund, who ruled from 1608 to 1619, became Duke of Prussia and
thus heir to the charred ruins left by the Teutonic Knights. By the
same marriage, he acquired some valuable territories on the Rhine,
the Ruhr, and the Maas. His heir, George William, could do little to
weld these holdings into a coherent state, however, for he and they
were now engulfed in the Thirty Years War. The Habsburg emperors
were determined to subdue the followers of Luther, and that decision
was fiercely resisted not only by the Protestant princes of northern
Germany but by all those neighboring nations that hoped to gain
advantage by prolonging the devastation of the Empire. George
William of Brandenburg hoped to remain neutral, but he soon decided
that he had no choice but to ally himself with the invading armies of
Gustavus Adolphus. Then he fled to what he considered the safety of
East Prussia.

And the war raged on. This was more than a terrible religious
war, though it was certainly that. It was a kind of national self-
destruction, an assault that left Germany hacked open with wounds
that would not heal. In that, it was comparable to the French Revolution or the American Civil War, though probably more damaging than
either. "The religious war has lasted sixteen years, and Germany has
lost half its inhabitants," Bertolt Brecht wrote in a stage instruction
about halfway through his chronicle of the disaster, *Mother Courage.*
"Those who are spared in battle die by plague. Over once-blooming
countryside hunger rages. Towns are burned down. Wolves prowl the
empty streets. . . ."

In the thirteenth year of the war, the Hohenzollern territories were
inherited by Frederick William, who was then twenty but had already
learned the tactics of Mother Courage: deception, guile, survival. For
these, he came to be known as "The Great Elector." He broke off the
alliance with Sweden and formed a new alliance with Sweden's arch-
enemy, Poland. No less important, he secretly organized and trained a
Brandenburg army of 8,000 men, which he made available to the
highest bidder. In a state of anarchy, an available army of 8,000 men
can be a very influential force.

After the various Scandinavian invaders retired, French subsidies
and interventions kept the war going through the 1640s, but exhaustion finally triumphed, and the powers of Europe gathered in the city
of Osnabruck to decide how the wreckage of Germany should be
divided. Under the Treaty of Westphalia in 1648, the fragmentation of
Germany was made quasi-permanent by the international recognition
of more than 300 different duchies, baronies, bishoprics, and free

cities, all nominally subject to the Habsburgs' decrepit Holy Roman Empire. In the shuffling of territories, though, the chief gainers were the French. The emperor ceded to them all his rights and possessions in Alsace, notably including Strasbourg and the fortified bishoprics of Metz, Toul, and Verdun. But the Great Elector's "independent" policy of following the highest bidder brought him handsome rewards as well: the entire coastal province of East Pomerania. And Brandenburg-Prussia now established itself for the first time as a power to be reckoned with.

Nobody did a great deal of reckoning, however, to the chagrin of Frederick III, a hunchback who hid his deformity under a flowing wig and devoted much effort and money to his dream of becoming a king. After several years of negotiations with the emperor, he finally won imperial approval for this rise in rank, which he celebrated in Königsberg in 1701, squandering some 4 million thalers on the festivities that ended with his placing a royal crown on his own head. As King Frederick I, he spent the rest of his reign imitating the pomp and extravagance of the French court at Versailles. The Hohenzollerns seemed to alternate, though, between extravagant dreamers and frugal empire builders, so Frederick was succeeded by Frederick William I, who dismissed his father's courtiers and scrimped to build an army. His one eccentric indulgence was a passion for soldiers of unusual size, whom he recruited all over Europe at a cost of several thousand thalers per man. This absurd expense led him to explore a radical alternative, raising troops from among his own subjects. By the time of his death in 1740, he had created an army of 80,000 men, roughly one twenty-fifth of Brandenburg-Prussia's population of 2 million (by contrast, only about one Frenchman in 150 served in his king's armed forces). To pay for all this, he left a war chest of 6 million thalers. Unlike many army builders, though, Frederick William was so conscious of how much his troops had cost him that he tried to avoid wasting them by sending them into battle.

That changed quite dramatically when the Prussian crown passed in 1740 to Frederick II, who was a military genius as well as an ardent flautist, composer of French verse, and would-be philosopher-king. Frederick had hardly been crowned before the death of Emperor Charles VI left a vacancy in the Habsburg palace that could only be filled by Charles's twenty-three-year-old daughter, Maria Theresa, who became archduchess of Austria and queen of Hungary and Bohemia but was forbidden by law from becoming empress. Frederick seized the opportunity to invade the fertile and prospering province of Silesia, which he called "a matter only of carrying out designs that I have long had in mind." In a more candid moment, he confessed that he had seen and seized "a means of acquiring reputation and of increasing the power of the State," but that he had also acted out of "the desire for glory, even curiosity." He spent the last night of peace at a masquerade ball, then galloped off toward the south, promising his officers that he would meet them at "our rendezvous with glory."

It was a rendezvous that Frederick had been long awaiting. His upbringing was of a harshness that modern guardians of innocence would categorize as child abuse. His frugal and ascetic father, Frederick William I, regarded his intellectual and somewhat dandyish son as an "effeminate fellow." With a disapproval that bordered on hatred, he periodically attacked and beat the young prince with his cane. "I am king and lord and will do what I wish," said Frederick William. When Prince Frederick tried to flee the country, the king not only court-martialed his son and two young officers who tried to help him but forced the prince to watch one of these officers being beheaded. Young Frederick acquired a certain hardness that would prove all too necessary when he reached the throne and went to war.

King Frederick defeated Maria Theresa without much difficulty, but her rage at the humiliating loss of Silesia inspired her to rally most of the great powers of Europe into an anti-Prussian coalition. The Seven Years War (1756–1763) raged from Canada to India, but on the battlefields of Germany, it was largely a war to punish Frederick. Vastly outnumbered by the allied armies of France, Austria, and Russia, Frederick learned to exploit all the possibilities of rapid movement and surprise. The cadets of Moltke's day studied such Frederickian victories as Leuthen and Rossbach in Clausewitz's military academy, and younger cadets have been studying them ever since. Prussia's wars, Frederick optimistically wrote in his *Principes Généraux de la Guerre,* should be "short and lively." Despite all of Frederick's daring and ingenuity, though, the implacable hatred of Empress Elizabeth of Russia, along with that of Maria Theresa, turned the Seven Years War into a war of attrition, and wars of attrition depend more on quantity than quality. There comes a point when every casualty is irreplaceable, no matter how high a price was exacted for the loss. In seven years of campaigning, Frederick won battle after battle but lost much of his army in the process. In the Peace of Hubertusburg, he kept Silesia and did not have to surrender a single village to the great powers that had fought so hard to overwhelm him. But the Prussia that he now ruled lay devastated, and Frederick had to devote the rest of his long life to its resuscitation and reconstruction.

This he did. Fulfilling his slogan that the king was merely "the first servant of the state," he built large numbers of schools and highways. He drained the marshlands of the Oder River valley, bringing thousands of acres of recovered land under cultivation, and he sent nearly 60,000 colonists, including many Huguenot refugees from France, out to cultivate them. He distributed corn seed for new crops, established a royal bank, and subsidized new factories to produce silk, wool, and linen. He made Prussia's industry the fourth largest in Europe.

He sponsored a thorough revision and codification of Prussian law, the *Codex Fredericianus,* which decreed, after all the horrors of the Thirty Years War: "Every inhabitant of the state must be granted complete freedom of religion and conscience." But though he liked to call himself *"l'avocat du pauvre,"* he never doubted his own divine right to decide every detail of his subjects' lives. And though he rode far and wide across his kingdom to hear and correct grievances against arbitrary actions by royal officials, that was because he knew that benevolent despots gain authority by demonstrating the benevolence of their despotism. He strongly believed that only aristocrats were fit to serve as officers in his army. As for the ordinary soldiers, they could be hired anywhere and flogged into shape. They represented what he often called, in his favorite language, the *"canaille,"* or rabble.

Frederick perpetrated one last grand territorial theft, which he was now old and wily enough to accomplish with virtually no bloodshed. In 1772, he joined Russia and Austria in the first partition of Poland. This united distant East Prussia to Brandenburg for the first time by extending Berlin's rule to the territory of West Prussia. It was not a permanent transfer, however, for West Prussia eventually became known as the Polish corridor and provided Hitler's pretext for starting World War II.

In Frederick's penchant for getting his way, one can see a foreshadowing of the future Field Marshal von Moltke. The bright and watchful eyes, the habit of sarcasm, the contempt for bombast, the ruthless intelligence—one recognizes them all. There is no documentary evidence that Moltke consciously modeled himself on Old Fritz, but it would not be surprising, for the king was a hero to most Prussian generals, then and in the future.

Frederick didn't much like his wife Elizabeth (he asked to be buried alongside his pet greyhounds), and so they both died childless. Absolute rule over Prussia passed to his nephew, Frederick William II, a worthless princeling who soon squandered both the money and the prestige that his predecessors had painfully amassed. The French Revolution, which caught him by surprise, also passed him by, and so it was Frederick William III, another prince with little claim to the Hohenzollern reputation for disciplined military skill, who came to power in 1797 and consequently suffered the sad experience of encountering Napoleon at Jena. Napoleon did not seriously plan to dismember Prussia, but he had other ways of punishing the Hohenzollerns. While the French and Russian emperors held their peace conference on a raft anchored in the middle of the Niemen River, where Napoleon could look across the frontier and eye the Russian territories that he falsely promised never to attack, the king of Prussia had to spend three hours waiting on the riverbank in the rain. When everything was settled, on July 9, 1807, Frederick William was made to sign the Peace of Tilsit, by which he surrendered nearly half his territory, partly to a Napoleonic Duchy of Warsaw in the east, partly to the new Kingdom of Westphalia under Jerome Bonaparte. He also had to accept a French occupation army of 100,000 men until he could pay the French an indemnity of deliberately unstated size. And finally he had to declare himself a military ally of his conqueror.

One of the few benefits in this humiliation was the creation of a Prussian Military Reorganization Commission, both to investigate what had gone wrong at Jena and to punish those officers who had fled or simply surrendered without a fight (208 of them were eventually purged). This was a benefit because the commission was dominated by Scharnhorst, one of the few commanders who had resolutely resisted the French invaders, and who was already the most magnetic of that extraordinary group of idealists who came to be known as the Prussian reformers. They took it as their mission to rebuild the nation out of the wreckage of the French occupation. "The great spiritual turning-point . . . was brought on by the disaster of the moment, not by any 'tradition of Frederick the Great,'" according to Gerhard Ritter in *The Sword and the Scepter*. "That tradition had been buried . . . by a mild brand of humanitarianism as early as the turn of the century. The world of new ideas arose from the depths of national defeat."

Scharnhorst undertook to build an army very different from that of Frederick the Great. He wanted to import the French idea of "the people in arms" by creating a mass militia, known as the Landwehr. And to command the new soldiers, he was determined to bring the merit system into the Junkers' ossified officer corps. He saw it as his duty "to raise and inspire the spirit of the army, to bring the army and the nation into a more intimate union and to guide it to its characteristic and exalted destiny." And further: "We must interject a feeling of independence, to destroy the old forms, to dissolve the bonds of privilege, to lead and nurture and unfetter the free development of regeneration—there can be no higher purpose."

Slowly, very slowly, Scharnhorst began changing the rules. Though the French forbade his plan for universal conscription, he inaugurated a plan of rotating recruits through training camps so quickly that he soon had a force of 35,000 ready reserves. The new training manual of 1808 emphasized target practice and the new French tactic of skirmishing by individual infantrymen rather than the mass charges of King Frederick's day. Infantry officers had to dismount and march with their troops, carrying their own knapsacks. They also had to pass exams in order to win their commissions. And no longer were they allowed to profit from the purchase of their troops' supplies. The old disciplinary system of flogging was abolished. Though some reformers went as far as urging the election of officers by their troops, however, King Frederick William was deeply opposed to any radical liberalization of his army, or anything else. But when Napoleon insisted that his puppet ally dismiss his moderately anti-French prime minister, Prince Karl August von Hardenberg, an important political change took place, the rise to power of a far more forceful, more liberal (and even more anti-French) minister, Baron Heinrich vom und zum Stein.

"Where is Stein?" asked Frederick William's assertive Queen Louisa during one crisis, while the king wallowed in uncertainty. "He is my last hope. A great heart, and encompassing mind, perhaps he knows remedies that are hidden to us." Minister of Economic Affairs since 1804, Stein had, in fact, been dismissed by the king earlier in 1808 as a "refractory, insolent, obstinate and disobedient official." Stein was all of those things but also an experienced administrator, courageous and farsighted. In October 1807, he had cajoled the king into issuing a remarkable decree promising his people that in the next three years the cities of the realm would begin to govern themselves, and on the broad estates of the countryside there would be no more hereditary serfdom, no more restrictions on what work a man might do or what land he might buy or sell. "After 11 November, 1810," the decree said of Prussia's future, "there will be only free people." To carry those sweeping promises still further, Stein began drafting plans for an elected legislature and a council of ministers responsible for their actions. As for the army, he totally supported Scharnhorst's hopes of ending the iron domination of the Junkers. "What can we expect," Stein wrote, "from the inhabitants of these sandy steppes—

these artful, heartless, wooden, half-educated men—who are really capable only of becoming corporals or book-keepers."

The reformers' efforts to renovate the Prussian regime were resisted not only by their king and aristocracy but by their all-powerful ally. Napoleon's agents discovered letters in which Stein expressed hope for a national uprising against France, and so Frederick William was forced to dismiss him (replacing him, once again, with Hardenberg). Beyond that, Napoleon proclaimed Stein an international criminal, seized his estates, and demanded his arrest. Stein fled to Austria, then to the safer sanctuary of Russia, where he began organizing resistance to Napoleon, first a Committee for German Affairs, then a Military German Legion. In June 1812, the emperor of France marched across the Niemen and invaded Russia at the head of a somewhat reluctant coalition. Of the 600,000 troops in his *Grande Armée,* some 180,000 were Germans of one kind or another—Prussians, Austrians, Saxons, Swabians—and thousands more came from the German-ruled territories in Poland and Italy. King Frederick William of Prussia, stricken by the recent death of Queen Louise, offered no objection to this new debasement of the Prussian army.

Napoleon's 20,000 Prussians marched under the command of Count Hans David Yorck von Wartenburg, himself a figure of rather mixed loyalties. English in origins, as his name suggested, Yorck had been dismissed from the Prussian army for disobedience in 1779, then joined the Dutch and fought for them in the East Indies. Accepted back by the Prussians, he had been wounded and taken prisoner in the Napoleonic campaign that ended at Jena. He had then joined Scharnhorst's reformers, but not to the extent of favoring any real liberalization. "If your royal highness robs me and my children of our rights," he once asked his sovereign, "on what, pray, do your own rights rely?"

The repeated twisting of German loyalties during these Napoleonic years would long reverberate through the history of the German army, right up until 1945. Yorck and his fellow officers had sworn personal fealty to King Frederick William, and they had shed blood to defend his lands against the invading French. What were they to do, then, when their king ordered them to follow those same French in marching against Russia? Yorck marched. Scharnhorst did not; forced to resign as head of the War Department in 1810, he went on indefinite leave. But that was a dim answer for younger and more spirited officers like Clausewitz. Though engaged to the Countess Marie von Bruhl, whom he would not be allowed to marry until 1816, he became one of 300 officers who renounced their pledged loyalty to the king of Prussia and offered their services to Tsar Alexander. "The idea that France can be opposed has almost completely disappeared in Prussia," Clausewitz wrote angrily in his *Political Declaration* of 1812. "Everyone believes in the necessity of an unconditional alliance, of throwing ourselves on their mercy, and finally of sacrificing the dignity of our own ruling house. They accept this progression of evil with a shrug—blushing deeply, their eyes on the ground. . . . I formally renounce this opinion and mood. . . . I renounce the facile hope of being saved by chance. . . . The childish hope of taming the tyrant's anger by voluntarily disarming. . . . The sinful neglect of all responsibility for the common good. . . . I believe and confess that a people can value nothing more highly than the dignity and liberty of its existence. That it must defend these to the last drop of its blood. . . . That a people courageously struggling for its liberty is invincible."

Brave words, typical of the passion and idealism that was to characterize the Prussian reform movement. "Poor Germany, tamed into slavery by your rulers," Gneisenau said of those heading eastward to serve Russia, "henceforth your best sons can fight only for an alien land." "I cannot condemn your decision," Scharnhorst wrote to one of the defectors, "because everyone must first see that he remains true to himself."

This question of "remaining true to oneself" is often treacherous. King Frederick William considered the exiles to be deserters, and the Russians welcomed them with the chilly disdain that is often the destiny of defectors. Unable to speak any Russian, Clausewitz became an aide-de-camp to Baron Carl Ludwig Pfuel, who had entered Russian service soon after Jena. So Clausewitz witnessed the Russian defeat at Borodino and the retreat to Moscow. Tolstoy rather scornfully portrayed him in *War and Peace,* riding past a Russian encampment after Borodino and speaking in German about various theoretical possibilities: "*Der Krieg muss in Raum verlegt werden,* [The war must be extended widely,]" says one of two Prussians distantly glimpsed on horseback. "*Oh, ja . . .*" says the other, "*so kann man gewiss nicht den Verlust der Privat-Personen in Achtung nehmen.* [So of course one cannot take into account the loss of private individuals.]" Prince Andrei Bolkonski, who overhears the Prussians' comments, observes bitterly that their talk of "extending" the war threatens his whole family. "That's all the same to him!" he adds "with an angry snort." Tolstoy was equally contemptuous of all the Prussians who had volunteered to join in the defense of Mother Russia. "Pfuel and his adherents," as he put it, in an analysis that was several decades out of date, "[were] military theorists who believed in a science of war with immutable laws—laws of oblique movements, outflankings, and so forth. . . . iThey saw only barbarism, ignorance, or evil intention in every deviation from that theory."

When Napoleon's invasion eventually ground to a halt, when captured Moscow went up in flames, forcing the French (and Prussians) to begin retreating through the snow, Clausewitz finally got his chance to challenge Yorck von Wartenburg's role in the invasion—or rather to subvert Yorck's role, to give Yorck an opportunity to do what no Prussian officer was ever supposed to do: betray his overlords. Despite all his traditional soldierly characteristics, Yorck impressed Clausewitz as someone with a penchant for intrigue. He was "a man of some fifty years, distinguished by bravery and military competence," Clausewitz later recalled in his account of the affair, *The Campaign of 1812 in Russia.* "A violent, passionate will that he hides under seeming coldness," Clausewitz wrote, "enormous ambition that he hides under constant resignation, and a strong, daring character distinguish this man. General Yorck is an upright person, but he is morose, melancholic, and secretive and therefore a bad subordinate. Personal attachment is rather foreign to him; what he does, he does for the sake of his reputation and because he is naturally competent. The worst is that under a mask of bluntness and rectitude he is basically very cunning."

As Napoleon's retreating forces neared the Polish border, at a point where Yorck's surviving 14,000 Prussians might still have helped the French to make a stand, Clausewitz suddenly appeared at Yorck's headquarters, wearing a Russian officer's uniform and bearing letters that showed how the Russians planned to cut him off and isolate him. Such a military threat, Clausewitz later recalled, "would have made no impression on a man like Yorck," but it had interesting political possibilities: "As a military pretext it meant a good deal, should the Prussian court wish to excuse itself to the French," he wrote. In other words, the Russian military threat was in itself feeble, but it might serve as an excuse for a Prussian capitulation.

Like any general called upon to betray his commanders, Yorck worried that the seducers might not be able to protect him.

"Keep away from me!" he shouted at Clausewitz when he saw the newcomer arrive with his messages, "I want nothing more to do with you. Your damned Cossacks have let a letter . . . through them which brings me an order to march. . . . Your troops do not advance. You are too weak. I must march, and I must excuse myself from all further negotiations, which would cost me my head."

Clausewitz temporized. He said he did not disagree with anything that Yorck said; he only asked for some candles so that he could show Yorck the new letters he had brought. Yorck scowled and ordered candles, but he showed no sign of any willingness to read Clausewitz's letters—which, remember, provided a pretext for Yorck to betray his French commanders. Clausewitz, by his own account, was exquisitely formal. "Your Excellency," he quoted himself as saying, "will surely not place me in the embarrassing position of departing without having carried out my Commission."

Yorck paused, then called for his chief of staff, Colonel von Roeder, either as an adviser or as a witness. Then he and Roeder read the letters. Another long pause.

"Clausewitz, you are a Prussian," Yorck finally said in the flickering candlelight. "Do you believe that General d'Auvray's letter is honest [that was the letter outlining how Yorck's force might be cut off and destroyed] and that [General] Wittgenstein's troops really will reach the places named by the 31st?" In other words, is it really safe to change sides?

"I pledge myself for the sincerity of this letter upon the knowledge I have of General d'Auvray and the other men of Wittgenstein's headquarters," Clausewitz again quoted himself as showing the solemnity of a foreign minister. Then he added a qualification characteristic of the future author of *On War:* "Whether these dispositions will really be achieved I cannot guarantee, of course, for Your Excellency knows that in war we must often fall short of the line we have drawn for ourselves."

Clausewitz reported another long silence. Yorck must have contemplated the young envoy—Clausewitz, in his Russian uniform, was still only thirty-three—and thought: What kind of an answer is that? Or, Who does he think he is? Or, Where will this all end? Yorck suddenly made up his mind. He stuck out his hand and said, "You have me. . . . I am now firmly determined to separate myself from the French and their cause." Yorck called in a cavalry officer and told him of his plans. Pacing up and down the room, he asked the young cavalryman, "What say your regiments?" The cavalryman promised that every man would cheer the idea of breaking with the French. "You young people may talk," Yorck said, "but this old man's head is shaking on his shoulders."

The next day, December 30, Yorck went to a mill near the town of Tauroggen and signed a document breaking off relations with the French. "Now or never is the time to regain liberty and honor," said he. There are uglier words for what history tactfully calls the Convention of Tauroggen—treachery, betrayal, desertion—but from other perspectives, Yorck can just as legitimately be considered a courageous patriot. He genuinely thought he was acting in the best interests of Prussia, and he hoped that King Frederick William would formally approve his decision. No such approval came. On the contrary, when the king heard the news of Yorck's defection, he relieved him of his command and ordered him arrested. "With a bleeding heart," said Yorck, "I tear the bonds of obedience and wage war on my own."

Yorck's defection was almost universally seen as an act of insubordination, if not outright rebellion.[1] The news not only startled and angered both the Prussian king and the French emperor but amazed all the leaders of a society where orders were expected to be carried out. Theodor Fontane gave a vivid account of how that news swept through that society in his panoramic novel of the Berlin of that period, *Before the Storm*. "Yorck has capitulated . . ." a Polish privy councillor announces to some friends at a ball. "That is to say, he has gone over to the Russians." A Polish count named Bninski, reflecting Polish support for the French creator of the Duchy of Warsaw, reacts with fury: "And that is what they call loyalty in this country!"

The novel's hero, Lewin, goes to his law classes at the University of Berlin the next day to hear the famous Johann Gottlieb Fichte deliver one of his lectures on "The concept of the Just War." "The little man with the sharp profile and the blue but penetrating eyes . . . had difficulty in fighting his way up to the platform. 'Gentlemen,' he began, after having, not without a smile of contentment, allowed his glance to glide over the full auditorium, 'gentlemen, we all have in our minds at this moment a piece of great news. . . . General Yorck has capitulated. . . . I, for my part, am certain that, while it may seem to humiliate us, this is in fact the first step on the road which will lead us out of humiliation to renewal and revival. . . . Let us be full of hope that gives courage, and full of courage that gives hope.'" (Long before

---

[1]Harold Nicolson, whose views are not to be taken lightly, regarded this entire episode as a Prussian exercise in duplicity. "A legend has in fact arisen," he wrote in *The Congress of Vienna*, "that General Yorck acted entirely upon his own initiative and in a burst of patriotic fervour. This is untrue. There is little doubt that the General had received verbal but precise instructions from his sovereign. Frederick William at the moment was striving desperately to place a foot in each camp. If we are to understand how so indecisive a man came to take so dangerous a decision we must examine for a moment the great surge of popular emotion which at the time was sweeping over Prussia and which in the end forced Frederick William to bow before the hurricane of the Befreiungskrieg." Fortunately, Nicolson offered no evidence in support of his argument.

Yorck's defection, Fichte actually said much the same in his *Addresses to the German Nation* in the winter of 1807: "We are conquered. . . . If we will it, a new struggle of principles, of morals, of character now begins.")

Clausewitz became familiar with Fichte's views, in due time, because the two of them shared an interest in, of all people, Machiavelli. Fichte wrote an essay in praise of Machiavelli in 1807 in a periodical published in Koenigsberg, which was then the last redoubt of Prussian independence from the French. Clausewitz wrote to express his agreement. "There can be no doubt that the art of war in Germany is in decline," he told Fichte. "It must be animated by a new spirit if it is to serve us, and justify the toil, effort, and sacrifices that any war requires." Unlike Machiavelli, Clausewitz wrote, he believed that a modern commander "should not cling to methods that were successful in the past . . . but rather seek to restore the true spirit of war. . . . This true spirit of war seems to me to consist in mobilizing the energies of every soldier to the greatest possible extent and in infusing him with warlike feelings, so that the fire of war spreads to every component of the army instead of leaving numerous dead coals in the mass. . . . The modern art of war, far from using men like simple machines, should vitalize individual energies as far as the nature of its weapons permits. . . ." Scharnhorst could hardly have said it better; it was to become the new doctrine of Moltke's army.

Back in Napoleonic Prussia, though, the news from Tauroggen ricocheted not only through Berlin but to other capitals as well. No sooner had Yorck made his move than the tsar asked the contentious Baron Stein, who had persuaded him to march westward beyond the Russian frontier, to become provisional administrator of liberated East Prussia, and Stein promptly convened an assembly of local representatives to authorize the creation of a Landwehr, or militia, just as Scharnhorst had long wanted. Stein's actions were technically quite as treasonable toward the king of Prussia as Yorck's defection had been, but Stein sounded defiance. "I have but one fatherland, and that is Germany," he declared in December 1812, at a time when no such thing as Germany existed. "I am completely indifferent, in this historic moment, to the fate of dynasties. . . . You may do with Prussia what you like."

The king of Prussia, under the guidance of the crafty Hardenberg, saw by now that he would have to shift his own position—without provoking French retaliation—starting with a prudent move of his royal court from French-occupied Berlin to the Silesian capital of Breslau, some 200 miles to the southeast. In mid-March, he finally agreed to join Tsar Alexander in resisting the French. All his soldiers, he now declared, "will fight for our independence and the honor of the *Volk* [people]. Both will only be secured if every son of the fatherland participates in this battle for honor and freedom." As Napoleon's empire crumbled, this became a time for ambitious proclamations, none of which seemed to endure more than a few months. A week after Frederick William's announcement that he would "fight for independence" against his ex-ally, the Russian commander, Michael Kutuzov, issued an edict in the names of both the tsar and the king of Prussia, promising "honor and freedom" to the governments and peoples of all the various German principalities, both those that had supported Napoleon and those that had resisted him. The Russian edict expressed the hope that "every German worthy of the name would quickly and forcefully accept." If not, there would follow "destruction through the strength of public opinion and the power of righteous arms."

Whatever the hypocrisy, these appeals to the people to take arms represented a victory for the once-radical ideas of Scharnhorst, who was now called back to active duty as chief of staff to the seventy-one-year-old General Gerhard von Blücher, one of the last surviving Hussar officers from the wars of Frederick the Great. The renewal of fighting between Prussians and French went badly for the supposedly revitalized Prussians, however. Napoleon narrowly won the Battle of Lützen, and Scharnhorst suffered a wound that took his life a few months later. The change in alliances rewarded Yorck von Wartenburg, though. Instead of being court-martialed for insubordination, he was handsomely rewarded, becoming a count in 1814 and finally a field marshal in 1821. Clausewitz, too, slowly won his way back into the Prussian service.

Regarded by King Frederick William as disloyal, Clausewitz was still wearing his Russian uniform when he served as an adviser to Blücher in 1813 at the start of what German historians still like to call "the war of liberation." That campaign finally brought together Blücher's 270,000 Prussians, 130,000 Austrians, and 110,000 Swedes against Napoleon's 450,000—the biggest confrontation in history up to that time—in the three-day "battle of nations" outside Leipzig. "Crowds of corpses lay around," Wilhelm von Humboldt wrote to his wife after wandering among the 100,000 casualties, "most of them partially clothed or completely naked, often piled one on top of another. Most lie with outstretched arms over the face, so that one grasps for the first time the meaning of Homer's lines, bite the earth with the teeth."

When Napoleon retreated from Leipzig, he retreated all the way to the Rhine and beyond, thus ending another decade in which the wars of French ambition had been waged on German soil. As in the conquests of Louis XIV, this meant wars fought at the expense of German farms and German crops and German villages. Beethoven probably summed up the general feelings about *la gloire* at the end of his *Missa Solemnis,* written between 1818 and 1823, when the relentlessly martial rhythms of drums and trumpets inspire the soloists to passionate cries of *"Miserere."*

Clausewitz yearned to join in Blücher's victorious march to the heights of Montmartre, at which point Napoleon finally offered his abdication, but King Frederick William readmitted him to the Prussian army only in 1814, and then he was assigned to command a collection of miscellaneous troops called the German Legion, serving in northern Germany rather than France. Only after Napoleon escaped from Elba and terrified Europe by recruiting a new imperial army did Clausewitz get back into the Prussian General Staff and become chief of staff to General von Thielman's Third Army Corps. This outnumbered force fought an inconclusive defensive battle on the left flank of the allied army that finally confronted Napoleon in Belgium. If the hero of Stendhal's *Charterhouse of Parma* is famous for not knowing whether he was actually taking part in the great Battle of Waterloo, Clausewitz knew his own part in the historic battle as one of obscure failure.

But if war is the continuation of politics by other means, as Clausewitz later summed up his famous idea, politics is also the continuation of war by other means, and the sequel to Waterloo took place at the Congress of Vienna. Under the aegis of Austria's Count Clemens von Metternich, the victorious powers endeavored to restore the status quo of 1792. But there were, as there usually are, exceptions. In abolishing the Napoleonic Duchy of Warsaw, the assembled diplomats transferred most of Poland to Austria. Prussia, in turn, acquired not only a slice of Poland but also Swedish Pomerania, nearly half of Saxony, much of the Rhineland, and all of Westphalia, enriching the Hohenzollerns with the future industrial treasures of the Ruhr. Prussia thus received, as Friedrich Meinecke wrote in *The Age of German Liberation,* "the mission of defending Germany's Western frontier against France. In the long run this solution did probably more for Prussian penetration of Germany than the acquisition of the entire Saxon kingdom would have done. By being drawn farther west into Germany . . . Prussia was divided into two separate land masses, but she was also woven more firmly and intimately into the texture of the whole German nation."

Napoleon had abolished the moribund Holy Roman Empire in 1806 (replacing it with a French-dominated Confederation of the Rhine), and though the delegates to Vienna had no great desire to revive the Habsburgs' empire, they did agree to replace the Napoleonic Confederation of the Rhine with a properly Teutonic German Confederation. For this, the 300–odd fragments of the old empire were cut down to thirty-eight—the five kingdoms of Prussia, Saxony, Bavaria, Hannover, and Württemberg, an assortment of duchies and principalities, and the free cities of Lübeck, Frankfurt, Bremen, and Hamburg. Only seven members of the German Confederation had populations of more than 1 million while twenty-one had less than 100,000, the smallest being Liechtenstein, with 5,000. By general consent, this loose confederation was to be presided over by Austria.

Deprived of political leadership, Prussia took a subterranean revenge by organizing in 1818 a *Zollverein*, or customs union, among its scattered territories and possessions. This not only brought in large revenues (15 million thalers in 1821) but spurred production and trade to such an extent that neighboring states soon wanted to join. Prussia gradually converted this desire into an economic leadership that prepared the way for the political union of 1871.

"What Is War?" was the title of Clausewitz's opening chapter. "War . . ." he wrote in answer to his question, "is an act of violence intended to compel our opponent to fulfill our will."

That may seem self-evident to the point of banality, but Clausewitz was writing in opposition to a whole tradition of eighteenth-century maneuvering. Most military campaigns by the professional soldiers of the prerevolutionary era had been relatively small and short, or limited, more exactly, to an army's stored supplies and the seasons of combat weather.

"An act of violence intended to compel our opponent to fulfill our will." Unable to forget the smashing attacks that Napoleon repeatedly inflicted upon his enemies, Clausewitz was determined to keep that fundamental idea at the center of all talk about strategic theory. "Violence arms itself with the inventions of Art and Science, in order to contend against violence," he wrote. "Self-imposed restrictions, almost imperceptible and hardly worth mentioning, termed usages of International Law, accompany it without essentially impairing its power. . . . He who uses force unsparingly, without reference to the bloodshed involved, must obtain a superiority if his adversary uses less vigor in its application."

Networks of military supply bases were of little importance to

Clausewitz; neither was the occupation of enemy territory. The main targets were what he called "centers of gravity." This meant mainly the enemy's military forces but could also include the enemy's capital or his connections with an ally. In attacking these centers of gravity, the commander must not just maneuver for advantage but seek the decisive battle, the all-out attack that would cripple the enemy and end the war. That was, after all, the goal of all theory: "The end for which a soldier is recruited, clothed, armed, and trained, the whole object of his sleeping, eating, drinking, and marching *is simply that he should fight at the right place and the right time*." The goal of military planning was correspondingly simple: "The best strategy is always to be *very strong*, first in general, and then at the decisive point."

Despite Tolstoy's sneering references to Prussian pedantry, the battle-tested Clausewitz was by no means dogmatic in presenting his ideas. On the contrary, he repeatedly emphasized the variables in any battle.

The first source of trouble was the lack of intelligence about the enemy's location and strength. "Many intelligence reports in war are contradictory; even more are false," Clausewitz wrote, "and most are uncertain. What one can reasonably ask of an officer is that he should possess a standard of judgment, which he can gain only from knowledge of men and affairs and from common sense. He should be guided by the laws of probability. . . . In short, most intelligence is false, and the effect of fear is to multiply lies and inaccuracies." Moltke was to confirm that on the battlefield of Königgrätz, where the Prussians managed to lose sight of the entire Austrian army until it was almost too late for Moltke's judgment and common sense to save them.

False intelligence typified a problem that Clausewitz called "friction." "Everything in war is very simple, but the simplest thing is difficult," Clausewitz wrote. "The difficulties accumulate and end by producing a kind of friction that is inconceivable unless one has experienced war. . . . Countless minor incidents—the kind you can never really foresee—combine to lower the general level of performance, so that one always falls far short of the intended goal. . . . Friction is the only concept that more or less corresponds to the factors that distinguish real war from war on paper. . . . Friction, as we choose to call it, is the force that makes the apparently easy so difficult."

One cause of friction that immediately leaped to Clausewitz's mind was the weather. "Fog can prevent the enemy from being seen in time, a gun from firing when it should, a report from reaching the commanding officer." This is a common excuse, of course, and it has often been noted that the Russian winter was just as cold for the Russians as it was for either Napoleon or Hitler. Still, an artillery piece that cannot move through mud is an artillery piece lost to friction just as decisively as if it had been lost to enemy action, as Moltke was to learn when he had to fight his first major battle, at Königgrätz, in pouring rain. "Action in war is like movement in a resistant element," Clausewitz wrote. "Just as the simplest and most natural of movements, walking, cannot easily be performed in water, so in war it is difficult for normal efforts to achieve even moderate results."

Clausewitz made little effort to provide rules or lessons on how to win a battle. Generally, he dismissed such things as "a matter of tactics," which he seemed to regard as beneath consideration. "We cannot formulate any principles, rules or methods," he wrote at one point. "History does not provide a basis for them. On the contrary, at almost every turn one finds peculiar features that are often incomprehensible, and sometimes astonishingly odd. Nevertheless it is useful to study history in connection with this subject, as with others. While there may be no system, and no mechanical way of recognizing the truth, truth does exist." And again: "No rules of any kind exist for maneuver, and no method or general principle can determine the value of the action; rather, superior application, precision, order, discipline, and fear will find the means to achieve palpable advantage."

It is often said, usually with some contempt, that generals like to spend their time planning to refight the last war. This is particularly true of generals who want to base their plans on actual experience rather than "mere theory." How should it be otherwise, when their experience of reality is precisely that of combat in the last war? The same applies, of course, to theorists, and for the same reason. So Clausewitz, who spoke with the combat veteran's customary contempt for theory, based his own theories on his experience of the Napoleonic wars. He repeatedly showed immense admiration for Bonaparte, "this juggernaut of war, based on the strength of the entire people." What he admired about Bonaparte was what Moltke later emulated, his boldness in attacking, his swiftness of movement, his concentration of force on one vulnerable spot, his flexibility in responding to difficulties combined with an iron determination in carrying out a basic idea. Clausewitz may well have been thinking of Napoleon when he wrote passionately of the elements in a successful attack: "Blow after blow must be aimed in the same direction: the victor, in other words, must strike with all his strength and not just against a fraction of the enemy's. Not by taking things the easy way—

using superior strength to filch some province, preferring the security of this minor conquest to great success—but by constantly seeking out the center of his power, by daring all to win all, will one really defeat the enemy."

But though Napoleon haunted his whole era, as Adolf Hitler later haunted his, the essential fact about his series of triumphs was, of course, that he eventually lost everything, and for many of the same reasons that were to lead Hitler to the same crushing defeat: megalomania, loss of judgment, loss of control, all acted out in the disastrous idea of invading Russia. Imagine Clausewitz at Stalingrad! He had seen a similar vision at Borodino, in Napoleon's triumphant march into Moscow, and his humiliating retreat westward through the snow.

And though Clausewitz could become quite rhapsodic in writing about Napoleon's offensive across Prussia in 1805–1806, he nonetheless had to deal with the fact that although his hero had dared all to win all, he ultimately lost. This led Clausewitz to the odd idea that defensive warfare is easier and more effective than an offensive campaign. Not only did he see this demonstrated by the Russians in 1812 but also by the campaigns of his earlier hero, Frederick the Great. "It is easier to hold ground than to take it," he wrote. "It follows that defense is easier than attack. . . . Time which is allowed to pass unused accumulates to the credit of the defender. He reaps where he did not sow. Any omission of attack—whether from bad judgment, fear or indolence—accrues to the defenders' benefit. This saved Prussia from disaster more than once during the Seven Years War. . . ."

Clausewitz concocted a variety of reasons to support his theory: the defender knows the terrain better, he can guard his supplies better, he benefits from the support of the local population. But none of his reasons rings true, and there is no sign that Moltke ever paid the slightest attention to them. On the contrary, he took to heart Clausewitz's two basic principles for offensive warfare: "The first principle is: act with the utmost concentration. The second principle is: act with the utmost speed. No halt or detour must be permitted. . . ." Not only were those Moltke's principles in attacking France in 1870, but they remained true when Heinz Guderian's panzer divisions slashed through the same territory along the Meuse in 1940.

In trying to analyze why some armies win, Clausewitz naturally emphasized the most basic reasons—manpower and firepower, but he kept coming back to the temperament of the commander. Since Clausewitz attached immense importance to combat experience, and since Moltke had less combat experience than the commanders he defeated, one can reasonably conclude that the qualities that Clausewitz thought could only be learned in combat were actually Moltke's birthright. "Habit," Clausewitz wrote almost as though describing his prize pupil, "breeds that priceless quality: calm, which, passing from hussar and rifleman up to the general himself, will lighten the commander's task. In war the experienced soldier reacts rather in the same way as the human eye does in the dark: the pupil expands to admit what little light there is, discerning objects by degrees, and finally seeing them distinctly."

What Clausewitz basically outlined, then, was not a series of rules for winning battles but rather a quality of mind, which Moltke easily recognized and developed. The successful commander, Clausewitz argued, was, first, a man who was prepared for surprises and did not become upset when the inevitable mishaps occurred. "If the mind is to emerge unscathed from this relentless struggle with the unforeseen," Clausewitz wrote, "two qualities are indispensable: first, an intellect that, even in the darkest hour, retains some glimmerings of the inner light which leads to truth; and second, the courage to follow this faint light wherever it may lead."

Over and over again, Clausewitz insisted that the commander cannot provide what the civilians want: certainties, accurate prophecies. That was what Bismarck yearned for, and what he asked of Moltke before the Austrian war. Moltke calmly told him that nothing was certain in war, a judgment that contributed to Bismarck's mistrust of war itself as an instrument of policy. "War is the realm of uncertainty," said Clausewitz; "three quarters of the factors on which action in war is based are wrapped in a fog of greater or lesser uncertainty. A sensitive and discriminating judgment is called for; a skilled intelligence to scent out the truth." And again: "The absolute, the mathematical as it is called, nowhere finds any sure basis in the calculations in the art of war. From the outset, there is a play of possibilities, probabilities, good and bad luck." And again: "War is the realm of chance. No other human activity gives it greater scope: no other has such incessant and varied dealings with this intruder. Chance makes everything more uncertain and interferes with the whole course of events."

How, then, does a "skilled intelligence" acquire "a sensitive and discriminating judgment"? First, of course, by learning to recognize the "intruder," by being ready to recognize mishaps and misfortunes. Then by remaining cool when they occur, and by remaining flexible in his responses to whatever does happen. But never losing sight of the overall strategic goals. The general may look with envy on the architect watching his building grow, says Clausewitz, or even on the doctor who "knows his medicines and the effects they produce. By contrast, a general in time of war is constantly bombarded by reports both true and false; by errors arising from fear or negligence or hastiness; by disobedience born of right or wrong interpretations, of ill will, of a proper or mistaken sense of duty, of laziness, or of exhaustion; and by accidents that nobody could have foreseen. . . . *Perseverance* in the chosen course is the essential counterweight. . . . Only great strength of will can lead to the objective."

But perseverance must not turn into mere stubbornness. The dogged pursuit of a course that events have proven wrong. The great need in such times of crisis is intelligent boldness, which Clausewitz described as the mark of a hero. "This kind of boldness," he wrote, and Moltke's whole life testified to his agreement, "does not consist in defying the natural order of things and in crudely offending the laws of probability; it is rather a matter of energetically supporting that higher form of analysis by which genius arrives at a decision. . . . A distinguished commander without boldness is unthinkable. No man who is not born bold can play such a role, and therefore we consider this quality the first prerequisite of the great military leader."

Perhaps no element of war involved more uncertainty, Clausewitz realized, than the element of politics. "War is not merely a political act," he wrote in what became his most widely quoted and most widely misunderstood statement, "but also a political instrument, a continuation of politics by different means." Hostile critics have often taken this to mean a Prussian penchant for substituting war for diplomacy. Clausewitz emphasized that he meant the opposite, that war was not a substitute but an addition to other forms of political action. "We want to make it clear that war in itself does not suspend political intercourse or change it into something entirely different. . . . The main lines along which political events progress, and to which they are restricted, are political lines that continue throughout the war into the subsequent peace. . . . War cannot be divorced from political life."

What cannot be divorced, though, cannot remain happily married, either. While soldiers and statesmen both profess to be working as allies, each respecting the other's separate field of special knowledge and authority, a politician can see any question as political, while a military commander can judge the same question as purely military. The two followers of Clausewitz who passionately fought out this dilemma were to be Moltke and Bismarck. Both agreed that war was a continuation of politics by other means—Moltke diplomatically defined strategy as "the practical adaptation of the means placed at a general's disposal to the attainment of the object in view"—and that was why they fought so bitterly against each other. Moltke accepted the idea that war was fought for a political end, and that Chancellor Bismarck was responsible for that end, but while a war was being fought, he insisted, no politician had a right to interfere in the army's actions. Bismarck, on the other hand, repeatedly had to stake his political life on his right to control the uses to which Moltke put his soldiers.

After dealing with every possibility that might confront a Prussian commander, Clausewitz finally confronted the fundamental issue: Who is the enemy? For the survivor of Jena and Borodino and Waterloo, there could be only one answer. To go to war against France, he imagined that the Prussians would require a vast coalition, embracing Britain, Austria, "the rest of Germany," and the Netherlands, to assemble an army of 725,000 men. But it could be done, and then the invasion could begin. "The center of gravity of France lies in the armed forces and in Paris," Clausewitz wrote. "The allied aim must, therefore, be to defeat the army in one or more major battles, capture Paris, and drive the remnants of the enemy's troops across the Loire. . . . The major concern of the commanders-in-chief must be to seek the necessary major battle and fight it with such superiority of numbers, and under such conditions, as will promise decisive victory. Everything must be sacrificed to that objective. . . ." He did not design this great campaign against France as an entirely capricious venture, Clausewitz insisted, but only so that France could be "taught a lesson any time she chooses to resume that insolent behavior with which she has burdened Europe for a hundred and fifty years."

If Clausewitz could have imagined that one of his pupils at the *Kriegsschule* in Berlin would undertake such a campaign without any help from the English or Austrians, he would surely have been pleased and proud of the results. And if Moltke could imagine any ghosts looking down over the battlefield of Sedan, they would include not only his father but also Carl von Clausewitz.

3

"I Must Have a Horse"

EVEN AFTER TRANSFERRING TO THE PRUSSIAN ARMY, EVEN AFTER ABSORBING all the teachings of Clausewitz's *Kriegsschule,* young Lieutenant Moltke inevitably discovered that there was very little fighting to be done. While the veterans of the Napoleonic wars grew old and recounted their memoirs, the statesmen who had gathered at Vienna imposed on Europe a new balance of power, designed by Prince Metternich of Austria to keep the peace indefinitely. That balance was also designed to keep power in the hands of conservatives. So reaction ruled Prussia, as it ruled most of Europe, with its customary deference to sloth and inertia.

The Prussian army, devastated at Jena, triumphant at Waterloo, now experienced what might be called a period of convalescence. Scharnhorst was dead, and so was his idealism, but many of his ideas lived on, a promising legacy to more cautious heirs. Most fundamental was that universal conscription had finally been ordered in 1814. This had been a Prussian principle since the days of Frederick William I, but there had been so many exceptions that the authorities relied on mercenaries and soldiers of fortune to fill their ranks. And while they did not order conscription to strengthen the idea of democracy, though they liked to cite the examples of Sparta and Rome, the move did have that effect. More important, probably, it wove the idea of military service into the fabric of Prussian life, when such contemporary societies as France, and, for that matter, the United States, permitted any moderately wealthy young man to hire a substitute to serve in his stead.

Whatever other effects it may have had, universal conscription now provided the Prussian army with a substantial supply of manpower. Though social caste still dominated the selection of officers, the heirs of the reformers continued to exert pressure for a lifting of educational standards, and the authorities sharply increased the funds available for the schooling of impoverished aristocrats. At the top level, Scharnhorst's successors continued the development of the general staff until it was rated as the best military planning organization in Europe. It created a historical section and a topographical section, and as early as the 1830s it began studying the use of the new railroads to speed up future mobilizations—all special interests of young Lieutenant Moltke. Also in the 1830s, it analyzed and approved the new breech-loading "needle gun" that Moltke's infantry would use with powerful effect in the wars of 1864 and 1866. And by regularly rotating young staff officers between Berlin and the forces in the field, the army turned its fledgling planners into a kind of central nervous system. This, too, Moltke would see, approve, and build on.

At regimental headquarters in Frankfurt-on-the-Oder, though, he led a dull and peaceful life. He was assigned in 1827 to teach at a local military school. "As I have now taken up surveying and drawing," he wrote to his mother, "I have no lack of work; I have fourteen lectures and eight inspections a week, as well as the surveillance of thirty-one youngsters, who, however, like me, and whom I keep in proper respect and good order."

Feeling himself established, though quite penniless, and not in the best of health, Moltke now began to fret about the careers of his younger brothers. "I hope that he [Adolf] and Ludwig will decide on not trying to make a career in Denmark . . ." he wrote his mother. "I shall never regret having given up the comforts of home, and so having secured prospects of advancement, little as may have come of it hitherto."

The hoped-for advancement came just two months later. "I have been quite unexpectedly appointed . . . to the Survey Office," he wrote in May 1828, "and by June 1 I must be at Namslau, in Upper Silesia. As you may suppose, it was a delightful surprise to me." The life of a military surveyor seems to have been a rather pleasant one. Moltke moved at a leisurely pace across the fertile fields of Silesia, staying with the local gentry and living the life of characters in Chekhov.

"In the last four or five weeks I have been living here on the estate of one Herr von Kleist, who makes me as much at home as a child of his own . . ." Moltke wrote that summer from Gruttenberg, northeast of Breslau. "At half past four in the morning a coffee-pot is brought in to me, with two plates on which slices of bread and butter and cakes are piled up to a considerable height, irresistibly suggesting the hospitality of a Highland chieftain. Then I sally forth attired in unbleached gaiters, a gray dust cloak, white foraging cap, and gloves without finger-tips, armed with an instrument case and a good Ramsden telescope. Behind me my servant with the plane-table. . . . Every mayor is enjoined to provide us with horses, quarters, and two men every day. As soon as I get in we sit down to dinner, when my only anxiety is how to manage to eat some of each dish, there are so many . . . and good Hungary wine in plenty."

There was clearly an artistic streak running through Moltke, and if he had been born in another time and place, he might well have found himself a very different career. His artistic gift was not really creative or original, but rather descriptive and analytical. "I have had the opportunity of copying many pretty pictures . . . " he wrote of his wanderings through Silesia. "I brought with me a Holy Family by Rubens; it is the largest thing I have yet done, and includes four heads of life-size, of the greatest beauty—not counting the head of the Dove." A splendid accomplishment for a young Prussian lieutenant but still only copying. There is perhaps more real artistry in the maps he loved making all his life, not only more craft but more feeling. He took sketchbooks on all his surveying trips, and all his other travels, too, and filled them with a great variety of skillfully drawn scenes, landscapes, portraits. But here, too, one senses the analytical rather than the expressive temperament. He is recording exactly what he sees, neither more nor less.

Moltke's artistic instincts took other forms as well. He loved music, poetry, the theatre, and he was delighted when the call of the general staff brought him back to Berlin in the autumn of 1828. The labors were not too demanding. "Work at the office goes on till two," he wrote his mother that Christmas, "drawing, reducing plans or taking problems from the staff officers of the General Staff. . . . Then come our private studies. I am attending, gratis, a course on French literature, one on modern history at the office, and one on Goethe at the University . . . My other lessons, besides these, cost me thirteen thalers, sixteen silver groschen a month; namely Russian, riding, and dancing. This last is only for the sake of the Mazurka, which I must know in case I go to Poland next summer. . . . Russian I consider of the first importance. Russia is to Prussia of the first consequence, and very few are familiar with its language; I work at it with great zeal . . ."

The idea that he needed to learn the mazurka in case he was assigned to Poland suggests that he was at least exploring the possibilities of finding a wife, but his natural reticence combined with the formalities of the age to fill him with caution. As early as his *Kriegsschule* days, when he escaped for a fortnight to the spa of Ober-Salzbrunn, he wrote to his mother: "There is a young girl here worthy to be your daughter-in-law. She is a Countess Reichenbach. She is lovely and well educated; you would take her to your heart. But unluckily she has no fortune. . . . I do not know whether you have ever had much to do with Poles; nothing can be pleasanter; you are made at home at once . . . and yet I should not like to give you a Polish daughter-in-law. . . . My finances . . . require the strictest economy. . . ."

These nervous explorations by the penniless lieutenant galvanized his unfocused artistic inclinations to produce one of his oddest creations, a rather stiff novella of wartime adventure and romance titled *The Two Friends*. The two friends are Prussian officers engaged in some desultory fighting in Austrian territory during the last days of Frederick the Great's Seven Years War. One of them, Gustavus, sends his friend Ernest to propose marriage to the young Countess Ida von Eichenbach, whom he had courted during a previous visit to the Eichenbach Castle. Ernest dutifully carries out his commission without mentioning that he, too, had once stayed at the castle and he, too, had fallen in love with the countess. Having outlined this rather espaliered romance, Moltke soon pushes it into the background so that he can concentrate on developments more to his taste and interest: a series of chases, battles, scaling of walls, fording of rivers, and so on. At the end, when he finally must resolve the conflict between the two suitors, he suddenly lets the rivals discover that they are in love with two different Countesses Ida von Eichenbach, and since the war providentially comes to an end, the Prussian officers and the Austrian ladies can all live happily ever after.

Since the literary claims of this little work are not large, admiring scholars have raked through it for autobiographical clues. The name of the Eichenbach family naturally aroused suspicions that Moltke felt more strongly than he had admitted about that Countess Reichenbach whom he had described to his mother three years earlier as "lovely and well educated" and "worthy to be your daughter-in-law." At about this same time, Moltke wrote his mother of the Polish aristocrats he met in Silesia: "While we regard them as feather-brained and boastful, they can but look upon us as excessively pedantic, and even somewhat hypocritical. In forming an estimate of the young ladies especially, it behooves a man to be on his guard. Betrayed by their friendliness, and an absence of formality which surprises a foreigner, a simpleton might be led to believe that he had but to pursue and conquer. . . ."

Passages like that have led biographical analysts of *The Two Friends* to regard Ernest, the more introspective of the two, as a kind of self-portrait of Moltke in his twenties. "His companion was a slim youth, the real type of a northerner," Moltke wrote of this Prussian officer. "His expressive face was surrounded by fair curls. Without being handsome, his features were noble and full of earnestness. His bearing was elegant, and he was quite at home in his handsome uniform." As for the more outgoing Gustavus, who was "tall and powerfully built," with "an easy good humor founded on a certain self confidence," literary scholarship has even identified him as one of Moltke's friends named Count Wartensleben, whom Moltke visited several times at his home in Schweidnitz, a few miles from Kreisau.

Seeking literary models that Moltke might have used, German scholars have cited E.T.A. Hoffmann, Ludwig Tieck, and, inevitably, Goethe, but none of this matters a great deal, since Moltke never finished another story. He published *The Two Friends* in 1827 as a serial in a Berlin periodical called *Der Freimütige,* which never paid him. Moltke's literary career, like his military career, was soon shaken by contemporary political events, specifically the rebellion in Paris in July 1830, which led to the abdication of King Charles X and his replacement by Louis Philippe; the following month Belgians rebelled against their forced union with the Dutch under the rule of King William I of the House of Orange. There was no good reason why any outsider should feel obliged to intervene in these upheavals, but they both challenged the post-Napoleonic equilibrium that had been carefully worked out at the Vienna conference of 1815. Once again, cries of revolution emanated from Paris; once again, the monarchs of the continent felt themselves threatened.

Moltke had only a marginal view of these events. "In May I was sent out to drill the Landwehr recruits . . . at Frankfort," he wrote his mother. "Here elegant youths with umbrellas and straw hats and canes were put into blue jackets and so licked into shape that they now look like soldiers." But though Prussia mobilized in response to King William's appeals for help—the Hohenzollerns also had a family connection to the House of Orange—the various factions in the Low Countries spent the summer in maneuvering and negotiating. Moltke watched with an acute interest. "In the event of war," he wrote his mother that Christmas, "I may flatter myself that I should at once be appointed to the General Staff." And he was looking forward to that prospect with all the enthusiasm of a peacetime officer contemplating a sudden justification for his existence. "The prospects of war seem increasingly near," he wrote his mother in February 1831. "The Belgian question is becoming so complicated that nothing but a regular European war will cut the Gordian knot at last. . . . Whatever comes of it, Prussia is armed . . . Though she did not strike, though it was Prussia that maintained peace in Europe, if she herself should be attacked, she can count on the approval of all . . . and public opinion in these days is worth as much an army. . . . The night before last tremendous applause broke out at the performance of [Schiller's] 'Maid of Orleans,' at the passage: 'The nation must sacrifice itself for its King!'"

What Moltke expected was French intervention on behalf of Belgian independence, but the new King Louis Philippe had no such intentions, and so the great powers conferred in London on what to do next. Moltke's contribution—little noticed by the contemporary authorities—was his first major effort at political analysis. It had cost him a great deal of work. "I have read about a thousand pages quarto and nearly four thousand octavo," he wrote. "To establish a single simple fact, I have often had to turn over whole volumes, and only that the reader may skip every other sentence, and not read it after all."

Having been cheated out of his fee for *The Two Friends,* Moltke decided to publish his "small pamphlet" on the Belgian crisis himself. And so the firm of Mittler published in January 1831 a pamphlet with the forbidding title of *Holland and Belgium in Their Mutual Relations with Each Other Since Their Separation Under Philip II, Until Their Reunion Under William I.* The results were probably predictable. "Thoroughly impressed by the value of our work," he wrote, "we are astonished to hear the booksellers talk of unsuccessful ventures, of the depressed condition of the book trade. . . ."

In fact, Moltke's essay served as a justification for Prussian intervention, but it was rather too circumspect to achieve any of the success he hoped for. "When a people of its own free will despises the blessings of peace and renounces its own rights," he began, "when severing the bonds of society it returns to the primeval state of force, in a word when it launches itself on a sea of revolution . . . then it is right for us to search for the causes." He thus stated a basic thesis that the Belgian revolution had no self-evident causes, a thesis contradicted by the subsequent two centuries of Belgian history.

In trying to retell the complicated story of the Low Countries since Philip II, Moltke became hopelessly entangled in events as diverse as the Spanish Inquisition and the murder of William the Silent. Out of that tormented history came the obvious causes of conflicts between Dutch and Belgians, differences in religion and language, economic competition, political rivalries. But the very obvious reason for the Belgian revolution of 1830 was that the Dutch and Belgians had been very unwillingly united just fifteen years earlier by the great powers that drew the map of post-Napoleonic Europe at the Conference of Vienna. This suited the British and the Prussians, who both wanted to keep Belgium out of the grasping hands of the French, but it hardly suited the Belgians, who found themselves not only ruled by a Dutch king but saddled with the enormous Dutch debts.

In Moltke's history, the Belgians are consistently petty and irrational while the Dutch are both shrewd and valiant. William the Silent is "the only great man that the Netherlands possessed," while the Belgians possessed no real leader at all. They were repeatedly misled and dominated by the French. Moltke loathed the French Revolution for all "those sufferings which it had heaped upon the world," but he disapproved of all revolutions. "Regeneration must issue from above, not from below," he wrote.

What may strike a modern reader as simple prejudices, typical of a Prussian officer in the post-revolutionary era, Moltke undoubtedly regarded as high principles, intelligently conceived and intelligently argued. He believed in monarchy, in stability and order. But it was not entirely coincidental that his views supported not just monarchy but the Hohenzollern monarchy. Moltke's presentation of Belgian history not only justified Prussian intervention but made such intervention seem natural, almost unavoidable. King Frederick William III, having survived the Napoleonic occupation, did not live up to Moltke's assertive ideals. The British convoked a peace conference in the fall of 1830, and Louis Philippe soon made it clear that France would not cause trouble, so the great powers, including Prussia, agreed in January 1831 to recognize Belgium's independence. Overtaken by events, Moltke's pamphlet ended on a note of equivocation: "Here no judgment ought to be passed upon an event which is so near to us in time. . . ."

At about the same time, a similar event occurred in Poland—another revolution—and the recurrent German nightmare of war on both western and eastern frontiers may well have increased Frederick William's willingness for a settlement in Belgium. Prussia's relations with neighboring Poland originated in centuries of aggression, hatred, guilt, and fear. The same might be said of Poland's relations with all its neighbors, the Swedes, the Hungarians, and particularly the Russians, but the conflicts between Poland and Prussia are the oldest and most bitter.

The Polish nobles had a passion for fighting with each other, however, and they were unable to resist the rapacity of their larger neighbors. Queen Maria Theresa of Austria started the final pillaging by simply seizing a piece of Polish territory. Frederick the Great and Catherine of Russia then joined in by taking adjoining territories for themselves. The First Partition of 1772 cost Poland one-fifth of its population and one-fourth of its territory.

After two decades of trying to accommodate their despoilers, the Poles finally rebelled in 1791, but Catherine of Russia responded with an invasion. The Prussian heirs of Frederick, who had pledged themselves to defend Poland against any attack, now did nothing except to join the victorious Catherine in the Second Partition of 1793, which reduced Poland to about one-third of its original size. Thaddeus Kosciusko, a hero of the American Revolution, led a new insurrection against the dismemberment, but Russian troops soon overpowered him. In the Third Partition of 1795–1796, Prussia moved as far east as Warsaw, Austria took Galicia, and Russia swallowed up everything else.

Napoleon disrupted this settlement by reestablishing a Grand Duchy of Warsaw, with the king of Saxony as grand duke and the French in charge of administration. The Poles obligingly provided 80,000 men for Napoleon's march on Moscow and loyally supported him to his final defeat at Leipzig. The Congress of Vienna abolished the Grand Duchy of Warsaw and largely re-created the partitions of the eighteenth century; it turned a small section of central Poland into what became known as the Congress Kingdom, a supposedly autonomous state that was required to accept the tsar of all the Russias as its king.

It was against this renewed Russian domination that a band of Warsaw military cadets, perhaps inspired by the rebellions in Paris and Brussels, rose in revolt on November 29, 1830. They were surprisingly successful, drawing nearly 100,000 Polish troops to their side and driving the Russian Grand Duke Constantine from the country. It was only a matter of time, though, for the Russians to reorganize and invade. Then came the inevitable massacres and maneuvers. Prussia's irresolute Frederick William mobilized for intervention but did not intervene. He favored the Russians and did his best to block any aid for the insurgent Poles. Fighting dragged on through the spring and summer of 1831.

It was now Moltke's job to think about such things, for he was gradually being taken into the General Staff. By March 1831, he was writing his mother that he was "now at work in the office of the General Staff, without being attached to it. . . . I must have a horse." A year later, he confirmed that he had been formally appointed to the General Staff, "perhaps as a first lieutenant." Once again, he worried about how a lieutenant's pay could support such an honorific position. "The appointment brings with it very serious expenses; in the first place I must have a horse." A relative had already loaned him 200 thalers for expenses, and so he had spent them on "a really capital black horse," plus saddle, bridle, and stable furniture.

"But where is the second horse to come from? That a second is indispensable you will easily believe, when you consider that the journey of the General Staff . . . through Thuringia involves a ride of 280 English miles and that it is neither customary nor possible to travel without a servant. Occasionally whole days are spent on horseback, and it is not regarded favorably if any order is not carried out at full gallop. One horse cannot suffice for this, and many officers think it scarcely possible to do with two." The result of all this, in the following paragraph of his letter, was "to beg you, if possible, to help me with 200 thalers." The loan was "not necessary—not indispensably necessary," for he could always acquire a horse on credit, but that would be expensive and awkward "so this certainly is the moment when I most need help, and I hope it will be the last."

Moltke also hoped to earn a little money by writing a pamphlet on the Polish crisis. He wrote about Poland with considerably more verve than he had written about Belgium, for he knew the country. He had climbed its mountains and surveyed its fields, and he felt a certain fondness for its temperamental people; he wrote of them with the same sort of patronizing affection that a broad-minded British colonial officer might have shown in speaking of the Indians or the Chinese.

In surveying what he called *An Account of the Internal State of Affairs and of the Social Condition of Poland*, Moltke was fascinated by the way in which the warriors of the Polish nobility had made themselves virtually synonymous with the state. While certain economic functions like moneylending were assigned to the Jews, for which they were widely hated, no real middle class had ever been formed "to bridge over the terrible gulf yawning between lord and serf. . . . This is the only explanation why a country could continue to be poor . . . which possesses abundance of corn, wheat, wax, honey, hops, fish, furs, numerous herds of the finest cattle, the most excellent horses, an inexhaustible supply of salt, and immense supplies of timber for ships and houses. . . . The abundance of its produce was of no aid to it for, it had no highways by which to carry it away, no ships to transport it, nor factories to work it up. . . ." The nobles held all political rights, but if any of them engaged in trade, he lost his nobility. "The republic . . . was without a treasury and even without a fixed government revenue."

Moltke's conclusion from all this was that the Poles were unfit to govern themselves. "We are only astonished that it could have existed so long," he wrote. In Prussia, by contrast, Moltke viewed the seizure of Posen province as bringing a wave of benefits.

Prussia had a right, almost a duty, to intervene and restore order in its turbulent neighbor. But while such implications seem natural to the ambitious authors of policy papers, a saving caution guides the rulers who must commit their armed forces to such projects. The feckless Frederick William sent the aged Count Gneisenau with four army corps to guard the Prussian-Polish frontier, a move that led to the death of Gneisenau and his chief of staff Clausewitz, then contented himself with watching the Russians.

Moltke wrote his pamphlets not only to assert himself but also to earn a little money in the process. He reported "a fair sale" from the pamphlet on Belgium, but that hardly met his new expenses. "I am saving at every margin to buy a horse," he wrote his mother, "but where I am to get three from, Heaven alone knows. I may manage to scrape together enough for one." There was no fortune to be made, though, in publishing historical pamphlets on various contemporary crises. "One wretch of a bookseller would have nothing to say to it now that Warsaw has fallen," he wrote in January 1832; "another had no money; however, he proposed to share profits and expenses. . . . So this is more risk . . ." The work was finally published later in 1832 by the Berlin firm of G. Fincke, which went out of business a few years later.

"Of more importance . . . is an undertaking I have just begun," Moltke wrote in that same letter of mid-January 1832. This was nothing less than a German translation of a twelve-volume edition of Edward Gibbon's *Decline and Fall of the Roman Empire*. It was an astonishing undertaking, for a promised advance from that shaky firm of Fincke of 500 thalers, particularly for a man who was supposed to be fully employed as an officer on the Prussian General Staff, but Moltke seems to have felt rather like Shakespeare's Richard III about his need for a horse. No sooner had Moltke accepted the project, however, than he began trying to subcontract parts to his younger brother Ludwig, who was just beginning a career as a minor government official. In a rush of enthusiasm, Moltke described the task of translating Gibbon's masterpiece as relatively simple. "With the magnitude of the task always confronting me," he wrote to Ludwig, "I have translated since the New Year twelve chapters, over 600 pages, with a certain nervous rapidity, and have arrived at the conclusion that by exerting the utmost diligence and speed—unfortunately more than is prudent—a volume may be finished every four weeks. . . . As to difficulties, to be frank, I have so far met with none. Although my whole acquaintance with the English language was gained by a four months' course of lessons and the reading of a few novels, I translate more easily from the English than the French, which I think I know pretty well. The relationship between the two languages assists one so much that one need hardly read the sentences through, the German ending fits on so easily to the English beginning. I might almost say that with the translation it is more important to know your German thoroughly than to literally understand the English. . . ."

If Moltke showed an uncharacteristic sloppiness about the work confronting him, he was no less gullible about its financial aspects. The publisher made his own intentions fairly clear when he wrote to Moltke that he thought it "of more importance to you to produce a work which will further the interests of learning than to receive a large sum for it." To further the interests of learning, the publisher flowed on, he would have to keep the price of the book low, and he could offer a payment of only 500 thalers when the translation was published and another 250 after 500 copies had been sold. Moltke, who placed his interest in learning somewhat lower than his interest in a horse, agreed.

In September he wrote, "I see that I can never finish the work unaided. I am working myself to a wreck over it." His regimen did not sound too arduous, though. "My daily life is as follows: at seven in the morning I have my breakfast and set to work. Lately I have been very busy with a *précis* of military history, entrusted to me by the General Staff. At nine o'clock, whatever the weather, I mount one of my horses, both very good beasts, and take a brisk ride of a mile or two [four and a half to nine English miles], and dismount at the office of the General Staff, where I am on duty till two o'clock. . . . Then I go to the café for dinner, and afterwards find another horse waiting for me at my door, and go for a short ride in the Tiergarten. Then I work from four to eight at my translation, and after that usually go into society. . . ."

A few months later, he offered a more detailed description of these ventures into society.

"During the last fortnight I have been to eleven balls, and have danced every dance while there, and I find it agrees with me. Last Sunday evening I was commanded by the king to a *déjeuner dansant.* These parties are small and select, and it is esteemed a distinction to be included. . . . You go at eleven o'clock, dance one waltz, then the gentlemen go into one room and the ladies into another; everyone receives a very pretty flower (artificial), leads the lady who has the flower that matches to the table which is decorated with the same flower. The so-called breakfast is really a luncheon, with . . . turtle-soup, oysters, caviar, paté de foie gras, and other happy results of the cook's art, and suitable drinks. Then all join in a grand Polonaise in the dancing-room, where a formal ball commences. . . . Concerning Gibbon, I wish ardently to be rid of it."

Moltke won a promotion to first lieutenant that April. This brought him an increase in pay, but "I must keep a servant and two horses, must live in the most expensive garrisons in the kingdom, and have been obliged to equip myself in the very handsome but expensive uniform." The idea that Gibbon would pay some of these expenses began to seem increasingly chimerical. Now nearly finished with the seventh volume, he asked about Ludwig's progress with the eighth. He said he "hoped" to pay Ludwig as soon as he finished his share of the work "although I as yet have not received a pfennig."

Moltke's relations with his publishers came to an almost inevitable conclusion. "I have begun a lawsuit against my publisher," he wrote in March 1835, more than three years after the great project had begun. "I am curious to see whether justice will help me." That, too, came to an inevitable conclusion. "I have come to a legal compromise with my publisher," he wrote that June, "by which he is to pay me the really miserable sum of 166 thalers; but then I am released from finishing or revising the work. . . . The whole sum is little more than half what I have had to pay for my grey. . . ." Not only did Moltke never get paid more than a fraction of what he had been promised, but the work seems to have ended in the wastebasket. Though Moltke once mentioned the first volume being "in print" a subsequent search of the Royal Library in Berlin found no trace of the work.

But to Moltke, now thirty-five and newly promoted to captain, was granted an opportunity that had never come to Gibbon. After a royal review of the Prussian and Russian armies at Kalisch on the Polish border, he was given a six-month leave to visit the capitals of Gibbon's saga, not only Rome but Athens and Constantinople.

• • •

The journey from Berlin to Constantinople in the autumn of 1835 was no simple jaunt. Getting to Vienna with another lieutenant named von Bergh was easy enough, but then came a turbulent passage down the Danube on a faltering steamer that went as far as Budapest. Moltke and Bergh then joined a Hungarian merchant in buying a wagon to carry them to Bucharest. And the rains came, and the wagon wheels sank in the mud, and the horses began staggering. The rains turned to snow, and when the three travelers lurched into some Romanian village at twilight, they considered themselves lucky to find a house where they could spend the night. By the time they saw Constantinople glittering on the horizon, they regarded it with as much awe as the Visigoths had felt on their first emergence from the Bulgarian wilderness some fifteen centuries earlier.

Despite his companion in hardship, though, Moltke was not traveling like an ordinary Hungarian merchant. He bore letters of introduction to various Prussian official outposts in the Balkans and he rightly expected to be treated as befit a baron serving on the general staff. The ambassador in Constantinople, Count Königsmark, provided a place to stay with a wealthy Armenian merchant on the outskirts of the plague-ridden capital. He also eased Moltke's introduction to the leading officials of the Ottoman regime. The most important of these was Chosref Pasha, the chief adviser to Sultan Mahmoud II. The octogenarian pasha told Moltke that he had a *Kriegspiel*, or war-game apparatus, that had been sent to him by the king of Prussia, but he had no idea how it was supposed to work. Moltke did. The pasha was charmed. He asked the young Prussian to return for further discussions.

Moltke soon found himself overwhelmed by Turkish hospitality. Chosref Pasha, he wrote his mother, "presented me with a snuff-box set with brilliants, which must be worth, I should think, at least 100 louis d'or, and will cover the expenses of my journey so far. He has also placed at my disposal a horse out of his stable with a handsome bridle and red velvet saddle. . . . A Kavass, armed with a cutlass and loaded pistols, walks in front of me wherever I go in Constantinople, so that I can scarcely ever be rid of him."

While he was charmed by Turkish *courtoisie,* Moltke showed a typically Western disdain for the Ottoman methods of administration. "Business gets done very slowly here . . ." he wrote. "Writing is generally done about as fast, and in very much the same way, as ladies' worsted work at home; that is to say, sitting on a sofa with your legs crossed and a long strip of paper on your knees, on which the characters are made with a reed-pen, from right to left." Even the bright young men at the Prussian embassy had already succumbed to the local lassitude. "We loiter into one of the numberless cafés, sit down on low cane stools, smoke nargilehs or hubble-bubble pipes, look at the vessels passing through the Bosporus and the dolphins which play about them in hundreds. The circulation of ideas is extremely limited; everyone knows beforehand all that his neighbor can know, so when we have told each other whether the wind is from the north or south . . . we loiter home again. . . . This is the land of lazy ease, a whole nation in slippers. . . ."

Despite the Turks' nonchalant ways, it seems likely that they were observing Moltke at least as carefully as he was observing them. He had originally planned to stay three weeks, then three months, but the Turks kept thinking up new projects for him. On learning of his experience as a surveyor, they let it be known that their whole capital needed to be surveyed, both the city and all its surrounding fortifications, and the Dardanelles, too. Moltke was quite willing to oblige. "The Pasha of the Dardanelles, to whom I was recommended, has given up to me a pretty little house on the shore . . ." he wrote early in 1836, "where the great merchant ships, with flags of every nation, are incessantly passing to and fro."

Having by now undertaken to learn Turkish, Moltke felt free to wander. He inspected the ruined site of Troy and sent his mother a spray of olive from the supposed grave of Patroclus. Sultan Mahmoud II invited his visitor on several tours of European Turkey. The Turks had good reason for their hospitality: the sultan was trying to modernize his decrepit army, indeed his whole regime. In April 1836, Moltke wrote that Mahmoud had officially asked Berlin "to spare him a few Prussian officers." Moltke told the Turks "that it was not a thing I so particularly desired that I should ever ask for it," but that if the Turkish ruler thought he could be of use, "I would certainly do my utmost to earn his approbation." Moltke seems to have thought that this meant he was declining the Turkish invitation; the Turks thought otherwise.

Sultan Mahmoud knew that he needed help, for he was being pressed on all sides. Indeed, he had rarely known anything else.

Anarchy in the capital naturally furthered insurrection in the outlying provinces of an empire that stretched from the Danube to the upper Nile and the Persian Gulf. The Greeks rose in rebellion in 1821; Bosnia was in revolt; so was Arabia. Egypt had fallen under the control of an Albanian warlord named Mehemet Ali, who offered only token allegiance to the sultan. Russia kept encroaching on the Black

Sea and pressing forward into the Balkans. The French seized Algeria in 1830. Britain repeatedly threatened force to protect its commercial lines to India.

Unable to rely on his Janissaries but determined to suppress the Greek insurrection, Mahmoud took the risky step of appealing for help to Mehemet Ali in Cairo, who responded by sending an army under his son Ibrahim Pasha. This porcine envoy succeeded in reconquering much of the Peloponnese, but after what may have been a series of local misunderstandings, an Anglo-French-Russian fleet destroyed Ibrahim Pasha's naval support at the Battle of Navarino. Greece won its independence. The sultan then turned to another brief and disastrous war with the Russians, who wrested away control of Moldavia and Wallachia.

As a committed reformer, Mahmoud naturally had other things on his mind besides warfare. He opened embassies all over Europe to establish contact with new ideas; he rewrote the legal codes to provide secular rules for society; he created Turkey's first school of medicine and its first newspaper; he started a music conservatory, which hired as one of its instructors Donizetti Pasha, brother of the composer of *Lucia di Lammermoor.* In the midst of all this, he managed to organize a new army that succeeded in suppressing his disloyal Janissaries.

But when the sultan tried to reassert Turkish rule over Egypt, Mehemet Ali sent Ibrahim Pasha to Syria, where he soon conquered Aleppo and Damascus and threatened to invade Turkey. Sultan Mahmoud, with only a feeble army under his own command, pleaded with the hated Russians to defend him, and so a Russian army landed at the Bosporus. The British and French, fearing a Russian seizure of Constantinople, insisted on a compromise. Mehemet Ali halted his invasion in exchange for the hereditary governorships of Crete, Tripoli, and Damascus. Both sides began preparing for another round of fighting.

In 1838, the sultan sent Moltke and another Prussian officer named Mühlbach to serve as advisers to a local commander in the east named Hafiz Pasha, who was trying to collect an army at Kharput, on the upper Euphrates Valley. Its nominal purpose was to keep order among the eternally restive Kurds; its real purpose was to defeat and drive away Ibrahim Pasha.

Hafiz Pasha, like his colleagues in Constantinople, set the Prussians to surveying, and Moltke roamed far and wide, as far east as Mosul in what is now Iraq.

"A few days ago, on a clear starry night, I stood upon the ruins of the ancient Roman fortress of Zeugma," the translator of Gibbon wrote to an army friend. "Far below in a rocky ravine glistened the Euphrates, and its rushing filled the silence of the evening. Then passed by in the moonlight Cyrus and Alexander, Xenophon, Caesar and Julian; from this same point they had seen beyond the stream the empire of the Chosroes, and seen it exactly as I saw it, for nature here is of stone and does not change. I determined to sacrifice to the memory of the mighty Roman people the golden grapes which they first brought to Gaul, and which I had carried from the western to the eastern border of their wide empire. I flung the bottle down from the height; it dived and danced and glided along the stream toward the Indian Ocean. . . ."

The Turks had not commissioned Moltke simply to fling champagne bottles into the Euphrates, however, but rather to determine whether it was navigable for their troops. Several Turkish guides apparently declared the rapids too dangerous to cross; they refused even to attempt it. "At dinner the Pasha suggested that I might try my hand," Moltke wrote, and so he departed that same night, supervised the building of a raft by torchlight, then launched it onto the turbulent Euphrates just after midnight. Not until sunrise did he reach what he called "the awkward places," where the rapids turned into waterfalls. Moltke had to take the raft apart and have it carried downstream for two hours, then launched again. "We had hardly pushed off from the bank when off went the raft like an arrow. . . . The whole mighty mass of water rushes headlong through this funnel, pouring over blocks of stone that cause powerful whirlpools and waves. In some places the water leaps up five feet into the air while the boiling stream shoots past on each side. The waves literally broke over our heads, and the raft was sometimes under water. . . . Steering was out of the question; two of the men fell overboard, but they were tied with ropes. . . . the raft went on about a mile *istedi gibi*—'as it thought fit'—until Allah guided us aside into a whirlpool and there twirled us round and round a dozen times, which enabled us to come to ourselves again. We now plied the oars with every exertion, but it seemed for a long time doubtful whether we should reach the land or be carried by the stream to a fresh cataract. The poles which form the framework of the raft are two inches thick, but three of them were broken; four of the sheepskins had burst and two had been carried away. At last we happily neared the shore. . . ."

All this exploring was only a preliminary, though. Moltke spent the winter months of 1838–1839 in training the imperial troops—many of them reluctant Kurdish conscripts—into some semblance of discipline for an attack. And occasionally there were forays that brought Moltke near to his first experiences of actual combat.

As for the main task of driving out Ibrahim Pasha, Moltke planned a defensive strategy, based on his surmise that Ibrahim would aim toward the Taurus mountains in southeastern Turkey. To counter that, he urged Hafiz Pasha to establish his forces at Biradshek, a strong defensive position with both flanks covered by the Euphrates. Ibrahim could not pass without exposing his rear lines, and so he would have to attack at a point where the Turks would have an advantage. Hafiz's attendant mullahs disagreed, however. They argued that it would be shameful to wait for the enemy to attack, and that Hafiz should advance to meet Ibrahim and his Egyptians at Nisib, just north of the Turkish-Syrian frontier. Moltke was now ill with dysentery, and the mullahs persuaded Hafiz to follow their plan.

When the two armies met just outside Nisib, Ibrahim began an encircling maneuver. Moltke strenuously urged Hafiz to fall back to a defensive position along the Euphrates. The mullahs once again urged Hafiz to be more aggressive, and they once again convinced him. Moltke promptly resigned from all responsibility for Hafiz's overall strategy, though he did agree to command the artillery that bombarded Ibrahim as he moved into position. It was useless. Once the Egyptians attacked, the Turks, whether governed by fear or bribes, simply ran away. Moltke felt that he had little choice but to join in the flight. When he rejoined the defeated Hafiz Pasha, he learned that their whole campaign had been overtaken by events. Sultan Mahmoud had just died and been replaced by a sixteen-year-old son; Moltke's own mission was canceled; as for the struggle between Constantinople and Cairo, the Western powers intervened to force another compromise. On what had actually happened in the hills outside Nisib, we really have only Moltke's version, but the handful of other Prussian officers in Turkey trusted it completely. "Moltke has behaved in all circumstances as a *chevalier sans peur et sans reproche*," one of them wrote later. "Though ill and by rights in bed . . . he was always with every reconnaissance, daring and dashing. The Turks looked on him as a sort of legendary hero. . . . I cannot understand how he has endured the fatigues."

Relieved from the pressures of war, Moltke finally suffered a physical breakdown on the slow journey back to Germany. "The sudden change from a Syrian summer to the late autumn in Germany, the very unhealthy sojourn in quarantine at Orsova, and the results too, no doubt, of great fatigue, brought on a severe attack of low fever," he wrote to his brother Adolf from Vienna in late November 1839. "I had to remain three weeks at Pesth [Budapest], and could hardly drag myself to Vienna, where I had to begin a course of radical treatment. Now, I can get up, and out a little, and eat like a wolf. . . ."

One reason he wrote this to Adolf was that his mother had died during his campaigning in Turkey. She had died like a Moltke, keeping her illness secret from everyone. Even on her last evening, she said nothing. Returning from an outing, she sent her daughter off to bed, and was found dead on the living room floor the next morning. Moltke was deeply affected, but he, too, went on with his work and said nothing. Returning to Berlin haggard and convalescent, he had to wait until the spring of 1840 before resuming his duties at the General Staff.

If he was a legendary figure among the Turks, he was hardly less so in Berlin. A young cousin named Marie Ballhorn remembered all the letters from Turkey being copied by her father and sent on to other relatives. "They made a deep impression upon us when we were children, even by their looks, for they were pierced through and fumigated to prevent spreading the plague then raging in Turkey," Marie wrote many years later. And then came the returning hero himself, visiting the Ballhorn house in Berlin just at Christmastime. "I well remember the tall handsome man with a Turkish fez on his head," Marie wrote, "entering the room where our Christmas tree was, laden with all the treasures of the East, so at least it appeared to us children. For my mother he had brought a tube with attar of roses. . . ."

Such family scenes in Berlin may have caused Moltke to think more seriously about marriage. In his younger years, he had been rather skittish. He had watched the disintegration of his parents' marriage, after all, and as a penniless young lieutenant, he had written his mother "that every marriage is a risk which we blindly rush into. That we should know and judge calmly of the being with whom we join our lot is too much to ask, since we do not love, know, or judge ourselves, and since what we find in married life depends perhaps as much on ourselves as on our partner. If we call only cold reason into council, it is impossible not to see that it is granted to very few men to meet in real life with the ideal of which each certainly dreams once. . . ."

These are, of course, the musings of a young man preoccupied mainly with himself, but Moltke was nearly forty now, and his mother was no longer there to criticize anyone he might choose. One of her last letters to him, five months before her death, had urged him to make a choice. "I am sitting quite alone in my lonely little room thinking of you . . ." she wrote him on New Year's Eve of 1837. "What will the new year have in store for us? God's blessing and health for you, my beloved Helmuth, that is what I pray for at this hour, and soon a loving companion at your side, who will make your home cheerful and happy. May Providence then grant you a wife who will be worthy of your noble heart!"

Moltke carefully saved this letter, but his most heartfelt answer went to his younger sister Augusta. "Marriage is a lottery, nobody knows what he will draw," he once told her. "If ever I should marry, I should like to choose a girl brought up by you." It so happened that Augusta now had just such a girl available. Augusta had married an English widower named John Burt, who owned estates in the West Indies but now lived quietly in the town of Itzehoe in Holstein. By his first marriage, he had three children, one boy who died young, and two girls, who had been reared by Augusta. The younger girl, Bertha Marie Wilhelmine, had been born at Kiel in 1826, so she was just eight when her father married a stepmother who kept receiving dramatic letters from a brother waging war in Turkey. This distant brother naturally acquired a heroic image for Marie, but nothing she imagined could surpass the returning warrior himself. "Thin and tall of stature," one contemporary account describes him, "with a sharp, bronzed face, and with lips that seldom opened, grave, taciturn and self-contained."

At fifteen, Marie was a coltish girl, with cascading brown curls, who liked to warn her friends and relatives, "I am wild today." When this legendary soldier suddenly appeared in her life, she was swept away by a wave of adolescent admiration, and Moltke, having passed forty under military discipline, was apparently vulnerable to just that. Marie's devotion knew no limits. "I am afraid of not being able to be everything to you when I am your wife, as I am so young and inexperienced," she once wrote him. "But for that reason I will now endeavor not to be obstinate or willful, that I may be able to give way to you when I am in the wrong. I have no manners for society yet, and I shall be so glad to be directed by you. But you will need much patience to excuse all my blunders. . . ."

The modern sensibility scorns such declarations as unworthy of a woman approaching marriage. And Freudian suspicions question the motives of a sixteen-year-old girl marrying a forty-two-year-old man, particularly when the man's previous romantic life remains almost totally unknown. Must we also be suspicious, then, that the officer and his bride were separated for long periods and died childless? Perhaps, but many nineteenth-century couples remained blissfully ignorant of the suspicions that a later age would heap on such situations. What documentary evidence there is of Moltke's marriage suggests a relationship of constant and enduring happiness.

"Tell me, why are you melancholy, and how can you be so?" Marie wrote him during their engagement. "Are we not going to lead a beautiful, happy, peaceful, and God-fearing life of mutual love? If I am not to be happy, it will be my fault, and I ask God to give me the power and talent to make you so in our married life. I cannot imagine a greater blessing for a woman than that of making her husband happy. You, above all men, deserve happiness, and I realize the high and holy duty that God has assigned me in making me your companion for life." If this sounds one-sided, the supposedly taciturn soldier could be just as devoted in his many letters to his fiancee. "Sweet Marie," he wrote, "when you look toward the South at nine o'clock in the evening, you will see a magnificent star rising on the horizon. This is the same star that my blessed mother so often admired. I never saw it without thinking of her because of it, and I have a belief that it is my lucky star. So then think of me." Sometimes he addresses her in English as "My own dear, dear sweet little Mary," and his tone is consistently gentle and tender.

If Marie impressed anyone as merely a flighty child, however, it was a false impression. A contemporary portrait shows us an essentially serious girl, with large and intelligent eyes, a high forehead, a long and shapely nose, a pale face; not an overwhelmingly pretty girl but a likable one.

And Moltke was perceptive enough to realize what he was acquiring. "My little wife is my greatest joy," he wrote to his brother Adolf five years after their marriage in the spring of 1842. "In five years I have rarely seen her sad, and never cross. She has no 'whims' and takes no notice of them in other people. But if she were seriously wronged by anybody, she would never forgive it; for with all her cheerfulness she has a strength of will and a depth of character which would show itself if anyone crossed her. God preserve her from such. But I know what I possess in her." By this time, their childlessness was apparent, and Marie accepted it as stoically as she could. "If God does not give us any children," she wrote, "I know He does it to prevent me from thinking too much of this world. He knows how to guide us all; something must be wanting somewhere, or we should become too fond of earthly pleasures. A wish that is not fulfilled reminds us of the imperfection of all earthly things."

Appointed in 1840 to the staff of the Fourth Army and promoted to major on his wedding day in 1842, Moltke remained on duty in Berlin without a great deal to do. "I draw slightly better pay and . . . have a pass into the Court box at the theatre," he remarked to Adolf. He and Marie lived very quietly, riding together in the Tiergarten, reading the Bible to each other in the evenings.

Reaching out for new enterprises, Moltke invested some 1,500 pounds that he had saved during his Turkish wanderings in the new Hamburg-Berlin railroad. Being Moltke, he studied every aspect of railroad building and even wrote a long study, *Considerations in the Choice of Railway Routes* (1843). As early as 1833, a Westphalian named Friedrich William Harkort was writing about the British development of steam engines and how much more quickly troops could be concentrated by railroad trains than on foot. Moltke absorbed all this, in his quiet way, becoming not only a stockholder in the Hamburg-Berlin Railway but a member of the board of directors. When he ultimately became the Prussian chief of staff, he would make the mastery of railroads an essential element in his victories.

But Moltke had many other things to write about during these piping times of peace. He published in 1841 a collection of the letters he had written to his family under the title *Letters About Conditions and Events in Turkey in the Years 1835–39*, a collection widely praised not only for its evocative descriptions of a remote empire but for its succinct prose. On a more professional level, he published in 1845 an analysis of the war that had preceded his own arrival in Turkey, *The Russo-Turkish Campaign in European Turkey, 1828–29*.

The most interesting and important of all these interwar writings—though its importance would not become clear for another thirty years—was an essay that he published in 1841 in the *Deutschen Vierteljahrschrift (The German Quarterly Review)* under the innocuous title *The Western Boundary*. Taking up the question of repeated French claims on the Rhineland, Moltke assaulted the ancient enemy just as emotionally as if the Napoleonic sacking of his father's house in Lübeck had occurred the day before yesterday. Moltke took the argument back to Roman times, because, as he put it, the French labor "under the delusion that they are the direct descendants and heirs of ancient republicanism." Moltke, by contrast, portrayed that heritage as one of degradation. "Gaul shared the misery of slavery and the worst demoralization with all other Roman provinces. It was first by the fusion of the slavish population sunken in vice with the free and strong Franks, Goths, and Burgundians that healthful life returned to the people of Gaul." The religious wars that rent Germany in the sixteenth century "soon gave France a new opportunity for brigandage," he wrote. It was by a combination of "stratagem and force" that King Henry II of France seized control of Metz, Toul, and Verdun. "Metz, till now a free German imperial city, subsequently became inclined to Lutheranism, lost its ancient freedom and was changed into a French provincial city. . . . The Lutheran faith was forbidden on pain of death." Lacking the powers of prophecy, Moltke could hardly have known when he wrote those lines that Metz would one day be besieged and recaptured by his own Prussian armies.

Moltke's indictment of the Bourbons' aggression was more general, though. He reviled Cardinal Richelieu for sending French troops to support the German Protestants in prolonging the horrors of the Thirty Years War. "France acted," he wrote, "like a thief that enters a burning city, not to extinguish the fire, but to steal." The Peace of Westphalia in 1648 was supposed to settle all these disputes, but Moltke saw it as only another stage in the continuing aggression.

"The court of Louis XIV was surrounded with memories of Roman antiquity, and with imitations of ancient art," he wrote. "Ancient mythology was brought to life again. Statues and pictures of ancient gods filled the palaces and gardens; the plays, operas and poems were fashioned after this model. It was . . . the second birth of the Gallic-Roman spirit. But this spirit . . . was godless, immoral and heathen, despotic and servile. The French court wallowed in all the vices of the ancient world, and presented a scene of shameless public life. . . . Unfortunately Louis XIV also adopted the ancient Roman system of conquest . . . and while he regarded himself as heir to the ancient Roman culture, it pleased him to see in the Germans again only 'barbarians' that he had a right to subject to himself by stratagem and force, just as the Roman emperors had exercised the same right."

Being a dedicated conservative, Moltke naturally regarded the ensuing French Revolution as "a catastrophe," but even this could be fitted into his overall view of Franco-German relations. "The Revolution," he wrote, "was a revival of the old Franconian, that is, Germanic element of popular freedom and popular representation, so long suppressed in France. . . ." Because the Prussians failed to resist the revolutionaries' aggressiveness, though, the French kept expanding, "and stole, stole like ravens." And so Napoleon rode to triumph because "he understood . . . how to flatter the two chief passions of the nation, desire for fame and covetousness. He led them to victory everywhere, and he gave them the plundered booty of all countries."

Prussia's obeisances to Napoleon after the defeat at Jena should "cause the German nation to be deeply ashamed," Moltke wrote, but the eventual outcome was inevitable because "when such a great people as the Germans become angered and arise in a body, France must tremble even though it had ten Napoleons." Though Prussia then gained a good deal of territory at the Vienna peace conference, Germany as a whole failed to regain the territories lost over the past centuries. "France kept not only Italian Burgundy and Italian Lorraine but also German Alsace and German Lorraine," Moltke complained. Now that France had recovered from the defeat of Napoleon and was again claiming a frontier on the Rhine, Moltke expected new conflicts. "Whenever they differ with us, they seize the sword," he wrote. And the next time that happened, Moltke concluded, with a remarkable prediction of what he himself would achieve three decades in the future, Germany should "not sheathe the sword until our whole right has become ours, until France has paid its whole debt to us."

But the time for Moltke to avenge the Napoleonic sack of Lübeck had not yet arrived. Instead, he was surprised to receive in 1845 one of the most benignly peaceful sinecures in the command of the Prussian army. Prince Henry of Prussia, a brother to the late King Frederick William III, was incurably ill, a convert to Roman Catholicism, and living out his remaining years in Rome. His aide-de-camp had recently died in a fall from his carriage, and protocol decreed that the prince must be assigned a new one. This plum was suddenly awarded to Moltke, who thus revived his decade-old plan of visiting the main sites of Gibbon's great history. His duties as an aide-de-camp to an invalid prince soon proved almost nonexistent, so Moltke found his own ways to occupy his time.

He read, he reflected, he searched, he wandered. "I am studying Niebuhr's Roman History," he wrote to his brother Ludwig.

On a more practical note, Moltke happily reported that his drafting table had arrived, and that he was "hard at work mapping the environs of Rome." This was apparently something that no professional cartographer had attempted in modern times, and it was a large project. When Moltke had finished the first ten square miles, he wrote to Ludwig that he still had about ten times more area to cover "and shall have to work at it for a very long time, more especially as in summer the heat is too great for such work. I wander up hill and down dale in enormously high boots, against thorns and snakes, and meet with no interference but occasionally from sheep dogs or herds of oxen. . . ."

Moltke seems to have undertaken this for no reason except the satisfaction of accomplishing it, but he had now reached a point where almost everything he did had political possibilities, and so, when the French army attacked the Roman Republic a couple of years later, in 1849, Moltke sent his map to Wilhelm Humboldt at the University of Berlin for forwarding to King Frederick William IV so that His Majesty might follow the course of Garibaldi's defense of the holy city. The king was appropriately appreciative. Indeed, Moltke's map of Rome was long considered the best in existence. It can still be seen in the library of the American Academy of Rome.

The ailing Prince Henry did not last long. In Moltke's second year, 1846, he died, leaving his aide-de-camp no further duties except to escort the corpse back to Berlin. Moltke set sail across the Mediterranean on a corvette, but he became so seasick that the captain put him off in Gibraltar, and he voyaged overland across Spain and France to receive the prince's coffin when it reached Hamburg.

Promoted to colonel and appointed to the staff of the Eighth Corps at Coblenz, Moltke now could look forward to little more than a few years of provincial tedium. "I do not want to rise any higher, and shall then retire," he wrote to Adolf in October 1847. And six months later, long before the acquisition of Kreisau: "My cherished idea is that by degrees we should gather together on an estate somewhere or other, where each of us should contribute in capital or working power whatever he could bring. I would rather that this possession should be on the beloved soil of Germany. But if matters should become still worse in the home-country . . . I have no objection to the other hemisphere."

What inspired Moltke to consider the extravagantly unlikely prospect of moving to the Americas was that revolution now threatened to overthrow the monarchy he had sworn to uphold.

4

The Year of Revolution

LIKE 1989, WHEN THE BERLIN WALL SUDDENLY CRACKED OPEN, 1848 was a year in which revolution spread from nation to nation with almost unimaginable speed. With revolution spread hopes and fears, appeals to reason and appeals to violence, hopes betrayed and fears fulfilled. The revolutionaries of 1848 fought for a bewildering jumble of different causes. Industrial workers wanted more pay and shorter hours; artisans wanted a halt to the disruptions of the Industrial Revolution; peasants wanted freedom from their debts and feudal obligations. Progressives of all kinds demanded constitutional and representative government, free elections, and basic civil rights. No less impassioned were the awakening nationalities. Hungarian and Bohemian patriots cried for an end to Habsburg domination; Italians sought complete independence from the hated Austrians; the ethnic Germans of Schleswig-Holstein protested against being incorporated into Denmark; the Poles wanted their partitioned country re-created and restored.

The preceding years 1846 and 1847 had been among the worst of the century: crop failures, business failures, unemployment, hunger. A potato blight that arrived from America in 1845 turned the basic food of the poor into black mush. The "potato famine" caused more than 20,000 deaths by starvation in Ireland and drove tens of thousands more into exile across the Atlantic. In 1847, there were hunger riots in Berlin, Stuttgart, and Ulm. The price of potatoes doubled in Paris; bread went up 50 percent. Some 700,000 people in Belgium survived only on public welfare handouts, and one-third of Cologne lived on the dole. The hungry in Flanders ate grasses and carrion.

Revolutions do not generally break out in the depths of despair, though, but rather when there are signs of improvement, and the beginning of 1848 seemed to bring some of those signs. Food prices dropped slightly. The carnival season in Cologne passed with unusual good cheer. While economic hardships naturally strengthened the sense of discontent, the prevailing spirit—as in 1989—was one of political dissatisfaction. The general settlement of 1815, by which Prince Metternich and the Conference of Vienna tried to destroy and bury the consequences of the French Revolution, had outlived its usefulness. Many of the restored autocracies no longer commanded loyalty or even obedience. The redrawn maps no longer charted national identities.

The first actual outbreak of 1848 occurred on January 12 in Palermo, then Naples, where thousands of demonstrators demanded that King Ferdinand II grant a constitution. French liberals had already won similar concessions in the revolution of 1830, which replaced the Bourbons with their cousins of the House of Orleans, but now a liberal campaign for freedom of speech led to barricades, street clashes, and finally, on February 24, the ignominious flight of King Louis Philippe, disguised as "Mister Smith" in a plain hat and goggles, into exile in London. The rebels in Paris proudly proclaimed the birth of the Second Republic.

The news of this upheaval naturally shook Vienna, where the septuagenarian Prince Metternich still presided over a regime that permitted no constitution, no representative government, and no guarantees of individual rights. *"Eh bien, tout est fini,"* the white-haired prince is supposed to have said when an agent of the Rothschild Bank told him of the flight of Louis Philippe. Inspired not only by the events in Paris but by nationalistic speeches from the Hungarian Louis Kossuth and a group of Czech liberals, crowds of workers and students swarmed through the streets of Vienna, fought with imperial guards, and demanded Metternich's resignation. Within a week, on March 14, Metternich too boarded a coach to safety in London.

The basic demand throughout Germany was for a better life, but the liberals of the professional classes, the lawyers and writers and progressive public officials, interpreted that to mean mainly an end to princely absolutism, a shift to constitutional government and civil rights. In the Grand Duchy of Baden, which was overpopulated, economically troubled, and close to the disturbing influence of France, the liberals won the elections at the end of 1846, and the radicals convened in 1847 to demand the right of assembly, free speech, and religious choice; the grand duke did his best to delay reform, but the fall of the French monarchy inspired mass meetings in Mannheim to renew the liberal demands. Though the grand duke obligingly named a liberal cabinet, the protest movement soon turned more violent. Crowds of peasants attacked manor houses and burned the records of their debts. It was the liberals, then, who called out troops to restore order.

Through all the thirty-eight states that made up the German Confederation, the agitation swept from town to town. In Saxony, Württemberg, Hesse, Hannover, there was the same sequence of shouting crowds, broken windows, leaping flames, and frightened princes giving way, appointing liberal ministers. In Bavaria, the popular anger also focused on Lola Montez, an Irish-born Spanish dancer who had not only bewitched the aged King Louis I but become a power in the royal government. Student riots in Munich forced the king first to exile her, then to abdicate.

The demands for change reached even tradition-bound Berlin, which a visiting American student named Henry Adams found to be "a poor, keen-witted, provincial town, simple, dirty, uncivilized. . . . The condition of Germany was a scandal and nuisance to every earnest German, all whose energies were turned to reforming it from top to bottom."

The most notable and most puzzling of those earnest Germans was Prussia's King Frederick William IV, who promised his people a constitution largely because his father had made but not honored the same promise at the time of the struggles against Napoleon. Frederick William IV had taken a small part in those campaigns (he was twenty at the time of Waterloo), but his main interests seemed to be intellectual and artistic. He studied painting and architecture under the eminent Karl Friedrich Schinkel, as well as law and finance under other experts, and when he came to the throne in 1840, he gave many signs of a new and more liberal era. He released political prisoners; he eased restrictions on the press; he installed the old reformer Hermann von Boyen in the ministry of war. His admirers credited him with high intelligence, political skill, and personal charm, but when he finally announced his plans for the first Prussian legislature in February 1847, he made it clear that he still believed in the enlightened despotism of Frederick the Great. This legislature was not to be directly elected but to combine the existing provincial assemblies. It was to meet only at the king's pleasure, to approve new taxes and state loans, to address petitions to the throne and give advice on government actions. Nothing more. "No power on earth," the king said at the opening session in April 1847, "will ever force me to transform the natural relationship between prince and people into a conventional constitutional one; neither now nor ever will I permit a written piece of paper to force itself . . . between our Lord God in heaven and this land, to rule us with its paragraphs and, through them, to replace the ancient loyalty."

This unpromising opening of the Diet was accompanied by a so-called potato rebellion, when Berlin mobs enraged by the high price of potatoes went on a three-day rampage that could be ended only by the army. The legislators took all this into account as they engaged in an unprecedented debate on their various grievances against the monarchy. Finally, they asserted their new prerogative by refusing to approve a state loan needed to build a new railroad from Berlin to the East Prussian capital of Königsberg. And all this took place before the year 1848 even began.

When revolution broke out in Paris and then in Vienna, the authorities in Berlin naturally began worrying about what to do if similar uprisings occurred there. Large but peaceful crowds were gathering every day in the unusually mild March sunshine in the Tiergarten to listen to speeches calling for political reforms and more help for the unemployed. The king's aides warned against leniency. "The only way to combat revolution," said the king's chief military adviser, General Leopold von Gerlach, "is to avoid concessions of any kind, and instead of calling in legislators, to assemble an army." The king's brother, Prince William, was no less stern. "The masses must see that they can accomplish nothing against the military," he said.

The king, easily cowed, agreed to the generals' demands for reinforcements, and so the streets were soon filled with marching columns from garrisons in Potsdam, Frankfurt-on-the-Oder, Halle, and Stettin. The street crowds, for their part, were swollen by more than 10,000 unemployed workers from other cities. But the vacillating king would not agree to the generals' request that he leave the city while they turned their troops loose to "restore order." So the troops marched around and looked threatening while various politicians organized political meetings, and the two forces inevitably kept colliding. Citizens shouted slogans, and officers waved their swords. Three weeks after the fall of Louis Philippe, the turbulence in Berlin was fully self-sustaining. On March 13, cavalry charged a political meeting on the central boulevard known as Unter den Linden; on March 14, cuirassiers attacked a group of civilians in the Brüderstrasse; on March 15, infantrymen fired into a crowd gathered outside the *Schloss* (the royal palace at the eastern end of Unter den Linden); on March 16, cavalry used force to disperse another demonstration near the *Schloss* and soldiers killed several people by firing into a crowd that was fighting with police outside the opera. The following day, March 17, the king shocked his commanders by deciding to give in to many of the demonstrators' demands. In a document signed late that night, he announced that he was recalling the United Diet into session on April 2, that he would grant a written constitution, and that he was ending all restrictions on the press. Although this seemed a royal surrender, the king also reorganized his own forces, putting them all in charge of one of his most assertive commanders, General Karl von Prittwitz.

March 18 started as a day of popular festivities. Delegations of citizens called on the king to thank him for his benevolence. Crowds gathered at the *Schloss* for the same purpose, or perhaps simply to watch whatever was happening. As the crowds pressed into the Schlossplatz, General von Prittwitz began to worry about the personal safety of the king—or so he later said. On the easy assumption that a Prussian general could face down any crowd of civilians, Prittwitz led a group of mounted cavalrymen slowly across the plaza, shouting at the crowd to disperse. The festive crowd suddenly became less festive. There were answering cries of "*Militär zurück!* [Soldiers, get back!]" Then the crowd surged forward and surrounded Prittwitz. A general on horseback may seem a commanding figure when he stands alone on a hillside, but a shouting crowd easily demonstrates his helplessness. Seeing Prittwitz surrounded, a Major von Falkenstein decided on his own to help out by marching in two companies of the Kaiser Franz Infantry Regiment. The crowd blocked their way. Amid the pushing and shoving, two rifles went off. The crowd recoiled in a moment of fear. Then somebody shouted, "Treachery!" and the cry spread. More firing. More shouting and pushing. Several officials came running out of the palace and tried to restore order. They were ignored.

The infantry proceeded systematically to clear the Schlossplatz. But the retreating crowds soon gathered new strength and began erecting barricades on all the main streets leading to the castle. Prittwitz sent groups of soldiers to smash the barricades, which were indeed fragile obstacles, manned only by students and workers armed with nothing more than bricks and clubs. But the soldiers found what soldiers often find in street-fighting, that barricades might be easily smashed but they could just as easily be rebuilt, that rebels who fled from gunfire soon reappeared at some other streetcorner, and that soldiers who could fight bravely against a recognizable enemy soon became demoralized by jeering women and pots of boiling water. Trying to clear the Konigstrasse from the *Schloss* northeastward to the Alexanderplatz, Prittwitz found that it took his troops four hours to subdue the seven-block area. They killed about 300 people in the process, most of them young artisans: cabinetmakers, tailors, and shoemakers.

That evening of March 18, Prittwitz held a long conference with the king and outlined the standard military argument. He needed reinforcements, which he knew would jeopardize the security of other cities; he could crush the resistance but only with great bloodshed; he recommended evacuating the city and then besieging the rebels within it. The king was dismayed. He refused to authorize an all-out offensive; he also refused to leave the city. Instead, he retired to his study and began composing an emotional address to his rebellious subjects, whom he called "my dear Berliners." (The belligerent Prince William, who opposed all of his brother's concessions, was bundled off to London on a quasi-diplomatic mission that served as quasi-exile.) But if the events in Berlin in March 1848 seemed like a defeat for the army, they were scarcely a victory for the people or for the idea of revolution.

The king's message blustered and complained against "rebellious and insolent demands," which he blamed on "a rabble of rascals, for the most from abroad." But he also offered a thinly disguised surrender. He asked the rebels to dismantle their barricades and send him "men of the real old Berlin spirit" who would recognize him as their "king and most loyal friend." Once such talks were under way, he said, he would remove most of his troops from the city.

On the morning of March 19, various civic groups came to the palace to offer their services, and then their followers began dismantling a number of street barricades. Prittwitz, worried about an erosion of his position, did not wait to be dismissed. At noon, he sent word to the king that he himself was removing all troops from the city, leaving even the royal palace virtually undefended. "But that is not possible!" cried the king. Some of his advisers urged the king to join the troops in quitting the capital, which he could recapture from the safety of Potsdam, but by the time the shaken king agreed to this plan, his escape route was closed by mobs of citizens shouting for the king to come and see the bodies of people whom his soldiers had killed the previous day. Seven or eight wagonloads of bloody corpses were hauled up to the gates of the *Schloss* for his inspection. The king reluctantly appeared on his balcony. "Come down and salute the dead!" the crowd yelled. And this humiliation he also had to undergo. Bareheaded, abandoned by his army, he had to descend from his balcony and stand silent in feigned mourning for the victims of his rule. As for the future of his nation, he vaguely promised that "Prussia will merge into Germany."

The leaders of the Prussian army never forgot this humiliation, which they blamed not only on the insolence of the crowds but also on the cowardice of a king who had refused, as they saw it, to let them restore order and protect his throne from the *canaille*. The crowds might have won the test of strength in the streets—if only because neither side was ready for all-out combat—but translating that victory into political reality would take more time and talent than were readily available.

Ever since the first stirrings of revolt in Baden that spring, German liberals had been appealing for two principal goals, the unification of Germany and the establishment of constitutional government throughout the nation. On March 5, even before the crisis in Berlin, a meeting of progressives in Heidelberg made the first appeal for the election of an all-German parliament. On March 10, the Diet of the Confederation acquiesced in the idea of convoking a new assembly to replace it. It asked all German states to send "men trusted by the public" to Frankfurt to help draft a new German constitution. If this seemed rather vague, it gained considerable force from the fall of Metternich in Vienna and the street-fighting in Berlin during the following week. About 500 men answered the summons to Frankfurt— the first such representative assembly in German history—and their warm welcome inspired them to call themselves a *Vorparlament* (preparliament) and to draft an election law for a constituent assembly. This granted the vote to every "independent" adult male, though it left local authorities to decide what constituted "independence."

Despite all the faults and all the dangers, these elections did take place, producing some 800 delegates to a "German Constituent National Assembly," which convened on May 18 at St. Paul's Church in Frankfurt. This assembly has been widely derided as a "parliament of professors" because it did love to talk and because it ultimately failed to accomplish anything permanent. Technically, the description of these intelligent and dedicated men is untrue because only forty-nine of the delegates were professors—most were lawyers, many of them in government service—but the patronizing charge is unfair for broader reasons. The delegates had no precedents in all of German history to guide them, and the precedents in other nations were few and unreliable.

The French Revolution was hardly an inspiring example, and the more promising American experiment had yet to prove its value. Only sixty years had passed since the Philadelphia Convention that drafted the U.S. Constitution, and it is hard to imagine what would have happened there if, say, Washington, Jefferson, Madison, and Hamilton had all been reigning princes who opposed any major changes in the Articles of Confederation. Besides, the government that resulted from the Philadelphia Convention was already hurtling toward civil war.

It is partly the function of constitutional conventions to conduct windy debates about abstractions, but the Frankfurt Assembly was particularly handicapped by its lack of experience. There were no political parties to herd the hundreds of delegates toward decisions, no rules or traditions that could get the job done, or even explain what the job was. Most important of all was the Assembly's lack of real authority. From whom did it have a mandate, and to do what?

One of the delegates, Friedrich Dahlmann, a lawyer and professor from Mecklenburg, had drafted a constitution for a hereditary monarchy with a bicameral legislature, but this draft never came before the full Assembly. Instead of actually creating a government to rule the united Germany that they envisioned, the delegates spent the summer of 1848 debating something that they considered more important, the individual German's civil rights. It was as though James Madison's Bill of Rights had come first rather than last at the Philadelphia Convention of 1789, not a contemptible mistake in judgment but one lacking in what would come to be known as *Realpolitik*.

As though aware that their efforts were somewhat disconnected from the realities of German political life, the delegates decided on June 29 to create a sort of shadow government. Though there was no emperor of Germany, they elected as "imperial regent" the Archduke John, a liberal younger brother of the Austrian emperor Francis. Archduke John in turn appointed a "government" under Prince Carl von Leiningen, with an Austrian foreign minister, Anton von Schmerling, and a Prussian war minister, General Eduard von Peucker. This "war ministry" issued orders telling all German states to have their troops parade on August 6 and to read to them a declaration claiming Frankfurt's supreme command. The main armies, Prussia, Austria, Bavaria, and Hannover, simply refused. (Britain and France, incidentally, both refused to receive accredited ambassadors from Frankfurt, and only the United States offered to exchange ministries.)

In the midst of all this erupted a crisis beloved of Victorian humorists, the Schleswig-Holstein problem. Though supposedly incomprehensible, the problem was basically simple: both Danes and Germans claimed the two states that lay just south of Denmark's Jutland peninsula. When King Christian I of Denmark had been chosen Duke of Schleswig and Count of Holstein in 1460, he had signed an agreement that the two lands would never be separated. But Holstein, the southernmost of the two states, had a predominantly German population; it was part of the Holy Roman Empire and its successor, the German Confederation. The crisis arose when King Christian VIII died in January 1848 and was succeeded by his son, Frederick VII, who had no male heirs. The Danish crown could pass through female successors, but the German states were governed by the so-called Salic law that required a male heir. Salic law would have transferred both Schleswig and Holstein to the German Duke of Augustenburg. In March, just as the Prussians were preoccupied by the rioting in Berlin, the new King Frederick of Denmark tried to settle at least part of the problem by simply annexing Schleswig, which was about one-third Danish in population. Rebellion soon broke out in both territories, and the rebels set up a provisional government in the Baltic port of Kiel. When Danish troops moved in to support their king, the Duke of Augustenburg hurried to Berlin for help, and nationalists all over Germany howled their support. The Diet of the German Confederation formally recognized the Kiel government and requested that Prussia enforce Augustenburg's authority. The Prussians sent an army under General Friedrich von Wrangel, supported by contingents from Hannover and Brunswick, marching into Holstein.

Not only did the Danes have their own nationalistic view of the situation, but the rulers of Britain, Russia, and Sweden disapproved of any disturbance of Danish rule at the mouth of the Baltic. Wrangel, not the most gifted of commanders, found that he could dominate the disputed territories, but the Danish fleet blockaded the coast and prevented him from pushing on into Jutland. When the Russians threatened to send in troops to support the Danes, King Frederick William of Prussia gave way and signed the armistice of Malmö on August 26. The armistice abandoned the provisional government in Kiel and provisionally turned Schleswig and Holstein over to a mixed commission dominated by the Danes. This may have seemed to Frederick William a sensible cutting of losses, but Schleswig-Holstein had become an issue on which German nationalists were no longer sensible. Though we now associate nationalism with conservatism, German nationalism in the mid-nineteenth century was primarily a liberal cause. So the "oppression" of Schleswig-Holstein became entangled with the oppression of the working class. And the parliamentarians who had gathered in Frankfurt to right all these wrongs became correspondingly indignant over what Benjamin Disraeli sneered at as "dreamy and dangerous nonsense." Not only had Frederick William heartlessly abandoned the citizens of Schleswig-Holstein by making peace but he had done so without consulting them, the new "government" of Germany. The legislators angrily voted on September 5 to reject the armistice of Malmö. The "government" of Prince Leiningen resigned. The parliament then decided to accept reality and voted to endorse the armistice. This seemed to many a shameful surrender to Prussian autocracy, and so crowds began rioting in Frankfurt. Two leading legislators were murdered before Prussian and Hessian soldiers restored order.

But what of the constitution that the delegates were supposed to be drafting? The delegates had spent all summer debating what they called *Grundrechte*, or basic rights—in effect a German bill of rights to sweep away the remnants of feudalism and standardize the meaning of citizenship in thirty-eight different states, starting with freedom of speech. While Madison and the delegates in Philadelphia had been content to proclaim that "Congress shall make no law . . . abridging the freedom of speech," the parliamentarians in Frankfurt wanted it explained in detail that every German now had the right "freely to express his opinion in words, writing, print and pictures." They went on then to guarantee the right to assemble and form organizations; they forbade arbitrary searches and arrests; they promised complete freedom of religion. Going into smaller detail, they outlawed all class privileges, ranging from aristocrats' demands on peasant labor to such special cases as hunting rights. Though many historians have sneered at the Frankfurt delegates for their lack of "realism," this elaborate charter of civil rights was one that Germans might well have remembered with sorrow when so many of those rights were later denied them.

The list came to fifty articles in all, and though the parliamentarians had not yet created any real government to carry them out, they had them all published as laws. By mid-October, though, they had to confront the problems of creating a national government. They wanted a constitutional monarchy with a bicameral legislature—vaguely modeled on what the British had achieved after several centuries of conflict—but their efforts to create a government were immediately entangled in the question of what lands they proposed to govern. Specifically, Austria had long been accepted as head of the German Confederation, heir to the Holy Roman Empire, but how could a new government of Germany include the Austrians' restless subjects in Hungary, Bohemia, Italy? After some heated debates between the factions known as *grossdeutch* (greater German) and *kleindeutch* (lesser German), the delegates voted to exclude all non-German territories and to make the king of Prussia their emperor. The church bells of Frankfurt tolled in honor of the new constitution for a new Germany. A delegation voyaged to Berlin in April 1849 to offer Frederick William the imperial crown.

During the year of constitutional deliberations, though, the political situation in Germany had greatly changed. The frightened princes had stopped making concessions to street crowds and protesting delegations. They had fallen back on their military forces, and those forces had carried out their orders. The most important of these reversals occurred in Vienna, which had witnessed not only the outbreak of nationalist rebellions in Bohemia, Hungary, and Italy but a radical seizure of the imperial city itself. In early October, a mob attacked the war ministry, murdered the minister, and seized 30,000 rifles from the city armory. The imperial court fled to Olmütz in Moravia to await the army's revenge. Prince Alfred von Windischgrätz, who had crushed an insurrection in Prague that summer, now attacked Vienna with similar results: brutal cannonading, brutal street-fighting, brutal executions of anyone suspected of rebellion.

All this had its effect in Berlin, where the fate of the monarchy was still being debated. While the national delegates met in Frankfurt, the Prussian legislature gathered in Berlin in May 1848 to write a constitution for Prussia. King Frederick William, who had promised his subjects a constitution, was dismayed to see the legislators start attacking some of the Hohenzollern traditions. They proposed abolishing noble ranks and ending the designation of the king as "by grace of God." Emboldened by the Austrian army's recent victories in Vienna, the king of Prussia appointed one of his cousins, General Frederick William von Brandenburg, as his new prime minister, and this paladin promptly announced that because of political pressures from street crowds, the legislature would move from Berlin to the provincial town of Brandenburg, where he could keep a protective eye on its deliberations. General Wrangel reinforced Brandenburg's words by moving 13,000 troops into Berlin. When a number of legislators still refused to leave their capital, the king dissolved the Prussian parliament on December 5. At the same time, he responded to the demands for a constitution by issuing one of his own. This document made various gestures toward the liberals, proclaiming freedom of speech and religion and equality before the law, but it retained for the king full control over the executive, over the army, and over all cabinet ministers. It also granted the king large tax exemptions to make him financially independent. To show his openmindedness, the king said he would discuss this constitution with the next session of the legislature; he then proclaimed a new electoral law that divided all voters into three categories according to how much they paid in taxes. The richest 5 percent, who paid one-third of the taxes, chose one-third of the deputies. In Berlin, this richest third totaled 2,000 voters, the second 7,000, and the third 70,000. The bias in favor of the rich and conservative weighted every future election until the Hohenzollern monarchy itself was swept away in 1918.

So it was in a post-revolutionary state of truculence that King Frederick William received the thirty delegates from Frankfurt on April 3. To their dismay, he said only that he would think about their offer of an imperial crown, adding that he could not act without the agreement of his fellow princes. Some twenty-eight German governments then approved the Frankfurt constitution, with Frederick William as emperor, but the king finally refused the crown. He may have been influenced by a fear that the newly assertive Austrians would go to war to prevent the Prussians from claiming a leadership that had long belonged to the Habsburgs. Another problem was that the Frankfurt parliamentarians wanted to break up Prussia into eight parts so that it would not dominate the new empire. But Frederick William also had very personal reasons for his refusal. He felt strongly that he was king of Prussia by God's will, and he scorned any title offered by an elected parliament. "This so-called crown is not a crown at all," he wrote to Ernest Augustus of Hannover, "but actually a dog-collar, with which they want to leash me to the revolution of 1848."

There were scattered uprisings in support of the doomed constitution and the principle of constitutional rule. In Baden, scene of the first disturbances of 1848, Prince William of Prussia returned from his semi-exile in London to command a Prussian army that overwhelmed all opposition. In Dresden, the king of Saxony was chased out of his capital by rebels who included the young conductor of the royal opera, Richard Wagner, but Prussian reinforcements helped Saxon troops to crush the insurrection within a week (sending the future composer of *Der Ring des Nibelungen* into prolonged exile).

Both Prussia and Austria ordered their delegates to Frankfurt to return home. A rump parliament of 136 legislators tried to continue their session, but the Frankfurt authorities said they were no longer welcome there. The stubborn delegates moved south to Stuttgart and called for the election of the first German Reichstag on August 15.

They hoped to stay in session until then, but they were dispersed on June 18 by soldiers of King Charles of Württemberg. So ended in disarray and disgrace the admirable attempt to create a constitutional and representative government for Germany. The delegates to Frankfurt have been repeatedly condemned and ridiculed for their failure, as though that failure were their personal fault, or the fault of their "impractical" ideas. They deserved better, and so did the German people who believed in them.

Helmuth von Moltke was only a minor player in these upheavals, though they created the situation that would bring him to the center of power. By now a major on the staff of the Eighth Army Corps, stationed in Coblenz, he looked on the uprisings of 1848 with a mixture of loathing and contempt. This is fairly standard among professional soldiers, who are trained to believe in hierarchical order and discipline. But Germany was now wallowing through the political and constitutional arguments that had recently shaken France, Italy, and the United States—what is the origin of power, and how should it be exercised? On such issues, Moltke stood with his comrades-in-arms; as he put it, "I do not think that the worst of all enemies, democracy, has much chance with us."

In the early days of turbulence, Moltke and his fellow officers suffered what the military mind most resents, indecision and vacillation at supreme headquarters. In Berlin, generals like Prittwitz demanded in vain the authority to suppress the rebellious crowds at all costs. They had no sympathy for the king's doubts and hesitations about massacring so many of his subjects—or about whether such a massacre would indeed restore order. In the provinces, far from the center of decision, officers like Moltke could only look on in bewilderment and anger. It was this as much as anything that inspired his talk of moving to the Americas. In a letter to his brother Adolf in July 1848, he referred to "the shriekers in Frankfurt" and protested against the new idea that Prussian soldiers should swear allegiance to a constitution rather than to their royal commander. "If we are required to swear a fresh oath to a new constitution, I too shall retire." A month later, in Berlin, he ridiculed the popular demonstrations. "All these demonstrations prove nothing, or very little. Only a small number of people attend them, and always the same. But popular feeling is much excited; antagonisms are strongly pronounced, and the street tumults, which were half lulled, have broken out again. It is a pity that so much mud sticks to the tricolor flag, and that it should be offered by the hands of demagogues. . . ."

By September, now chief of staff for the Fourth Army Corps and stationed at Magdeburg, Moltke was cheered to find the tide turning. "The poor Fatherland!" he wrote to Adolf. "The better sort of the nation are silent, the scum come to the top and govern. . . . Berlin was almost unendurable. . . . The feeling here is very good; they look with contempt on Berlin. It must all end in war; and it is some comfort to think that the first gun-shot will put an end to the part of all these praters. God forgive them for all they have brought on our poor, unfortunate country. Then Prussia will either go under, or come out at the head of Germany, her proper place." And two weeks later: "Power now lies in Berlin, with a full right to use it. If they fail to do so now, I am ready to set out with you for Adelaide."

In his new post, Moltke could play a larger part in the repression that was going on throughout Prussia. "I have plenty to do, for democracy is moving here too . . ." he wrote to Adolf from Magde-burg, an industrial city ninety miles southwest of Berlin. "But we step in firmly with our splendid soldiery. The insurgent towns are kept in order by mobilized columns, whole troops of armed citizens and shooting-corps are disarmed, the ringleaders captured, and the rebels plainly taught that the law still has the upper hand."

By November, though, the battle was still far from over. "We are, it is certain, at a serious crisis," he wrote to Adolf. "It has come to a refusal to pay the taxes. The next step will be a red republic. And all this with the full sanction of the press, accompanied by addresses from all parts of the kingdom, and backed up by the bayonets of the armed citizens. . . . For all this, I am more hopeful than I have been for the last six months. The state of things has been so insufferable that one longs for it to be decided—as it must be now, one way or another. I hope to Heaven that reason and right may prevail. The Brandenburg Ministry may be an unpolitical measure, but its resolute attitude makes up for everything. This is the first time since March 18th that we have seen any show of firm determination, and it stirs the hearts of millions. . . . Wherever our troops appear, order is at once restored; the well-intentioned come to the fore and the most noisy have vanished. . . . The storm at our own doors has necessarily driven the Schleswig-Holstein business into the background. Our papers give us little or no news from that quarter. . . ."

Moltke's letters give very little evidence that he ever remembered his days as a Danish army cadet or a Danish court page, pledged to defend the Danish monarchy against all enemies. In January 1848, as the crisis was just beginning, he wrote to Adolf in full support of the legalistic Prussian position: "Considering the ultra anti-German policy to which Denmark has adhered for the last fifty years, and the endless obstructions by which it has hampered German efforts toward development . . . we here can only desire a closer union of the Duchies [of Schleswig and Holstein] with the common Fatherland. . . . It was not the Germans who abrogated the Salic law [against succession through a female]. Positive rights are on their side; they are fighting for their hereditary dynasty, for legitimate succession. . . ."

When the Schleswig-Holstein forces created their provisional government, however, Moltke seemed aloof and pessimistic. "If the Provisional Government should be broken up . . . such a peace would be but a wretched one, but, in the present state of Germany, how can anything better be aimed at?" A former clerk to the chief court of Holstein, Adolf took part in the Danish-dominated government created after the armistice of Malmö. Moltke expressed some misgivings about his brother's participation in "what seems to be such a thoroughly revolutionary, constitution-mongering assembly," but he saw no purpose in further fighting. "That it should be supposed in Holstein, that general war will be made for the sake of its petty interests, when matters are so serious all over Europe, is really too much!"

5

Bismarck Takes Charge

WHILE MOLTKE PLAYED A RELATIVELY MODEST PART IN THE CRISIS OF
1848–1849, the consequences of that crisis led to his rise to supreme
command of Prussia's military power. But not immediately. After all
the turbulence, the early 1850s were a time of retrenchment in Germany. Despite a good deal of pressure from Britain and France, Prussia managed to stay out of the Crimean War (1853–1856). It was a
time for making money, for investing and profiting. The German railway network, in which Moltke took such a powerful interest, doubled
during the 1850s, from 3,660 to 6,930 miles, and that helped Prussian industrialists to exploit both the Ruhr coalfields that Prussia had
unwittingly acquired at the Congress of Vienna and the Silesian coalfields that Frederick the Great had just as unwittingly acquired a century earlier. In just the six years from 1851 to 1857, Prussian coal
production soared from 5.8 million to 14.8 million tons. Steel production increased proportionately, and so did the output of textiles.

But the great political changes that would soon propel Moltke
into the supreme command depended on the rise to power of two
men. The first of these was the prince of Prussia, William of Hohenzollern, who, as commander of the Fourth Army Corps, had watched
with admiration Moltke's enthusiastic participation in the suppression
of the rebels of 1848. Younger brother of King Frederick William IV,
Prince William had spent most of his life as a soldier. Appointed an

officer as early as 1807, when he was ten, he had accompanied his father in the anti-French campaign of 1814 and the triumphal entry into Paris. He had received an Iron Cross for personal bravery at Bar-sur-Aube and joined the last fighting against Napoleon in 1815. There was a certain amount of nepotism in this, of course, but William nonetheless showed enough dedication to become a colonel at twenty and a general at twenty-one. He was a figure of honor and integrity, but as he showed in 1848, his mind was no broader than the parade ground that had served as his university.

In 1856, almost ten years after those years of revolution, King Frederick William suffered a series of strokes. He couldn't remember names, had trouble finding the right word, suffered paralysis of the right hand and periodic losses of consciousness. Being childless, he decided to make William the regent, and so the soldier-prince who was already sixty became ruler of a kingdom that he hardly knew. The peasants of East Prussia were as alien to him as the coal miners of the Ruhr. In the first days of 1861, he became King William I.

His only ambition seems to have been the expansion, strengthening, and nurturing of the Prussian army. As early as October 1857, the new regent asked the war ministry for recommendations on improving the army. The ministry responded with a few ideas in February, mainly a request for more conscripts, since the population of Prussia had nearly doubled since 1820 while the number of recruits still remained at 40,000 per year. Shortly after this, perhaps by coincidence and perhaps not, William received a long memorandum on the same subject from a friend and colleague named General Albrecht von Roon. A fiercely moustachioed professional, Roon demanded not only an increase in manpower but a transformation of those recruits into disciplined regular troops. The militia, or Landwehr, to which the liberal reformers had attached so much political importance, imagining it as a means for uniting the army and the people, was in Roon's view "militarily false" and "politically false." It had demonstrated several times in 1848 that it could not be relied on because "every *Landwehrmann* has become a voter." This was exactly what the reformers had planned back in the days of Scharnhorst, of course, but Roon argued that the militia lacked *"eigentlichen richtigen festen Soldatengeist,"* a nearly untranslatable term that might be rendered as "the real spirit of real soldiers." To inculcate that spirit, he said, the period of service should be increased from two years, where it had stood since 1834, to three.

William liked Roon's ideas, but he soon discovered that there was opposition. General Eduard von Bonin, the liberal minister of war, declared that the Prussian legislature would never accept such changes or vote the funds to pay for them. As regent, William could overrule the war ministry's worries, however. He created a special committee under Roon in September 1859 to draft a military reform bill. When Bonin resigned, the regent named Roon as the new minister of war, a post in which he would play an important role for years to come. Before accepting the job, Roon told William that he did not believe in "all of this constitutional business," and that he could not "bear the thought of my King and master subordinating his will to that of another."

Roon's reform bill was just what William wanted. Recruitment would be increased from 40,000 to 63,000, the term of service would be increased from two years to three, the regular army almost doubled in size, and the Landwehr greatly reduced. The cost of all this would mean an increase in the military budget of 9.5 million thalers. The Prussian legislature reacted much as Bonin had predicted it would. It sent the draft bill to its military committee, and there the legislators began suggesting improvements, which they said would cut 6.8 million thalers from the costs. William was apoplectic. Not only was the legislature disputing his judgments as to what his army needed but he was not ready to admit that it had any right even to consider such matters. Just as he was king by grace of God, the army was *his* army, and he was convinced, not without justification, that he knew more about its needs than any legislators did. To the surprise of those legislators, he simply withdrew the whole bill. The finance ministry asked the legislature, however, to grant a one-year "provisional" military budget increase of 9 million thalers, leaving all questions of reorganization unsettled. The legislators unwisely agreed.

The king and his generals were getting most of what they wanted, but instead of savoring their triumph, they raged over the fact that the legislators had dared to criticize them and restrict them. Having promised (in order to get the one-year financing) not to undertake any actual reorganization without parliamentary approval, they not only created several new regiments but announced that the battle flags of these new regiments would be dedicated at the tomb of Frederick the Great. When a parliamentary delegation protested about all this to General Edwin von Manteuffel, the chief of the king's military cabinet and perhaps the most ultra of all the military ultras, the general loftily replied that he could not understand what the legislators wanted. "His majesty has ordered me to arrange a military ceremony," he said. "Am I to renounce this because there are a number of people sitting in a house in the Dönhoffplatz who call themselves a *Landtag* and who may be displeased with this ceremony? I fail to see how these people concern me. As a general, I have never yet been ordered to take my instructions from these people."

The legislators saw they could do nothing, but Manteuffel was not finished with them. When a liberal official named Carl Twesten published a pamphlet favoring the two-year term of service and accusing Manteuffel of helping to produce "an atmosphere of distrust and hostility between the military and civil society," Manteuffel challenged him to a duel, shot him in the arm, and then demanded that he himself be ceremonially "punished" for his action. While Manteuffel served a term of mild detention at a fortress in Magdeburg, King William wrote frantically to Roon about the loss of the general's services. "To have him hunted out of my presence by the triumph of democracy . . . these are things which can rob me of my senses."

This may all seem silly, but Manteuffel and his comrades seem to have believed that a new revolution was brewing. To prevent it, they convinced King William to authorize the establishment of a large military force in Berlin: nearly 35,000 infantry, 16,000 cavalry, and one hundred cannon. Their hope was to stage a coup d'état, abolish the hated constitution of 1849, and return to royal absolutism. All they needed, then, was some pretext to start firing, to start the battle that would reverse the results of 1848. One of the events that most alarmed the generals was the creation of the German Progressive Party, which won the elections in late 1861 and became the strongest party in the Prussian legislature. The legislature then rejected the government's budget and the three-year term of service but it avoided any action that would justify the generals' yearning to stage a coup d'état.

The king dissolved the legislature; new elections in May 1862 only strengthened the Progressives. And when the king contemplated the idea of massacring the voters, he blanched. He began to talk bitterly of abdicating. Roon also proved less steely than he sometimes seemed. He tried consulting with the legislators to see whether some compromise might not be found. By September, he was able to announce one: if the legislature would vote the needed funds, the term of service might remain at two years. But the king refused to give up the three-year term. If he could not organize his army according to his own best judgment, he declared, he would abdicate. Roon then abandoned the compromise, and the angry legislators retaliated by again rejecting the military budget.

So neither side would give way on this small and technical issue, which both king and legislature regarded as large and symbolically significant. And without a compromise—or a resort to force—there seemed to be no way of deciding on a budget. At this point, Roon had an inspired idea that he had long planned to invoke when the inevitable moment came. So now he sent a telegram to a friend and protégé, Otto von Bismarck, who was idling in the south of France: "*Periculum in mora. Dépêchez-vous.* [Delay is dangerous. Hurry up.]"

Just two days earlier, a similar telegram had been sent by Prussia's foreign minister, Count Albrecht von Bernstorff: "The king wants you to come here, and I advise you to come at once." That message had been ignored. It was only when Roon sent his telegram to Bismarck that the second new figure in Moltke's rise to power returned to Berlin.

King William disliked and distrusted Bismarck, not only as a reactionary but as an arrogant, temperamental, and ruthless power-seeker. The cabinet and the legislature felt much the same. So did the king's wife, Queen Augusta, to whom the king had promised that Bismarck would not be made a minister. But when Roon told him that Bismarck was back in Berlin and "ready to serve your majesty," William felt that he had to at least talk to the one man whom Roon recommended as willing and able to overpower the legislature.

From previous discussions, William knew that Bismarck would demand a free hand in foreign policy, so he drew up a list of both foreign and domestic issues on which he demanded Bismarck's support. Besides, he wanted to keep Bernstorff as foreign minister. And to overawe Bismarck, as he had overawed Roon, he drew up his abdication. On September 22, 1862, two days after Bismarck's return from France, the two men met at the king's summer palace in the suburb of Babelsberg. Instead of listening to the king's statement of policy, Bismarck simply told him that the only issue was the choice between "royal government or the supremacy of parliament." If he became the king's minister president, he said, he would guarantee the triumph of royal government over parliament. The king was impressed; he thought he had found a man who would carry out his wishes against all opposition. He knew that Bismarck was difficult, but Bismarck did promise that he "would always submit to the king's orders in the last resort even if he disagreed with them." Bismarck did not really mean it, but the king did not yet realize that Bismarck had no compunctions about lying for reasons of state, and Bismarck's first reason of state was that he intended to rule over both king and parliament. That day, he rose to power, and he clutched that power for nearly thirty years.

In retrospect, there always seems a kind of inevitability in a great man's rise to success, and yet Bismarck's origins hardly promised such a career. He was now forty-seven, with almost no experience in domestic problems, parliamentary politics, civil or military administration. He was immensely intelligent and immensely shrewd, a skilled negotiator and tough as a rhinoceros, but few people knew of those abilities. He cultivated the image of a rugged Junker soldier, with his spiked helmet and his fierce moustaches, but he actually spoke in a high, thin voice and was prey to nervous outbursts and fits of weeping. Despite the helmet, he had done his best to escape military service and knew nothing of military affairs. His ambitious mother, who prided herself on being the daughter of Ludwig Mencken, a trusted adviser to Frederick the Great, resolved that a Junker upbringing in the countryside was not good enough for her sons. She set up house in Berlin so that young Otto could be properly educated at the Friedrich Wilhelm Gymnasium, then at the Gray Cloister. This duly led to Göttingen, a highly esteemed and liberal university in Hannover, where Bismarck read widely but distinguished himself mainly for drinking, chasing girls, running up debts, and fighting some two dozen duels. Appointed to a civil service post in Aachen, he frittered away a few months, then had to confront the requirement for military service. He tried to escape it by claiming a muscular weakness. "I feel pain when I raise my right arm," he said. Unimpressed, the army assigned him to garrison duty in Potsdam, where he won his only medal for military achievement by rescuing a corporal who had fallen into a ditch. He did manage to spend a useful amount of time at the royal palace, though, and there to establish a friendship with the future Frederick William IV.

At the end of that year of military service, Bismarck abandoned not only the Prussian army but the Prussian civil service. He likened himself to a musician in some orchestra and then added: "I will play music the way I like, or none at all." Since he was still only twenty-four, and the prospects for inexperienced conductors were small, Bismarck had little choice but to return to the management of the family estate, which his incompetent father had seen occupied by the French and was now in the process of reducing to bankruptcy. In the course of the next eight years, Bismarck and his brother managed to regain a state of solvency, but only by lots of drudgery and boredom. "I learned only from experience that the Arcadian life of a landowner . . . was an illusion," Bismarck later wrote. He spent the long evenings in exotic reading, notably *Tristram Shandy,* or in riding through the woods and trying to seduce peasant maidens. He also drank large quantities of Black Velvet, a mixture of stout and champagne, of his own invention.

He became much involved, though, with a twenty-year-old neighbor named Marie von Thadden, who was engaged to one of his friends and was one of the most prominent members in a circle of devout Pietists. She did her best to convert the scapegrace Bismarck to the faith, but her project was interrupted by the sudden attack of a fatal disease. She bequeathed the Bismarck problem to one of her best friends, Johanna von Puttkamer. Bismarck duly proposed to her, and was duly accepted, on condition that her father must approve. Bismarck thereupon wrote to the father one of his most remarkable letters, an outpouring not only of romantic devotion but of deep piety. "I am firmly and manfully resolved," he said, among other things, "to seek to live in peace with every man, and seek also that holiness without which no man shall see the Lord." Historians have subsequently debated whether this letter represented a true conversion or simply an early example of Bismarck's readiness to say whatever seemed necessary to get what he wanted. Perhaps both. Bismarck's Christianity, as demonstrated from that day forth, was a faith that seemed to confirm and support whatever aggressions and deceptions he deemed necessary for the greater good of the Prussian monarchy. This does not necessarily convict him of hypocrisy, however, for it was the age of "muscular Christianity." Bismarck's Christianity was not very different from that of, say, Cecil Rhodes or Teddy Roosevelt. In any case, his statement of it impressed Heinrich von Puttkamer, who surrendered his daughter to her suitor.

It was a happy marriage, for Johanna saw her mission as keeping house, supporting her husband in all things, and never protesting when he wandered off to the south of France to spend idyllic hours with Katharina Orlov, wife of the Russian ambassador to Brussels. But the life of a Junker inevitably bored Bismarck, and so he inevitably drifted toward his vocation. Even before his marriage, he had wangled a seat in the Magdeburg Estates and thus become a delegate to that United Diet that King Frederick William IV had convened in the spring of 1847 to get the funds for a railroad line from Berlin to Koenigsberg. As an unknown provincial of thirty-two, Bismarck made his maiden address a *succès de scandale* by disputing the idea that the Prussian people had fought for constitutional government in 1813. When liberal deputies protested this attack on a national legend, Bismarck casually picked up a newspaper and pretended to read until the uproar died down.

Such debates were all swept away, however, by the upheavals of 1848, in which Bismarck played a small and ignominious part. He was at the family estate in Schönhausen when he heard of the street clashes in Berlin. Apparently persuaded that he could lead a loyal peasantry against the disaffected urban proletariat, he spent several days touring local villages to collect weapons and arm the peasants. When military headquarters in Berlin declined his offer of help, Bismarck hurried to Potsdam to urge a bizarre coup within the royal family. In an agitated interview with Augusta, wife of Prince William, he argued not only that the hapless King Frederick William should be pushed aside in favor of his brother but that Prince William should then retire in favor of his sixteen-year-old son, Prince Frederick, in whose name the army would crush all signs of revolution. Augusta not only spurned Bismarck's scheme but never forgave him for urging it. King Frederick William also retained baleful memories of Bismarck's intrigues. He once referred to him as a "red reactionary, with a scent for blood, only to be used when the bayonet rules."

That was not a total condemnation, however. Once the Prussian army had suppressed the revolution, Bismarck's steadfast conservatism gradually came to seem more acceptable at the royal palace. And the king needed all the support he could find, for he now faced a new challenge from the south. Having crushed the rebellions in Italy and Hungary, as well as in Vienna, Prince Felix zu Schwarzenburg set about reestablishing the Austrian-led German Confederation after its hibernation during the sessions of the Frankfurt Parliament. He found a splendid opportunity when the elector of Hesse appealed to the Confederation to help restore order in his territories, and the Confederation asked Austria to provide troops for the task. King Frederick William of Prussia angrily ordered a mobilization to resist the Austrian intervention, for Hesse lay athwart the highway connecting Berlin to its Rhineland possessions. But when Russia hinted that it might intervene on the Austrian side, Frederick William's advisers persuaded him that he should back down, that Prussia was too weak to fight such an array of enemies. The Prussians met Schwarzenburg at the Moravian fortress of Olmütz and agreed to all Austrian terms, withdrawal of Prussian troops, and reactivation of the Confederation.

"The humiliation of Olmütz," as many Prussian nationalists called it, had a deep effect on Moltke, who scorned the Prussian generals' belief in Austrian invincibility. "A more disgraceful peace was never signed," he wrote. "And such an army as we had collected! . . . If only Frederick the Great had had such men! . . . But the worst government cannot ruin this nation. Prussia will yet stand at the head of Germany."

The fulfillment of that prediction still awaited the rise of the "red reactionary" whom King Frederick William so mistrusted. It was with very mixed feelings that he asked the tempestuous Bismarck to undertake the difficult post of Prussian delegate to the German Confederation's headquarters in Frankfurt—and with mixed feelings that Bismarck accepted his first important post. He was supposed to assert Prussia's equality in the leadership of the Confederation, but he soon found that Austria's Count Leo von Thun-Hohenstein, the Diet chairman, never considered such equality possible. Thun was immensely rich, and his family had been patrons of Haydn and Beethoven, so he assumed and displayed his superiority as a birthright. Bismarck responded like a coarse frontiersman. He frequently lit cigars at meetings where tradition held that Thun was the only man who smoked; he would even ask the Austrian for a match. He stripped off his jacket whenever he found Thun receiving guests in his shirtsleeves; and any time the count kept him waiting for an appointment, Bismarck left.

Bismarck actually was thought to be pro-Austrian when he first came to Frankfurt. Vienna was a capital of conservatism, after all, and Bismarck's own king was quite prepared to accept Austrian leadership of a united Germany. Bismarck's natural combativeness soon changed all that, as did his evolving view that Prussia must take command.

"I am a Prussian and want to remain Prussian," he said of the liberal agitation for German unification. As for the conservative penchant for an alliance with Austria, Bismarck's opposition was unequivocal. "I should be alarmed," he wrote in 1854, "if we sought protection from the approaching storm by tying our neat seaworthy frigate to Austria's worm-eaten old battleship." The first step was to escape from the German Confederation, and Bismarck wrote bluntly in 1856: "Germany is too small for us both."

Bismarck was not yet advocating war, but the idea obviously attracted him. "Great crises are the very weather for Prussia's growth," he wrote, "if we take advantage of them fearlessly and, perhaps, very recklessly." And then: "The great chance has come for us again, if we let Austria get embedded in war with France and then march south, setting up the Prussian frontier-posts either on Lake Constance or wherever protestantism ceases to predominate." The simplest statement of his plans was recorded by Benjamin Disraeli, who may have only imagined Bismarck's words after many of them had come true: "I shall declare war on Austria, dissolve the German Confederation, subjugate the middle and smaller states, and give Germany national unity under the control of Prussia."

This was hardly possible without the leadership of the Hohenzollern monarchy. Bismarck lost that wavering support when King

Frederick William suffered a stroke in October 1857 and had to give way to the regency of his younger brother, Prince William. The regent believed in an alliance of the main German monarchies, Prussia and Austria. To win a measure of popular support, though, he appointed a liberal cabinet to oversee a thaw in domestic affairs. Both strategically and philosophically, then, Bismarck found himself isolated. The regent offered him an only moderately attractive escape, appointment as ambassador to St. Petersburg. Shrugging before the inevitable, Bismarck undertook the study of Russian.

His grand strategy was unworkable anyway as long as it was based on the army that had backed down in "the humiliation of Olmütz." The man who would rescue it from that humiliation, Moltke, was seen by Frederick William not as a great strategist but as an impressive courtier. He appointed Moltke in 1855 to serve as a personal aide to Prince Frederick of Prussia, then twenty-four, the ill-fated champion of those who hoped for a liberal Prussia in some post-Bismarckian future. Moltke's first duty now was to join the prince at Balmoral Castle in Scotland. In his letters to Marie, he offered all the usual insights on his first visit to a Western capital—the House of Commons was too small, British weather atrocious, the wine too expensive but the beer excellent—but he remained discreetly silent about the prince's principal mission, the maneuvers that led to his marriage three years later to Queen Victoria's oldest daughter, "Vicky," the princess royal.

Moltke returned to England the following year for more of the ceremonial that attends a royal courtship. Queen Victoria reviewed her troops at Aldershot, and the Prussian visitor observed that the parade "eloquently betrayed the English love of pageantry." Of the infantry, he noted that there were five German regiments along with two English and one Swiss. These were apparently from the German Legion, a collection of volunteers who had served in Crimea. Described as a compliment to the nationality of the visitors, this demonstration may just as well have been a pointed British reminder that the visitors' government had stayed out of the recent war.

Prince Frederick had other missions. In July 1856 he took Moltke to St. Petersburg for the coronation of Emperor Alexander II. Moltke was impressed by the devotion with which Russian soldiers had died at their posts in fires and floods because nobody had ordered them to move to safety. At the end of that same year, Prince Frederick made a state visit to France, and Moltke caught his first sight of the enemies who had burned his father's house. Moltke scorned the empire of Louis Napoleon as a "magnificent swindle" and he was only mildly impressed by the emperor himself. "He has a good-natured kindly smile, which is anything but Napoleonic . . ." he wrote. "In conversation he seems even slightly embarrassed. He is all an emperor, but never a king." Moltke was not only observing but observed. "A general called Moltke or some such name . . . talks but little [but] is always interesting, and surprises one by his apt remarks," wrote the Empress Eugénie. "The Germans are an imposing race. Louis says they are the race of the future. Bah!"

It was only the death of General von Reyer in 1857 that opened up the position of Prussian chief of staff, which was not then the commanding position that it became under Moltke. General von Manteuffel, who then headed the army's Department for Personnel Affairs, recommended Moltke for the position, and Moltke's cordial contacts with the royal family reinforced the choice. Though the appointment was not officially confirmed until September 1858 (three weeks before William became regent), Moltke started immediately to carry out the chief of staff's main function, to plan and organize any future wars. One of his main moves concerned the general staff itself. It was a small organization, numbering only sixty-four officers, but that made it possible for Moltke to supervise the training of each one. And each one assigned to a division or corps—to commanders who often owed their titles to political or family power—remained Moltke's agent, loyal to Moltke and responsible primarily to him for his authority. Collectively, then, Moltke's staff provided the nervous system of the entire Prussian army, each nerve sending signals to the brain that was Moltke's.

His other main move was to speed and streamline the system by which the Prussian army mobilized for war. It was this system that gave an army the ability to strike first, when and where it chose. The mobilizations before Olmütz and during the Franco-Austrian war of 1859 showed all too much lethargy and confusion. The solution, Moltke saw, lay in the railroads, and he made it his business from the first to oversee the construction of every new line, every bridge, every crossing. Moltke approached the planning for war, in the words of a French military analyst, as *"une affaire industrielle soumise aux règles précises de calcul* [an industrial operation subject to precise rules of calculation]."

If Clausewitz was right in arguing that war was a continuation of politics by other means, then Moltke's calculations remained meaningless without a master politician to put them into effect. The master politician was biding his time as ambassador to the court of St. Petersburg. When the Prussian legislature refused to approve the money for the new King William's reinforced army in 1862, William dissolved the legislature, summoned Bismarck home from Russia, and offered him the prime ministry but without control of foreign affairs. Bismarck declined, explaining later that he was "not absolutely sure that the king would go with me through thick and thin." The king sent him off as ambassador to Paris, and the deadlock in Berlin continued. The king's ministers said they could not go on without a budget, the new legislature refused to approve the budget, and the king again talked wildly of abdicating. War Minister Roon kept trying to achieve a compromise, but the king kept refusing to yield any ground on what he considered *his* army. It was at this point that Roon's telegram summoned Bismarck home from France.

He then went before the defiant legislators and told them that the king's plans for the army were not a matter of choice but of necessity. "Germany does not look to Prussia's liberalism but to her strength," he said in his thin, high voice. "The great questions of the day will not be decided by speeches and the resolutions of majorities—that was the great mistake from 1848 to 1849—but by iron and blood." The legislators were shocked and angry, not because what he said was not true but because he seemed to be threatening them with a reopening of 1848, with the coup d'état that the army ultras had long yearned to execute. The waves of liberal indignation reached even as far as Baden-Baden, where King William was taking a holiday to celebrate his wife's birthday. The king wanted no violence. Bismarck protested, probably falsely, that he had not intended any threat of fighting, only a warning that the army needed more money.

The king decided to return immediately to Berlin. Bismarck, seeing his new grip on power threatened, decided to intercept the king's train before anyone in Berlin could get access to him. Bismarck made a bizarre foray to the unfinished railroad station at Jüterbog, some fifty miles south of Berlin, where he sat on an overturned wheelbarrow amid planks and piles of bricks until the royal train came chuffing through the dusk. Uninvited, he clambered aboard. "I can see how all this will end," the king said gloomily when Bismarck tried to explain his course. "Out there in the Opernplatz under my windows they will cut off your head and soon afterwards mine." Bismarck was nothing if not courageous. "We all have to die sooner or later," he said, "and what better way than that? I myself fighting for the cause of my king and Your Majesty, in sealing your royal prerogative by the Grace of God with your own blood, whether on the scaffold or the battlefield. . . ." This was largely rhetoric, of course. On another occasion, Bismarck compared his sovereign to a balky horse who "takes fright at an unaccustomed object, will grow obstinate if driven, but will gradually get used to it." The king was impressed by Bismarck's rhetoric, however; he remained in harness. "It is not easy," he said many years later, in the wry wisdom of old age, "to be emperor under such a chancellor."

And now Bismarck unveiled his grand scheme, a probably illegal scheme that undermined any future hopes for German democracy. What little authority the Prussian legislature had was its constitutional power over the budget, but Bismarck announced that he had discovered a "gap" in the constitution. When the king and the legislators could not agree on the budget, he said, the king's ministers had no alternative but to keep collecting the taxes and administering the laws as they saw fit. It was the same conflict over the "power of the purse" that had started revolutions in seventeenth-century England and eighteenth-century France, but Bismarck enjoyed an advantage over Charles I and Louis XVI, the steadfast loyalty of the Prussian civil service. The constitution of 1849 did in fact allow the crown to collect taxes regardless of a budget, and though it did not authorize expenditures without parliamentary approval, that was not the concern of the Prussian civil service. In case any Prussian official might waver in these troubled times, Bismarck made a point of dismissing several men who seemed to have liberal views; the rest understood what was wanted of them. The legislature again rejected the budget in 1863, and new elections gave the liberals new strength, but Bismarck ignored them all. The deputies might make all the speeches they liked. "We will take the money where we find it," said Bismarck.

In carrying out the king's desire for a stronger army, Bismarck saw an important weakness in the parliamentary opposition. The liberals resisted funds for the army, he reasoned, because they thought that the main use to which the army would be put was the suppression of popular demonstrations. This had indeed been virtually its only use for nearly half a century. But what if the army were to be strengthened for the assertion of Prussian power against other nations? How could the liberals object? How could any patriotic Prussian object?

Bismarck liked to say that a statesman's main task was "to listen until he hears the rustle of God's robes, then leap up and grasp the hem of the garment." So the listening Bismarck thought he heard an interesting rustling when Denmark's King Frederick VII died childless in 1863. His childlessness had been the central issue in the brief Prussian-Danish war of 1848, and then the Western powers had imposed a compromise that favored Denmark. The German claimant, the Duke of Augustenburg, had accepted a handsome sum of money to renounce his claims. Still more complicated deals followed. The sister of the late King Christian VIII renounced her rather feeble claims, and those of her son, to the son's sister, who then transferred all her rights to her husband, Prince Christian of Glücksberg. All the great powers approved these deals in a document known as the London Protocol of 1852. If that seemed to settle the question of the Danish succession, though, it left unresolved the problem of the relations between Denmark and the two territories of Schleswig and Holstein, which were supposed to be eternally bound to each other, even though Schleswig was almost part of Denmark while Holstein remained part of the German Confederation.

After a certain amount of arguing and exchanges of notes between Copenhagen and the German Confederation, Denmark's King Frederick had issued a new constitution in September 1863 for "our kingdom of Denmark-Slesvig"—and then died. Prince Christian of Glücksberg not only claimed the Danish throne as King Christian IX but endorsed his predecessor's dubious new constitution. And out of limbo sprang the new Duke of Augustenburg, who claimed that he had never been consulted about his father's renunciation of the family claims to Schleswig-Holstein.

All this maneuvering excited the growing body of nationalists, who noisily proclaimed it to be Prussia's duty to lead the unification of Germany. Every possible fragment of this fragmented nation naturally formed an essential part of what had to be united. "I wish Prussia to take an intelligent and honest step," declared the historian Heinrich von Treitschke, "and to start now the war, which will in any case break out within a few years. Prussia should—at the risk of a terrible struggle—finally, finally demand that Denmark pay its debt of honor to Germany. Should the war with Napoleon then follow, let it come. Our hands are clean, and the struggle will be a popular war which will bring Prussia immeasurable moral gains if not the German crown."

Burbling with nationalist fervor, the Diet of the German Confederation asked Saxony and Hannover to send troops marching northward "pending the settlement of the succession." This was not exactly what Bismarck had planned. "It is no concern of ours whether the Germans of Holstein are happy," he remarked. But he did have some very definite ideas on what he wanted and did not want. He wanted to preempt the liberal demands for German rule in Schleswig-Holstein and more generally for German unification. He wanted to increase and expand Prussian power, so he wanted Schleswig-Holstein not to become an independent state under Augustenburg but to be annexed by Prussia; but he could not admit any of these goals lest the Western powers intervene against him. The Danes' new constitution gave him a perfect excuse not to annex Schleswig-Holstein—not yet—but to demand the preservation of the London accords of 1852. For safety against Western intervention, he inveigled the Austrians into joining him, which they did reluctantly, and only in the hope of controlling him. Bismarck scorned all efforts to control him. When a liberal deputy in the Prussian Diet declared that the legislators would not support any war against Denmark, Bismarck answered: "Let me assure you and also the world that if we find it necessary to carry on a war, we shall do so with or without your consent." When the Danes ignored a Prussian-Austrian ultimatum, the German allies marched across the Eider River into Schleswig-Holstein on February 1, 1864.

Roon had written to Moltke as early as November 1862 to ask how he might wage a war against Denmark. Moltke responded the following month with two memoranda on how to attack. If the Danes decided to defend the Schleswig-Holstein border, they could be quickly encircled and destroyed, Moltke said. But if they withdrew to the strongly defended fortresses of Düppel and Fredericia, the best strategy would be to bypass the fortresses and invade the Jutland peninsula and attack Denmark proper. "So long as our navy is unable to cover a landing upon Zeeland, where we could dictate peace in Copenhagen itself," Moltke declared, "there remains only the occupation of the Jutish peninsula, which, to be effective as a constraint upon Denmark, must be of long duration, but which in that case may provoke the . . . interference of other powers." That possibility greatly worried Bismarck, not only that other powers might intervene but that the mere prospect of such intervention might cause the nervous Austrians to back out of the joint attack. King William decided on a compromise: the field commander, Wrangel, was instructed only to attack the Danes and destroy them before they could withdraw to Düppel. The Danes succeeded in withdrawing to Düppel, however, and Wrangel had no desire to assault them there. The Austrians said they did not want any invasion of Jutland, so Wrangel was ordered to halt at the frontier. There followed then one of those common cases in which generals either do not receive or do not respect orders they do not want to obey. Wrangel was by now eighty, and not in full command of his faculties, but it was a subordinate General von Mülbe who ignored the wishes of Berlin and marched into Jutland to attack the town of Kolding.

Bismarck could hardly countermand this fait accompli; he could only press the Austrians to accept it, which they grudgingly did. On the other hand, the Prussian advances prompted the British to call for a truce conference. Bismarck had to agree to talk, but he was reluctant to do so until the Prussians had won some major battle. The likeliest possibility was a storming of Düppel, a target that most of the Prussian generals wanted to bypass. "It will cost a lot of men and money," protested Prince Frederick Charles, the king's younger brother who was assigned to command the attack. "I don't see the military necessity." Moltke agreed. "Any reasonable soldier must see that a quick decision at Düppel is not to be expected and that time is needed . . ." Moltke wrote. "A good rider doesn't encourage his best horse to make a jump which will break its neck."

It is often hard for generals to see the political aspects to a military situation, and sometimes they succeed in denying them. As Moltke was to learn again and again, though, Bismarck's political views tended to prevail over any military objections. King William found himself persuaded that the capture of Düppel was a matter of honor—the Prussian army had not fought a major battle in the half century since Waterloo—and Manteuffel put the royal views in the most strenuous terms to Prince Frederick Charles. "This is a matter of the renown of the Prussian army and the position of the King in the council of Europe," he wrote. "The prize is worth streams of blood, and for its sake that blood will be spilled with joy by everyone from the highest officer down to the drummer boy."

The question of joy might be debated, but if the king of Prussia wanted his soldiers' blood spilled, then blood would flow. The Prussians stormed the fortress at Düppel on April 18, and despite a fierce Danish resistance, the attackers overran all opposition. "The endurance and devotion with which the [Danish] army held its opposition at Düppel must excite the admiration even of their opponents," Moltke wrote to his brother Ludwig a week after the battle. "Their troops suffered indescribably, far more than ours, which had the initiative of attack, and which, being superior in numbers, could relieve each other in the arduous task. But were the Danish authorities, in their insular security, justified in demanding such sacrifices? Was it even a just cause for which they demanded them?"

Interesting questions, which might just as well have been addressed to Bismarck, who now had the victory that enabled him to start the London talks on the following week. Like many truce conferences, it was an exercise in threats and bullying. Bismarck offered a number of minor concessions in the shrewd belief that he would never have to make good on them. The Prussian military objected to every compromise on the ground that they were being denied the spoils of the victory they had won at Düppel. The Danes, denying the victory, refused to concede anything, and so, after two months of wrangling, the London conference ended in failure.

The Prussians had taken advantage of the pause to reorganize their command structure on the quiescent Danish front. General Manteuffel felt there was too much confusion at Wrangel's headquarters, so he urged Roon to send Moltke there to replace Vogel von Falckenstein as chief of staff to the ancient field marshal. Shortly after that, Wrangel himself was replaced by Prince Frederick Charles, with Moltke staying on as the prince's chief of staff. There was only one remaining operation, an invasion of the coastal island of Alsen. Under Moltke's guidance, that rolled off smoothly, and the Danes sued for peace on July 12.

Bismarck had by now long abandoned all talk of restoring the London treaty of 1852, of Schleswig-Holstein remaining autonomous under the Danish crown. His terms had become quite different. By a treaty signed in Vienna on October 30, the king of Denmark renounced all claims to the two duchies in favor of the emperor of Austria and the king of Prussia, who were somehow supposed to rule the territories jointly. Lord Robert Cecil, who later became prime minister of Britain as the Marquis of Salisbury, described this as "one of the most wanton and unblushing spoliations which history records" but he sadly noted that "England stands aloof."

Just as Moltke generally swelled with rage against any prospective enemy of the Prussian crown, he also tended to feel sympathy with any enemy who had been conquered. His sympathy for the Danes who had ruled his boyhood sounded worthy of Lewis Carroll's walrus. "Poor Denmark! Poor king!" he wrote to his brother Adolf. "The founder of a new dynasty, who begins his reign by losing one half of the realm! . . . Indeed, it is doubtful if this state can continue to exist as an independent kingdom."

Moltke apparently did not yet realize that the Danes were mere pawns in Bismarck's master plan, which now called for the downfall of Prussia's supposed allies, the Habsburg empire in Austria.

6

"Vienna Lies at Your Feet"

"THIS IS ALL VERY WELL," A PRUSSIAN DIVISIONAL COMMANDER IS SUPPOSED to have said on receiving an order at the Battle of Königgrätz, "but who is General Moltke?"

If this report is true, it may simply be testimony to the self-effacing modesty of the Prussian chief of staff. It may also be evidence of Moltke's faith in the delegation of authority, in the decentralization of command. He believed strongly in letting field commanders follow their own initiatives and their own judgments. "An order," he once said, "shall contain everything that a commander cannot do by himself, but nothing more." Or finally, the report of the divisional commander's question about Moltke may simply prove that the Prussian army, like any other, had its inevitable quota of idiots.

Appointed chief of staff in 1857, Moltke had now held that position for nearly a decade, and the power of the position kept increasing in his hands. Traditionally, the chief of staff's main function was to plan possible wars of the future. He communicated directly neither with the king nor with commanders in the field; until 1859, even his messages to and from the minister of war had to go through the bureaucracy of the War Ministry. The only personal reports that Moltke received on the early days of the Danish war came from his private correspondence with Count Leonhard von Blumenthal, the chief of staff to Prince Frederick Charles. Only during the siege of

Düppel did War Minister Roon ask King William to invite Moltke to all royal councils on the war. And only on the eve of the war with Austria did the king decree that orders from the General Staff should go directly to troops in the field and not through the war ministry. Thus did Moltke finally take charge of the Prussian military machine.

Moltke had no desire to fight the Austrians. Like other conservatives, like the king himself, he regarded them as "brother Germans," potential allies in any new war against the perpetual enemy in Paris. Mindful of how the army had pleaded to avoid war in the crisis that led to Olmütz in 1850, Bismarck was keenly interested in how Moltke now evaluated Prussia's prospects in a conflict with Austria. As early as 1860, Moltke drafted a memorandum predicting how war might come, and how the Prussians could win it. Still the pupil of Clausewitz, Moltke anticipated that the Austrians would strike directly at Berlin in an effort to destroy the Prussian monarchy. Moltke proposed attacking the invaders' flanks and pushing them eastward toward Silesia. He also proposed, quite cold-bloodedly, a preemptive Prussian attack against the kingdom of Saxony. "If we could occupy Dresden before the Austrians and establish ourselves there," Moltke wrote, "we could compel the Saxons to go with us. . . . We would make ourselves masters of the rich resources of the country."

Moltke was assuming, of course, that the Austrians were going to attack, and that their forces were larger. Such assumptions generally make preemptive attacks seem not only justifiable but imperative. "Prussia's advantage lies in the initiative," Moltke wrote in another memorandum on the same subject in 1862. "We can mobilize our forces more swiftly than any of our German opponents. Success depends entirely upon their immediate and unconditional employment." And again two years later: "As soon as one of our neighbors begins to arm, we should declare war and announce mobilization simultaneously, for in no case should we permit ourselves to lose the initiative."

The gap in this logic was that the Austrians had no real intention of attacking. They took their leadership of Germany for granted, but they were reluctant to assert it by force. Beset by continuing disturbances in Hungary and Italy, they also found themselves in serious financial difficulties. With Bismarck at the head of the Prussian government, however, none of this mattered. If he wanted the Austrians to fight, then he would find ways of making them fight. Bismarck's maneuverings to this end were even more complex than usual. Meeting at the Schonbrunn Palace in Vienna with the Austrian foreign minister, Count Johann Bernhard von Rechberg, Bismarck boldly demanded that Austria acquiesce in Prussian annexation of the so-called Elbe duchies, Schleswig and Holstein. Rechberg, eager to appease the tiger of the north, responded to this essentially outrageous proposal by an equally cynical proposal of his own, that Prussia guarantee the increasingly wobbly Austrian rule of Venetia, and that it back an Austrian reconquest of Lombardy (lost in the Franco-Austrian war of 1859). Hastily weighing the pros and cons of such an involvement in Italy, Bismarck agreed, but the reigning monarchs balked. Emperor Francis Joseph would not agree to Prussian acquisition of Schleswig-Holstein unless he received compensatory territory elsewhere in Germany. King William, unwilling to give up an inch of his lands, disavowed Bismarck's claim on Schleswig-Holstein, saying that he "had no right over the duchies."

Having lost the treaty he thought he had won, Bismarck was correspondingly sulky in the next encounter, over the *Zollverein* treaties that were due for renewal in 1865. The *Zollverein* (customs union) had originally been created by Prussia in 1818 to integrate the Rhineland territories acquired at the Congress of Vienna into the Brandenburg motherland. As the customs union grew, Prussia and its north German neighbors prospered. Like the Britain of our own time, Austria first ignored this common market, then tried to create a rival trading bloc, and finally petitioned to join. Bismarck, who was generally indifferent to economic forces, had played no part in the growth of the *Zollverein,* but he saw now that membership was something Austria wanted. He vaguely promised to help, considering it "an inexpensive act of friendship." When Prussia's economic ministers raised objections to Austrian membership in the flourishing enterprise, however, he pretended to the Austrians that he could do nothing. It suited him perfectly well, of course, for Prussia to be supreme in north German trade, for its merchants to expand outward into the North Sea and the Atlantic, while Austria remained focused on the Danube and the Balkans. But the *Zollverein*'s rejection of Austria was also a serious diplomatic blow. Foreign Minister Rechberg resigned, bequeathing his ministry to Count Alexander von Mensdorff-Pouilly, a man even less qualified than Rechberg to parry the diplomatic thrusts of Bismarck.

Schleswig-Holstein once again came into play. Mensdorff thought it would be useful to support the ambitions of the younger Augustenburg as lord of the two duchies. Bismarck quickly agreed—if Augustenburg would agree to Prussian military control of his territories. When the two men met to discuss the prospects, Bismarck grandly greeted the duke as "Your Royal Highness." When Augusten-

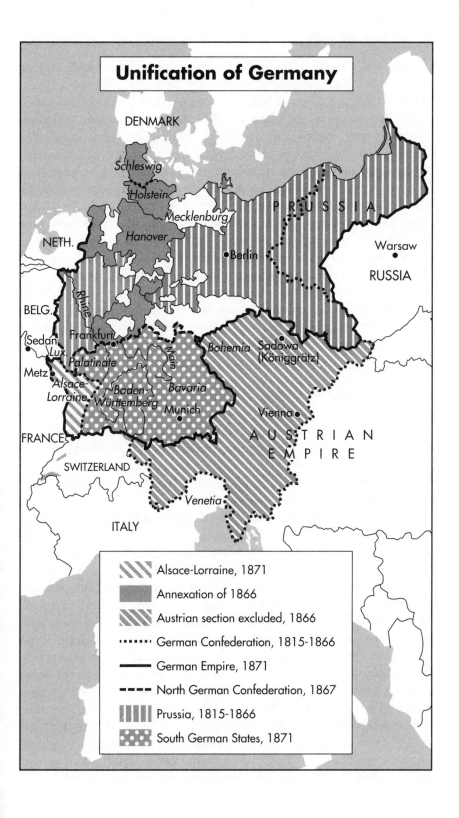

Unification of Germany

DENMARK

Schleswig

Holstein

Mecklenburg

NETH.

Hanover

P R U S S I A

Berlin

Warsaw

RUSSIA

BELG.

Rhine

Sedan
Lux.

Frankfurt

Palatinate

Bohemia

Sadowa
(Königgrätz)

Metz

Alsace-
Lorraine

Main

Baden-
Württemberg

Bavaria

Munich

Vienna

A U S T R I A N
E M P I R E

FRANCE

SWITZERLAND

Venetia

ITALY

Alsace-Lorraine, 1871
Annexation of 1866
Austrian section excluded, 1866
German Confederation, 1815-1866
German Empire, 1871
North German Confederation, 1867
Prussia, 1815-1866
South German States, 1871

burg proved difficult, thinking he had the support of not only Austria but the whole German liberal movement, Bismarck still more grandly addressed him as "Your Highness." When they parted, finally, Bismarck bade farewell to "Your Excellency." And when the Austrians sponsored pro-Augustenburg demonstrations, Bismarck demanded that the duke be expelled from Holstein. Austria refused. Bismarck thereupon denounced the Austrians for violating their alliance with Prussia. An Austrian official let it be known that Augustenburg would rather plant potatoes than be the Duke of Schleswig-Holstein on Bismarck's terms. Bismarck may well have smiled as he contemplated the duke's prospects as a potato farmer.

Prussia and Austria were supposed to be joint rulers of Schleswig-Holstein all this time, but Bismarck kept stirring up troubles, not only in Schleswig-Holstein but in Hungary and Italy, wherever the Habsburgs' shaky rule extended. Bismarck's personal banker, Gerson Bleichroeder, assured him from his pipelines into the Rothschild empire that the Austrians were too impoverished to fight, and this seemed to be true. Instead, the two sides repaired to the Austrian spa of Bad Gastein, and there they decided to separate the two supposedly inseparable Elbe duchies. Prussia would rule Schleswig and Austria, Holstein. This not only abolished the "legitimacy" for which the two German monarchies had fought Denmark; it also left Austria with an isolated possession entirely surrounded by Prussian territories. "I never imagined I should find an Austrian diplomat who would put his name to such a document," Bismarck remarked as he signed the Bad Gastein agreements.

From there, he went to Biarritz and ascertained that Napoleon III would not intervene in any Prussian-Austrian war. By the following February, 1866, the Prussian Crown Council was openly discussing the prospects of war with Austria. Crown Prince Frederick sounded deeply opposed, declaring that such a war "will be a war between brothers, and the interference of foreign powers is certain." Most of the courtiers, however, supported Bismarck's argument of inevitability. "A war with Austria must certainly come, sooner or later," Bismarck said. "It is wiser to undertake it now, under the present favorable conditions, than to allow Austria to choose the moment most auspicious for herself." Bismarck had already asked Moltke whether the army was ready to fight, and Moltke said it was. But now that war seemed imminent, Moltke argued that Italy should first be brought in as an ally, to create a second front against the Austrians. Bismarck promptly got the Italian government to agree that it would attack Austria if war to the north broke out within three months.

Now that he was under a time limit, Bismarck became even more devious in his maneuvering. On April 20, Vienna suddenly heard reports from northern Italy, apparently spread by Bismarck's agents, that the Italians were mobilizing along the frontier with Venetia. Austria responded with a southern mobilization of its own. Bismarck roared that Prussia was being threatened and had to mobilize as well.

"War is inevitable," Moltke wrote to his brother Adolf toward the end of May. "I do not think that it is in the power of man to prevent it. The destiny of Germany is now to be decided. The passion of the Germans for separation, observed by Tacitus, necessitates decision by force of arms. . . . Fifty years of peace have shown that union can never be achieved by means of a peaceful understanding."

The Austrian-led German Confederation now made an ungainly intervention and voted to demand that Prussia explain its mobilization. Austria further asked the Confederation to take charge of Schleswig-Holstein. Bismarck claimed this was a violation of the Bad Gastein agreements, and so he ordered an invasion of Holstein. Austrian troops withdrew into Hannover without a fight. Prussia now went all-out at the Confederation Diet in Frankfurt. It asked the Diet to support a united Germany without Austria. The Austrians responded by asking all members to mobilize against Prussia. Prussia demanded that the Confederation be dissolved. On June 15, it announced that it would march through Hannover, Saxony, and Hesse-Kassel to fight Austria, and that any resistance by the lesser kingdoms would mean war.

Moltke had never commanded even a regiment in combat, and now he had undertaken to attack what many considered the strongest force in central Europe. The Austrians boasted of an army of some 850,000 men, tested and hardened, if not exactly victorious, in the recent wars against France in northern Italy. But Moltke had several good reasons for the confidence he expressed to Bismarck. For one thing, the Austrians' numerical superiority was imaginary. When Vienna mobilized its forces in the summer of 1866, it could raise only 528,000 men. When service forces, garrisons, clerks, and other noncombatants were subtracted, the total of combat troops numbered only about 320,000 against Moltke's 350,000, and these troops also had to fend off whatever the Italians could mobilize on the southern front. It was true that the Prussians had less combat experience—in their only war of the last fifty years, their performance against Denmark had been no more than adequate, often inferior to that of their Austrian allies—but there were intangible advantages. While the Prussians were a coherent force with good morale, the Habsburgs' army was a polyglot accumulation of Austrians, Hungarians, Croats, and Italians, many of them disaffected from their rulers, many unable even to speak a common language.

Moltke also knew that technology was on his side. He had five railroad lines to mobilize his troops on the northern side of the Bohemian mountains while the Austrians had only one on the southern side. And while he kept his troops spread over an expanse of more than 125 miles, Moltke's studies of Grant's campaigns in the recent American Civil War had shown him how the new electric telegraph enabled a commander to keep closer control over his troops than any Napoleon or Frederick the Great had ever enjoyed. Most important of all, perhaps, Moltke's infantry was equipped with a rifle known as the *Zündnadelgewehr,* the needle gun. This was a breech-loading rifle that used a long, sharp firing pin. Invented in about 1835 by Nicholas von Dreyse, it achieved about 65 percent accuracy at 300 paces, and the Prussian army began ordering it as early as 1841. Partly for financial reasons, partly because of tradition, the Austrians clung to their Lorenz muzzle loaders, which were more accurate over longer distances. But the needle gun had two enormous advantages that would prove critical in the impending battle. It could be loaded much faster than the Austrian weapon, about five shots rather than one per minute, and it could be loaded while the infantryman remained under cover on the ground. Copying the tactics that the French had used in Italy, the Austrians relied heavily on bayonet charges after the first round of firing; quick reloading by the Prussians would have a murderous effect.

All this technology was necessary to control the vast armies that technology had made possible. Only about a century earlier, Frederick the Great on horseback had invaded and conquered Silesia at the head of an army of 30,000 men. From Berlin, Moltke now commanded a force more than ten times that large against an equally large Austrian horde. This metastasis in armies was largely a consequence of the French Revolution and its discovery of the energies inherent in "a nation in arms." As in so many things, Napoleon seized and perverted the revolutionaries' discoveries. The "Grand Armée" that he led into Russia in 1812 numbered nearly 700,000 men, and though less than 100,000 staggered back to the Prussian border, the age of mass warfare had arrived. Nearly 500,000 troops fought at the Battle of Leipzig, which drove Napoleon out of Germany. If Napoleon knew that an army marches on its stomach, his successors of the Moltke generation had to translate that into trainloads of food, bullets, shoes. Only technology could perform the translation.

Finally, Moltke probably gained confidence from knowing his adversary, Ludwig von Benedek. Now sixty-two, Benedek was a Hungarian Protestant and a veteran of the Italian wars, highly popular with his men, the public, and the press. He knew that he lacked the skills to command a large army on unfamiliar territory, and he protested when he heard that the emperor had political reasons for assigning the Italian front to his uncle, Archduke Albert. "So now I am supposed to study the geography of Prussia!" Benedek complained. "What do I know about a Schwarzer Elster and a Spree? How can I take in things like that at my age?" The emperor convinced him that it was his duty to accept the northern command. Though the prospects might fill Moltke with confidence, however, that confidence was not universally shared in Berlin. "The king in command at the age of seventy, with the decrepit Moltke at his side!" one Prussian general fretted. "What will come of it all?"

Moltke, too, had intangible problems, apart from his own age and inexperience. The most important of these, as in many wars, was the question of authority. Who was really in charge? Theoretically, King William, an experienced soldier, who often insisted on having his own way. William was no Frederick the Great, however. At his side, there was always Bismarck, whose rages and sarcasms had a powerful influence on the king and who tolerated no interference by anyone less than a king. While Moltke accepted Bismarck's primacy in political matters, the distinction between political and military questions was often difficult to define. William did not want to go to war against Austria, and it took all of Bismarck's gifts to persuade him that Emperor Francis Joseph was treacherously determined to attack him. Even when William was convinced of that, he rejected what Moltke called "the initiative," rejected the idea of a Prussian surprise attack; he did not want to appear the aggressor against his "brother" in Vienna. So Moltke's long efforts to enable the Prussians to mobilize in three weeks rather than the Austrians' six were largely wasted. The only result was that he wasn't actually caught defenseless when the Austrians began mobilizing on April 21 and King William dithered about what to do. Not until May 12 was Moltke allowed to respond, with all his railway lines pressed into service.

Hardly less important than timing was the question of where to concentrate the troops. Moltke expected Benedek to march on Berlin, but he could only guess the route the Austrians would follow. He guessed they would march into northern Bohemia, but if he concentrated on blocking them there, he would have to leave neighboring Silesia virtually undefended, and King William explicitly declared that this would be politically unacceptable. The territory that Frederick the Great had snatched from Maria Theresa of Austria could never be abandoned to her heirs.

Moltke's solution was to arrange his forces along a huge arc stretching across Bohemia, Saxony, and Silesia. From there, they would advance southward in separate units, joining together only when the Austrians' intentions became clearer. More experienced strategists grumbled that Moltke was breaking the basic rules of war. "It is a principle," Napoleon had written, "that the unification of diverse army corps must never take place near the enemy." The danger, of course, was that the enemy who confronted such scattered forces might thrust himself between them and destroy them separately before their unification could ever take place. Moltke knew the risks of letting the Austrians acquire interior lines, but he decided to defy them. "To profit by the inner line of operations," he explained later, "it is necessary to have enough space to enable the army thus situated to have a sufficient zone of maneuver to enable it to seek one of the opposing armies *at a distance of several days' march,* and also to be free to countermarch to meet the other. If this space is too constricted, there is the risk of having to deal with both adversaries at once. When an army on the field of battle is attacked in front and flank, the possession of the inner line is of little practical value. . . ." In other words, if Moltke united his scattered forces only at the last moment, the Austrians not only could not defeat them separately but would find themselves surrounded. So the question dominating Moltke's plan was where and when to unite, and the risks of disaster were substantial. "Great successes in war," said Moltke, "are not achieved without great risks."

Moltke organized his forces into three armies (later consolidated into two). In the west, the Army of the Elbe (46,000 men) would guard Dresden and the road to Berlin. To its east, Moltke assembled the Third and Fourth Corps into his main striking force, the First Army (93,000 men). This was commanded by the king's nephew, Prince Frederick Charles, an experienced commander but also cautious to a fault, arrogant, and stubborn. Another of Moltke's problems was that he not only could not choose his commanders—that was the king's prerogative—but that he had very limited authority to tell them what to do. To the east, guarding Breslau and the approaches to Silesia, Moltke's Second Army of about 115,000 men came under Crown Prince Frederick. Moltke had become friendly with the prince during their travels to Britain and Russia, but neither of them could ever forget which one was heir to the throne. According to Moltke's master plan, these three forces were to pursue their separate courses through the mountains that form the northern border of Bohemia and onto the tableland between the Elbe and the Iser rivers. Their goal was to join forces at Gitschin, a pleasant market town on the Cidlina River, once the home and headquarters of the almost legendary Duke Albrecht von Wallenstein, imperial commander during the early days of the Thirty Years War.

Once King William had been persuaded to go to war, Moltke's military machine worked as smoothly as one of the Krupp plants that were providing his cannons. On June 16, the day after Prussia declared war on Saxony, Hannover, and Hesse, three divisions of the Elbe army swept across the Saxon border and headed for Dresden. The Saxon army prudently withdrew into Bohemia. On June 22, the Prussian First Army reached the Bohemian frontier marking the border of Austria.

"A toll house with a black and yellow crossing barrier marked the border between Saxony and Bohemia," recalled one witness to the scene. "Here the Prince [Frederick Charles] stopped. Uhlans, who formed the advance guard, crossed the border first; then came the infantry. Whenever the forward ranks of a battalion reached the barrier and saw the Austrian colors, they raised a joyful shout, which was taken up by the rear ranks and repeated over and over, until the troops reached the toll house and saw their 'soldier prince' standing by the border marker. At the sight of him, the hurrahs turned to a jubilant roar, which stopped only when replaced by the sound of a war song which was taken up and repeated by every battalion as it crossed to Bohemian soil. . . ."

One of the oddities in Prince Frederick Charles's caution was that he mistrusted the standard tactic of using his cavalry for reconnaissance; he thought his horsemen should be saved and protected until a battle was actually under way. The result was that he had very little sense of where either his allies or his enemies were to be found. Marching southward, he approached with great caution the town of Reichenberg only to find it undefended. He then decided to wait there until someone established contact with the rest of the Elbe army, somewhere off to his right.

What saved him during this snaillike advance was that Benedek was being equally wary. The Austrians were still headquartered at Josephstadt, some fifty miles to the southeast, where Benedek's staff officers persuaded him that he should remain until his rear guard caught up. None of this corresponded to Moltke's plans for the Prussian forces to speed toward a meeting at Gitschin. From Berlin, the chief of staff sent Frederick Charles a scolding telegram that his delays might leave the crown prince's Second Army vulnerable to attack while it struggled through the mountains. "Only a vigorous advance by the First Army [can] disengage the Second," Moltke warned. Rebuked, Frederick Charles sent a division forward toward Turnau, the nearest bridgehead across the Iser River. Despite a skirmish with some Austrian cavalry, Turnau also proved undefended. Established on the Iser, still about twenty miles from Gitschin, Frederick Charles decided to wait some more.

Benedek seems to have foreseen little danger from the crown prince's Second Army, but it soon proved far more assertive than Frederick Charles's First Army. Emerging from the mountains near the border town of Nachod, the troops of the Prussian V Corps under General Karl Friedrich von Steinmetz seized a commanding plateau, and their needle guns mowed down the Austrians who attempted to root them out with bayonet charges. The Austrian casualties of nearly 6,000 came to more than five times the Prussian losses, and the Prussians held the plateau.

Gitschin was still the main target for the unification of the two main Prussian armies, and Moltke was still urging Prince Frederick Charles to get his First Army moving. "His Majesty expects," Moltke wired the lethargic commander, "that the First Army will by the speediest possible advance disengage the Second Army, which despite a number of victorious fights is still momentarily in a difficult position." The prince had already sent six cavalry squadrons toward Gitschin, which they found defended by force under Crown Prince Albert of Saxony. Attacked from both north and west by Prussian infantry, Albert staged a spirited defense but suddenly received orders to retreat to the east. Prince Frederick Charles rode into Gitschin the next morning and discovered conditions that inspired one member of his staff to write: "The battlefields were dreadful to look at, and the worst thing is that there was no means of carrying the wounded to lazarets as quickly as one would have desired. Often one finds these hapless people days later lying half dead in the fields. The inhabitants have all fled, and there are seldom people in the villages, and when there are, they themselves have nothing to live on, so how can anything be done for the sick and the wounded?"

The Austrian setbacks in these preliminary encounters seem to have had a still more punishing effect on Benedek. "I beg Your Majesty urgently to make peace at any price," he cabled the emperor. "Catastrophe for the army is unavoidable." Francis Joseph was understandably scornful. "To conclude peace is impossible," he answered. "I order you, if it is unavoidable, to begin a retreat." To this one of the emperor's aides added a rebuking but obvious question: "Has a battle taken place?"

Now that Prince Frederick Charles had finally reached Gitschin, now that he could only await the arrival of the crown prince from the mountains to the east, Moltke decided (or the king decided) that it was time to leave Berlin and take command in the field. "I come to you today . . . and offer you my royal greeting . . ." the king declared in a general order issued on June 30. "Soldiers! Countless foes stand arrayed against us. Let us therefore trust in God the Father, the ruler of all battles, and in our just cause. . . ."

It took six trains to carry the leaders of the Prussian war machine southward—King William, Bismarck, Roon, Moltke, the chief of the military cabinet, the quartermaster general, the inspectors general of artillery and engineers, as well as representatives of the foreign ministry and the diplomatic corps, doctors, cooks, and attendants of all kinds. Bismarck had great confidence in Moltke, whom he once described as "unconditionally reliable and at the same time cold to the very heart," but he worried about all the activities over which he had no control. "If we are beaten," he somewhat vaingloriously said to the British ambassador, Lord Augustus Loftus, "I shall die in the last charge." Hearing rumors that there were Austrian troops within six miles of the railroad line carrying the royal retinue southward, Bismarck asked Moltke whether this was not dangerous. "*Ja*," said Moltke, cold to the very heart, "in war everything is dangerous."

Bismarck was not the only self-appointed adviser. Hardly had Moltke installed his headquarters in Gitschin than he received a visit from Count Leonhard von Blumenthal, chief of staff for the crown prince's First Army, who was now full of fire over the victory at Nachod. In his diary, he wrote: "I said straightforwardly to the King: 'Your Majesty should just lay your ruler on the map in a line between Gitschin and Vienna, draw your pencil along the ruler, and march straight along that line!' He laughed in his kindly way, and doubtless thought that I was not in earnest. Headquarters was to me not an impressive experience. A crowd of long-faced loafers is always an odious sight, especially when they greet one in a sort of condescending manner, fancying themselves omniscient, and apportioning blame freely, in some cases either not knowing or not understanding the circumstances. . . ."

From Blumenthal's trip to Gitschin, it becomes clear that Moltke's great gamble had worked. The First and Second armies had finally made their connection; if not exactly united, they had established contact, with their headquarters about thirty miles apart. Moltke promptly issued instructions to both forces: "The Second Army is to maintain itself on the left bank of the upper Elbe, its right wing ready to unite with the left wing of the advancing First Army over Königinhof. The First Army will advance without pause in the direction of Königgrätz . . . "

This orderly plan, however, failed to take into account a remarkable new development. Though the Prussian First and Second armies had managed to find each other, they had also managed to lose all contact with the enemy. It may seem hard to believe that an armed force of 250,000 men can lose sight of an equally large force somewhere in the Elbe valley, but these two managed it. The crown prince had apparently been surprised when the Austrians retreated after the last fighting, and Prince Frederick Charles persisted in not using his cavalry for reconnaissance. The result was that the entire Austrian army disappeared from sight. Neither Moltke nor his field commanders knew where it was.

While most of the soldiers were promised a rest on the following day, July 3, the king and his chief advisers conferred futilely in Gitschin on what to do about the missing enemy. Several units of the Seventh Division had already started out from their headquarters north of Sadowa to see what they could find in the Bistritz River valley. They saw campfires on the heights to the east. Next morning, they clashed with an Austrian infantry unit and captured a prisoner who told them that the Austrian Third Corps had established itself nearby. When this news reached First Army headquarters at Schloss Kamenetz, a Major von Unger of the general staff set off with a lance corporal and sixteen Uhlans to see what he might discover in the Bistritz valley. They soon encountered an Austrian cavalry patrol, which apparently mistook them for their Saxon allies and started to pass on. An overanxious Uhlan opened fire on the Austrians and downed two of them before the rest fled. These two captives told the Prussians that not one but four Austrian corps were established nearby. As the Prussians rode on, they kept passing more Austrian cavalrymen, who kept mistaking them for Saxons and waving cordially while they rode past. The Prussians thus managed to reach the top of a hill at Dub, from which they could see a whole Austrian army camped on nearby hills. By this time, though, some of the Austrian cavalry had begun to realize that there were strangers in their midst, and reinforcements set out to capture them. Major Unger and his Uhlans fled the pursuing Austrians through field and forest until they finally reached Frederick Charles's headquarters at Schloss Kamenetz at twilight and blurted out their story.

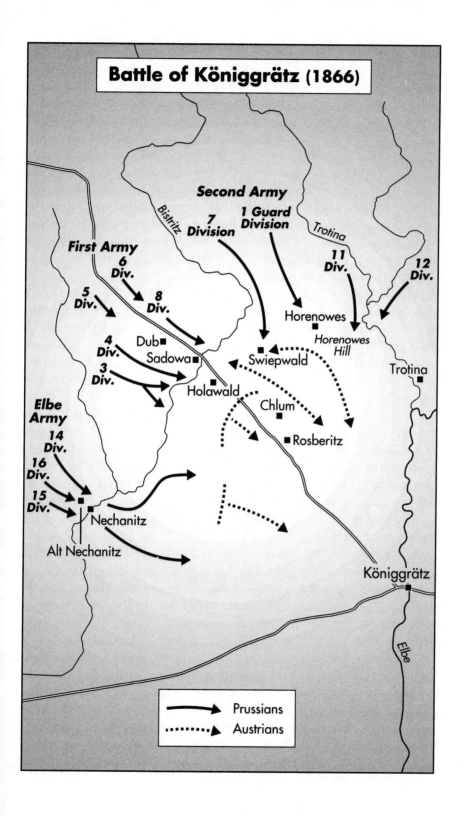

Battle of Königgrätz (1866)

Second Army

7 Division

1 Guard Division

Trotina

First Army

6 Div.

5 Div.

8 Div.

11 Div.

12 Div.

Bistritz

Dub■

Sadowa■

4 Div.

3 Div.

Horenowes
■

Horenowes Hill

Swiepwald
■

Trotina
■

Holawald
■

Elbe Army

14 Div.

16 Div.

15 Div.

Chlum
■

■ Rosberitz

Nechanitz
■

Alt Nechanitz

Königgrätz
■

Elbe

——▶	Prussians
·······▶	Austrians

The prince, presumably nettled by the constant scoldings from Moltke, apparently felt relief at discovering a real enemy in front of him and decided to launch an immediate attack. After spending all evening issuing orders to all his commanders, he sent a message asking the crown prince, almost as an afterthought, to add any assistance he could. He then sent an emissary to royal headquarters in Gitschin to inform the king of what he was doing. The emissary arrived there after 10 P.M. and found that the king had gone to bed. When he insisted that the king be awakened, an aide-de-camp did disturb the royal slumber. The king bestirred himself only enough to decree that the message be taken to his chief of staff. Moltke, though suffering from a cold, received the news with relief. *"Gott sei dank!"* he said as he began to reorganize his plans.

Moltke's main judgment—providential, as it turned out—was that Frederick Charles was underestimating the enemy, that he would not need just a little help from the crown prince's forces but all the help he could get from the entire First Army. He issued immediate orders to the crown prince to "move with all forces against the right flank of the presumed enemy order of battle, attacking him as soon as possible."

At the crown prince's headquarters, Moltke's jostling proved very necessary. The prince and his chief of staff, Blumenthal, had both gone to bed when the original messenger from the First Army arrived. Prince Frederick Charles "prayed me to come to his aid," Blumenthal later recalled. "I . . . told [the messenger] that the Prince could only have the cavalry and the First Corps to support him, for we needed the whole of the rest of our troops to support our own reconnaissance in force on the left bank of the Elbe.

"At 4 A.M. Count Finkenstein arrived from Gitschin, with a written communication from Moltke, saying that four full Austrian Corps d'armée were opposed to Prince Frederick Charles, and directing us to support him. I immediately woke up the Crown Prince, and then dictated aloud to my staff the orders for moving the whole of our army across the Elbe to the support of Prince Frederick Charles. . . .

"At seven o'clock the whole of the troops were in motion. . . . It was very cold but bracing. I had no feeling now of weariness, although the previous day I had driven 56 miles, had eaten hardly anything, and had only a short hour's sleep from 5:30 to 6:30. The heavy atmosphere prevented our hearing the sound of cannon; but towards nine o'clock we saw the smoke of battle all the way from Horonowes along the heights of Sadowa and all had the feeling that an important engagement was imminent. . . ."

So Moltke, on being awakened out of a cold-ridden sleep, had made the crucial decision—a mysterious combination of instinct, caution, shrewdness, the Clausewitzian doctrine of maximum force, and luck. Unknown to him, while he was correcting Frederick Charles's miscalculation, Benedek was making much the same miscalculation. While Frederick Charles anticipated that he would not need more than moderate assistance on his left flank, Benedek was anticipating that he would not get more than that moderate assistance. And so he unwisely sent only two corps to protect his right flank from the major attack that Moltke was sending the Second Army to inflict on him.

Benedek had arrayed his forces along the Bistritz River, a minor tributary of the Elbe, in an area about fifty miles east of Prague. The Bistritz formed one line in a large X; the other was the road from Gitschin to Sadowa, where it crossed the river, to Königgrätz (which is why the impending battle was later known as both Sadowa and Königgrätz). Benedek anchored the Austrian center on a height called Chlum, commanding the north side of the highway. There he concentrated 44,000 men and 134 cannon. His left wing extended along the river as far as Nechanitz, seven miles to the southwest. He was sure the attack would come from there. Bands played as the Austrians took up their forward positions in a drizzling rain, and W. H. Russell of the London *Times* admired the "squares and parallelograms of snowy white, dark green, azure, and blue on the cornfields like the checker work of a patchwork quilt." It was the last time in history that an imperial army would go into combat in the gaudy colors of a medieval tournament, infantrymen in white coats and blue pants, Uhlans with brightly colored flags on their lances, staff officers with green plumes on their cocked hats. On the Prussian side of the Bistritz, another *Times* correspondent reported: "A person standing this morning on top of the ridge saw Sadowa below him, built of wooden cottages, surrounded by orchards, and could distinguish among its houses several water mills; but these were not at work, for all the inhabitants of the village had been sent away, and a white coat here and there among the cottages was not a peasant's blouse, but was the uniform of an Austrian soldier. . . ."

The Prussians started with a probing cavalry attack just after seven on this rainy morning. The *Times* correspondent reported them advancing down toward the Bistritz "at a gentle trot, slipping about on the greasy ground, but keeping most beautiful lines, the lance flags of the Uhlans wet with rain, flapping heavily against the staves. At the bottom of the hill the trumpets sounded and in making their movements to gain the bridge the squadrons began wheeling and hovering about the side of the river, as if they courted the fire of the enemy. Then the Austrian guns opened upon them from a battery placed in a field near the village at which the main road crosses the Bistritz, and the Battle of Sadowa began."

It began, though, with all the disorder that one might expect of a half million men trying to organize a battle in the rain. Prince Frederick Charles didn't see any hurry, so he had planned to feed his troops and then order them into action at about 10 A.M. He was correspondingly annoyed to get an order from Moltke at eight, ordering an immediate attack all along the Bistritz. An outburst of cannon fire brought Moltke his first news that his orders were being carried out. Bismarck, who could claim no rank higher than major in the Landwehr militia but had outfitted himself in a cuirassier's helmet and a long gray coat, now came riding up on a reddish-brown horse to demand information. "Do you know how long this towel is whose corner we have grabbed here?" "No . . ." said Moltke, blowing his nose into a red silk handkerchief, "perhaps the whole Austrian army." An Austrian shell exploded nearby, and the king's courtiers' horses reared and whinnied in fear. "I owe that one to you, gentlemen," the king remarked as he prudently moved to a safer position.

The first Prussian success came on the extreme right, where seven battalions of the Elbe army launched an attack on the riverside village of Nechanitz, which controlled the nearest bridgehead south of Sadowa. The Saxon defenders slowly withdrew, but only after tearing up the floor of the wooden bridge and setting the whole structure on fire. The Prussians put out the fire and quickly reinforced the wreckage with fencing, but once they had occupied Nechanitz, they cautiously halted, waiting for all their supporting troops to get across the river. Their commander apparently feared an Austrian counterattack that would cut off his line of retreat. Such a delay was not at all part of Moltke's plan, which envisioned the advance into Nechanitz as one wing of a huge encirclement, but it illustrated once again how a commander's orders can change as they pass down the line.

Toward the center of the battlefield, near to the road from Sadowa to Königgrätz, the advancing Prussians encountered stronger Austrian resistance. "Before 9:30 the whole range of hills and valleys and slopes, for nine miles or more, was as if the earth had been turned into snow wreaths agitated in a wintry gale," a London *Times* correspondent reported. "Before 10 o'clock a thicker and darker cloud rose from the trees and villages on the right."

The Prussian Fourth and Eighth divisions nearly surrounded Sadowa itself, but the Austrian defenders managed to retreat into some nearby hills, where their artillery pounded the attackers as they tried to advance through a small forest known as the Holawald. "We looked for cover," one Prussian soldier later recalled, "but where was one to find it in this kind of fire! The bombshells crashed through the clay walls as if through cardboard; and finally, raging fire set the village ablaze. We withdrew to the left, into the woods, but it was no better there. Jagged hunks of wood and big tree splinters flew around our heads. . . . We all felt we were in God's hands."

That Austrian bombardment pinned down the Prussians in the Holawald all morning, but there was worse fighting in a nearby wood called the Swiepwald, a mixture of oaks and firs rising steeply from the riverbank to the northeast of Sadowa. The Prussian Seventh Division pushed into this forest at about 8:30 A.M.—"Fresh fish! Fresh fish!" cried their commander as he urged them on—only to find it defended by an accumulation of Austrian Jaegers, Hungarians, and Italians supported by a powerful array of artillery on a nearby hill overlooking the woods. In about an hour of fierce fighting, six Prussian battalions smashed about ten Austrian battalions, but the Austrians seemed determined to hold the line here, and they had substantial reinforcements ready to send into the shattered forest. So did the Prussians, and so the killing went on.

By late morning, the Prussian leaders began to fear that their attack might fail. The Austrian left and center had been beaten back from the river, but they held fast on the slopes that rose to the east of it. On a height known as the Roskosberg, King William anxiously asked Moltke what he thought of the situation, and Moltke coolly said, "Your Majesty will win today not only the battle but the campaign." The king continued fretting, as well he might, for Moltke's optimism rested largely on his confidence that the crown prince's Second Army would soon arrive and attack the ill-defended Austrian right flank, but the hours kept passing with no sign of the prince. The king finally asked whether Moltke had made preparations for a retreat. "Here there will be no retreat, here we are fighting for the very existence of Prussia," Moltke supposedly answered, though there are skeptics who suspect that these unfailingly optimistic promises are the handiwork of later legend-makers. If nothing else, the chief of staff had a bad cold. Bismarck silently offered him a box of cigars, and Moltke carefully picked out one of the best.

Shortly before noon, the news that Moltke was awaiting reached Austrian headquarters: a telegram from Josephstadt reported that large numbers of Prussian troops were marching westward and should soon reach the battlefield. Benedek obviously should have recognized the danger, but he was apparently so preoccupied with his plans to launch a counterattack against the First Army outside Sadowa—a counterattack that never actually started—that he simply ignored the prospect of the Second Army smashing into his right flank.

Wallowing along through the rain and mist, the Prussian crown prince also seemed only faintly aware of what lay ahead. He thought he was simply offering a little help to his cousin, Prince Frederick Charles. It was only when he reached a hill overlooking the town of Horenowes that he could see eight Austrian batteries firing westward, and thus see the scope of the fighting. "This is the decisive battle," said Blumenthal, his chief of staff. The crown prince's army was marching toward a junction with the First Army, but he now realized that this would take too long, and the battle might be over before he got there. Taking as his guidepost two linden trees standing alongside a large crucifix, he ordered his troops to shift about twenty-five degrees to the left and head straight into the flank and rear of the Austrian defenders.

In his telescope on the Roskosberg, Bismarck could see through the rain and mist what looked like a line of trees advancing up a ridge toward a tall linden. He handed the instrument to Moltke, who took a long look, then rode over to the king. "The campaign is decided," he said in another one of those almost-too-well-remembered prophecies, "and in accordance with Your Majesty's desires!" The king frowned. He grumbled that he didn't know what Moltke was talking about, and this was no time for rosy predictions about some distant future. "No, the success is complete," Moltke said. "Vienna lies at your feet."

It was one of Moltke's characteristics, though few recognized it then, that a lifetime of war games and strategic planning had accustomed him to seeing not only a present array of forces but also the effects of any change, how such a change would make things look in an hour or twenty-four hours or a week. That was why, when Prince Frederick Charles requested reinforcements to increase his attack on the Austrian center, Moltke refused him. He wanted the Austrian center held in place, not pushed out of the pincer that Moltke hoped to close on it. And that was how, when Moltke saw the line of trees moving up the ridge toward the crucifix, he saw, like Macbeth confronting Birnam Wood, Vienna lying at King William's feet.

In some ways, it seemed almost too easy. When the Second Army's First Guards Division swept into Horenowes, just north of the Austrians' right flank, the corps chief of staff ordered the guards to stop and wait for more troops to catch up with them. The guards' divisional commander, Hiller von Gärtringen, complied by ordering some of his men to halt, but he simultaneously ordered others to continue pressing forward. Ahead of them lay a major Austrian defensive post, the village of Chlum on a height overlooking the Sadowa-Königgrätz road. Chlum was oddly constructed in that the town's most sheltered defensive position had no view of the approaches to the north and east, and there the Austrians established themselves, all facing toward the Prussian forces in the west. When there were reports of Prussians spotted advancing through the wheatfields on the slopes to the east, the Austrian regimental commander, Colonel von Slaveczi, was scornful. "You are all seeing phantoms," he said. When the phantoms emerged from the smoke and fog covering the wheatfields, Slaveczi's Hungarian troops seemed paralyzed. "Instead of fighting back with determination," one Prussian captain later recalled, "they stood undecided and without firing a shot, and then turned and struggled away in every direction." Their officers beat them across the shoulders with their swords and shouted at them to stop being cowards, but they could not stop the panic and flight.

It was about 3 P.M. when one of Benedek's staff officers brought him the news that the Prussians had captured Chlum.

"Nonsense!" retorted Benedek, who was still in the midst of planning his great counterattack. He ordered another aide to go and check on the report. Then he galloped off to do the checking himself, with his staff hurrying after him. "The key of the position was in the hands of the enemy, and consternation was on every face," reported one of the three London *Times* correspondents on the battlefield. "No one was cooler than Benedek himself, as, attended by all who caught sight of him, he rode off to bring up some of the reserves and to retake the position. The bullets still fell thickly, as the Staff galloped after their chief; and on their approaching a small farm with outhouses, which should have sheltered them, they were saluted with a fresh volley of balls from the Prussian tenants, one of which wounded the Archduke Wilhelm in the head. . . . This unexpected apparition of the enemy in our very midst, when the Austrian army seemed on the point of victory . . . created some confusion."

Benedek's reaction was fury. Thinking that he was near victory, he had been about to attack, and now he found his men on the run from the Prussians in their midst. He galloped to the vicinity of Chlum, where he found some of the beaten Hungarians. Ignoring the Prussian bullets flying around him, Benedek harangued the Hungarians and ordered them back into battle. Some of them followed him to the outskirts of the village, but there the Prussian fire drove them back again. Back at the Roskosberg, Moltke could see the Chlum village church on fire, but he had no clear news that the Prussians had captured the village. Nor was Benedek accepting that defeat. He ordered a massive bombardment of Chlum and the neighboring village of Rosberitz, then sent reinforcements to recapture them. With horns sounding the charge and the Deutschmeister regimental band providing accompaniment, the Austrians managed to recapture Rosberitz. "The air was literally filled with shells, shrapnel and cannister," one Prussian officer recalled later; "branches of trees, stones, splinters flew around our ears and wounded many, and for good measure, Prussian shells also landed. The shells crashed through the buildings; walls collapsed and buried . . . the wounded; big clouds of dust rose in the air, made up of pulverized plaster and bricks and mingled with the smoke of the powder. It was as if the world were coming to an end. . . ."

The Prussians finally retreated from Rosberitz up the hillside to Chlum, and there nothing could dislodge them. General Hiller von Gärtringen had to watch some of his artillerymen withdraw because they had run out of ammunition, but he also saw gray columns of infantrymen marching to his aid from the north. "*Gott sei dank!* There you are!" he welcomed the newcomers. "What have you got for me?"

"My battalion," said its commander, Major von Sommerfeld, "and right behind us, the whole Avantgarde of the First Army Corps."

"Now everything will be all right," said Hiller von Gärtringen. Then his men saw him jolted in his saddle, and he raised a hand to his breast. "Help me, comrade, I'm wounded," he gasped as he slid from his saddle, dying from a shell splinter that had pierced his chest.

At Prussian headquarters, Bismarck was still worrying, not only about the fate of Moltke's armies but about the immediate dangers of the battlefield. Specifically, he knew that his seventeen-year-old son Herbert was serving as an officer somewhere on the battlefield, and, as he said at one point, "it makes me sick at heart to think that Herbert may be lying like this someday." The only figure on whom he could vent his anxiety was the old King William, who insisted on watching the gunfire from his saddle. When Bismarck fretted to one of the monarch's military aides, the officer coolly answered, "His Majesty rides where he wishes." Despite his modest military rank, Bismarck decided to confront his sovereign. "As a major, I have no advice to give Your Majesty in time of battle," he said, "but as Minister President, it is my duty to beg Your Majesty not to expose yourself to danger in this way." Legend has it that Bismarck furtively whacked the king's horse with a branch until it carried the king to greater safety, but historians doubt the tale. The king was able to control his own horse as well as his subordinates. Without admitting any withdrawal, however, he did, as usual, heed Bismarck's advice.

Only now that the battle was almost over did Benedek finally send his reserve cavalry into combat. Their main mission was to deflect the Prussians advancing along the Sadowa-Königgrätz road, and this they did, though their loss of 1,000 men came to more than twice the Prussian cavalry casualties. In a final gesture, the infantry of the Austrian First Corps made a desperate effort to recapture the height of Chlum. With flags flying and drums beating, they charged up the ravaged hillside. The Prussians with their needle guns waited until the Austrians were almost upon them, then opened fire. Within twenty minutes, the Austrians lost more than 10,000 men.

These devastating clashes did enable Benedek to extricate most of his army from Moltke's pincer. About 180,000 managed to get back across the Elbe, though in a sad state of disarray. A London *Times* correspondent reported seeing "wounded on all sides, fragments of regiments marching, the roadsides lined with weary soldiers asleep, dressing their wounds or cooling their feet; on both sides of us, waggons, guns, cavalry of all kinds. Tyrolese Jägers, Hungarians, Croats, Italians. . . . The *débris* of an army." Moltke, still nursing his cold, gave no orders to the weary Prussians to pursue the retreating Austrians. He knew that he had won, and that was the decisive fact. The king, heading for a reunion with his son, descended from thirteen hours in the saddle and remarked, "One feels that one's youthful years are over." As for Bismarck, he discovered after the battle that nobody had assigned him a place to spend the night. Wandering around in search of a room, he fell into a manure pit. An emissary from the Grand Duke of Mecklenburg finally found him napping under the colonnade of the marketplace in Horitz and took him to the grand duke's quarters.

The casualties for the day were lower than one might have expected for a battle of such size. The Austrians and their allies suffered losses of nearly 45,000, the Prussians nearly 10,000, but the Austrians never recovered from the defeat. Though fighting went on for another month, Prussian victory was never in doubt. Both King William and Moltke wanted to end the war with a victory parade through Vienna, but Bismarck characteristically refused to allow it. Unlike his sovereign and his generals, he had no desire to humiliate the Austrians or to make their enmity permanent. Bismarck never avoided wars, but he waged wars for specific political purposes, and when those purposes had been won, he warred no more. "If only we don't push our demands too far and think we have conquered the world, we shall get a peace worth having," Bismarck wrote home to his wife. "But . . . I have the thankless task of pouring water into the sparkling wine and trying to make it plain that we are not alone in Europe but have to live with three other powers who hate us and envy us."

Moltke and his supporters were not convinced. At one conference, a general offered the traditional military argument that became all too familiar during our own Cold War, that the Prussian borders would never be secure unless the enemy was pushed far back from them. Why stop there? Bismarck retorted. Why not march on into Hungary? And why stop at Hungary? Why not march on to Constantinople and create a new Byzantium?

Still King William remained adamant. Having finally been persuaded by Bismarck that Austria was a treacherous enemy, and having been shown by Moltke how Austria could be defeated, the king insisted on punishment, the annexation of Austrian territory. Having argued, scolded, mocked, and argued some more, Bismarck walked out. As he climbed the stairs to his quarters on the fourth floor, he considered the pros and cons of resigning. Once on the fourth floor, according to his own subsequent account, he began to consider not just resigning but throwing himself off the balcony. Instead, he sat with his head in his hands, presumably waiting for somebody to come and console him. And in due time, his wish was fulfilled. He heard footsteps; he felt a reassuring hand on his shoulder.

"You know that I was against this war," said Crown Prince Frederick, whose timely arrival on the battlefield had won the day at Königgrätz. "You considered it necessary, and the responsibility for it lies on you. If you now think that our end is attained and that it is time to make peace, I am ready to support you and defend your views against my father." Bismarck could only welcome the crown prince's new arrival on this new battlefield. The prince strode off to continue the arguments. When he returned, he said, "It has been a very difficult business, but my father has consented." So Moltke was put in his place.

Bismarck's peace terms demanded no Austrian territory, but they ended Austria's claims of domination over Germany. Specifically, the Habsburg emperor agreed to "the dissolution of the hitherto existing German Confederation and [gave] his assent to a new organization of Germany without the participation of the Austrian Imperial State." He agreed to Prussia forming a "narrower federal relationship . . .

north of the Main." He agreed to Prussian annexation of both Schleswig and Holstein, plus the states that separated Berlin from its territories on the Rhine, Hannover, Electoral Hesse, the Duchy of Nassau, plus the free city of Frankfurt, which had presumed to welcome the parliamentarians of 1848. At the Austrians' insistence, their allies in Saxony lost no territory, but the treaty required the Saxon army to be henceforth commanded by the king of Prussia.

"The war of 1866," Moltke wrote later, "was entered on not because the existence of Prussia was threatened, nor was it caused by public opinion and the voice of the people; it was a struggle long foreseen and calmly prepared for ... not for territorial aggrandizement but for an ideal end—the establishment of power. Not a foot of land was exacted from conquered Austria, but she had to renounce all part in the hegemony of Germany."

Some saw that immediately as a monumental change. "Thirty dynasties have been swept away," the London *Spectator* said of Austria's fall at Königgrätz, "the fate of twenty millions of civilized men has been affected forever, the political face of the world has changed as it used to change after a generation of war ... Prussia has leaped in a moment into the position of the first Power of Europe."

"I never in my life breathed a more invigorating air than the one that blew through North Germany in the fall of 1866," according to the recollections of Julius von Eckhardt, a Baltic German journalist, anticipating the euphoria that all too many Germans felt in the heady days of 1933. "It cast an incomparable spell over us. One felt as if one were standing at the threshold of a new period, a period which promised miracles. One lived under the impression of a surprise which had come so suddenly and with such overwhelming fullness that the patriots who a short time before had been full of fears and sombre premonitions suddenly felt like dreamers."

This sudden growth in Prussian power was not universally acclaimed, of course. Many Germans themselves saw the extension of Bismarckian autocracy as a grievous disintegration of the older and more peaceful Germany that had accepted and even taken pride in regional differences. "It is not wise to overlook out of patriotism, the fact that the events of 1866 have revived for the continent and for our age the dangers of a system generally held to be in decline. . . ." wrote the liberal historian Georg Gottfried Gervinus in a memorandum submitted to the Prussian royal family. "After the hopes and labors of half a century to outgrow the military systems of former times, there has been here created a permanent military power of such tremendous superiority as the world has not known even in the iron age of the

Napoleonic wars. . . . It would be a woeful perversion if Germany turned from a people dedicated to culture to a people trusting in power, and thus become involved in war after war."

"The year 1866 seems to me the beginning of many errors from which we suffer today," Rainer Maria Rilke wrote to a friend more than a half century later. "For that year marks the birth of the terrible Prussian hegemony which by brutally unifying Germany suppressed all the simple and likable Germanies of the past. Prussia, the least civilized and least German state, this incorrigible *parvenu,* has succeeded in imposing upon hardly formed faces the coldly fixed mask of a greedy demon who attracts and provokes doom."

Prussia was in the middle of an election campaign when the war began, and though the voting took place before anyone knew about the Battle of Königgrätz, the electoral results that were announced on the same day as the results on the battlefield strengthened Bismarck's political position as decisively as the battle did. The conservatives gained 114 seats in the Landtag, while the progressives and their allies lost 105. Both conservatives and liberals split apart, and out of the storm came the National Liberal Party, which would provide Bismarck with his parliamentary power base for years to come. At the same time, Bismarck promised the crown prince that he would end his long maneuver of ruling without parliamentary approval. A month after Königgrätz, he had a bill submitted to the legislature acknowledging that he had acted unconstitutionally in ignoring the parliamentary rejections of his budget and asking that these past measures now be accepted. The liberals inflicted another deep wound on parliamentary government by hastening to agree. "I have convinced myself," said one eminent Prussian official, "that Bismarck's actions were necessary: what seemed to us, the uninitiated, to be criminal arrogance turns out to have been the indispensable means to the end." Treitschke, on the other hand, wrote to his brother-in-law: "You know how passionately I love Prussia but when I hear a shallow Junker like this Bismarck boast of the iron and blood by which he intends to dominate Germany, I can only say it is hard to tell whether he is more vulgar or ridiculous."

All this, directly and indirectly, from the orders that Moltke sleepily sent out to the crown prince's Second Army. After Königgrätz, all Germany north of the Main would be led from Berlin.

7

"The Rustle of God's Robes"

BERLIN WELCOMED MOLTKE'S RETURN WITH ALL THE EXCITEMENT OF A city that had just become the capital of central Europe. The troops assembled for their triumphal march at the Brandenburg Gate on September 21. At their head, of course, rode King William, but he was closely surrounded by the men who had made the cheering possible: Crown Prince Frederick and Prince Frederick Charles, Bismarck and Roon, and Moltke. They had not only won a great victory, Prussia's first in more than fifty years, but they had won it in the best possible way—quickly. The cheers expressed relief as well as triumph.

The public praises embarrassed Moltke, partly because he was not a vainglorious man, but perhaps also because he knew how small a role a commander actually plays in his army's victory, how much his triumph depends on accident and luck. Moltke liked to call that the will of God. "Yes, the Bohemian campaign is a great and deathless page in the world's history . . ." he wrote after the shouting died down. "I just did my duty, and my comrades did theirs, too. God's omnipotence led our banner on to victory. . . . And when I listen to all the exaggerated flattery which the public sees fit to bestow on me, I can only think how it would have been if this victory, this triumph, had not been ours. Would not this same praise have changed to indiscriminate censure, to senseless blame?"

Yes, it undoubtedly would, but now the crowds cheered. The

139

Prussian legislature expressed its gratitude by voting Moltke the sum of 200,000 thalers. After a fruitless search through the ancestral lands of Mecklenburg, he discovered the estate that pleased him at Kreisau, just south of the Silesian garrison town of Schweidnitz. And he began planting and building. "I am going to lay out a park," he wrote to his brother Adolf, "in which bridges must be built, roads made, and 10,000 trees planted. I shall not live to walk in their shade, but there are some fine old oaks already. I rejoice every day to see the sun rising higher over the roofs. . . ."

Moltke's planning for his own estate, and for improvements in the village of Kreisau, made the summer of 1868 one of the happiest of his life, but one autumn afternoon, he and his wife were caught in a heavy rainstorm while out riding. Marie von Moltke had to continue on to some local festivity in her wet clothes, and this was later blamed for her suddenly falling sick with a severe fever. She seemed to get better, then suffered a relapse, and on Christmas Eve, she died. She was forty-two and had been married twenty-six years.

"Our dear Marie died this afternoon," Moltke wrote to his brother Adolf, "after sixteen days of severe illness, but a short and painless death-struggle. A dreadful fever snatched her from us after all means of medical skill and careful nursing had been exhausted. Several days ago, while yet fully conscious, she took leave of us, and prayed for us in her worst delirium. I cannot desire her to wake again. She has led a life of rare happiness and escaped the sadness of old age. Her open, true, and pious character made her beloved by everybody, and her death has caused much grief."

The following week he wrote to Adolf's wife, Auguste, with more details of his plans to commemorate Marie: "Nothing more beautiful can be imagined than she looked after all was over, and the sweet and tranquil look on her face. She seemed to be only asleep. She is now in her coffin in the little Catholic chapel at Kreisau, surrounded with innumerable wreaths of flowers and palms. . . . I hope in the spring to finish a little vault for Marie and myself; I had always thought Marie would do this for me. The mausoleum will be erected on the top of a small wooded hill near the house, from whence there is a wide and beautiful view of the estate and mountains. . . ."

While the building and harvesting continued at Kreisau, though, Moltke still had to manage the Prussian war machine. To start with, he had to review and analyze and correct all the mistakes of the Austrian war. The Prussian mobilization had been swift, but there had been all too many cases of troops hastening into position and finding no food or ammunition. There had been too many intelligence failures, too many breakdowns in communications, too many instances, in short, where the army did not know what it was doing. It was the essence of Moltke's planning to repair all that; it was the essence of his staff system to provide the army with a central nervous system so that it always knew what it was doing, and knew how to react to what the enemy was doing.

The enemy in 1866 had been Austria, sluggish and overconfident, but Moltke knew that the next great war would be against the eternal antagonist on the far side of the Rhine. He had probably felt that way ever since that day when the army of the great Napoleon had sacked and burned his father's home. If the hunger for retribution was partly unconscious, though, Moltke's hostility toward France had become quite open by 1841, when he wrote his long essay, "*The Western Boundary.*" "Whenever they differ with us, they seize the sword," he had charged then, promising that a future Germany would "not sheathe the sword until our whole right has become ours, until France has paid its whole debt to us."

When Moltke became Prussian chief of staff in 1858, he and the other military authorities in Berlin still regarded France as a potential invader. This was not unreasonable, for the new Emperor Napoleon III not only boasted that "the name of Napoleon is in itself a program," but did his best to revive the legend of Napoleon the Conqueror. In 1859, he attacked the Austrian occupiers of Italy, and in 1861, he invaded Mexico. Moltke's military plans of 1858, 1860, 1861 repeatedly dealt with the question of how to block a French invasion of the Rhineland. It was not long before he began thinking about a preventive war. "If the former German provinces of Alsace and Lorraine were conquered," he reflected, "it is conceivable that we might keep them."

This all lay within Bismarck's field of command, however, and Bismarck made his moves with great care. Once Moltke's armies had crushed the Austrians, it was Bismarck who had to deal with the French. Napoleon felt that it was unacceptable for the Prussians to change the European balance of power without French approval. He had offered to mediate the Austro-Prussian dispute, and when his efforts were overtaken by events, by Moltke's offensive, he demanded compensation for having kept France out of the war. Specifically, he asked for the restoration of the 1814 French frontier on the Rhine and the evacuation of Prussian troops from Luxembourg, a former member of the German Confederation but owned by the king of Holland. Napoleon was stunned when Bismarck turned on him. "If you want war, you can have it," said the Prussian leader, who now felt able to use Königgrätz as diplomatic capital. "We shall raise all Germany against you. We shall make immediate peace with Austria, at any price, and then, together with Austria, we shall fall on you with 800,000 men. We are armed; you are not." Napoleon, who was already beginning to feel the debilitating effects of a painful and incurable bladder ailment, recoiled, retreated, accepted the embarrassing failure of his maneuvering. Shrewd old Adolphe Thiers, who had served as minister to King Louis Philippe and would rule France once again after Napoleon was gone, foresaw the consequences. "It is France that was defeated at Sadowa," he said.

Bismarck relished Moltke's victory at Königgrätz, but it also presented him with a nest of new problems. The structure of Germany that had been worked out at the Congress of Vienna in 1815 now lay in ruins, and it was up to Bismarck to create a new one. His first step was the simple annexation of those states that lay between Berlin and its Rhineland possessions: Hannover, Nassau, and Hesse-Kassel. But now that he had destroyed the German Confederation, he had to create a new North German Confederation to unite Prussia's twenty remaining neighbors north of the Main River. As for the states south of the Main, Bismarck negotiated secret military alliances with the principal ones, Bavaria, Baden, Württemberg, and Hesse-Darmstadt—giving Moltke an additional 200,000 troops to organize—but these states were to be left in a condition of twilight independence.

The main problem was the creation of the North German Confederation, for that required a new Prussian constitution as well. And Bismarck was very sick. After the victory parade in September, he suffered agonizing stomach cramps, severe pains in his leg, and a general sense of disintegration. His wife bundled him off to a retreat on the Baltic island of Ruegen, where he sat staring into space for hours on end. "I cannot sleep," he grumbled, "I cannot eat, I cannot drink, I cannot laugh, I cannot smoke, I cannot work." He had already assigned legal experts in all the North German states to start drafting their views on the new constitution, however, and as the autumn progressed, sheaves of memoranda began flowing to and from Ruegen. By December, Bismarck had drafted his constitution, to be approved by the new Reichstag, which turned out to have a substantial bloc of seventy-nine National Liberals, as compared to fifty-nine Conservatives, twenty-seven Old Liberals, nineteen Progressives, and no Socialists. The new constitution that was now approved had been partly modeled on the American creation of 1789 and seemed at least as democratic as those of other European powers of the day, with a Reichstag elected by universal suffrage, but Bismarck had arranged everything so that he remained in charge—as long as he could bully the legislature as he had always bullied the king. Friedrich Engels did not hesitate to compare Bismarck to Bonaparte as a new kind of ruler. "The bourgeoisie has not the stuff in it for ruling directly itself," he wrote, "and therefore where there is no oligarchy as there is here in England, to take over, for good pay, the management of state and society in the interests of the bourgeoisie, Bonapartist semi-dictatorship is the normal form. It upholds the big material interests of the bourgeoisie even against the will of the bourgeoisie, but allows the bourgeoisie no share in the power of government. The dictatorship in its turn is forced against its will to adopt those material interests of the bourgeoisie as its own. So now we get Monsieur Bismarck. . . ."

Bonapartism has its attractions for the mass of voters as well as the merchants, which is why both Bismarck and Napoleon III liked to rely on elections to assert their power against the pretensions of princes and aristocrats, but a Bonapartist regime cannot easily coexist with a Bonapartist neighbor. Both rulers and supporters require the imagery of dynamic growth. For Bismarck, this meant German unification under Prussian rule, a goal that had inspired little interest in his younger days. Napoleon, on the other hand, presumed to claim for France the right to decide whether Germany could be united. Since Napoleon knew that he really could not prevent it if the Germans were determined to unite, he was reduced to demanding "compensation" for any German moves in that direction. Denied in his first attempt to acquire Luxembourg, he resolved to try again.

Bismarck led him on. He indicated to the French ambassador that Prussia would not object to the king of Holland selling Luxembourg to France, which would require a withdrawal of the Prussian garrison there, as long as it was strictly a deal between Napoleon and the king of Holland, with Prussia neither approving nor being asked to approve this marketing of theoretically German territory. The king of Holland was a little embarrassed, but he agreed in early 1867 to Napoleon's request to buy Luxembourg for 5 million gulden—if the king of Prussia agreed. To assist this change, French agents in Luxembourg organized a series of anti-Prussian demonstrations. But the king of Prussia distinctly did not agree. The National Liberals in the Reichstag protested loudly against the loss of territory that had "at all times been German." Bismarck himself said that "we must, in my opinion, risk war rather than yield."

Moltke openly favored war. He thought it inevitable, his army was tested, and he worried that French military reforms would soon strengthen Napoleon's ability to fight. And military strategists generally attach great importance to striking first. That captures the initiative, forces the enemy to retreat and react. Opposing moral arguments always have to be paid for in soldiers' lives. "Nothing could be more welcome to us than to have *now* the war that we must have," Moltke said.

Bismarck's concepts of strategy were broader and more sophisticated. "Unhappily I believe a war with France must come before long— her vanity, wounded by our victories, will drive her towards it," he wrote. "Yet, since I know of no French or German interest which calls for a resort to arms, I do not see it as certain. . . . No statesman has a right to start a war simply because, in his opinion, it must inevitably come within a given period of time." As for the specific quarrel with the French, he made a gloomy prediction: "I shall avoid this war as long as I can; for I know that once started, it will never cease."

Moltke remained unconvinced. If war was inevitable, why wait rather than striking? "Bismarck's point of view is unchallengeable, but some day it will cost us many lives," he said. Bismarck, however, managed to get his way without war, as so often happened. Napoleon had to back off from Luxembourg, not only thwarted but humiliated. And Moltke continued refining his plans. He still expected a French invasion, but now he planned not just to resist it but to anticipate it with an invasion of his own. The political realignments that followed the Austrian war increased the forces at his disposition by some 200,000 men. With the six railway lines available to him, he estimated that he could concentrate nearly 400,000 men on the Rhine within a month. The French were not resting idle, either. For all his diplomatic setbacks over Luxembourg, the ailing Napoleon was just as active as Moltke in planning for the inevitable. He was encouraged in this by the Austrians, who talked of avenging Königgrätz by joining in a French invasion.

While Bismarck said that "no statesman has a right to start a war simply because . . . it must inevitably come," he thought he heard once again the fateful sound of God's robe. The sound seemed to come from Madrid, where an army coup in the fall of 1868 had expelled the corrupt and dissolute Queen Isabella II, the last member of the Bourbon dynasty that King Louis XIV of France had established on the Spanish throne in 1701, and now the army leaders, Juan Prim and Francisco Serrano y Dominguez, were searching for a replacement. French agents naturally played a role in this search, but so did two of Bismarck's aides, who arrived in Madrid as early as December 1868. The Prussians' efforts may have been assisted by the fact that they had 50,000 pounds to dispense, but no documents have ever shown exactly what roles they played. Nevertheless, after the Spanish king-seekers were rebuffed by their first choices in the ruling families of Portugal and Italy, they began considering Prince Leopold of Hohenzollern-Sigmaringen, of the Catholic branch of the family, which had remained in Swabia when a more ambitious Hohenzollern moved north in the fifteenth century to become margraf of Brandenburg. The two Hohenzollern branches had remained close. Leopold's father, Prince Charles Antony, had served for a time as minister-president of Prussia, and he now was military governor of the Prussian provinces of Rhineland and Westphalia. As for Prince Leopold, he was an officer in the Prussian army.

He had no great desire to be king of Spain, perhaps because the throne was so unstable, perhaps because he mistrusted the generals who were searching for a king. When the Spaniards secretly sounded him out early in 1869, he politely declined. His father, Prince Charles Antony, had grander visions of what the two branches of the Hohenzollern family might rule. "A dynasty," he wrote, "which represents the center of gravity of Central Europe and whose scions flourish by the Black Sea and beyond the Pyrenees—the one ruling over a nation of developing civilization, the other ruling over one whose civilization belongs to the past—a dynasty such as has not been known in history since Charles V—on such a dynasty, therefore, rests the responsibility of a high mission willed by Providence."

Charles Antony knew that the French would object, of course, so he insisted on getting the support of King William of Prussia, but the king had no great interest in extending the Hohenzollern rule from Prussia to Spain. He also had no interest in provoking a quarrel with the French. Bismarck would not give up, however. He told the king that it was "to Germany's political interest that the House of Hohenzollern should gain an esteem and an exalted position in the world such as does not find its analogy . . . since the days of Charles V." As for any French objections, Bismarck loftily wrote in his memoirs that "it was hard to find in the law of nations a pretext for France to interfere with the freedom of Spain to choose a king." When the Spaniards renewed their offer to Leopold in February 1870, William summoned his chief officers to a dinner. Bismarck, Moltke, Roon; they all favored Leopold's accepting, but the king remained opposed, as did his son, the crown prince. Still Bismarck persisted, and after several more discussions, the king grudgingly agreed—"with a heavy, a very heavy heart"—that "as soon as any prince of the House of Hohenzollern showed any inclination to accept the crown he would raise no opposition whatsoever to this inclination."

That concession, announced by Bismarck to Charles Antony on May 28, enabled the intriguers to pursue their intrigue. King William retired to the spa at Bad Ems and Bismarck to his estate at Varzin, leaving it up to Charles Antony and his son to meet in secret with the Spaniards to work out the details. Within a month, the chief Spanish negotiator happily telegraphed from Berlin that he would return to Madrid with Leopold's written acceptance and William's approval to be put before the Spanish Cortes "about the 26th," meaning June 26. The plan was to present the world with a fait accompli, after which it would be hard for the French to deny the Spaniards' right to choose their own king. But an obscure cipher clerk at the Prussian Embassy in Madrid then made a major error, so that the June 26 arrival of the Spanish envoy was translated as July 9. It was so hot in Madrid that the president of the Cortes balked at the idea of keeping his legislators in session for another three weeks. So he prorogued the Cortes until November, leaving the whole question unresolved.

And the secret, which had remained remarkably well-kept, began to leak out. The Parisian press heard of it on July 3, a Sunday, and the Monday morning papers raised an uproar. The new French foreign minister, Antoine Agénor, the Duke de Gramont, whom Bismarck once described as "the stupidest man in Europe," responded by firing off a telegram to Berlin, demanding to know whether the Prussian government was involved in this scandalous intrigue in Madrid. Since Bismarck was in the country, one of his foreign-ministry functionaries answered that the Prussian government "knew absolutely nothing about this affair," and that "so far as the Prussian government is concerned, the affair did not exist." This was a lie, of course, but Bismarck's official line was that Prince Leopold's future was purely a private concern of the Hohenzollern family. Though diplomatic lies do often serve a purpose, a lie that is very obvious can have the effect of infuriating the recipient. Gramont considered the Prussian disavowal "derisory"; as for Bismarck, he found the French minister's question "impudent." "The intervention of France . . . was internationally unjustifiable and exasperating," Bismarck wrote later, "and proved to me that the moment had arrived when France sought a quarrel against us and was ready to seize any pretext that seemed available."

Gramont refused to accept Berlin's pretense of innocence. He said the whole affair was "nothing less than an insult to France." When a member of the opposition raised the question in the French legislature, Gramont declared that the prospect of a Hohenzollern king of Spain would "imperil the interests and honor of France." To prevent it, he continued, he would rely on German wisdom and Spanish friendship, and if those failed, "we should know how to do our duty without hesitation and without weakness." Bismarck was having breakfast at his country estate in Varzin when the newspapers arrived with their accounts of Gramont's threat. "This looks like war," he said. "Gramont could not have spoken so recklessly if war was not decided."

There was some question, indeed, whether the French excitement had any real basis in Spanish dynastic politics. "From Paris," the Prussian crown prince noted in his diary on July 13, "I heard a few days ago the Emperor Napoleon said to one of his former ministers . . . that at the present moment Spanish concerns are practically unimportant, inasmuch as the question really at issue is the struggle for preponderance of power as between France and Prussia. If this is authentic, we should be fully justified in concluding that France is resolved on war at any price."

The Empress Eugénie, who was much concerned with the military glory of the Bonaparte dynasty, spoke volubly of the need to fight, and Premier Émile Ollivier told the legislature that he would accept the responsibility *"d'un coeur léger"* ("with a light heart"). Napoleon himself was less sanguine. He had been shocked by the carnage in the Italian war of 1859, and by the humiliating failure of his Mexican expedition. His own illness was painful and exhausting and dispiriting, and after fifteen years in power, he felt that the attractions of the imperial throne were beginning to pall in comparison to those of a quiet retirement. Still, the game had to be played. His empress demanded action, and so did the press, the politicians, the crowds in the street. Bismarck's banker reported that the French government was outfitting warships in Toulon; other agents said the army was buying up horses, ordering forage and other supplies.

Then as now, European statesmen liked to spend much of the summer in idleness far from their centers of conflict. Moltke was at Kreisau during the middle of July, and he was driving through his fields with his brother Adolf when a messenger signaled their carriage to stop at a ford in the River Peile. When the messenger handed Moltke some papers, the general silently read through them and then stuffed them in his pocket. Adolf and his family later recalled that Moltke drove rather recklessly on the way home, but he said nothing about the message he had received, and none of them had the temerity to ask him about it. Only when the carriage had returned to the manor did Moltke make a brief announcement: "It is a stupid thing, but I must go to Berlin tonight."

Thus did Moltke learn that all his plans seemed to be coming true.

The king's message had just notified him that the French maneuvers seemed so alarming that he wanted to mobilize the army. Back in Berlin, though, Moltke had dinner with Bismarck and Roon, and there he learned that the king planned not to fight the French but to give in to them. Unknown to Bismarck on his country estate—or to Prince Leopold on vacation in the Alps—the king had been consulting with Leopold's father, Prince Charles Antony. The king made it clear that he had no desire to involve the Hohenzollern family in Spanish politics, much less to fight the French for the sake of Bismarck's intrigues. Now, on July 12, had come word that Charles Antony was renouncing, on behalf of his vacationing son, any claim to the Spanish throne.

Bismarck was appalled. He spoke to Moltke and Roon of resigning "because after all the insulting provocations of recent days, I saw in this surrender to blackmail a humiliation for Germany." Moltke and Roon did their best to encourage him, and he soon decided to go on the offensive. ("I saw by that time that war was a necessity, which we could no longer avoid with honor.") He told his ambassador in Paris to demand "a completely satisfying statement as to the intention of France" or he would ask the king to convene the Reichstag to consider the next step, implicitly war.

This bluff was unnecessary because Gramont soon proved himself unable to realize that he had already won everything he could reasonably expect. His threats had persuaded the mighty Hohenzollerns to withdraw; there would be no Prussian prince on the throne of Spain. Instead of accepting his victory with a smile of satisfaction, Gramont sent an ill-considered telegram to his ambassador to Berlin, Count Vincent de Bénédetti, demanding that King William officially associate himself with Charles Antony's renunciation and "give us assurance that he will not authorize a renewal of the candidacy."

Bénédetti was already in Bad Ems and he already had an audience scheduled with the king for that afternoon of July 13, but he decided that Gramont's new demand was too urgent to wait. He accosted the aged king as he went strolling through the shaded paths of the Kurpark along the River Lahn. The king, recognizing him, paused and raised his hat. Bénédetti, clearly a man of some audacity, undertook to present there and then Gramont's rather peremptory demands. The king politely answered that he would not consider any such promises. The ambassador tried to argue, but the king cut him off, declaring that he had nothing further to say. He then raised his hat once more and walked on, accompanied by his wife and entourage. He told an aide to telegraph Bismarck an account of what had happened. "His

Majesty leaves it to Your Excellency," the telegram said, "whether Bénédetti's fresh demand and its rejection should not at once be communicated to our Ambassadors and to the press."

Bismarck was again dining with Moltke and Roon—all three of them in a state of depression over the renunciation of the Spanish throne—when the telegram from Bad Ems arrived. It was bland enough, but Bismarck saw at once that it could serve his purposes. "I saw by that time," Bismarck recalled later, "that war was a necessity, which we could no longer avoid with honor." With a little editing, Bismarck thought, the Ems telegram could have the effect of what he called "a red rag on the Gallic bull." He reached for a pencil and started to work.

This editing was subsequently denounced by Bismarck's critics as a fraudulent provocation and even a forgery, but all Bismarck did was to delete the niceties of diplomatic discourse and emphasize the bare facts of what had happened. The French ambassador had pressed extravagant demands on the king, and the king had completely rebuffed him. Moltke and Roon both approved of Bismarck's alterations. Moltke said that the telegram "sounded before like a parley; now it is like a flourish in answer to a challenge." Roon was even more emotional. "Our God of old still lives, and will not let us perish in disgrace," he cried.

Bismarck asked Moltke once again whether his army was ready to fight and able to win. Moltke said that if there was to be a war, he saw no benefit in delaying it.

"I believe that we are superior to them," Moltke said, but he could not resist adding a qualification: "But I make this reservation, that no one can foresee the result of a great battle." He knew immediately that this was not the kind of response that Bismarck wanted to hear, needed to hear. So Moltke struck his hand against his chest and offered a more warlike pledge, which oddly resembled Faust's bargain with Mephistopheles: "If only I can live to lead our armies in this war, then the devil may come directly afterwards and fetch away this old carcass."

Bismarck's version of the confrontation at Ems made headlines throughout Europe the next day, which happened to be Bastille Day, July 14. Gramont came rushing into Ollivier's office and cried that the Prussians had administered a "slap in the face." Street crowds sang the forbidden revolutionary anthem, "La Marseillaise," and chanted warlike slogans, "To Berlin!" and "Down with Prussia." Despite the popular hysteria, a strong peace faction in Paris had been trying to restrain the rush to war. Just the day before, when the cabinet had reluctantly approved the aggressive instructions that Gramont had already sent to Bénédetti, the ministers added their view that "the demand for guarantees was susceptible of mitigation and any honorable transaction would be welcome." The cabinet also voted down, by eight to four, a proposal for military mobilization. Only on the next day, when they read Bénédetti's reports together with Bismarck's belligerent version of the meeting in Bad Ems, did the ministers decide to approve the mobilization. Even after the marching orders were issued, they went on arguing for hours whether they should cancel the move and appeal for a conference of the great powers. They finally decided to accept what now seemed inevitable.

The legislature still had to approve the necessary financial credits, but legislatures do not often withhold such approval. The septuagenarian Adolphe Thiers, who would rise to rule France before this war ended, now was one of the few who spoke against the call to battle: "Do you want all Europe to say that although the substance of the quarrel was settled, you have decided to pour out torrents of blood over a mere matter of form?" It was in response to this that Ollivier delivered his jaunty remark about going to war with a light heart. War Minister Edmond Leboeuf, in an unconscious echo of Moltke's views, declared that the enemy was gaining strength, and so it would be better to fight the inevitable war now rather than later. So France declared war on July 15, and the Parisian crowds cheered at the news.

Despite all the cheering, Napoleon III seemed rather gloomy as he started out from his private railroad station in St. Cloud, with no public ceremony, to take command of his armies in the east. "We are beginning a long and difficult war," he said. With him was his fourteen-year-old son, Loulou, the prince imperial, newly commissioned as a lieutenant. Empress Eugénie made the sign of a cross on the boy's forehead as he boarded the train. Then she called out in their general direction: "Do your duty, Louis."

If the mood of the invader was filled with foreboding, the French declaration of war created an almost festive atmosphere in Prussia. In contrast to 1866, when the average citizen had difficulty in believing that a war against Austria would actually take place, the prospect of fighting the French seemed almost welcome. This was the arrogant enemy that had repeatedly invaded and plundered Germany, and the name of Napoleon still aroused memories of Jena and Tauroggen and Leipzig. The entire student body of Bonn University, some 1,000 strong, now marched off to enlist en masse. "The crowd stood shoulder to shoulder all the way from the station to the Royal Palace," Crown Prince Frederick wrote of his departure from Berlin to take up his military command, "uttering one unbroken storm of cheers that gave witness to their enthusiasm for the coming struggle."

Richard Wagner, nearing the end of the radiant third act of *Siegfried*, began denouncing French belligerence and dreaming up patriotic marches to inspire the Prussians.[1] "The more one hears of the French behavior, the more angry one becomes; a tissue of lies, ignorance, insolence, and conceit," his mistress, Cosima von Bülow, wrote in her diary, scarcely mentioning that she received her divorce that same week from the conductor Hans von Bülow and thus became free to marry the father of her infant son, Siegfried Wagner. (Cosima herself was largely French by birth and upbringing, being the illegitimate daughter of Franz Liszt and the Countess Marie d'Agoult; her sister Blandine married the future prime minister, Émile Ollivier.) "R[ichard] says he is beginning to feel hopeful; war is something noble, it shows the unimportance of the individual." At fifty-seven, Wagner was somewhat too old to don a Prussian uniform, but his twenty-six-year-old friend and protégé, Friedrich Nietzsche, shared his delusions about the nobility of war. Nietzsche could not join Moltke's army because his recent appointment to a professorship in classical philology at the University of Basel had required him to adopt Swiss citizenship. Anxious to join in the national defense, though, he signed up as a military nurse. As for Cosima, she rolled bandages while Wagner pressed on with the composition of the Norns' song of destiny at the start of *Götterdämmerung*. In her diary, she recorded, along with reports of burning villages, Beethoven quartets, and illness among the children, "We drink a toast to General Moltke."

This widespread outburst of patriotism was not mere chauvinism. There was a general feeling among the Germans that theirs was a *moral* cause, a struggle against the corruption and evil of Bonapartism. "God so willed," Crown Prince Frederick wrote in his journal, that the defeat of France and the consequent unification of Germany should enable "a free German Imperial State" to "march at the forefront of civilization and . . . bring to bear all noble ideals of the modern world, so that through German influence the rest of the world should be humanized, manners ennobled and people diverted from those frivolous French tendencies." This may all have been a case of Protestant righteousness, or simply national delusion, but the Prussians were not alone in their fervor. Thomas Carlyle, for example, had written extensively about both countries and now contrasted "vapouring,

---

[1]Even the amiable Brahms wrote a *Triumphlied* for chorus and orchestra, which he dedicated to the kaiser.

vain-glorious, gesticulating, quarrelsome, restless and over-sensitive France" to "noble, patient, deep, pious and solid Germany." The *Times* of London condemned the French declaration of war as "the greatest national crime . . . since the days of the First Empire." Queen Victoria saw it as a conflict "of civilization, of liberty, of order and of unity," by which she meant Prussia, against the French characteristics of "despotism, corruption, immorality, and aggression." These moral judgments were not universally shared, of course. With the benefit of considerable hindsight, we can see that there was more shrewdness as well as more compassion in the views of Giuseppe Verdi, who wrote to a friend: "It is true that the *blague,* the impertinence, the presumption of the French was and is, in spite of all their misfortunes, unbearable; but after all, France has given the modern world its freedom and its civilization. . . . Let our littérateurs and our politicians vaunt the knowledge and the science and even, God forgive them, the arts of these conquerors [the Prussians]; but if they would only look a little below the surface they would see that in their veins still runs the old blood of the Goths, that their pride is beyond measure, they are hard, intolerant, despisers of everything that is not German . . ."

Though it was the French who declared war, the German enthusiasm for this conflict was so ardent that it has inspired many analysts to accuse Bismarck of deliberately provoking the French into war. His goal, in this view, was to galvanize the lesser German states into supporting the unification of Germany under Prussian rule. Bismarck declared in his memoirs that "in view of the attitude of France, our national sense of honor compelled us . . . to go to war." If he had avoided the war, he added, "we should lose . . . the entire impetus towards our national development won in 1866." The eminent German historian Erich Eyck has argued that Bismarck's responsibility for the war was far greater than he admitted. While Napoleon and Gramont "have to bear their share of the responsibility," Eyck has written, Bismarck "kept the initiative by knowing beforehand how the others would react to his moves. He made them his tools, and they did what he wanted them to do. . . . His superiority towers above them, head and shoulders. Therefore, the primary responsibility rests with him alone." Nothing about Bismarck can be so simply judged, however, and it seems a little odd to blame him for such accidents as the error by the cipher clerk at the Prussian embassy in Madrid. The Oxford historian A. J. P. Taylor wrote that "there is not a scrap of evidence that he worked deliberately for a war with France, still less that he timed it precisely for the summer of 1870." To the extent that Bismarck later claimed responsibility for the war, Taylor observed, he was just boasting. A more judicious assessment of Bismarck's intentions is that of Hajo Holborn of Yale: "No adequate evidence has been produced that he initiated [the Spanish candidacy] in order to start a fire that would end in war between France and Prussia. But the Spanish candidacy was a move designed to harass Napoleon and Bismarck was fully aware that it would engender great political tension . . ."

Since Bismarck did get what he wanted, it has been easy for both his admirers and his critics to claim that everything was a result of his strategic planning. But Bismarck was not an inhuman calculator, either. He was no lover of war, and though his daily reading of the Bible may seem hypocritical, the bodies of the dead at Königgrätz did make him shudder over the fate of his son. "No one who has looked into the eyes of a man dying on the battlefield," he once said, "will again go lightly into war." On the other hand, he was always willing to risk war for political gain, and he was always a stoic about accepting the unavoidable. And those men who think war unavoidable most often find themselves waging it.

Moltke, of course, not only thought a war with France unavoidable but necessary and even desirable. All his life, he had regarded the French as insatiable, a constant threat. The only defense against them was to smash them. Now that Napoleon had stumbled into a reckless declaration of war, Moltke finally got his chance to settle old scores.

8

"To Attack the Enemy at Once, Wherever Found"

ON TAKING COMMAND OF THE FRENCH ARMIES, EMPEROR NAPOLEON III spoke with complacent pride of the repeated invasions that so rankled in Moltke. "Whatever may be the road we take beyond our frontiers, we shall come across the glorious tracks of our fathers," he said to his troops. "We shall prove worthy of them. . . ." As though to corroborate this, the maps issued to French officers covered only Germany, not the eastern regions of France.

Like Moltke, Napoleon expected that victory would go to the army that was best organized to go into combat. He thought, naturally, that this would be the French army. His war minister, Edmond Leboeuf, had promised him that his soldiers were "ready down to the last gaiter button." It took him only a few days in the field to realize that this was a delusion. To the Empress Eugénie, who had relentlessly insisted that he ignore his painful bladder stone and assume personal command of his army, he sent a bitter message: "Nothing is ready. We do not have enough troops, *Je nous considère d'avance comme perdus.*"

"The French intended to cross the Rhine at once, at and below Strassburg," Moltke wrote many years later in his analysis of the war. "To execute this plan, it would have been imperative to assemble the main forces of the French army in Alsace. Railway accommodation, however, was so inadequate that in the first instance it was only possible to carry 100,000 men to Strassburg; 150,000 had to leave the railways near Metz and remain there until they could be moved up."

By the time Napoleon reached his headquarters in Metz, he found only about 220,000 troops of the 385,000 he expected, and the situation kept getting worse. "It was often unknown at the railway stations where the regiments to which the reserves were to be sent were encamped," Moltke's account continued. "When they at last joined they were without the most necessary articles of equipment. The corps and divisions had no artillery or baggage, no ambulances, and only a very insufficient number of officers. . . . The Ministry of War in Paris was inundated with claims, protestations, and expostulations, and finally it was left to the troops to help themselves as best they could. *On se débrouillera* was the hope of the authorities. When the emperor arrived at Metz, a week after the declaration of war, the regiments were not yet complete, and it was not even exactly known where whole divisions were at that time encamped. . . ."

The realities of the French efforts to mobilize were even more deplorable than Moltke knew. Since troops and their equipment were assembled in different places, the mobilization brought chaotic disruptions and delays. The 86th Regiment, for example, was garrisoned in Lyon while its main depot was in Ajaccio, Corsica. An Alsatian reservist assigned to the Fourth Zouaves had to travel all the way to their depot in Algeria to get his equipment and then return hundreds of miles to join his regiment outside Strasbourg, where he had started his voyages. The railroads, not under military control, found themselves swamped with half-drunken soldiers demanding transport to distant assignments. Railroad cars filled with weapons and supplies crowded sidings where nobody was ready to unload them. Ambulances assigned to combat units found their medical supplies all stored at some distant warehouse. Infantry officers lacking maps were reduced to requisitioning them from local schoolhouses. They tried to requisition food as well, but supplies soon ran out. One hapless officer in Metz sent to Paris a desperate account of the available supplies: "Neither sugar nor coffee nor rice nor *eau de vie* nor salt, and not very much fats or biscuit." There was also, in some cases, no money to pay the troops. One parish priest offered a chilling summary: "Everyone behaved as he wanted. The soldier came and went as he liked, wandered off from his detachment, left camp and came back as he saw fit." One brigadier sent Paris a cry of utter helplessness: "Arrived at Belfort. Cannot find my brigade. Cannot find my divisional commander. Do not know where my regiments are. What shall I do?"

By comparison to the French confusion, Moltke's mobilization seemed a model of speed and efficiency. He and his staff had studied all the faults and mishaps of 1866 and ordered the necessary corrections. There were still confusions, of course, as there must be in any attempt to organize several hundred thousand men into an army ready for combat. On one route, for example, the soldiers arrived eleven hours late and only then received their first hot food in twenty-one hours. But in general, Moltke's long study of his railroad timetables brought him his rewards. By nine different railroad lines, his troops streamed toward the frontier. Between July 24 and August 3, some 1,200 trains carried westward fully 350,000 men, 87,000 horses, and 8,400 guns. "Thanks to the French dilatoriness," the crown prince noted in his diary, "the German armies are quite ready for battle; so it may well happen that, for all the French sabre-rattling and all their age-long preparation against a sudden onslaught, *we* shall be the aggressors. Who could ever have thought it?"

The basic strategy was clear. Clausewitz had left a plan for some future hero to invade France, like the sword that Wotan left embedded in the world ash tree until Siegmund came to claim it. The blade of Moltke's sword was a substantial superiority in manpower, nearly 400,000 to the French 300,000. As in Bohemia in 1866, he divided his forces into three armies between Luxembourg and Switzerland. On his right or northern flank, he assigned his First Army of 60,000 men to General Karl von Steinmetz, the headstrong victor at Nachod in 1866. In his center, based at Mainz, Prince Frederick Charles commanded the 135,000 troops of the Second Army. To the south, Crown Prince Frederick led the 130,000 men of the Third Army, which included a Bavarian brigade and two divisions made up of other south German allies. Behind them stood a reserve force of 65,000.

All these forces were ordered to push westward like a great harrow raking across the rich fields of eastern France. "In his plan of war, submitted by the Chief of General Staff and accepted by the King, that officer had his eye fixed, from the first, on the capture of the enemy's capital, the possession of which is of more importance in France than in other countries," Moltke later wrote of his own strategy in *The Franco-German War of 1870–71*. "On the way thither the hostile forces were to be driven as persistently as possible back from the fertile southern states into the narrower tract on the north. But above all the plan of war was based on the resolve to attack the enemy at once, wherever found." Crown Prince Frederick saw that

Moltke's plans were more complex and more audacious than the general said. "Moltke even thinks to set a mousetrap for them and be able to make prisoner the enemy's army," he wrote as early as August 26. "I cannot let *my* hopes soar so high as all that."

In planning his campaign, Moltke no longer enjoyed the advantage that the Prussian needle gun had given him at Königgrätz. The French had also observed the superiority of the Prussian rifle, and for once, they had drawn the right conclusion. A technician named Chassepot, employed at the artillery works at St. Thomas d'Aquin, had been working for more than a decade, without any official authorization, on a breech-loading rifle. The war minister, Count Randon, had raised all the traditional objections: a rifle that was too easy to reload would cause a shortage of ammunition, and besides, French élan was more important than improved weaponry. But Chassepot's rifle proved effective at 1,600 yards, almost three times the range of the Prussian needle gun, and it could fire eleven rounds per minute, so Napoleon overruled Randon in 1866 and ordered the Chassepot into production. The army had acquired a million of these rifles by the time the war started. It also had a semisecret new weapon called the *mitrailleuse*, a primitive machine gun made of twenty-six revolving barrels, which could fire 150 rounds a minute.

Content with their superiority in infantry weapons, the French ignored Friedrich Krupp's advances in artillery at his giant steel plant in Essen. Napoleon, who took a special interest in artillery, had equipped his army with new muzzle-loading cannons in 1858, but they were made of bronze, and nobody could convince him that Krupp's new technique for casting steel could produce weapons with twice as great a range and shells that exploded on contact, with no need for a time fuse. Krupp exhibited his new cannons at the great Paris Exposition of 1867, where Moltke and Bismarck and King William and the sovereigns of some thirty other states diverted themselves by watching Hortense Schneider cavort through the comic warfare of Offenbach's *Grand Duchess of Gerolstein,* but the French army remained indifferent to Krupp's displays. French officers observed the Krupp breech-loader in action that year at tests conducted by the Belgian army, but their reports on its superior range and accuracy went unheeded. Besides, the French legislature refused to appropriate the necessary funds. Having voted 113 million francs for the new Chassepot rifle, it cut the request for new artillery from 13 million to 2.5 million francs. When Krupp himself reported to the French government the following year on the excellence of his new gun, War Minister Leboeuf scribbled across the document that noth-

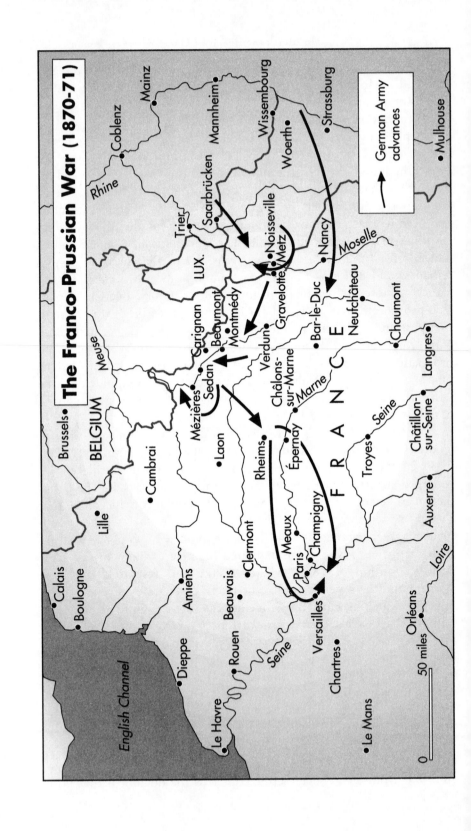

The Franco-Prussian War (1870-71)

German Army advances

English Channel

Calais
Boulogne
Dieppe
Le Havre
Rouen
Amiens
Beauvais
Clermont
Lille
Cambrai
Laon
Mézières
Sedan
Carignan
Beaumont
Montmédy
Verdun
Bar-le-Duc
Neufchâteau
Chaumont
Langres
Châtillon-sur-Seine
Auxerre
Orléans
Le Mans
Chartres
Versailles
Paris
Meaux
Champigny
Épernay
Rheims
Châlons-sur-Marne
Troyes
Nancy
Noisseville
Metz
Gravelotte
Saarbrücken
Trier
Woerth
Wissembourg
Strassburg
Mulhouse
Coblenz
Mainz
Mannheim
Brussels
BELGIUM
LUX.
FRANCE

Rhine
Moselle
Meuse
Marne
Seine
Loire
Seine

0   50 miles

ing could be done: *"Rien à faire."* And so nothing was done to prevent Prussia from entering the war with a decisive superiority in artillery.

As Moltke quickly saw, Napoleon began the war with a strategic plan roughly similar to his own, to cross the Rhine and strike the first blow wherever the enemy could be found. His hope was to reach as far as Nuremberg, there to join forces with invading armies from Austria and Italy, which he vainly hoped to have lured into the war by then. "The departure of the French troops to the frontier, before they were thoroughly prepared for service in the field, which is a very serious step to take, was evidently ordered for the purpose of surprising the German army . . . ," said Moltke, glacially unsurprised, "and thus interfering with the formation of their advance."

The French commanders seemed to have no coherent strategy for an invasion, however. Determined to do something, they started on July 31 a march toward Saarbrücken. The future capital of the coal industry was only lightly defended by one Prussian infantry division. When the French invaders arrived on August 2, the Prussians offered a minor cannonade from the hills south of the city and then withdrew. The dead numbered a total of eight Germans and eleven French. The French made no attempt to occupy the city, but the Parisian press nonetheless treated the army's arrival as an auspicious victory. "Our army has taken the offensive, and crossed the frontier and invaded Prussian territory," said the *Journal Officiel.* "In spite of the strength of the enemy positions a few of our battalions were enough to capture the heights which dominate Saarbrücken."

Not being guided by the Parisian press, Moltke pushed forward. His grand strategy was to wheel northward beyond Saarbrücken and encircle the French, but this was interrupted by two major clashes on August 6. In one, the French had withdrawn from Saarbrücken to the nearby heights of Spicheren, where they were discovered by German patrols. Underestimating French strength, the impetuous Steinmetz attacked. Though the Germans were originally outnumbered, according to Moltke's subsequent analysis, "the magnetic talisman of the thunder of the guns brought up reinforcements—some promised, others unexpected." It was a Prussian tradition, strongly supported by Moltke, for local commanders to march toward the sound of gunfire, thus to support each other wherever fighting began. French commanders were more likely to defend their own terrain and nothing more. As Bazaine remarked on this occasion, *"Le pion est dans la marmelade, qu'il y reste."* After waiting in vain for reinforcements while the battle grew larger from noon until dusk, the French commander, General Charles Auguste Frossard, finally decided to retire at nightfall. Armed with the Chassepot, his troops had inflicted 4,500 casualties on the Germans while suffering 2,000 of their own.

The second battle fought on that August 6 began just as haphazardly. Marshal Patrice MacMahon knew that he was threatened by Crown Prince Frederick's Third Army, but he seemed to have little idea of the size of the threat. One of his deputies even reported on August 3 that "the menace of the Bavarians is simply bluff." By that time, the Bavarians of the Third Army were pouring across the Rhine just southwest of Karlsruhe. It rained all that night, and they had to sleep on the sodden ground, but on the morning of August 4, they descended like locusts on the old fortress town of Wissembourg. The French division stationed in Wissembourg defended the town as best it could, but it was outnumbered by about four to one, and so it soon fled. "God be praised," the crown prince wrote in his diary, "our very first encounter with the enemy was a success."

MacMahon drew up his main forces into a strong defensive position in the hills around Wörth, about twenty miles southwest of Wissembourg, and in the evening of August 5 he solemnly declared to his staff, "The Prussians will be badly worsted." The crown prince was still assembling his forces and apparently had no intention of striking for another forty-eight hours, but the Prussian Fifth Corps, finding itself confronting the French center on the morning of August 6, boldly attacked. This may have been an impetuous decision by the local Prussian commander, or possibly just an accident. In any case, the Prussians were beaten back and called for help. A Bavarian unit emerged from some woods on the right, and then the Prussian Eleventh Corps appeared. As the battle expanded, the French held their ground so successfully that the crown prince sent orders for the Prussians to suspend their attack. But the Fifth Corps chief of staff, General von Kirchbach, refused to restrain his troops, and the fighting raged on through the afternoon. Several heroic French charges forced back the Prussian advance, but continual reinforcements kept strengthening the German numerical superiority—100,000 to 46,000 by the end of the day—and Prussian artillery provided deadly support for that superiority. The French fought well as long as they could, but when the breaking point came, they broke and ran. "I have today completely defeated Marshal MacMahon," Crown Prince Frederick wrote in his diary, "putting his troops to utter and disorderly retreat."

Some of MacMahon's troops fled as far as Châlons, where a French staff officer regarded them with contempt. "Disorder reigned supreme in the camp," he wrote later. "Instead of begilt generals there were commanders in dirty uniforms, who seemed afraid of showing themselves to their men. Instead of the fine regiments of other days there was a mass of beings without discipline, without cohesion, without rank."

The defeated always look grimy and disorderly to those far from the battle, but it is a mistake to assume that the victorious look very different. In a cattle car voyaging eastward from the battlefield at Wörth sat a twenty-six-year-old philology teacher from the University of Basel, Friedrich Nietzsche. "Yesterday we had an eleven-hour march to carry out our missions in Gersdorf and Langensulzbach and on the battlefield at Wörth," he wrote his mother on August 29. "With this letter comes a memory of the terribly devastated battlefield, sadly bespattered everywhere with human remains and reeking of corpses." To his newly acquired friend Richard Wagner, he offered a few more details. First he had to apologize to the "dear and honored master" for having failed to attend his marriage to Cosima von Bülow on August 25 and the baptism of their son Siegfried on September 4. "You know what stream it was that tore me away from you and made me unable to witness such holy and longed-for observances . . ." Nietzsche wrote. "In Ars-sur-Moselle we took charge of casualties and returned them to Germany. These three days and nights spent together with serious casualties were the climax of our efforts. I had a miserable cattle truck with six severely wounded men in it. I was alone with them for all that time, tending them, bandaging them, nursing them. The weather was bad, and the truck had to be kept shut or the patients would have been soaked. They all had shattered bones; several had four wounds. I could also see that two of them had gangrene. That I could survive in those pestilential vapors, and could even sleep and eat, now seems a marvel. . . ."

As soon as Nietzsche had delivered his patients to a hospital in Karlsruhe, he himself fell seriously ill. "I reached Erlangen with difficulty, to give various reports to my group," he wrote to Wagner. "Then I went to bed and am still there. A good doctor diagnosed my trouble as, first, a severe dysentery and, then, diphtheria. But we took strong measures against both infectious maladies, and today the outlook is hopeful. So I have made the acquaintance of two of those ill-famed epidemics at once; they weakened and enervated me so rapidly that I must for a start give up all my plans for working as a medical auxiliary and am obliged to think only of my health. . . . I prefer not to say a word about the German victories; these are the letters of fire on the wall, intelligible to *all* people. . . ."

There has been speculation, probably mistaken, that Nietzsche's confinement with these wounded men brought him the syphilitic infection that ultimately drove him insane. More probable is that it inspired his observation: "Whatever does not kill me makes me stronger." But it is hard to connect Nietzsche's views with his experiences. It was more than ten years after his harrowing experience of the battlefield at Wörth that he wrote in *Thus Spake Zarathustra* his fatuous apothegm in praise of war: "You say it is the good cause that hallows even war? I say unto you: it is the good war that hallows any cause."

Nietzsche was certainly no chauvinist. In sharp contrast to Wagner, he despised the Prussians and admired the French. "I believe only in French culture," he later wrote in *Ecce Homo,* "and regard everything else in Europe which calls itself 'culture' as a misunderstanding. I do not even take the German kind into consideration." And a few pages later: "Wherever Germany extends her sway, she ruins culture." Even while the war was still continuing, he wrote to a friend that the Prussia of Bismarck and Moltke represented the real enemy: "Confidentially, I consider the Prussia of today to be one of the powers most dangerous of all to culture." He urged this friend to leave "that fatal, anti-cultural Prussia, where slaves and priests sprout like mushrooms. Soon they will darken the whole of Germany for us with their vapors."

Whatever the consequences, Moltke still had a war to win. The two triumphs of Spicheren and Wörth brought a kind of pause, however. Moltke signally failed to follow up either victory with a pursuit of the fleeing French, for which he has been sharply criticized. One of his biographers, William O'Connor Morris, has written that "it is characteristic of him that he seldom attempted to crush a defeated enemy, the very opposite, in this respect, to Napoleon." Morris attributes this seeming lethargy neither to magnanimity nor to a sense of strategic design but simply to the fact "that Moltke was in his seventieth year." Perhaps, however, the answer is that Moltke failed to order the traditional pursuit of a retreating enemy because he regarded both battles as annoying interruptions of his master plan, and that as soon as the interruptions ended, he could resume that plan, to push the French toward the north and open the roads to Paris.

The French, on the other hand, came to a pause because they confronted a crisis in leadership. For Napoleon to assume the supreme command of all his forces had been a primarily political act, strongly urged by Empress Eugénie. He contributed very little to the army's military efforts, and his large retinue of chefs and wine stewards soon became a public nuisance. More important, Napoleon's bladder stone made it agonizing for him to ride a horse; even at rest, he was in considerable pain. His distraction was visible to everyone in his presence. "The Emperor, motionless, was gazing at the cloth," according to Emile Zola's account in *The Debacle,* "with the same vacillating, lacklustre, watery eyes he had already had at Rheims. . . . But he looked more tired. . . . An expression of secretly borne pain made his pale face look even more ashen."

When an aide finally persuaded the emperor to relinquish his command, he felt relieved; he dreamed of abandoning the campaign and returning to Paris. Empress Eugénie warned him, however, that any such retreat might lead to his overthrow. "Have you considered," she demanded, "all the consequences that would follow from your return to Paris under the shadow of two reverses?" Napoleon considered giving the supreme command to MacMahon, but the general's recent defeat at Wörth cast a dark shadow over his past successes in the Italian campaign of 1859, and so Napoleon finally settled on Marshal François Achille Bazaine. "Public opinion," he rather grudgingly announced to Bazaine, "combined with that of the army, marked you out as my choice."

Having enlisted as a private and worked his way up through the ranks in Algeria, Crimea, Lombardy, and Mexico, Bazaine did indeed have a reputation as a man of the people. This was somewhat reinforced by his appearance, the small and gleaming eyes, the jutting jaw, the beefy body. He had shown considerable bravery in combat, too, but no great aptitude for strategy or command. Sluggish in reaching decisions, he exhibited less boldness than doggedness. Threatened by Crown Prince Frederick's advances to the east of Metz, he withdrew into that fortress and waited stoically while MacMahon tried to mobilize a new force known as the Army of Châlons.

Both Eugénie's Regency Council and the Parisian press made it clear that MacMahon's chief duty was to rescue Bazaine and his 180,000 troops from Metz. Bazaine cautiously remained behind the walls of his fortress. Napoleon, who had also made his headquarters in Metz, kept prodding Bazaine to break out, but the commander dawdled. Only when he heard that the Germans were outflanking him by crossing the Moselle both north and south of Metz did Bazaine finally order a withdrawal on August 14. It was a scene of nightmarish confusion. The infantry began the evacuation at 4:30 A.M., but someone ordered the baggage trains to go first, and these creaking wagons soon blocked the narrow and winding streets of the old city. The combat troops could not move until 4 P.M., after twelve hours of standing at attention under the August sun, and then they came under heavy fire from the waiting Prussian artillery. Heavy rains had flooded the Moselle and knocked out several newly built bridges across the river, but the stream of wagons lurched onward through the shellfire and rain. Bazaine's goal was Verdun, about forty miles to the west, where he hoped to recover and reorganize, and to make connection with the new army that MacMahon was trying to organize at Châlons, another fifty miles to the west.

Moltke had not planned to contest this evacuation. He had already ordered his forces to march westward from Metz and the Moselle on a broad front about fifty miles wide. But since two hostile forces were moving westward along the road from Metz to Verdun, they inevitably collided. And though neither side was looking for a battle, the idea that Bazaine could escape from Metz without a shot being fired proved too much for Major General von der Goltz, commander of a brigade of the Prussian Seventh Corps. He resolved to attack. When firing started, General von Manteuffel's First Corps joined in. Bazaine was furious. "I absolutely forbid anyone to advance a yard," he said. General Steinmetz of the Prussian First Army also ordered his subordinates to break off the battle that had started near the village of Borny, but they found this almost impossible to do. By the time the firing died down at nightfall on August 14, the Prussians had suffered some 5,000 casualties, the French 3,500, but the results were inconclusive. While the Prussians had gained a few positions, the French had held a number of others. Both sides claimed victory.

At dawn the next day, the ailing Napoleon abandoned Bazaine and set off for Châlons with an escort of dragoons. He urged Bazaine to follow along the road to Verdun as quickly as he could. Instead of hurrying, though, Bazaine mysteriously ordered a delay in starting the march, and so he was caught by surprise when a Prussian cavalry unit swept down on the French camp at Vionville, alongside the Verdun road. The Prussian commanders, however, suffered from the illusion that they were attacking and trying to cut off nothing more than a rearguard; in fact, they were confronting Bazaine's whole army, which beat off their attack without much difficulty. Indeed, the French artillery fire from the north side of the highway to Verdun was so severe that it threatened to destroy the Prussian left wing. The only remedy that General Constantin von Alvensleben could propose was a desperate cavalry charge against the solidly defended French artillery. The only cavalry unit immediately available was a brigade commanded by a General von Bredow, and so he led the ferocious assault that became known as "Von Bredow's Death Ride," which Michael

Howard has described as "perhaps the last successful cavalry charge in Western European warfare." Partly concealed by a depression in the terrain north of Vionville, Bredow managed to lead his brigade to within a few hundred yards of the French lines before they started their thunderous charge. "Being received with heavy infantry and artillery fire," Moltke later wrote of Bredow, "he made a determined attack on the enemy's lines, riding down the foremost, breaking through their fire and securing the guns and their drivers. The second line of the French again could not withstand this onslaught, and even their remoter batteries prepared to limber up. But the triumph and excitement of success carried the small body of horsemen too far, and after an advance of 3,000 paces, they found themselves surrounded by the cavalry of the enemy, which attacked them from all sides. There was not space enough for a second charge, and so, after several encounters with the French, the brigade was forced to cut its way back through the French infantry, who followed them up with numerous volleys. Only one-half of the men reached Flavigny alive . . . having succeeded by their devoted bravery in stopping the French from further attack on Vionville."

The image of Moltke's forces moving irresistibly westward is misleading. As usual in warfare, every mile gained was gained in fear and confusion. The London *Times,* for example, published one unnamed Prussian infantry officer's recollections of the fighting near Mars-la-Tour on the Verdun road. "Marching forward, we soon heard the thunder of guns and the harsh grating of the mitrailleuse. . . . As we are turning a copse, we are suddenly in the thick of it. . . . Forward! Forward! Spreading out in their lines, we are running on while our breath lasts. We are exhausted even before we can see the enemy, so great is the distance, and so steadily ascending the long-stretching slope we have to go over. Stop! We are still at 1,000 paces from the French, and must take breath before we can proceed. Not a shot is fired. Now on again, a few hundred paces right into the potato field. Stop again, fire a few shots, and now at them at a run.

"At last we succeeded in getting near enough to see the heads of the French popping out of their ditches. As usual, they were in rifle-pits on the slopes and top of the hill. By this time very many of us had fallen, and we halted, on wholly unprotected ground, to exchange some rounds. Captain von Arnim was shot in the foot but remained sitting in our midst to direct the movements of the company. He soon got another ball in his breast, when he had to give it up. Finding we could not accomplish much, we got to our feet again and ran to within 500 paces of the enemy. Now, at least we had a fling at them. I measured the distance myself, took a dead man's rifle and popped away as fast and as well as I could. At this juncture, Major von Fabeck was shot, Captain von Hagen was shot, four men next to me were shot. We were in skirmishing order and beginning to melt away like wax. In front stood the French concealed in excavations up to their very eyes; behind us, for a distance of 800 paces, the ground was strewn with dead and wounded. . . . Captain von Berger, the adjutant of our Brigadier, came up at a gallop . . . ordering us to remain where we were if we wanted to escape being taken prisoners. So we just stood our ground until we saw troops coming to our support. Then we all advanced again and at 300 paces once more opened a murderous fire. All through this my men were very calm and self-possessed . . . though they could not but know that the greater part, and perhaps all, of them had got to die. . . . The fire was terrific, and Sadowa in comparison to it mere child's play. By and by our cartridges got exhausted, and we had to empty the pouches of the dead and wounded. As many of the latter as had a spark of life left did all they could to assist us in this. But everything has an end and so had our ammunition. I had given orders that every man was to reserve two cartridges in case the French took the offensive, and with these two cartridges in our possession we confronted the enemy even after we had ceased to fire. After a little while, which seemed to us terribly long, our support came up. They were skirmishers of Queen Elizabeth's Regiment, and the moment they joined us I heard their captain give the command in my rear, 'Charge with the bayonet!' I was lying on the ground with a shot in my left arm and shoulder blade; but as I heard those glorious sounds I jumped up and halloaing my men fiercely repeated the words of command, 'Charge with the bayonet!' But alas! There were only three men left to respond to my call. . . . I do not know whether the three survivors took part in the attack. As for myself, I could not do it, and sat down on the ground. The moment the Elizabeth Regiment charged the French jumped out of their ditches and ran away. . . . All the officers of [our] battalion are either dead or wounded. Of the 1,000 men with whom we went into the battle only 400 are left. . . ."

The fighting between Vionville and Mars-la-Tour continued throughout the afternoon as each side tried to outflank the other along the road to Verdun. This finally led to a tremendous cavalry battle on the Yron Valley—Moltke called it "the greatest cavalry battle of the war," though he himself could see little of the action; "a mighty cloud of dust," he wrote, "concealed the ensuing hand-to-hand encounter of 5,000 mounted men, swaying to and fro. . . ." As the confusion gradually died down in the gathering darkness, both sides claimed victory, but both had suffered grievous losses, nearly 16,000 among the Prussians, nearly 14,000 among the French. The Prussians took pride, though, in not only having checked the whole French army but in having cut the road to Verdun. The only escape route for Bazaine now lay northwest to Étain, and his forces wallowed in disorder. While many of his troops lacked food and even ammunition, his armada of some 5,000 supply wagons was scattered through the countryside, some overturned, some broken down, some looted, some abandoned. On the morning of August 17, Bazaine ordered his grumbling soldiers to recross the battlefields of the previous day and start marching back toward Metz. He claimed afterwards, when put on trial for his life, that he "believed . . . that by giving time to the Army of Châlons to form, it would reach a considerable size, which would allow it to come and relieve us." But if Bazaine had little idea of what to do, Moltke had plans for him. He still wanted to push the French northward, for his hope was to encircle them all. "The more enemy opposing Third Corps," he declared, "the greater the success will be tomorrow, when we can deploy against it Tenth, Third, Fourth, Eighth, Seventh Corps and eventually Twelfth." He ordered his pursuers to harry the retreating French "up to the Luxembourg frontier, and eventually on to the territory of that country."

MacMahon was quite aware, of course, that he was supposed to rescue Bazaine. That had been made quite clear by General Cousin de Montauban, who had been known as the Count of Palikao after leading a French expedition to China in 1860, and who became prime minister and war minister after Émile Ollivier was overwhelmed by the Parisian agitation that followed the first French defeats. But MacMahon knew better than Palikao and the pugnacious Empress Eugénie that his so-called Army of Châlons was quite inadequate to the mission envisaged for it. This army numbered some 130,000 men, but they were weary and disgruntled, almost mutinous. The few who had any energy were young recruits who had almost no training for combat. There were also eighteen battalions of *Gardes Mobiles* who still imagined themselves swaggering through the working-class districts of Paris. When they heard an exhortation of *"Vive l'Empereur!"* they were apt to respond with a rousing chorus of *"Un! Deux! Trois! Merde!"*

On August 17, the day after his arrival in Châlons, the ailing Napoleon summoned MacMahon and his top aides to a conference on future strategy. His cousin, the Prince Napoleon known as Plon-

Plon, insisted that the emperor must reassume command of his forces, must lead them back to restive Paris and install the popular General Louis Trochu as governor of the city. Napoleon vacillated and said that he wanted to consult Eugénie, the most outspoken alarmist about the political dangers threatening the regime.

"Aren't you the sovereign?" Plon-Plon demanded. "This must be done at once."

"I seem to have abdicated," Napoleon said vaguely. He had indeed installed Eugénie at the head of a regency council, and she had acted accordingly.

"You abdicated the government at Paris," said Plon-Plon, who nourished visions of himself as an heir to the empire. "At Metz you have now abdicated the command of the army." Plon-Plon's idea that Napoleon should lead the army back to Paris won support from Trochu, who claimed that MacMahon could maneuver more freely there.

That afternoon there came a message from Bazaine, claiming victory in the Battle of Vionville and proposing a temporary withdrawal back to Metz. Napoleon was skeptical. "Tell me the truth about your position so that I can act accordingly," he told Bazaine. Then came a telegram from Palikao, arguing nervously that a return to Paris would look like an abandonment of Bazaine and the whole of eastern France. "Could you not make a powerful diversion against the Prussian Corps, already worn out by several engagements?" he asked.

Trochu did return to Paris, taking along the mutinous *Mobiles*, whom he planned to disperse among various garrisons in the north. The empress and her chief minister gave him a frosty welcome. Palikao threatened to resign if Napoleon withdrew to Paris. The empress scornfully declared that only Napoleon's enemies could favor such a withdrawal. So Napoleon changed his mind again and canceled his withdrawal.

MacMahon asked Bazaine, the supposed supreme commander, for instructions on how the two generals might unite their forces. Bazaine pretended that they were both mere pawns in the hands of the distant Count Palikao. "I presume that the minister will have given you orders," he said, "your operations being at the moment entirely outside my zone of action." MacMahon became increasingly fretful at Bazaine's laconic leadership. "If, as I believe, you are forced to retreat in the near future," he said, "I cannot see, at this distance, how I can come to your aid without uncovering Paris. If you see the matter differently, let me know." It was like asking for orders from the Sphinx. Since Bazaine gave him no instructions or even information, MacMahon was reduced to asking local officials where his commander actually was. On August 21, after Prussian cavalry was reported within twenty-five miles of Châlons, he finally set out for Rheims, hoping that he might somehow discover what was expected of him. The influential president of the French Senate, August Rouher, rode to MacMahon's headquarters to see if he could be of any help. He found MacMahon in despair. "It is impossible to rescue Bazaine," he said. "He has no munitions, no supplies, he will be forced to capitulate, and we shall arrive too late." Rouher agreed with him that he should fall back on Paris.

Then came a new message from Bazaine, declaring that he now intended to break out from his sanctuary in Metz via Sainte Ménéhould, just beyond Verdun, or else by way of Sedan, some fifty miles to the north. MacMahon announced that he was marching to Montmédy, some twenty miles southeast of Sedan, to join forces with Bazaine and drive the Prussian invaders from French soil. Moltke was amazed at the news. He could hardly believe that MacMahon would deliberately march into the trap that he was preparing.

When medics were clearing away the 16,000 German and 14,000 French casualties at Mars-la-Tour, Bismarck was appalled to hear that they included his two sons. Herbert, not yet twenty, had been seen falling from his horse during a cavalry action, and Bill had fallen nearby. Frantic with worry, Bismarck set out from his camp at Pont-a-Mousson, south of Metz, and rode more than twenty miles through the night until he found both his sons slightly injured but quite alive. "Since God has so mercifully preserved our two I must not be bitter," he wrote home to his wife, then added a tirade against the commanders of the First and Second armies for their "squandering of the best soldiers in Europe."

After the ambiguous results at Vionville, Bazaine decided to establish a new defensive line from St. Privat to Gravelotte, just west of Metz. The fronts were now reversed—the French facing towards Paris and the Germans towards the Rhine. On the left end of Bazaine's defensive line, half a mile east of Gravelotte, his troops had established strong positions on a series of small farms connected by trenches and gun emplacements. They overlooked bare fields that could be raked by Chassepot fire. The crown prince's orders on the morning of August 17 told his troops to skirt this danger, to "set out . . . towards the north to find the enemy and fight him." His troops accordingly set out, accompanied by artillery fire from both sides. "Everywhere, along the whole range, guns sent out flashes and belched forth dense volumes of smoke," a German officer recalled afterwards. "A hail of shell and shrapnel, the latter traceable by the little white clouds, looking like balloons, which remained suspended in the air for some time after their bursting, answered the warlike greeting from our side. The grating noise of the *mitrailleuses* was heard above the tumult, drowning the whole roar of battle."

One man with a ringside seat for this battle was General Philip Sheridan, then thirty-nine, the Union army's celebrated cavalry commander in the recent American Civil War, who had asked for and received permission to act as an unofficial observer at German headquarters. He had arrived there just the day before the Battle of Gravelotte and accompanied King William to some high ground between Gravelotte and Rezonville. This seemed ideal except for one drawback: "the dead bodies of many of the poor fellows killed there two days before were yet unburied." Some of the king's escorts began hauling the corpses away, however, so the field was soon ready for new fighting.

Sheridan saw the French forces arrayed along the ridge of a crest that ran northward for about seven miles. The French left, nearest to the American's observation post, was also protected by a steep and wooded ravine. The Germans began their attack from their own left, where Frederick Charles's Second Army soon pushed the French back. "The French artillery and mitrailleuses responded vigorously to the Krupps, and with deadly effect," Sheridan later wrote in his memoirs, "but as far as we could see the German left continued its advance, and staff-officers came up frequently to report that all was going on well at points hidden from our view. These reports were always made to the King first, and whenever anybody arrived with tidings of the fight we clustered around to hear the news, General Von Moltke unfolding a map meanwhile, and explaining the situation. This done, the chief of staff, while awaiting the next report, would either return to a seat that had been made for him with some knapsacks, or would occupy the time walking about, kicking clods of dirt or small stones here and there, his hands clasped behind his back, his face pale and thoughtful. He was then nearly seventy years old, but because of his emaciated figure, the deep wrinkles in his face, and the crow's feet about his eyes, he looked even older, his appearance being suggestive of the practice of church asceticism rather than of his well-known ardent devotion to the military profession."

As the fighting continued all day, the German left kept pressing forward; only in mid-afternoon did the right launch a major attack across the ravine that protected the French defenders. When the French firing stopped the First Army infantry, General Steinmetz ordered a cavalry charge. "Crossing the ravine . . ." Sheridan recalled, "this body of horse swept up the slope beyond, the front ranks urged forward by the momentum from behind. The French were posted along a sunken road, behind stone walls and houses, and as the German cavalry neared these obstructions it received a dreadful fire without the least chance of returning it, though still pushed on till the front ranks were crowded into the deep cut of the road. Here the slaughter was terrible, for the horsemen could make no further headway; and because of the blockade behind, of dead and wounded men and animals, an orderly retreat was impossible, and disaster inevitable."

At about this time, the king moved his headquarters into the village of Gravelotte, and as soon as the royal party arrived there, "we first learned fully of the disastrous result of the charge which had been entered upon with such spirit." Sheridan, who must surely have become hardened to cavalry casualties by now, expected that Steinmetz would be relieved at once for having wasted his men, but he soon learned differently. "Steinmetz appeared in the village presently, and approached the King. When near, he bowed with great respect, and I then saw that he was a very old man, though his soldierly figure, bronzed face, and short-cropped hair gave some evidence of vigor still. When the King spoke of him I was not close enough to learn what he said; but his Majesty's manner was expressive of kindly feeling. . . . His fault had been overlooked."

The silence of the French artillery led several German officers to boast that they had knocked out all the enemy guns, but Sheridan was skeptical. "The Germans labored up the glacis slowly at the most exposed places," he wrote, "now crawling on their bellies, now creeping on hands and knees, but, in the main, moving with erect and steady bearing. As they approached within short range, they suddenly found that the French artillery and mitrailleuses had by no means been silenced—about 200 pieces opening on them with fearful effect, while at the same time the whole crest blazed with deadly fire from the Chassepot rifles. Resistance like this was so unexpected by the Germans that it dismayed them; and first wavering a moment, then becoming panic-stricken, they broke and fled, infantry, cavalry, and artillery coming down the slope without any pretense of formation, the French hotly following and pouring in a heavy and constant fire as the fugitives fled back across the ravine toward Gravelotte.

"With this the battle on the right had now assumed a most serious aspect, and the indications were that the French would attack the heights of Gravelotte; but the Pomeranian Corps coming on the field at this crisis was led into action by Von Moltke himself, and shortly after the day was decided in favor of the Germans."

When French artillery opened fire, many shells landed near King William and "made the place extremely uncomfortable." Following the traditional minuet of royalty in combat, the king's aides urged him to seek a safer place, but he "refused to listen" until he could made a show of "leaving the ground with reluctance." Bismarck made a similar show of "looking after some of the escort who had been wounded." When Bismarck and Sheridan finally galloped after the king, they found that he had stopped on the Châlons road to harangue a group of fugitives, an effort he repeated "in the same emphatic style [to] every group of runaways he overtook."

Passing through Rezonville, the royal party stopped just beyond the village. "There a fire was built, and the King, Prince Frederick Charles and Von Roon were provided with rather uncomfortable seats about it, made by resting the ends of a short ladder on a couple of boxes." There they waited anxiously for news from the battlefield. "But the suspense did not last long, for presently came the cheering intelligence that the French were retiring, being forced back by the Pomeranian Corps, and some of the lately broken rightwing organizations that had been rallied on the heights of Gravelotte. . . . It was not long before word came that Bazaine's army was falling back to Metz, leaving the entire battlefield in possession of the Germans."

Some of the fiercest fighting had taken place at the northern end of the French defensive line. Hampered by combat losses, the German cavalry had once again failed in the task of keeping close watch on where the enemy actually was. "Misapprehension . . . prevailed," according to Moltke's subsequent account, "as to the extension of their lines, and it was thought the French front did not reach beyond Montigny." When the Germans attacked near Montigny, therefore, they thought they were going to turn the French right wing but instead found themselves butting vainly into the French center. Further reconnaissance demonstrated that the French right wing extended as far north as St. Privat, a well-fortified village surrounded by sloping fields wide open to gunfire. When Prince Augustus of Württemberg arrived there with a Saxon contingent in late afternoon, he impetuously ordered a charge without waiting for artillery to soften up the French defenses. The Chassepot rifle dictated the results.

"Several ranks of riflemen, one above the other, were placed in front of the French main position, on the hedges and fences in a slope up the ridge," Moltke later described the hellish scene. "At their back towered St. Privat, castle-like, with its massive buildings, which were crowded by soldiers to the very roof. The open plain in front was thus exposed to an overwhelming shower of projectiles. The losses of the attacking Guards were, in fact, enormous. . . ."

"No sooner did the enemy notice our march than he opened fire upon us," one Prussian staff officer recalled later. "It was the most destructive quick-fire you can imagine. After a few minutes we had numbers of our comrades lying on the ground, and the nearer we proceeded the greater became our losses. Nor had we the satisfaction of retaliating upon our adversaries. Stationed as they were behind houses and walls, or crouching in ditches, they were perfectly invisible to us. . . . All the generals and staff officers were on horseback in front of the attacking party, and after a short time were either shot or had their horses killed under them. The enemy's fire came like a hailstorm of lead. . . . At last the village began to burn and we had some hopes of being able to penetrate through the shower of missiles which were still falling as fast and thick as ever. At half past six we resumed the charge. The enemy, though his flank had been turned by this time by the Saxons, still fought with desperate valor, and defended every single house in the place. Within fifteen minutes we dislodged him entirely, when his ranks suddenly broke, and the whole mass, which had made so long and obstinate a resistance, all at once fled in confusion towards Metz. But the cost of victory this time damped our joy in it. Nearly all the officers in our brigade were either dead or wounded. . . ."

Historians record that the Germans charged triumphantly into St. Privat, drums and bugles sounding together with the soldiers' cheers, flags waving in the setting sun, but both sides had to engage in the fearful business of counting casualties—20,163 on the German side, 12,273 on the French. "I have learned once more," Moltke said sadly, recalling Clausewitz, "that one cannot be too strong on the field of battle."

Having endured this bloodbath, Bazaine withdrew into the safety of Metz, which is probably what he had wanted to do ever since he had left the city a week earlier. Moltke, like a chess player moving a rook out into action late in a game, assigned Prince Frederick Charles's Second Army to keep Bazaine and his 180,000 troops confined within their sanctuary. Since that did not leave him enough troops to pursue MacMahon, however, he decided to reorganize his forces. He assigned about half of Frederick Charles's troops to a new Army of the Meuse under the crown prince of Saxony, who had shown himself a capable commander. He then supplemented Frederick Charles's depleted force by assigning to it Steinmetz's First Army.

He fully expected the fractious Steinmetz to resign at the prospect of being made a subordinate ("I should be surprised to see this turn out well," the crown prince observed), and he gave Frederick Charles full authority to dismiss Steinmetz at the first sign of trouble. When this occurred within a month, Steinmetz was shipped off to the obscure post of governor of Posen.

Once Moltke had reorganized his forces, he had to confront the challenge of trapping MacMahon and his new Army of Châlons. He heard that MacMahon had left Châlons, apparently retreating westward toward Rheims to take a flanking position on the road to Paris. He could not know that Palikao was strenuously urging MacMahon to march eastward toward Bazaine's headquarters in Metz. Only on the night of August 24 did Moltke receive a London *Times* report, based on stories in the Paris press, to the effect that MacMahon was "endeavoring to form a junction" with Bazaine. And only when he received *Le Temps* of August 23 did he read a semiofficial report that MacMahon was indeed marching forward to put his head in Moltke's noose. The story might be false, might even be a French effort to mislead the Prussian invaders, but Moltke decided to gamble that the reports were true, that MacMahon really was doing exactly what orthodox military doctrine said he should not do. Cautiously, Moltke suggested to the prince of Saxony that he might consider shifting toward his right; the prince promptly decided to do just that. Even before his cavalry scouts reported on MacMahon's whereabouts, he sent four infantry corps wheeling northward into the Argonne forest.

Pressing onward through persistent rain that turned the forest roads to mud, MacMahon fretted about the dangers that surrounded him. "I do not think I can move much further east without having news of you and knowing your plans . . ." he told Bazaine. Bazaine did not answer, but Palikao kept urging him on. "If you abandon Bazaine," said the message from Paris early on August 28, "revolution will break out in Paris. . . . You have nothing in front of you but a feeble part of the forces which are blockading Metz . . ." And then a direct order: "In the name of the Council of Ministers and the Privy Council, I require you to aid Bazaine." Onward into the quagmire MacMahon marched.

The two armies collided August 29 near the woods along the Meuse valley. At nightfall, the French withdrew into the woods, stumbling through the darkness until they reached the town of Beaumont, where they collapsed into the sleep of exhaustion. Bavarian infantry emerged from the woods at dawn and stared in amazement at the sleeping and unguarded French. They wondered whether it was proper to attack a sleeping camp, then suppressed their scruples and opened fire. At first, the French scrambled up and fought back, as well as newly awakened troops can fight, but they soon began retreating northeastward to the Meuse. The nearest crossing point was Mouzon. The French spent much of the day getting themselves across, losing thousands of troops in the process, along with horses, cannons, and supply wagons. About ten miles farther north, MacMahon had prepared a sanctuary for them, the venerable fortress of Sedan.

Located in a hairpin turn of the Meuse, Sedan was chiefly notable as the native town of Louis XIV's great commander, Marshal Turenne. The marshy valley of the Meuse seemed a strong protection for its defenders, but defensive strongholds, like Bataan and Corregidor, have a tendency to turn into traps. The nearby Belgian border also seemed a defensive barrier that Moltke saw differently. Bismarck notified the Belgian government on August 30 that any French troops who crossed the frontier would have to be immediately disarmed and interned or Moltke's forces would also cross the frontier in pursuit of them.

Once MacMahon had installed himself in the Sedan trap, Moltke began sharpening its teeth. Fully aware after St. Privat of the effects of the Chassepot rifle, Moltke now depended on the proven superiority of Krupp's cannons, which he began installing on the hills to the east of Sedan. MacMahon "did not intend to offer battle there," Moltke later wrote, "but it was indispensable to give his troops a short rest, and provide them with food and ammunition. Later on he meant to retreat via Mézières. . . ." French reinforcements were gathering at Mézières, but the only escape route in that direction lay through Donchéry, just beyond the hairpin turn that the Meuse took downstream from Sedan. When the crown prince's Eleventh Corps seized the railway bridge across the Meuse at Donchéry, Moltke knew that the last escape route to the west had been sealed. "Now we have them in a mousetrap," he said to King William, rubbing his hands as he spoke. MacMahon seemed only dimly aware of his fate, but one of his deputies saw it quite clearly. "*Nous sommes dans un pot de chambre,*" said General Auguste Alexandre Ducrot, "*et nous y serons emmer-dés.*"

Like many generals on the eve of victory—like Schwarzkopf at his television briefing outside Kuwait, for instance—Moltke liked to stage-manage an impending battle as a bit of theatre.

"It was now a superb day, and Moltke's staff had found for the King a vantage-point from which a view of the battle could be obtained such as no commander of an army in Western Europe was ever to see again," Michael Howard wrote in his authoritative account, *The Franco-Prussian War.* "In a clearing on the wooded hills above Frénois, south of the Meuse, there gathered a glittering concourse of uniformed notabilities more suitable to an opera-house or a race-course than to a climactic battle which was to decide the destinies of Europe and perhaps of the world. There was the King himself; there was Moltke, Roon and their staff officers watching the crown to their labours, while Bismarck, Hatzfeldt and the Foreign Office officials watched the beginnings of theirs. There was Colonel Walker from the British army and General Kutusow from the Russian; there was General Sheridan from the United States, Mr. W. H. Russell of *The Times,* and a whole crowd of German princelings; Leopold of Bavaria and William of Württemberg, Duke Frederick of Schleswig-Holstein and the Duke of Saxe-Coburg, the Grand Duke of Saxe-Weimar and the Grand Duke of Mecklenburg-Strelitz and half a dozen others, watching the remains of their independence dwindling hour by hour as the Prussian, Saxon, and Bavarian guns decimated the French army around Sedan.

"At first the morning mist and the smoke from the guns and fires at Bazeilles had hidden the battlefield, but as the sun mounted and the mist cleared the whole scene was unveiled: Sedan itself lying behind a glittering sheet of flood-water, so near that with a good glass one could look into its agitated streets; the slopes behind it thickly crowded with the bivouacs which the red trousers of the French troops made so conspicuous; the long line of the Bois de Garennes, outlining the summit of the crest; behind again, the open slopes above Illy and Givonne, which the two wings of the German army were beginning to crown with their batteries; and the dark crests of the Ardennes forming a backcloth to the whole scene. . . ."

The battle began at 4:30 A.M. on September 1, when the Bavarian General von der Tann sent his Bavarian I Corps to attack the village of Bazeilles, about three miles southeast of Sedan, the southernmost outpost of the French defenses. The village was fiercely defended not only by French Marines but by citizens firing from every house. The Bavarians' shells soon set the town on fire, and by noon they had captured the smoking rubble. A Bavarian shell fragment also felled the visiting MacMahon, piercing him in the buttocks. Disabled in this degrading way, MacMahon delegated his authority to his most experienced deputy, Ducrot, who thus assumed the responsibility for escaping from what he had regarded as a chamber pot. Ducrot promptly ordered a withdrawal to the west. Neither he nor MacMahon knew that Crown Prince Frederick had already severed that escape route at

Donchéry. Nor did they know that the authorities in Paris, specifically Count Palikao, had sent them a new commander, General Emmanuel Felix de Wimpffen,[1] until recently governor of Oran. Armed with secret orders that named him chief of the Army of Châlons in case of MacMahon's becoming disabled, Wimpffen now announced his takeover and canceled Ducrot's withdrawal. He had the advantage of knowing that the Germans were already in Donchéry, but his arguments were chiefly emotional. To Ducrot's protests, he answered only, "We need a victory." "You will be very lucky, *mon général,* if this evening you even have a retreat," Ducrot retorted. So the French were under orders to stand fast, but where they stood was under the murderous fire of Moltke's artillery.

Émile Zola, who interviewed many of the survivors and tramped over this whole area in search of physical details, vividly narrated much of what he called the debacle in terms of two cousins named Maurice and Jean. When they found shelter behind a hedge, a bullet killed one of their companions. "They had to kick him to one side," Zola wrote. "However, the dead no longer counted, there were too many of them. The horror of the battlefield, a wounded man they saw shrieking and holding his entrails in with both hands, a horse still dragging itself along on its broken legs, all this frightful agony had ceased to touch them. All they suffered from now was the overpowering heat of the noonday sun gnawing at their shoulders. . . ."

Hour by hour, Moltke's forces kept tightening the noose; his cannons kept intensifying their rain of destruction. Throughout the morning, Wimpffen clung to the idea of breaking out through the Bois de Garennes, which rose up in the valley to the east of Sedan. Shortly after noon, he sent a message to Napoleon beseeching the emperor to come and lead his troops out of Moltke's trap. The emperor refused; he wanted to end the killing and surrender. Very few French troops answered Wimpffen's summons either. They too wanted to give up the hopeless struggle. In late afternoon, General Ducrot, who had been forbidden to retreat, could think of only one last measure, a desperate charge by General Margueritte's reserves of cavalry from the Bois de Garennes down to the Meuse. General Margueritte was among the first to fall, severely wounded by a bullet that smashed his jaw and covered his face with gore. Held up by two aides, he raised an arm toward the waiting enemy and then collapsed. Among his dismayed horsemen, there arose a rumble of anger: *"Vengez-le!"*

---

[1]Moltke generally referred to him as Von Wimpffen, but perhaps that was just Prussian malice.

"The trumpets sounded and the mass began to move," Zola wrote in re-creating the scene. "Prosper was in the front rank. . . . When they had scaled the top of the hill and were beginning to go down the further side towards the broad plain he had a clear view, some thousand meters ahead, of the Prussian squares against which they were being hurled. For all that, he was riding in a dream, feeling as light and disembodied as a man in his sleep, with an extraordinary vacuum in his brain which left him without a single idea—in fact a machine functioning with irresistible impetus. They kept repeating 'Close up! Close up!' so as to close the ranks as tightly as possible and give them a granite-like solidity. Then as the pace quickened and changed into a mad gallop, the Chasseurs d'Afrique, as in the Arab fashion, uttered wild yells that maddened their mounts. This furious gallop soon turned into a diabolical race, hell's own stampede, with its savage cat-calls accompanied by the patter of bullets like hailstones on metal things, messtins, water-bottles, the brass on uniforms and harness. In this hail blew a hurricane of wind and din that made the earth tremble, and into the sunshine rose a smell of scorching wool and the sweat of savage beasts. . . ."

But the German lines held, an awesome demonstration of the new reality that modern rifles could withstand even the bravest cavalry charge. "Their foremost lines were broken through at several points. . . ." Moltke recalled, "but the reserves beyond checked their further progress." French military legend records that after the charge had failed to dislodge the Germans, General Ducrot asked the doughty General Gaston de Gallifet, who had replaced the injured Margueritte at the start of the unsuccessful charge, whether he could repeat the assault. "As often as you like, *mon général*," Gallifet supposedly answered, "so long as there is one of us left." So Gallifet reassembled his horsemen and repeated the charge. And again the Prussian infantry lines stood fast, forcing the charging cavalry to turn aside. A third time they charged, and a third time they failed. King William, watching from the box seat that Moltke had provided on the hilltop, is supposed to have been so impressed by the cavalrymen's courage that he exclaimed in their own language, *"Ah, les braves gens!"* Such, at least, are the words carved on a nearby memorial. It is not impossible, though, that the king was speaking of his own infantrymen refusing to yield to the onrushing stampede.

Those charges were the end of the famous French élan. It remained only for the German artillery to ravage the Bois de Garennes, driving out all those who had taken shelter there. "Long columns of French could be seen pouring down on Sedan from all the neighboring hills," Moltke recalled. "Irregular bands of troops were massed in and around the walls of the fortress, and shells from the German batteries on both sides of the Meuse were constantly exploding in their midst. Columns of fire soon began to arise from the city, and the Bavarians . . . were about to climb the palisades of the gate when, at about half-past four, flags of truce were hoisted on the towers."

Napoleon had really wanted to surrender some time earlier, as soon as he saw that the struggle was hopeless. But Wimpffen had resisted with all the ardor of a commander new to battle. "Your Majesty may be quite at ease," Wimpffen declared at the first talk of surrender. "Within two hours I shall have driven your enemies into the Meuse."

The French panic soon became irreversible. "As far as ever the telescopes could make out," Crown Prince Frederick wrote, "everywhere we saw men of all arms bolting headlong for Sedan; each quarter of an hour increased the number of the fugitives. . . . In the midst of this hurly-burly . . . I saw Zouaves taking prodigious leaps into the air. Infantrymen were already running about unarmed, restless and bewildered; to a soldier's eye the whole scene was a painful and repugnant one."

Rouged to disguise his pallor, Napoleon spent much of that day riding around the battlefield with an almost suicidal disregard for his own safety. The emperor was apparently accustomed to being disobeyed, but after two more hours of fighting, he complained to one of his generals, "Why does this useless struggle still go on? An hour and more ago, I ordered the white flag to be flown."

When Wimpffen first caught sight of an imperial white flag, however, he exploded. "Drop that rag!" he shouted. "I mean to fight on."

At about 3 P.M., King William decided that the battle was over and sent a staff lieutenant, Paul von Bronsart von Schellendorf, to request the surrender of Sedan. He found that Napoleon, ignoring Wimpffen's threats of resignation, had already sent an envoy, General Reille, with a message for King William. "A French officer approached from Sedan, preceded by a white flag and two German officers," General Sheridan recalled. "Coming up the road till within a few hundred yards of us, they halted; then one of the Germans rode forward to say that the French officer was Napoleon's adjutant, bearing an autograph letter from the Emperor to the King of Prussia. At this, the king, followed by Bismarck, Von Moltke and Von Roon, walked out to the front a little distance and halted, his Majesty still in advance, the rest of us meanwhile forming in a line some twenty paces to the rear of the group. The envoy then approached, at first on horseback, but when within about a hundred yards he dismounted, and uncovering, came the remaining distance on foot, bearing high up in his right hand the dispatch from Napoleon."

"*Monsieur mon frère*," Napoleon wrote to the Hohenzollern king, who would never have dreamed of regarding this powerless usurper as a brother, "having been unable to die in the midst of my troops, there remains to me nothing but to give up my sword into the hands of Your Majesty. . . ."

The Germans were stunned—Moltke later claimed that the emperor's "presence in Sedan had till now been unknown"—but Bismarck quickly dictated a response for his king. "While regretting the circumstances in which we meet," the Prussian letter said, "I accept Your Majesty's sword and ask you to name one of your officers with full power to arrange the capitulation of the army that has fought so bravely under your orders. On my side, I have designated General Moltke for this purpose."

Bismarck, for one, felt like celebrating, and when his nephew offered him a bottle of brandy that evening, he gratefully seized it. "Here's to the unification of Germany!" he cried as he lifted the bottle to his lips, "which sentiment," Sheridan observed, "the gurgling of an astonishingly long drink seemed to emphasize." When the nephew retrieved his bottle, he said, "Why, we can't pledge you in return—there is nothing left." Bismarck unapologetically apologized that "it was so dark I couldn't see."

When Count Reille returned to French headquarters, Wimpffen protested bitterly at the general assumption that he would have to be the one to negotiate the surrender. He agreed, however, to go to Prussian headquarters to see what Bismarck and Moltke would propose as their terms. The Prussians demanded that the entire French army submit to becoming prisoners of war. Wimpffen requested an "honorable capitulation," in which the army would march off with its arms, though pledging not to fight again for the rest of the war. Bismarck refused. He said Prussia wanted to end the war as soon as possible, and the best way to do that was to dismantle the French army completely. Wimpffen threatened to renew the fighting for Sedan. Moltke relentlessly pointed out that he now had 250,000 men to Wimpffen's 80,000 and that the French were not only outnumbered but demoralized, low on food and ammunition.

Wimpffen then appealed to Bismarck's sense of history. "A peace based on conditions which would . . . diminish the bitterness of defeat would be durable," he said, in words that might as well have been addressed to several future generations of both German and French leaders, "whereas rigorous measures would awaken bad passions and perhaps bring on endless war between France and Prussia." Bismarck was vastly unimpressed. "One should not, in general, rely on gratitude," he said, "and especially not on that of a people." If Napoleon enjoyed popular support, "we might be able to trust in the gratitude of the Emperor and his son." But Napoleon didn't seem to represent France, and neither did anyone else. "One can rely on nothing in your country," Bismarck scornfully declared, except that the French as a whole were "irritable, envious, jealous, and proud to excess. It seems to you that victory is a property reserved for you alone, that the glory of arms is your monopoly." The French had made war on the Germans thirty times in the past two centuries, Bismarck declared, and that must now end. "We must have land, fortresses and frontiers which will shelter us for good from the enemy attack." Wimpffen answered rather unpersuasively that this French penchant for war had changed under the empire, that "all minds have turned to speculation, business, the arts." Bismarck replied that the Paris press's enthusiasm for the current war belied any such change, and now he proposed to march on Paris. "The fortune of battle has delivered to us the best soldiers, the best officers of the French army; to voluntarily set them free, to risk seeing them march against us again would be madness." A little after midnight Wimpffen decided to retire to French headquarters, leaving the surrender document unsigned and the battle still theoretically unfinished. Of the parting of Wimpffen from Moltke and the other Prussian leaders, one French staff officer observed, *"Ce silence était glacial."*

Napoleon decided that it was up to him to avoid the degradation of total surrender. He arose at five the next morning, donned the dress uniform of a major general, complete with white gloves and gold-bordered kepi, and set forth in a two-horse open carriage to see if he could wheedle better terms from his "brother," King William. Bismarck heard of Napoleon's approach and scrambled out of bed to intercept him, "all dusty and dirty as I was, in an old cap and waterproof boots." Encountering the imperial coach on the highway, Bismarck stopped it and led it off to the nearby cottage of a weaver. For forty-five minutes, the two men sat and talked. Bismarck, gruff and gigantic, outlined his plans for the future. The serpentine Napoleon, nearly a foot shorter, chain-smoked cigarettes and tried to defend his gaudy reign. He insisted that he had not wanted this war but had been "driven into it by the pressure of public opinion." Bismarck inquired whether the sword that Napoleon had given up represented the French state or himself alone. Himself alone, said Napoleon. Bismarck remarked that all military questions would have to be discussed with Moltke.

At about 8 A.M., Bismarck took his leave, saying that he would return soon. Napoleon wandered to an upstairs room, where the weaver's wife found him sitting with his head in his hands. She asked if she could be of any help.

"Pull down the blinds," said the emperor.

Half an hour later, he came out of the cottage and began promenading around the potato patch behind the house, his hands clasped behind him. "He limped slightly on one leg," the weaver's wife recalled, "and he waddled sideways, the left shoulder forward." Perhaps he was remembering some of the bizarre moments in his bizarre career, the moment when his famous uncle had summoned thousands of supporters to the Champs de Mars to swear allegiance to him before he marched off to confront his enemies at Waterloo, or perhaps the moment when young Louis Napoleon appeared at a military barracks in Strasbourg, at dawn of an October day in 1836, and announced to the sleepy garrison that he was there to lead a march on Paris to overthrow King Louis Philippe, a march that soon ended when a loyal colonel contemptuously knocked off Napoleon's hat and arrested him. Perhaps the moment when, though still an exile in London, he won election to the National Assembly of the fledgling Second Republic, or the moment when he became president of that ill-starred republic, or the moment when he sent his army out into the streets to arrest the Republican leaders and open fire on the protesting crowds. The moment when he had led the beautiful Eugénie, her hair alight with diamonds and orange blossoms, down the central aisle of Notre Dame to be married by the archbishop of Paris. Or that chilly gray morning just two months earlier when Eugénie had accompanied her husband and their young son to the railroad station in St. Cloud to see them off to what she occasionally called "my war," making the sign of the cross on the boy's forehead, and then crying out to them, as the train pulled out, "Do your duty, Louis." When a squad of Prussian cuirassiers arrived to take Napoleon away, he bade farewell to the weaver's wife by giving her four 24-franc coins, saying mournfully that hers was "probably the last hospitality I shall receive in France."

Back at French headquarters, the generals were still arguing about who should officially accept the disgrace of defeat and surrender. Wimpffen persisted in declaring that he would resign rather than sign the humiliating document that Moltke had prepared for him. Ducrot could not resist his moment of revenge. "You assumed the command when you thought there was some honor and profit in exercising it," he said scornfully. "Now you cannot refuse."

A Prussian captain named von Zingler appeared in the doorway to proclaim Moltke's impatience. "I am instructed to remind you how urgent it is that you should come to a decision," he said. "At ten o'clock precisely, if you have not come to a resolution, the German batteries will fire on Sedan. It is now nine. . . ."

Wimpffen said that nothing could be decided until after the meeting between Napoleon and King William. "That interview will not in any way affect the military operations, which can only be determined by the generals," said Zingler. Neither he nor Wimpffen seemed to realize that the monarchs could not even meet until Bismarck allowed it. The terrible prospect of renewed Prussian shelling ended the French arguments. Wimpffen accompanied Zingler to Prussian headquarters, and there, with tears streaming down his cheeks, he signed the surrender. "My sad and painful duty having been accomplished," he wrote later, "I remounted my horse and rode back to Sedan, with death in my soul."

Only then was Napoleon allowed to meet William for fifteen minutes of royal exchanges. Napoleon told the king, as he had told Bismarck, that he had not wanted to go to war, that he had been forced into it by "public opinion." William politely agreed that the creators of public opinion were much to blame. As to the emperor's future, William proposed to house him in the castle of Wilhelmshohe, near Cassel. Napoleon accepted with gratitude, his main concern now being that he should go into exile by way of Belgium rather than through eastern France, where he feared insults and humiliation by his former subjects. His fear was not unjustified. As he left his empire, escorted by magnificent royal carriages bearing bewigged coachmen in scarlet uniforms, together with quantities of imperial linens and fine champagnes, he inevitably encountered columns of his soldiers, who shouted curses and insults at him as they marched glumly through the rain toward the stockade that the Prussians had established north of Sedan for more than 100,000 new prisoners. It was known by those prisoners as the *Camp de la Misère*.

9

On to Paris

HAVING SEALED UP NAPOLEON'S SO-CALLED ARMY OF THE RHINE INSIDE the fortress of Metz, about one hundred miles west of the Rhine, and having taken prisoner the entire Army of Châlons, Moltke might have felt entitled to think that the war was over, and that he had won it. The ancestral enemy had been punished. No force of any consequence stood between the Prussian army and Paris, nothing could prevent Moltke from leading a triumphal march through the vainglorious Arch of Triumph. But nothing was ever that simple, as Moltke undoubtedly knew, and nothing would be that simple now.

If France was truly defeated, the first question was who could sign on behalf of France a peace treaty that would embody the main Prussian terms, the surrender of Alsace and Lorraine? Just two days after the disaster at Sedan, mobs of Parisians chased the Napoleonic legislature out of its chamber and then marched on the Hôtel de Ville to proclaim the end of the Second Empire and the foundation of the Third Republic. The provisional "Government of National Defense" was headed by General Trochu with Interior Minister Leon Gambetta as its guiding spirit and Jules Favre as its foreign minister, and Favre had boldly announced that the new regime would not give up "an inch of her soil or a stone of her fortresses." As for Bismarck's demand for Alsace-Lorraine and the fortresses of Metz, Strasbourg, Toul, and Verdun, Favre was even more pugnacious: "There can be no answer to such demands but *guerre à outrance*." Bismarck was tempted to ignore the upstarts in Paris, who had no real legal standing or diplomatic recognition. For several months, he toyed with the idea of negotiating with the deposed Napoleon—what could be more satisfying than bargaining with one's prisoner? But though Bazaine theoretically still owed allegiance to the fallen emperor, Napoleon himself had wit enough to see that his sovereignty no longer existed. As long as the war dragged on, though, Bismarck feared intervention by the neutral powers, not knowing that both Britain and Russia had privately decided to remain neutral.

Guerre à outrance suited Moltke rather well, since all the armed force belonged to him while the French Government of National Defense had little more than the rhetoric of Gambetta, who promised to "set all our resources at work. . . . We must shake the countryside from its torpor. . . ." As in the war against Austria, Moltke wanted to march triumphantly from the battlefield to the enemy capital while Bismarck wanted to negotiate a peace settlement. In Austria, Bismarck had insisted on getting his way, and his threats of resignation had won the king to his side, but now Gambetta's blustering strengthened Moltke's view that the army must fight on until all of France lay conquered. He was not alone in this view, to be sure. "We can, for the sake of our people and our security, conclude no peace that does not dismember France," wrote War Minister Roon. Crown Prince Frederick foresaw a dangerous future: "France is henceforth for all time our natural enemy, who will seek any and every alliance to help them to avenge themselves on us; hence it is our immediate task to weaken France in such a way that she can never again bring the enjoyment of peace into the question." The prince's chief of staff, General Blumenthal, was correspondingly assertive: "We ought to crush them so that they will not be able to breathe for a hundred years." These were not simply expressions of Prussian militarism. The American General Sheridan echoed Blumenthal's views. "The proper strategy," he said, "consists in inflicting as telling blows as possible on the enemy's army, and then in causing the inhabitants so much suffering that they must long for peace, and force the government to demand it. The people must be left nothing but their eyes to weep with over the war."

The question of how to proceed against France brought out all the old differences between Moltke and Bismarck, each of whom accused the other of trying to invade his special area of responsibility. Bismarck opposed Moltke's march to Paris; he thought the Prussian army should occupy Alsace and Lorraine and then establish a strong defensive line so that it could wait while the various French factions began to quarrel, as he was sure they would. "My wish," he wrote to his son Herbert, "would be to let these people stew in their own juice, and to install ourselves comfortably in the conquered provinces before advancing further. If we advance too soon, that would prevent them from falling out among themselves." But Moltke, too, had his influence in the royal court, and Paris was still the enemy capital, and so, on September 7, the march to the west began. Two weeks later, on September 20, the forces that Moltke directed to move north and south around the capital met in St. Germain-en-Laye and completed the encirclement.

Even under siege, Paris in September can be bewitching. Crown Prince Frederick, who had visited the capital as a state guest during the International Exposition just three years earlier, could hardly believe himself at war. "Today, a splendid, hot Sunday," he wrote at his headquarters in Versailles on September 25, "a field service was held in the open, at the foot of the great terrace under thick chestnut avenues. I think Louis XIV would have turned in his grave if he had known how we heretics were using his creations for our devotions. The singing from hundreds of voices of gallant soldiers who had many a time looked death in the face, accompanied by instrumental music, while in the distance the gunfire from the Paris forts could be heard, gave the whole an extraordinarily solemn air."

It is a little difficult now to imagine a major European city under siege, but the Paris of 1870 was still a fortress surrounded by forty miles of walls more than thirty feet high. Its citizens herded thousands of cattle and sheep into its parks for food and then began cutting down the trees for firewood. Several hundred thousand armed volunteers guarded the walls, and fifteen outlying forts like Issy and Vanves could keep any attacker at bay. Even the strongest fortress can be conquered, however, either by shellfire or by hunger. Moltke favored hunger. It was more efficient. It would cost fewer casualties, particularly fewer Prussian casualties. Bismarck agreed that the decadent Parisians would not be able to stand much deprivation, not more than "eight days without *café au lait*," but he nonetheless favored shelling, partly because he thought it would bring a quicker surrender, partly because of a peculiar moral judgment, reinforced by letters from his pious wife, Johanna, that "that mad Sodom" *deserved* to have Prussian artillery rain brimstone and fire from the Lord out of heaven.

Moltke's view was generally supported by the military, but it is interesting to see how Bismarck prevailed. Crown Prince Frederick's chief of staff, Count Blumenthal, wrote in his diary as early as October that "we ought not to think of bombardment, but trust entirely to starvation." He said that Moltke "agreed with me entirely." From then on, in a remarkable demonstration of the military mind at work, which we will see again in the German generals' kowtowing to Hitler, Blumenthal began to see political circumstances that gradually changed his mind:

October 25: "The starvation tactics do not promise too early a conclusion. Human beings can hold out a very long time when they have a will, and that they seem indeed to have here. . . ."

November 18: "The Crown Prince . . . suggested that it might be well to commence the attack with a few of the guns just to frighten the Parisians. What irresponsible person has put this idea into his head I cannot tell, but I intend to combat the notion tooth and nail, as I consider it foolish in the extreme. This is exactly what the French want. They would like to pose with great effect as martyrs. . . ."

November 21: "After dinner Bismarck began about the bombard-ment, saying that he considered it necessary from a political point of view. I could only reply that I considered it would be a great military fault, and that I would rather retire than permit it. At the present moment I have the King and Moltke on my side. I have this evening written a memorandum of my views and sent it to Moltke, trusting it may carry some weight. . . ."

November 29: "This afternoon came a message from the King to Moltke and Roon, in which he expressed his concern at the tardy progress of the siege, and required a reply to certain questions as to the possibility of hastening operations. . . ."

November 30: "A written communication addressed by Bismarck to the King has just been communicated to the Crown Prince. It says that a bombardment of the forts has become a political necessity, as otherwise the neutrals will take it as a sign of weakness and may intervene, and so create difficulties. . . . It will be very regrettable if more men are to be unnecessarily slaughtered. My conscience is clear, however, and I cannot prevent it. . . ."

December 7: "The Crown Prince showed me a telegram from the diplomatic bureau in Berlin, which Bismarck had sent to him, wherein it was stated that the rulers in Paris themselves desired to be bom-barded, so that they might capitulate with honor. How this is known I should like to be told."

December 8: "I was able to have a long conversation with General von Moltke, and came away with the conviction that he and I agree thoroughly upon the general situation. He, too, thinks that the Parisians will yield in the course of this month from stress of hunger, and that it would be better to apply our heavy artillery to strengthening our positions rather than to commence bombardment. . . . In order, however, to meet halfway those who press for a bombardment, he is going to put the case to some of the artillerists as to whether a partial cannonading of Paris might not be possible without opening regular parallels. I imagine he overestimates the range of our weapons, and the moral effect that such a cannonading would have. . . ."

December 10: "As soon as the French are driven over the Loire they will not be in a condition for any more fighting. Then there must be a pause for at least four weeks, perhaps six, in which Paris must fall. If only we were not being harassed by ignorant and incompetent persons to bombard the town! It can hardly have any effect, as the guns will scarcely range as far, and, moreover, they will have to keep down the fire of between 300 and 400 of the enemy's guns. It will not only cost us the lives of a great number of men, but will also make us a laughing-stock to the world."

December 11: "As an instance of the determination with which Bismarck is pressing his point in the bombardment question, the following will serve. He is laid up with a bad leg, and so sent the Secretary of Legation, Abeken, to an audience with the King, with instructions to inform His Majesty that the excitement in Berlin on account of the delay in bombarding is so intense that they are in fear of insurrections. . . ."

While these arguments over the bombardment of Paris dragged on, Moltke confronted a similar problem that was no less complex and no less vexing, the problem of French civilian snipers. By all the traditional laws of war, soldiers were not supposed to use their weapons against civilians, but, conversely, civilians were not supposed to fire on soldiers either. Anyone who did so was considered no better than a murderer, subject to hanging. But although the Prussians had defeated the French army in open combat, the French people refused to accept their soldiers' surrender as the end of the war. Even as the Prussians were closing in on Sedan, civilians in the neighboring towns felt entitled to defend their homes with rifles, and to shriek in protest when Prussian guns were turned against them.

After the French surrender at Sedan, the Trochu "government of national defense" openly supported the recruitment of civilians for guerrilla warfare. "Harass the enemy's detachments without pause or relaxation," said Gambetta, "prevent him from deploying, restrict the area of his requisition, make him thin out before Paris, disturb him day and night, always and everywhere—that is the object for you to obtain." The Spaniards—and the Germans, too—had demonstrated during the Napoleonic years that guerrilla warfare could seriously impede even the most powerful armies of occupation, and so the recruitment of *francs-tireurs* or snipers became a patriotic passion all over France. Even such a sedentary figure as Gustave Flaubert recruited a band of partisans and marched them through the streets of Rouen. Within a few months of Sedan, some 300 guerrilla units, numbering about 57,000 members, had joined the crusade. Some affected the capes and plumed hats of Dumas' three musketeers; some carried black banners with the skull and crossbones of piracy. At the head of this raggle-taggle movement, which the republican government supported in much the same way that Queen Elizabeth had supported the piracy of Drake and Hawkins, stood the great warrior of the Italian Risorgimento, Giuseppe Garibaldi, who had offered his services to the cause of Republicanism. And at Tours, one Republican official urged the guerrillas to "harass the enemy and hang from trees all the enemies they can take well and truly by the neck, after having mutilated them."

All well and good for the advocates of guerrilla warfare, which was to become more widespread, more ruthless, and more generally condoned throughout the next century. From the Ukraine in 1943 to Cuba in 1953 to Vietnam in 1973, the refusal to surrender to military force came to seem the highest form of patriotism. But to a commander who thinks he has won a just war by all the traditional rules of battle, a civilian sniper hiding behind a tree can only seem a cowardly and treacherous terrorist, who deserves nothing better than a public hanging. Even before Sedan, Crown Prince Frederick complained of terrorist attacks. "Single shots are fired, generally in a cunning, cowardly fashion, on patrols," he declared, "so that nothing is left for us to do but to adopt retaliatory measures by burning down the house from which the shots came or else by the help of the lash and forced contributions. It is horrible, but, to prevent greater mischief, unavoidable. . . ."

Moltke had little hesitation in ordering harsh punishments for the *francs-tireurs,* and, when individual guerrillas could not be caught, collective punishment for any village that might have sheltered them. "Experience has established," he told the Second Army, "that the most effective way of dealing with this situation is to destroy the premises concerned—or, where participation has been more general, the entire village." And to another commander in Burgundy: "The very severest treatment of the guilty as regards life and property can alone be recommended to your Excellency, whole parishes being held responsible for the deeds of their individual members when these cannot be discovered."

If Moltke hated the French partisans, Bismarck hated them even more. Bismarck declared repeatedly that any French civilian who fired on German troops should be shot on the spot; villages that harbored snipers should be burned to the ground and their inhabitants shipped to Germany as prisoners. "It will come to this," he said at one dinner conversation, probably stimulated by too much Burgundy, "that we will shoot down every male inhabitant." Even that would not have satisfied his devout wife, who urged that all French should be "shot and stabbed to death, down to the little babies."

French officials only replied to the German indignation with Gallic shrugs. "We are hunting them down pitilessly," Bismarck said to Favre of the German search for snipers between Sedan and Paris. "They are not soldiers; we are treating them as murderers." The French foreign minister replied that German guerrillas had also engaged in sniping during the "Wars of Liberation" against Napoleon. "That is quite true," Bismarck said, "but our trees still bear the marks where your generals hanged our people on them."

Generations of generals have seen that such repression does not work, that the hanging of guerrillas only breeds more guerrillas. But what is a commander to do when his soldiers are fired on from behind trees? In October 1870, the Prussians retaliated against rebellion in Chateaudun by burning the beautiful Loire Valley town to the ground, but it became a Lidice of its time, its flames inspiring continued resistance. And there still remained the question of how to conquer Paris. Could it be subdued without being destroyed? Bismarck was now spreading the word that the opposition to bombardment could all be traced to the malign influence of the English crown princess and the Anglophile queen. "Hahnke received the impression at Headquarters that all were against me in the question of bombardment," Blumenthal wrote in his diary on December 12. "They appear to imagine that the Crown Princess and the Queen are influencing me to spare Paris. It is most extraordinary that men will not believe the naked truth. Science and Reason are the forces which deter me from a childish and purposeless bombardment. This they will not believe, but . . . attribute my attitude to female influence. . . ."

December 14: "The Crown Prince came to me in my room and told me that he had received a letter from the Crown Princess, in which she said that there was a very strong feeling in Berlin against herself and the Queen, because people thought that they, acting under the influence of the Queen of England, were discountenancing the so-called bombardment. I am convinced that this is some deep intrigue. . . . If the King yields to such an intrigue, it will be the turning-point of our fortune and our successes. With a bombardment we destroy ourselves, even if by any accident it prove successful. . . ."

December 16: "The everlasting question of the bombardment is still on the tapis, and tomorrow there is to be a conference on the subject at General von Moltke's quarters. I have requested the Crown Prince's leave to be absent, for I am considered a partisan, and everyone knows my opinion. . . . At 10:30 I was summoned to the King's presence and ordered to attend the conference. . . . It was very interesting to me to see how certain of the members were willing to compromise when they thought that the King was in favor of a bombardment. How seldom it is that men in such circumstances speak their minds truly and honestly, without regard to consequences! I, at least, have always tried to do so. . . . The professional soldiers all deprecated the useless and childish idea of a bombardment. The War Minister [Roon] alone was in favor of it, and he glared at us most angrily and resentfully. . . ."

December 19: "Count Bismarck . . . sat down beside me on a sofa, after dinner, and began to converse with me about the bombardment. . . . He said to me that it was never his wish to bombard; he was perfectly aware that the town could not be touched by our fire; but the political necessities of the case rendered it most important that we should show that we are in earnest. . . . Otherwise it would be impossible for him to prevent Foreign Powers—Russia and England he meant—from intervening. . . . My argument that such an idea did not justify us as soldiers from behaving foolishly, and acting in opposition to our better judgment, he would not listen to, as he said that war could not be carried on without a consideration of political results. . . ."

While the Prussians argued over the destruction of Paris, there was nothing to prevent the French from defending themselves by force of arms. Despite the loss of their two main armies, their reserves of manpower were formidable. When Gambetta's regime called up all unmarried men between twenty-five and thirty-five, it dealt with a force of more than 1 million, and its shipping routes to Britain and the United States gave it access to ample arms and ammunition. The trouble was that its potential armies were for the most part untrained in using those arms, or even in marching in step, or even in obeying orders. Against Moltke's trained and disciplined legions, then, it could oppose little more than a rabble in arms. Whatever their shortcomings, though, the ill-trained French began gathering in the woods to the south of Paris, and when Prussian cavalry patrols exploring southward from Fontainebleau ventured into those woods, they were ambushed and driven backward. Moltke sent General von der Tann, who had commanded the Bavarian First Corps at Wörth and Sedan, to clear out the Loire valley, but the French Army of the Loire by now numbered some 100,000 men, under the veteran General Claude Michel d'Aurelle de Paladines, and when the two forces clashed on November 9 near the village of Coulmiers, just west of Orleans, the French surrounded the Bavarians and forced them to retreat. It was the first clear French victory in the whole war. Aurelle promptly moved on and seized Orleans, thus replaying, as he and every French patriot knew, the great victory of Joan of Arc over the invading English. "We are now living through a very interesting time," Moltke wrote, "when the question of which is preferable, a trained army or a militia, will be solved in action."

As a professional soldier, Moltke could scarcely doubt the answer to that question. No matter how inevitable the superiority of a trained army might prove to be, however, the demands of a campaign to conquer France were becoming dangerously large. In marching directly from Sedan to Paris, Moltke had made virtually no effort to subdue the intervening countryside, but now that his main army was stretched out around the forty-mile perimeter of Paris, he found his three railroad lines back to Germany increasingly vulnerable to guerrilla raids from such unconquered fortresses as Thionville, Toul, and Soissons. And while Aurelle was causing disturbances along the Loire, yet another French army was forming around Amiens. Headed by Charles Bourbaki, a dashing commander who had led the Zouaves to repeated victories in the Crimea, this new force somewhat optimistically called itself the Army of the North.

Surrounded by new aggravations on all sides, Moltke suddenly benefited from a twofold stroke of luck, the fall of Strasbourg and Metz, the two chief fortresses of Alsace and Lorraine. Strasbourg was the more vulnerable, since its defenses had not been modernized since the time of the great seventeenth-century engineer Sébastien de Vauban, and it was guarded by a garrison of only 17,000. Moltke assigned a force of 40,000 under General Carl Wilhelm von Werder to capture it. Werder decided to start with the then novel tactic of shelling not just the fortress but the civilian areas of the city. Within four days, his artillery burned down the palace of justice and the famous city library and even set fire to the roof of the cathedral. Throughout September, the Germans kept bringing their guns closer and making their fire more destructive until, on September 28, with the fortress walls smashed open and the openings indefensible, the garrison surrendered.

Metz was more complicated, not only because Marshal Bazaine had some 180,000 troops and a large quantity of food and supplies but because Bismarck was still playing with the idea of pretending that Napoleon still ruled France, with Bazaine as his commander in chief, and that Bazaine might therefore negotiate the armistice that Bismarck so badly wanted. Moltke was fiercely opposed to any talk of compromise. He saw no reason to grant Bazaine any terms but unconditional surrender. After a series of messages to and from the exiled Empress Eugénie came to nothing, Bazaine could only agree with Moltke. Without the slightest attempt at a battle, he abjectly surrendered on October 29.

Moltke had a warm sense, entirely imagined, of the humiliation of defeat. "A vanquished commander!" he wrote of Benedek after Königgrätz. "Oh! if outsiders could form but a faint conception of what that means! The Austrian Headquarters on the night of Königgrätz—I cannot bear to think of it." Still, the capitulation of Bazaine could only have filled him with relief. Now he could transfer the besieging forces of Prince Frederick Charles's Second Army away from idleness outside Metz to strengthen his forces on the Loire and outside Paris.

Both sides seemed to agree that the course of the war now depended on the fate of Paris. When, after several days of denials, the government finally confirmed Bazaine's surrender of Metz, Paris reacted with its traditional political *geste:* mass rioting. A mob gathered outside the Hôtel de Ville and chanted those cries of the bellicose noncombatant: *"Pas d'armistice!"* and *"La guerre à outrance!"* The crowds thought for a time that they had overthrown the government—yet again—but when Trochu and Ducrot marched their troops to the city hall, the crowd had already evaporated.

Gambetta's master plan—to the extent that the interior minister in Tours was the man now commanding the French resistance, with enthusiasm and rhetoric more than with organized military force—was to coordinate an offensive on the Loire with a breakout to the south from Paris. His commanders had little hope of success. Their ill-trained troops were weary, hungry, and dispirited. Trochu numbly declared it their duty "if not to triumph, at least to succumb gloriously after having fought valiantly."

Gambetta's new commander on the Loire, General Antoine Eugène Chanzy, had more spirit than that. He ordered an attack at dawn of December 2 on the snow-covered fields that lined the road northward to Chartres. Moltke had also ordered an offensive, however, directing the cautious Prince Frederick Charles to drive the

French upstream towards Orleans. Wind and snow swept the disputed fields for the next few days and nights, and when the storms died down, the French were retreating toward Orleans. Messages from Gambetta's headquarters pleaded vainly for the French officers to "stiffen their [troops'] courage and patriotism by their own resolute example." It was a useless plea. When the Prussian 17th Division reached the northwestern outskirts of Orleans at about 8 P.M. on December 4, its commander formally warned the city authorities that he would begin a bombardment unless he received an immediate surrender. This was a bluff, since he did not have the cannon to attack Orleans, but there are times when bluffs work. At about midnight, Prussian troops marched unopposed into Orleans while the French forces slunk away.

Since besieged Paris could communicate with the outside world only through an erratic system of balloons and carrier pigeons, there was little coordination between General Trochu, nominal chief of the Government of National Defense, and the scattered forces along the Loire. Nonetheless, the Parisians attached an almost mystical importance to the idea of what the press kept calling a *"sortie torrentielle."* It was proposed that thousands of Parisians should simply venture forth, organized in social groups—a legion of judges, a legion of professors, even a legion of virgins, if one could be found and mobilized—and that the Prussians would not dare to open fire. Such advocates probably underestimated the pugnacity of Moltke's infantry, but the experiment was never put to the test.

It became increasingly clear, though, that some kind of sortie would have to be attempted. The politically outspoken National Guards were complaining about being cooped up inside the city walls, and their commanders dared not confess that they doubted their own soldiers' competence and courage. Word spread that General Ducrot was planning a grand sortie on November 28 to the Marne Valley southeast of Paris, aiming at a merger in Fontainebleau with the supposedly advancing Army of the Loire.

Ignoring any chance of surprise, Ducrot started with a huge cannonade. Edmond de Goncourt, the tireless chronicler of this period, climbed upstairs in his home in Autouil to see what he could see. "In the starless sky crisscrossed by the branches of big trees, from the Bicêtre fortress to the Issy fortress . . ." he wrote in his journal, "there is a succession of little points of fire, which flare up like gaslights and are followed by loud explosions. These great voices of death in the silence of the night are very moving. After a while the barking of dogs is added to the thundering of the cannons; the fearful voices of people who have been awakened begin to whisper; roosters send forth their clear notes . . ."

Ducrot's own crowing was plastered on walls all over Paris that morning. "I swear before you and the entire nation," he declared, "I shall only re-enter Paris dead or victorious. You may see me fall, but you will not see me yield ground. So do not halt, but avenge me. *En avant donc!* Forward, and may God protect us!" The higher powers did not support Ducrot's ambitions. Heavy rains had washed away the bridge across the Marne at Joinville, and its debris blocked the tugboat that Ducrot had assigned to haul his pontoon bridges into position. After three tries, the tug did finally get through, but not until after daybreak. The delay enabled Moltke to bring in a division of Saxons as reinforcements. Ducrot's forces captured the two towns of Champigny and Brie, but when they climbed to the Villiers Plateau behind the two towns, they found the German defenders well entrenched. "Such a scene as there grew up before me in a moment or two I hope I shall never behold again," one British correspondent reported. "The pavement was covered with wounded men, generally half-undressed, and lying there helplessly. . . . In the middle of the Place a seething mass of soldiers of all arms struggled and wrestled to get through the village, without order, without leaders, without any idea what to do or whither to go, unless it were to avoid the Prussians. Every moment the mob increased, with every moment the panic became greater and the struggle to get through fiercer."

Ducrot rode boldly along his front lines on a white charger, pushing his troops forward at saber point, but it was hopeless. After losing more than 5,000 men, more than double the German casualties, Ducrot gave up and withdrew back into the besieged capital. "Today everybody is withdrawn into himself," Goncourt wrote. "In the public vehicles nobody speaks; everybody is closed up, and the women of the common people seem to look blindly at what is going on around them."

After this resounding failure, Ducrot was hardly cheered by a polite letter from Moltke to Trochu, informing him not only that Metz had surrendered but that the Army of the Loire had just been defeated outside Orleans. If this was supposed to persuade Trochu to surrender, though, it had no such effect, and so the Prussian debate over the bombardment of Paris came to its predictable conclusion. Just after Christmas, General Blumenthal persisted in denying the inevitable. "I am more and more convinced," he wrote on December 26, "that my plan for reducing Paris, viz., by starvation, is the right one."

Blumenthal had ample reasons for his views. The sheep and oxen that had been herded into the Bois de Boulogne had long since disappeared, and it was not until October that the government began an ineffectual attempt at rationing meat; not until mid-December was there any rationing of bread. The only system actually in effect was that of black market prices, and so there was speculation and hoarding, and long lines in front of shuttered stores, and shouts and quarrels and furtive deals made by candlelight. Butter rose from 4 francs per pound at the start of the siege to 35 francs by mid-December; potatoes from 3 francs per bushel to 15; rabbit meat from 8 francs per pound to 40 (this in a time when a workman's wages averaged 5 or 6 francs per day).

Hunger plus profits challenged Parisians' ingenuity. "On today's bill of fare in the restaurants we have authentic buffalo, antelope, and kangaroo," Goncourt wrote in early December. Two fancy trotting horses that the tsar had presented to Napoleon now went to the butcher. Connoisseurs also explored the pleasures of eating camels and wapiti. The zoo killed its two prize elephants, Castor and Pollux, and they ended, like so many expensive delicacies, on the counter of the Boucherie Anglaise. "It's forty francs a pound for filet and trunk . . ." explained Monsieur Roos, the proprietor. "Oh, let me recommend the blood sausage. Don't forget that elephant blood is the most generous blood of all. His heart, did you know, weighed 25 pounds. . . . And there is onion, ladies, in my blood sausage." Goncourt said he settled for two larks for the next day's lunch. But at Voisin's that evening, "I see the famous elephant blood sausage again; indeed I dine on it."

While the rich were protected by their wealth, as usual, the poor had to scramble, also as usual. They caught dogs and cats, first the strays, then the pets. It became common for people to fish for rats, with hook, line, and sinker, through the gratings in the gutters. Victor Hugo published his recommendations on how rats might best be served (chopped up and baked in a pie, for example, with horseradish on the side). Those who couldn't afford rats could subsist on "osseine," a sort of soup made out of horse bones and gelatin, which sold for 1 franc per kilo. "People are talking only of what they eat," Goncourt wrote in December, "what they can eat, and what there is to eat. Conversation consists of this and nothing more. . . . Hunger begins and famine is on the horizon."

Nobody actually starved during the siege of Paris, but with the demoralizing hunger came demoralizing cold, from one of the harshest winters in many years. At the edge of the Bois de Boulogne, on the

Avenue de l'Impératrice (now the Avenue Foch), Goncourt encountered "a menacing crowd, surrounded by terrible female faces . . . giving the impression of Furies, among the rabble. . . . The explanation is a depot of wood for making charcoal, which they have begun to pillage. The cold, the freeze-up, the lack of fuel to heat their minute rations of meat, has thrown this female populace into a fury and they hurl themselves upon trellis-works, plank barricades, ripping up everything that comes to their enraged hands."

With hunger and cold, inevitably, came disease. Deaths from smallpox had averaged 158 during the first week of the siege; they rose to 386 during the tenth week. Deaths from flu and other respiratory ailments rose even more drastically, from 123 in the first week of the siege to 1,084 in mid-January.

But still the Parisians refused to surrender, and so the Prussians once more looked to their cannon. "We shall have to confine ourselves to a bombardment of the two forts which the king now desires to be fired at," wrote Blumenthal on December 29, hardly remembering that he had once talked of resigning rather than agreeing to a bombardment. Two days later the generals conferred, and Moltke formally came out in favor of a bombardment. He said it was necessary to end the siege as quickly as possible so that the besieging forces could be freed to end the warfare in the provinces. Crown Prince Frederick also offered a cautious approval: "The bombardment may perhaps lead to important results." The king's views were already known, of course, as were those of Bismarck. It seemed only fitting that Blumenthal should finally be assigned to carry out the task. "Immediately after lunch, at 2 o'clock, Kameke, Hohenlohe, and Schulz came to me to arrange about the plan of bombardment," he wrote on December 31, "which in the course of a few days will have to take place. The Crown Prince was here too, and we were soon agreed on what to do. . . ."

By now it was a matter for celebration. Blumenthal on New Year's Day:

"The King received all the officers present in the lovely Glass Gallery of the Château, and made a very touching speech. His Majesty also spoke to several officers singly. . . . He thanked me for all that I have done. . . . After the audience the Crown Prince told me that the 4th had been appointed as the date for the commencement of the bombardment. Although I would willingly have seen it deferred till some days later, still it is quite possible that the time has come when a bombardment of the forts and a portion of the city may be successful. . . . I dined at the King's table, when he was again most gracious, and at seven o'clock I held a conference . . . to settle all details of the bombardment. . . ."

January 2: "This morning I was overwhelmed with an amount of work quite unusual, and among other things had to issue orders regarding the bombardment. . . ."

January 5: "When I woke up this morning it all looked as foggy as ever, but it soon cleared up and the sun broke out. At 8:15 the first gun was fired, but the fire which succeeded was not very powerful. . . ."

January 8: "This afternoon I went for a walk . . . to the park of the Château. I have no wish to look on at the bombardment. It does not meet my approval on principle, and at the same time I cannot alter matters. At mid-day Moltke and the heads of the Siege Committee were here, and informed me that this night twelve cannon were told off to fire into Paris. To me this is a terrible thought, especially as I consider it will be a useless proceeding. . . ."

Like those generals who now boast of "surgical" air strikes, Blumenthal managed to turn his eyes away from the actual results of his "useless proceeding." The first shell fired on January 5 sprayed shell fragments over a baby asleep in its cradle in the Rue Lalande; another one of the first shells wounded a girl walking home from school near the Luxembourg Gardens. The Prussian guns could not reach much north of the Seine, but the whole Left Bank had been turned into a battlefield. The great domes of the Pantheon and the Invalides were smashed in; shells repeatedly hit the Salpetrière Hospital, despite the large red cross on its roof; others damaged the Odéon Theater, which was being used as a hospital, the Sorbonne, the Convent of the Sacred Heart, the Church of St. Sulpice, the orchid collection in the Jardin des Plantes. Trochu, who felt that the bombardment "dishonors German arms [and] dishonors civilization," wrote to Moltke to protest the attacks on hospitals. Moltke wrote back, in an unfortunate attempt at Prussian wit, that he hoped his cannon would soon get near enough to see the red cross flags more clearly. The Prussian commanders seemed unable to realize that it is a crime against humanity to fire artillery shells into the heart of Paris; the main concern was whether this atrocity would be "senseless and purposeless."

Which, of course, it was. In a month of shelling, the Prussians fired about 12,000 shells, which killed ninety-seven people and damaged 1,400 buildings and probably did not shorten the war by one hour. What brought Paris to surrender was not only shelling but the combination of shelling and hunger and cold, of fear and defeat and despair.

While Moltke waited out these last days in the test of wills, Bismarck turned to another project that he considered no less important than the fall of Paris, the unification of Germany under Prussian rule. This had been a major goal in leading the allied German states into war against Napoleon, and it was not a goal that he ever lost sight of for long. Now that he had King William and his ministers and a collection of twenty German kings and princelings all assembled in the Bourbon palace of Versailles, what better time to bring his dream to fruition?

This was not just a happy coincidence, of course. Bismarck had been working toward his goal for months. His interior minister, Rudolf von Delbrück, had long been engaged in delicate negotiations to bring the major South German states into Bismarck's North German Federation. There were endless little deals and concessions to be made—preserving one state's independent postal system or promising that another would always be consulted on imperial foreign policy—but eventually, everything was finished. On November 14, Baden and Hesse-Darmstadt signed the necessary treaties, with Bavaria following on November 23. Bavaria was important to Bismarck's plans not only because it had a long and proud history of independence but because Bismarck intended to use the unstable young Bavarian King Ludwig to win the support of King William of Prussia. Ludwig represented the Wittelsbach dynasty, which had ruled Bavaria since Count Otto V had established himself there in the twelfth century, and the Wittelsbachs were thus considered the senior family among all German ruling clans.

William himself had no burning desire to be emperor. Like his older brother who had scorned the imperial crown in 1848, he was immensely proud of being king of Prussia; the imperial title struck him as an empty honor. He did not follow Bismarck's reasoning that an imperial crown would greatly strengthen the economic and constitutional ties that Bismarck was already creating. The successful customs union known as the *Zollverein* was up for renewal in a few years, which gave Bismarck a powerful hold on the lesser German states, but William still resisted the birth of the empire with all the emotional stubbornness of a spoiled and pampered monarch. Bismarck recruited the crown prince, as he often had before, to argue his cause, and the crown prince became eloquent in his visions of imperial grandeur. ("The crown prince is as stupid and vain as anybody else," Bismarck tartly observed of his ally.) But Bismarck never relied on anyone's eloquence when more practical means were available. He knew that the young King Ludwig was obsessed with building expensive castles and monuments, notably a Wagner theater in Munich and the Wagner *Festspielhaus* in Bayreuth, and that this obsession had driven the senior German dynasty deeply into debt. He also knew that the Bavarian delegation at Versailles included a courtier named Count Max von Holnstein, who was infinitely corruptible. Reaching into his secret "reptile fund," Bismarck promised the vulnerable King Ludwig a simple bribe of 100,000 thalers a year (10 percent going to Holnstein for arranging the deal) to persuade King William of Prussia to do as Bismarck wanted. Specifically, Holnstein had to ride to Munich with a letter carefully drafted by Bismarck for Ludwig to copy out in his own hand. King Ludwig was confined to his bed with a toothache and tried to avoid seeing Bismarck's envoy, but Holnstein persisted until Ludwig did as Bismarck wanted. When Holnstein returned to Versailles, he bore Ludwig's letter begging the king of Prussia also to do as Bismarck wanted. So William was not to become emperor at the request of the German people or their elected Reichstag, but at the invitation of Germany's ruling princes. Knowing nothing of Bismarck's trap, William saw that he was trapped. He could not refuse such a request from the head of the Wittelsbachs.

Angry and sulky, the king insisted on only one trivial detail. He reluctantly agreed to be chosen either the emperor of Germany or emperor of the Germans. Bismarck, believing that the newly seduced southern states would not accept such a subordination, proposed that the title be simply German emperor. The king refused. On this one detail, he wanted to have his own way. His chancellor would not allow it.

The next morning, July 18, Bismarck played out his drama in the famous Hall of Mirrors of the Versailles Palace. Here, in the palace that is inscribed *"à toutes les gloires de la France,"* the Germans assembled under rows of their battle flags to celebrate themselves.

"It is 12 o'clock," wrote W. H. Russell of the London *Times*. "The boom of a gun far away rolls above the voices in the Court hailing the Emperor King. Then there is a hush of expectation, and then rich and sonorous rise the massive strains of the chorale chanted by the men of regimental bands assembled in a choir, as the King, bearing his helmet in his hand, and dressed in full uniform as a German general stalked slowly up the long gallery, and bowing to the clergy in front of the temporary altar opposite him, halted and dressed himself right and front, and then twirling his heavy moustache with his disengaged hand, surveyed the scene at each side of him."

He surveyed and was angry. It was not what he wanted. As king, he had been thwarted by Bismarck; as emperor, he would continue to be thwarted by Bismarck. When the ceremony was over, and the newly crowned kaiser paraded past the battle flags and regimental banners, shaking the hands of Moltke and Roon and all the others who had made his new powers possible, he studiously avoided the one man most responsible for everything, Bismarck. "His Majesty was so offended at the course I had adopted," Bismarck coolly wrote, "that on descending from the raised dais of the princes he ignored me as I stood alone . . . and passed me by in order to shake hands with the generals standing behind me." Now when the Grand Duke of Baden called for three cheers for Emperor William, the emperor was visibly furious. "I several times wished I was a bomb," Bismarck wrote to his wife, "to go off and blow the whole edifice to pieces." It took several days, Bismarck recalled, before "our mutual relations returned to their old form."

But Moltke still had a war to win, an elusive army to capture, a defiant capital to subdue. On this same day of imperial pageantry in Versailles, Trochu decided to turn loose all those zealots and romantics who kept clamoring for a mass breakout, an irresistible *sortie torrentielle*. Trochu was confident that this too would fail, but let the orders be issued, and let the gates open wide. Goncourt was at the Étoile to watch the troops march past the Arch of Triumph. "The monument to our victories, illuminated by a shaft of sunlight," he wrote, "the distant cannon fire, the immense parade, the last bayonets of which send sparkling light under the obelisk, all this was something theatrical, lyrical, epic. A great and proud spectacle, this army going to the cannons which we hear; among the men are white-bearded civilian soldiers, the fathers of families, beardless faces, who are their sons; and in the open ranks women carrying the rifles of their husbands and lovers slung over their shoulders. . . ."

The spectacle of white-whiskered veterans marching off into combat alongside untrained youths and a scattering of women may have stirred patriotic emotions in a Parisian novelist, but to the Prussian soldiers assigned to confront this challenge, it must have seemed little more than a bad joke. Even some of the French may have regarded the experiment as ludicrous. Loaded down with about eighty pounds of gear, many of the Guards had to stand and wait for hours until their commanders were ready to move; recent rains had turned the highways to mud, and the Parisians' clamor for battle soon faded. One of Trochu's staff officers described a scene: "The drummer beat the charge; the colonel gave the word of command, '*En avant!*' the regiment shouted, '*Vive la République!*' and—nobody stirred. That went on for three hours. . . ."

When it came to actual fighting, notably in the suburb of Buzenval, the French made little headway, and by the end of the day, they were ready to give up. "Hardly was the word retreat pronounced," General Ducrot wrote later, "than . . . the debacle began. . . . Everything broke up, everything went. . . . Across the open country the National Guards were taking to their heels in every direction. . . . Soldiers, wandering lost, searched for their company, their officers. . . ." "All Paris has gone out of doors and walks about waiting for news," Goncourt wrote on January 19. And on January 20: "Trochu's dispatch last night seems to me to be the beginning of the end; it poisons my stomach. . . . Men of the National Guard infantry companies march in, a bit stragglingly, without music, morose, all-in, harassed, covered with mud. . . . I encounter anew the despairing discouragement of a great nation which has done much to save itself by its own efforts . . . and feels that it has been lost by military stupidity." And on January 21: "I am struck more than ever by the silence, the silence of death, which disaster brings in a great city. Today you can no longer hear Paris live. Every face is that of a sick man or a convalescent; you see only yellowy pallor like horse fat."

Trochu's "dispatch" had been a request for a truce to bury the dead lost in the sortie. French casualties had been more than 4,000, as compared to German losses of about 700, a discrepancy that aroused suspicions that Trochu had had political reasons for sending the ardently republican National Guards off to be slaughtered. Bismarck curtly rejected the request, perhaps because he suspected Trochu of trying to negotiate with Moltke, perhaps simply because he was already engaged in broader and more complicated negotiations. The surrender of Paris was only a part, after all, of the surrender of France. Moltke did not really want any compromises with either Paris or France; he wanted both to be totally defeated, crushed. Bismarck, on the other hand, still worried about intervention by the neutral English or Russians. He wanted to arrange a peace, but with whom could he bargain? While both Moltke and the nationalist press in Berlin insisted on German annexation of Alsace and Lorraine, could any French government that accepted such terms survive in power? Bismarck had virtually abandoned his fantasy of negotiating with Napoleon or Eugénie or even Marshal Bazaine, but who was left? Inside Paris, Trochu no longer had any support, and the radicals kept talking about mass struggle and *guerre à outrance*. While Gambetta led the dying war effort in the provinces, the nearest thing to a national leader was Adolphe Thiers, the septuagenarian Orleanist who had been roaming around Europe in a vain attempt to recruit outside support for the shadowy government that now made its headquarters in Tours. New elections seemed the obvious answer, but how could elections be held until there was an armistice?

In this state of virtual anarchy, the authority of legitimacy somehow descended on the rumpled figure of Jules Favre, nominally the vice president and foreign minister in Trochu's "Government of National Defense." A tall, gaunt man customarily attired in a high hat and ill-fitting frock coat, Favre was a lawyer by profession, and he seemed to be regarded by all sides as a man of goodwill and good faith. Before his first encounter with Bismarck, Favre had declared that France would never surrender "an inch of her soil nor a stone of her fortresses," which might have seemed diplomatically gauche, but it actually lent him authority among various French factions without jeopardizing his relations with Bismarck, since the chancellor never took Favre's statement seriously.

The two had first met in September, at Favre's request, when the siege of Paris had just begun and Sedan was fresh in Prussian memories. Bismarck had laid down his basic terms, the cession of Alsace and Lorraine. Favre burst into tears and cried, "You want to destroy France!" He had no idea what Moltke would have demanded, but he was horrified at Bismarck's terms, the surrender of the forts at Toul and Strasbourg before any elections could be held, and the surrender of at least one Parisian fort before any food could be brought into the capital. Such terms, he said, would mean "an endless struggle between two peoples who ought to stretch out their hands to each other. I had hoped for another solution."

To Moltke and many of his generals, though, Bismarck seemed once again to be bargaining away what they had won. "I have never yet known such bitterness against any man," one of them observed, "as prevails against Bismarck at this moment." The generals had never really been cured of their resentment after Königgrätz, when the chancellor had prevented them from staging a victory march to Vienna. "The ill-feeling towards me, which had survived in the higher military circles from the Austrian war, lasted throughout the French war . . . " Bismarck later recalled. "As early as the journey to Cologne I learned by accident that at the outbreak of war the plan of excluding me from the military consultations had been settled." Bismarck learned this "by accident" because he "unwillingly overheard" two generals talking too loudly in an adjoining compartment of his train. One of them said that "arrangements have been made this time that the same thing does not happen to us again." From his furtive eavesdropping, Bismarck learned what the generals planned: "that I was not only not admitted to the military consultations . . . but strict secrecy about all military measures and intentions was generally observed towards me." Bismarck did not blame these maneuvers on Moltke, whom he credited with "unvarying tactful courtesy," but rather on "the 'demigods,' as the higher staff officers were then called." It was Moltke, though, who dropped his famous taciturnity at a dinner with the crown prince and protested vehemently against Bismarck's negotiations. Moltke's own terms for a truce were Catonian. He wanted Paris occupied and governed by German troops, its garrison sent to imprisonment in Germany, its citizens subjected to heavy reparations, so that he, Moltke, could concentrate on the total conquest and subjugation of France. "We must fight this nation of liars to the very end," he declared. "Then we can dictate whatever peace we like."

Bismarck thought that he was already within reach of the very end, and he was still obsessed with preventing any possible intervention by Britain or Russia, but Moltke worried far more about the continuing French resistance, that ragged troop still maneuvering in the east, and the damnable *franc-tireurs* who seemed to be hiding behind every tree. The crown prince tried to calm the angry general by suggesting that there were political reasons for Bismarck's moves. Moltke brushed that aside. "I am concerned only with military matters," he snapped.

In trying to reassert his traditional position that generals spoke only of military matters—but that in those matters their authority must be supreme, that once a war had started, the military commander must overrule political advisers—Moltke had forgotten Clausewitz's doctrine that all major military questions are ultimately political. It was a doctrine that Bismarck never forgot—and in political matters, Bismarck enjoyed not only supreme authority but supreme talent. Whenever he wanted to criticize Moltke's military decisions, he could find some apparently good reason to do so. But every time Moltke challenged him in the political field, Moltke lost.

The chief of staff unwittingly put his foot into one of the chancellor's many snares when he responded caustically to Trochu's protest about the shelling of Parisian hospitals. With his infinite guile, Bismarck pretended to believe that Moltke's crude jibe about hoping to get his cannon within better range of the red crosses on the hospital roofs constituted an attempt to enter into negotiations with the enemy and thus an illicit intrusion into Bismarck's political/diplomatic domain. He asked the newly crowned emperor to rein in his allegedly rebellious chief of staff. Though the emperor sympathized with Moltke, he did not dare provoke his chancellor, who was now engaged in complicated negotiations not only with the various factions in France but also with the German states that were being enticed into the nascent empire. So he explicitly ordered Moltke to keep Bismarck fully informed of all military plans—and to acknowledge Bismarck's right to express his own views on all those plans—and to notify the foreign ministry of any military messages of any political significance whatever.

Moltke was outraged. He called the kaiser's order *"ungnädig"* ("ungracious"). He denied all the wrongdoings implicitly charged to him and said that if Bismarck wanted to become a royal adviser on military as well as political affairs, he was quite ready "to leave the relevant operations and the responsibility for them to the federal chancellor alone." To this implicit threat of resignation, he added: "I await your Imperial Majesty's most gracious decision." Some internal censor persuaded Moltke to tone down this threat before sending his letter, however, and before the kaiser had a chance to answer, Bismarck had ended the game by negotiating a truce.

Favre had arrived at German headquarters in Versailles on January 23 with a very weak hand to play.

Just five days had passed since the coronation of the kaiser, just four since the disastrous sortie from Paris. Favre hoped mainly to arrange for an election, to prevent an immediate Prussian entry into Paris, and to block any attempt to disarm the National Guard. If he failed in those aims, he was prepared to threaten an indefinite continuation of the fighting. Bismarck was affable, and not at all averse to compromise. He said that German opinion would insist on a triumphal entry into Paris, for example, but that the German presence did not need to last long. When Favre started asking better terms because of the Parisians' heroic resistance, though, Bismarck snarled, "Do not talk to me of your resistance. It is criminal!" Over the next two days, the details were worked out, and on January 25, Favre signed, on behalf of all France, an armistice that would allow three weeks for the election of a new National Assembly. Moltke was then brought in to negotiate the details of the armistice, which he very grudgingly did. Since Bismarck had already abandoned much of what Moltke wanted, he had little choice. The Paris truce was to begin immediately, and the Germans would do whatever they could to bring food into the city, which would retain an armed French garrison of 12,000 men. It would have to pay a war indemnity of 200 million francs. In the rest of the country, both sides would withdraw ten kilometers from the line now dividing them.

To anyone who still cherished notions of the people's readiness to fight on for their republic, the election on February 8 was devastating.

Of 768 elected legislators, more than 400 were avowed monarchists. More generally, they were overwhelmingly conservative, rural, and in favor of peace at any price. Bismarck's price was high: the cession of most of Alsace and Lorraine and an indemnity of 5 billion francs. Moltke's army would parade down the Champs Elysées, and its occupation of the northern provinces would end only as the indemnity was gradually paid over the course of three years. "On the day of Moltke's victory parade, a number of Parisians still shammed resistance, closing their shops and draping their windows in black. One hostile crowd even surrounded and threatened Bismarck himself on the Place de la Concorde. Bismarck, no man to quail at a challenge, calmly took out a cigar, accosted the most baleful of the menacing Parisians and asked him for a light. The threat dissolved, and the parade continued."

The French Assembly chose the venerable Thiers as its leader, and so Thiers had to go to Versailles to sign Bismarck's armistice. He tried for a time to negotiate a few improvements. Could France keep Metz, for example, if it gave the Germans Saigon in exchange? But Thiers had no cards left to play. Throughout January, General Bourbaki had been trying to lead the last French army of 80,000 men to a sanctuary in the Jura mountains. When that failed, he shot himself, but the bullet only grazed his skull and left him helpless. A deputy then marched the surviving troops into internment in Switzerland. So Thiers sadly signed Bismarck's terms—generally regarded as milder than those Napoleon had imposed on Prussia in 1807—and started to work on rebuilding his country for the next war.

10

The Last Years: "Our Moltke"

IT IS POSSIBLE THAT THERE IS NO SATISFACTION KNOWN TO MAN THAT surpasses the satisfaction a general feels on his return home from a victory in war. Parades, honors, acclamations—*Ritorna vincitor!* His function in life, as he sees it, has been tested and fulfilled. His rulers and his people honor him as the savior of the nation. Critics and skeptics fall silent. Nothing interrupts the flow of admiration.

For Moltke's triumphal return to Berlin in 1871, an honor guard of 42,000 veterans of the French campaign assembled to march behind him through all the main boulevards of the delirious capital. With them, they carried eighty-one captured French eagles and banners. Even the king, now emperor, took his place behind Moltke, to whom he had given, on the fall of Metz, the title of count. Now the kaiser had just awarded Moltke the baton of a field marshal, directing him to carry it on this occasion, which he proudly did. At his side rode the only two men who could share his triumph, Bismarck and Roon. Moltke remained utterly imperturbable, of course. A witness who was watching him at this supreme moment said that he looked as though he were planning some new battle rather than accepting honors for a victory already won.

But if the German rewards for military victory can seem excessive, the excesses can also bring their own irritations. Moltke had to attend so many parades and reviews in his honor that weariness finally compelled him to petition the emperor for permission to go on leave. When the emperor agreed, Moltke put himself in the hands of his aide and nephew, Major Henry von Burt. "Let us go somewhere where we can have perfect rest," Moltke said. "Take tickets for us and the servant for X."

No sooner had they arrived in the town of X for their perfect rest than a man in white tie and tails boarded their train and identified himself as the mayor of X. "Your excellency, everything is prepared for your reception," he said. "Rooms have been ordered, and a carriage is waiting at the station."

"The town was decorated with flags," Burt recalled, "and some of the inhabitants were still engaged in putting up wreaths on the houses; school children were running after our carriage, and all X. was agog. The Mayor told the Field-Marshal that it was the anniversary of the veterans and also the vintage festival, and the people would be very cross with him if he did not persuade his Excellency to honor the feast with his presence. Rather hesitantly, Moltke accepted. . . ."

Once the carriage had arrived at the hotel, however, the hotel owner took charge, delivering his own little speech of welcome to his establishment and ceremoniously ushering his guests to their suite of rooms. The mayor pursued them with reminders of the official feast until Moltke irritably demanded: "Will you allow me at least to wash a little first?" When he had washed and returned to the street, where an open carriage waited to take him to the dinner, Moltke found that it had started to rain. It took an hour to creep through the crowded streets to the vineyard where the dinner was to be held. "We left the carriage and the policeman made room for us to go slowly and single file through the crowd," Burt recalled, "now and then we stumbled over a little dachshund who had lost his master and hoped to find him in the path that had been cleared for us."

By the time they reached the vineyard, it was raining hard. "An old woman offered the Field-Marshal her umbrella, which, however, he declined, being in uniform," Burt wrote. "A thundering 'hurrah' was his reward. Then we were taken to see some fire-works, which, however, did not go off well on account of the rain, and which altogether were not very effective as it was not dark enough." Somehow, the spectacle of the fireworks in the rain seems to have reprieved Moltke from his obligation to attend the mayor's dinner because he and Burt drove back to the hotel in the open carriage and ordered dinner for themselves.

"Now let us have a game of patience and then go to bed," said Moltke, still searching for his "perfect rest." No sooner had Burt dealt out the cards, though, than there came a solemn knock on the door. There stood the mayor, still in his white tie and tails, with white gloves as well. "The singing club of the town wishes to serenade your Excellency," he announced to the weary visitors, "and the fire brigade to give a torch-light procession. There is a balcony near this room, and it would be a great favor if you would show yourself there to the assembled crowd."

Could the conqueror of France refuse the tribute of the fire brigade of X? Burt discreetly slipped downstairs to give the singing club the names of some of the field marshal's favorite songs. The singing club sang, the fire brigade marched, and "after this festivity was ended we succeeded in finding quiet and rest in our beds."

The first light of dawn brought new knocking on the door, however. When Burt opened it, he once again found himself confronting the tireless mayor of X.

"The town band has assembled outside the hotel to serenade the field marshal," the mayor announced. Burt tried to restrain him, declaring that Moltke was past seventy and needed rest. The mayor was, as before, relentless in his hospitality.

"Have I come here to rest and am I not let alone for a moment?" Moltke protested, but Burt heard in the protest the sound of imminent surrender. "I appeased him as well as I could," he recalled, "reminded him of the fact that all was done with the best intentions, and that it would make a bad impression if he did not show himself pleased."

"Very well," Moltke said as he finally capitulated, "but after this we will leave by the very next train and go straight to Berlin."

"And so it was," Burt concluded his memoir. And so it continued. On another occasion, Moltke went to take the waters at the spa of Ragatz, then strolled through a forest to the neighboring village of Pfäfers. He felt so hot that he stopped at an inn for a drink. The landlord asked him whether he was staying in Ragatz. Moltke acknowledged that he was. "Moltke is said to be there," the innkeeper persisted.

"Yes," said Moltke, long noted for his lack of loquacity.

"What does he look like?" the innkeeper inquired.

"Well, what should he look like?" Moltke retorted. "Just like one of us two."

From Ragatz, he later went privately to visit the town of Lindau. Imagining himself unrecognized, he took a ground-floor room at the Bayerische Hof and went to bed. Unfortunately, he forgot to draw the blinds. He was just falling asleep when he heard the sound of a marching band approaching his hotel. He looked out into the darkness, which was no longer darkness. The torches of the Lindau fire brigade had banished night, and crowds were pressing against his windows for a look at the hero of Sedan. "The difficulty for him now was how to get dressed without being seen," Major Burt wrote. "He dared not strike a light. But, as he himself afterwards related, the glare of the torches lit up his room, and the curious crowd stood close to the windows, their noses pressed against the panes. In spite of all that, he felt that he must rise, and at each piece of dress that he put on loud and endless hurrahs were heard."

As soon as the snows melted in Silesia every spring, the old man escaped from the cheering and ogling by returning to Kreisau. He had observed many years ago that he would never live to enjoy the shade of the oak trees he had planted, but now he liked to get up early and wander out into the park and sit in the shade of his oak trees. And when he went walking, tall and straight in his black coat and dark gray trousers, he invariably took along a saw or a pair of garden shears, for he could not help seeing things that needed work. Pruning and trimming, that is what makes gardens grow.

The backcountry of Silesia is afflicted every summer by invasions of flies. The field marshal resisted them as resolutely as if they had been flaunting the French *tricolor*. Every day, he prowled around his room with a fly swatter, and broken windowpanes often provided evidence of the vigor of his attacks. Even at the dinner table, the old man pursued his offensive with sudden assaults that occasionally sent plates and glasses flying.

"The young crops are looking very well, and promise a rich harvest, if we could only have some warm, dry weather," Moltke wrote to his brother Ludwig in July 1879. "The violent rains have flooded the Peile [River] till all the meadows are under water. . . . The greater part of the abundant hay had to be thrown away. The continuous damp is of course most beneficial to the young trees in the plantations, and they are a mass of fresh green foliage. . . ."

Any practical landowner has to concentrate on the fundamentals, of course, on the wheat and the potatoes and the pigs, but there is always time for the pleasures of experimentation with exotic plants and rare animals. The sight of a little stream meandering through one of his meadows inspired the old field marshal to start imagining himself as a breeder of trout. A man named von Behr-Schmoldow had established himself in the business of selling fish supplies, so Moltke arranged with him for the purchase of 2,000 trout eggs. Behr also agreed to send what Moltke described, in a letter to his gamekeeper, as "a Californian breeding box." "The most important point," Moltke wrote from Berlin to the gamekeeper, warning him to prepare for the arrival of 2,000 trout eggs by means of the imperial postal system, "will be to take measures by which the water may be made to flow through the box without interruption for several months. According to Borne's calculations, one liter is needed every forty seconds, that is, three liters for every two minutes, and at least 2,000 liters = two cubic meters of water every twenty-four hours; that is to say, as much as would fill two boxes of one meter length, height and width each. My idea was to put up such a box, or one a little larger, near the pump in the yard, inside the wire fence, and to fill it twice a day, but Herr Behr is of the opinion that it would answer the purpose better to use the water that is raised by the American mill above the roof of the carriage-house; there only remains the question of how this is to be done."

Although Moltke claimed that he was leaving all these questions to the judgment of his tactical commander on the battlefield—that is, the gamekeeper—he proceeded to offer the same kind of detailed suggestions that he used to offer his tactical commanders: "The breeding box might be placed in the carriage house or in or near the verandah, a narrow pipe would be required to convey the water from the nearest tube into the box A. How wide or narrow the mouth of the pipe would need to be must be found out by experiment. The water must not flow in too violently so as to shake the eggs about, but it must gently run through, entering at the surface, and flowing out at the bottom. It might be sufficient to let the water run through a little tin gutter along the ground, from which it would flow into a funnel contrived over the box; it would need to be purified by being filtered through pebbles. In falling into the box the water would carry with it dissolved air from the atmosphere, which would be very desirable. The breeding time lasts three months, and the question is, whether we could count upon sufficient water to keep the large tubs half or two-thirds full uninterruptedly up to the month of June. . . . Another consideration would be the varying temperature. . . . You, being on the spot, will be better able to judge than I can do from here. Ask Unverricht's and the gardener's advice, which of the two plans would be the better one, and then take the necessary measures according to your own judgment. Order the workmen who will be wanted, and tell the carpenter that he will have to help; I should like at least to have the attempt made. . . ."

So the attempt was made. The elaborate network of gutters and pipes was built. The trouble was that Silesian weather did not provide the tranquillity necessary for the hatching of 2,000 trout eggs. Every time there was a thunderstorm, which was often, the ponds harboring the trout eggs overflowed, covering the adjacent meadows with sand. Worse, the infant trout swam forth into the Peile River, where hungry pike were waiting to devour them. The trout that actually reached the Moltke dinner table proved extravagantly expensive.

Cost-efficiency played little part in the old field marshal's plans, however. He was as frugal as any Prussian Junker, but being the lord of Kreisau meant not just harvesting crops but acting as seigneur to all the villagers. It dismayed him that the schoolchildren of Kreisau had to spend forty-five minutes every morning walking to class in the neighboring village of Gräditz, so he tore down a small farmhouse in Kreisau and built a new school there. He also donated enough nearby land to provide the schoolmaster with a garden and an income. To encourage the schoolchildren, he started a savings bank for them. Every child entering school received a bankbook with 1 mark already inscribed in it. The children then contributed whatever pennies they could save. Each time one of them saved a mark, the field marshal doubled it. He also built the children a free library, and what would now be called a day care center, where the villagers could leave their children while they went to work in the fields. And since the church at Gräditz needed a new spire, he got the emperor's permission to melt down some of the cannon captured in France, so the booty of warfare in Lorraine tolled the peaceful hours in distant Silesia.

Moltke's good deeds were not undertaken, however, without an almost Dickensian anxiety (Dickens remained one of his favorite writers all his life) about their corrupting effects. "I try to the best of my ability to help the people on my estate . . ." he wrote to his sister-in-law Augusta in 1875. "Small gifts to individuals are very apt to go to the wrong person, and to relieve them of the duty laid on them by God of providing for their own families by harder work and greater economy. Poverty and distress are necessary elements in the scheme of life—what would become of the whole social system if this stern necessity did not force men to think and work? We all send our love and wish you a happy Christmas."

Though Moltke loved his quiet days in Kreisau, the first snowfall every autumn drove him back to Berlin. He still had his duty, after all, as chief of staff to the army that he had made the most feared in Europe. When he passed the age of eighty, he submitted his resignation, so that a younger man might take over this responsibility. The kaiser responded by issuing a cabinet order declaring that the field marshal's services were so valuable that his resignation could never be accepted. So he remained chief of staff for another seven years until, at the age of eighty-eight, he wrote to the young Kaiser William II to say that he had grown too old to mount a horse, and asking that he be allowed to retire. The new emperor granted his request but appointed him to another advisory position as president of the Committee for National Defense. In doing so, he declared that Moltke's service as chief of staff would be remembered with honor "so long as there was a Prussian soldier or a Prussian heart left in the world."

The labors of a chief of staff to a victorious army in a time of peace were probably not very onerous—the chief enemies being complacency and inertia—and Moltke combated those not only in the war ministry but also in the legislature. Berlin, with its long tradition of voting against conservatives, rejected Moltke as one of its representatives in the Reichstag ("I can forgive the town of Berlin if I fail," he wrote to his brother Adolf), but three other constituencies, Memel-Heydekrug, Fürstenthum, and Bitterfeld-Delitzsch, were more admiring. Moltke represented Memel from the election of 1866 until his death in 1891. He also sat in the upper chamber, the Herrenhaus or House of Lords, from 1872 on, and in the Prussian legislature and the Zollparlament, the legislature of the *Zollverein*. Though he scrupulously attended legislative meetings, listened to debates, and studied the relevant documents, he did not often speak (only forty-one times in his twenty-one years in the Reichstag and only three times in the Herrenhaus), and then not at great length. The rarity and brevity of his speeches gave them all the more weight.

As might be expected, he was a tireless advocate of greater military strength. He urged more construction of military railroads; he urged strengthening the fortifications of Cologne and Strassburg against the dangers of a French attack. To rebuild their forces after Sedan, the French had imitated the Prussians and inaugurated a system of universal conscription, a measure that could hardly help but worry a German commander. But in the Reichstag, the debate focused on fortifications. "Military interests, as regards the extension of the city's enceinte, are not matters of present debate," Moltke said of Cologne, "extension is demanded in the most imperative interests of the town itself." He was hardly less intransigent about the duty of the south German states to follow Prussian leadership: "I am not referring to the fact that North Germany possesses the greater war strength; that is a matter of course. We maintain an army; you merely furnish contingents. We have a War Lord, you have a Commander-in-Chief. The difference is a great one. . . . We offer you what we have purchased with our blood, what no power will again wrest from us . . . a Fatherland."

Is there not something rather sad about this? When Bismarck insisted that German public opinion demanded the annexation of Alsace and Lorraine, he was really carrying out the army's traditional wish for a defensive zone on the border, which he knew would lead to a French hunger for revenge; now here was the general who had conquered those cursed provinces, tormented in his old age, like a white-haired Macbeth, by the ghosts that he had created by the fulfillment of his own ambitions.

French and British historians tend to scold Bismarck—and implicitly Moltke—for the wars he fought and won, as though this somehow created a tempting model for the aggressions of Adolf Hitler. But Bismarck's record in foreign affairs is really rather good. While the culpability for the wars of 1866 and 1870 can be debated indefinitely, the Prussian responsibility is no more than partial. And once those battles were won, Bismarck, like Frederick the Great, successfully devoted most of his life to keeping the peace while he repaired and reconstructed his country.

On the country that he reconstructed, though, he left a dark shadow. The Bismarckian Reich, supported and upheld by Moltke's army, was a deplorably autocratic state. It has been harshly criticized by liberals for being conservative, but that hardly seems a crime in the age of Disraeli and Thiers and Grant. It has been even more unfairly criticized by liberals as being the ancestor to Hitler's Third Reich. It certainly was not that, but it did share with Nazism a deep aversion to parliamentary government and a deep indifference to individual citizens' rights.

As early as the 1860s, when Bismarck was engaged in a fierce battle with the legislature over military budgets, he began using every political weapon he could find against his enemies. After the 1863 elections, seventeen East Prussian deputies were prosecuted and fined for a campaign pamphlet that criticized the cabinet. A leading radical, Johann Jacoby, was sentenced to six months in jail for lèse majesté. Eight liberals among the nine men elected to the Berlin City Council in 1865 were denied their seats, and so were a number of liberal mayors chosen by their local governments. Commercial firms suspected of liberal sympathies lost out on military contracts. Progressive doctors failed to get jobs in public health services. Judiciary pay raises went only to judges who cooperated with the government. When criticized for such maneuvers, Bismarck explained, "The government must reward its friends and punish its enemies."

If this makes Bismarck sound like a dictator, he was not. On the contrary, his enemies included a number of generals who hoped and planned for a military coup d'état by General Edwin Manteuffel, who quite openly favored shutting the Reichstag and restoring the absolute monarchy that the Hohenzollerns had enjoyed until 1848. William I was not unsympathetic to this goal, but he did not dare act without Bismarck's support, which Bismarck declined to give to the plotters. Still, when Bismarck and Moltke returned in triumph from France in 1871, they regarded themselves as the true authorities of the Reich that they had created. How startling, for them, to hear members of the Reichstag, civilians who had taken no part in the great war, delivering speeches implying that *they* somehow deserved the power to govern.

"The foreign policy of a great country cannot be put at the disposal of a parliamentary majority," Bismarck declared. On another occasion, he referred to his having "to undergo the chronic suffering of parliamentary activity." Though he believed this as a matter of political philosophy, Bismarck's tendency toward autocracy was also a matter of personal feelings. "He treats everyone with a certain arrogance," Prince Hohenlohe wrote in his diary. "He is the terror of all diplomatists." Another colleague, Gustav von Diest, thought that Bismarck's "whole nature" had changed after the victory over France. "He no longer tolerated contradiction," Diest wrote, as though tolerating contradiction had once been one of Bismarck's notable characteristics. "He was accessible to flattery, even the smallest, alleged disregard for his ego and his position exasperated him."

Moltke, for his part, spoke bitterly about what he called "that ill weed Democracy" and "the nightmare of the prevailing Democracy." Bismarck, ironically, had insisted on the democratic mechanism of universal suffrage in his constitution of 1867 because he was convinced that this would confound the liberals; the workers and peasants, he thought—quite wrongly, as it turned out—would always vote for their conservative masters. Bismarck himself belonged to no party, and he ruled at the pleasure of the kaiser, not the Reichstag. Still, he needed a parliamentary majority to vote for the bills he wanted passed. This majority consisted of patchwork coalitions that changed from vote to vote, and now it had little stability. The National Liberals, whom Bismarck used as his primary party during the 1860s, won only 120 seats out of 382 in the elections of 1870; the Conservatives won 54, and the so-called Free Conservatives 38.

The essential controversy, just as it had been a decade earlier, was the need for the Reichstag to approve a national budget, meaning a military budget, since the army needed nearly 90 million of the 117 million thalers requested in the budget for 1872. It had been said in the days of Frederick the Great that while other countries had armies, Prussia was simply an army with a country attached to it. Since then, the military had grown fivefold, and the latest funds for Moltke's standing army of 400,000 were needed within two months of the budget request. Since a large part of the army was still serving in France, the legislators felt they had little choice but to pay its bills. They felt, however, that the military budget could be trimmed down in the future by reducing the term of military service from three years to two, and by other little frugalities that they were happy to suggest. Moltke balked; Kaiser William balked; and so the Reichstag began to debate, which further irritated Moltke and the emperor and Bismarck as well. If the Reichstag couldn't discuss these matters, one legislator tartly observed, Germany would be one-fifth constitutional monarchy, four-fifths military dictatorship. Bismarck's goal, on the other hand, was a permanent military budget that never needed to be altered, questioned, or discussed. In 1867, both sides had agreed to compromise on a three-year budget, and this was renewed in 1871. In 1874, however, Bismarck demanded an end to such debates; the Progressives consequently revived their old demand for an annual budget review; the National Liberals, who had traditionally supported Bismarck on most issues, held a party caucus and split wide apart. Bismarck suddenly fell ill with a painfully inflamed leg. His doctors blamed it on gout. Bismarck disagreed. He told the press that he was a victim of "vexation, not at his enemies and political opponents, with whom he knew how to cope, but at those who ought to support him in their own interests and for the good of the country, but who everywhere harmed him and left him in the lurch." If this controversy continued, Bismarck warned, he would have to resign. The kaiser was no less querulous. On his seventy-seventh birthday in March 1874, he told a gathering of generals that it grieved him, in the "evening of life," to have his military judgment challenged by mere parliamentarians. He vowed that he would fight them to his last ounce of strength. Public opinion had a very limited power in Bismarck's Germany, but these public declarations by both Bismarck and the emperor prompted a number of citizens' groups and private individuals to petition their Reichstag representatives in support of a permanent military budget. The Reichstag deputies looked to the horizon, as they periodically did, and found no signs of support from anywhere for their challenge to the constituted authorities. And so, as often happened, they shrugged and surrendered.

Or rather, they compromised. If Bismarck's government would not submit to an annual parliamentary review of the military budget, or even a triennial review, then could everyone agree on a review every seven years? This measure, known as the *Septennat,* proved to be the solution, or at least an agreement that all sides could pretend to regard as a solution.

Apart from Progressives, and Socialists, the great nuisance to Bismarck in these years was a new grouping called the Center Party, which was born out of the conflicts that followed the claim by Pope Pius IX and the Vatican Council of 1870 that the pope, speaking ex cathedra on spiritual and moral issues, was infallible. The Vatican then demanded that the so-called old-Catholic priests who rejected this new ideology be expelled from their pulpits. Bismarck, on the other hand, decided to demand secular control over all church schools. He denounced Catholicism as "a hypocritical, idolatrous papism full of hate and cunning." He declared in his memoirs that he never opposed the Catholic religion, but that the church and its officials "constitute a political institution under clerical forms, and transmit to their collaborators their own conviction that for them *freedom* lies in *dominion,* and that the Church, wherever she does not rule, is justified in complaining of Diocletian-like persecution."

This was the famous *Kulturkampf* or clash of cultures which reawakened memories of those terrible struggles between church and empire in the Middle Ages, and then of the butcheries of the Reformation and the Thirty Years War.

Bismarck seems to have been the aggressor, though his aggressions hardly approached the persecution that his enemies charged. He, on the other hand, seems to have been motivated by a paranoid fantasy of "ultramontane" conspiracies that linked the Vatican and the Center Party to the fractious Poles, the Bavarian separatists, to Austrians seeking revenge for the war of 1866, and to Catholic support of French guerrillas in Alsace and Lorraine. His most hotly disputed measure was to abolish church supervision of schools, but he also added to the criminal code a paragraph making it illegal for any priest to speak on public issues "in a manner endangering public peace." He insisted on secular regulation of ordinary life, as in civil marriages. He also took action against that favorite target of conspiracy theorists, the Jesuits. All Jesuit centers in Germany were shut down, and the government claimed the right to limit the stay of individual Jesuits in Germany, and to ban non-German Jesuits altogether.

The *Kulturkampf* reached its height in 1873 with the passing of the so-called May Laws in Prussia. These required several years of study at a German state university before any priest could be assigned to a parish. They also banned Vatican jurisdiction over the church in

Prussia and assigned all disciplinary authority to German government agencies. The German bishops, with the support of the Vatican, protested vehemently against these measures and refused to acknowledge their legality. The Vatican, like the popes of the Middle Ages, declared the new laws illegal and threatened to excommunicate anyone who obeyed them. Bismarck tightened the screws, banning all monastic orders except those devoted exclusively to medicine and teaching. And Bismarck's empire wielded greater coercive powers than Frederick Barbarossa had enjoyed. By 1876, all the bishops in Prussia were either imprisoned or exiled, and 1,400 of the 4,600 Catholic parishes had no parish priest. Still, though the church was seriously divided by the controversy over papal infallibility, Bismarck soon discovered that he had underestimated his antagonists. Bismarck not only miscalculated that he could hobble the Center Party by putting pressure on the Vatican, which he then expected to rein in its political party; he not only miscalculated the effects of repression on the Catholic Church, which has traditionally been strengthened and unified by political pressure; he also miscalculated the effects of his anti-Catholic laws on many Protestants, who saw the government's anti-clericalism as a threat to their own schools, their authority, and their privileges. To them, as much as to the Vatican, it seemed a new assault by the forces of modernism, secularism, and materialism. When the Prussian government finally proposed to suspend the traditional subsidies to the church—except for those bishops who promised in writing to obey all the *Kulturkampf* laws—many Protestants joined in voting against the measure.

On July 13, 1874, a young Catholic cooper named Eduard Kullmann fired a pistol at Bismarck while he was waving to supporters from his carriage in the spa of Bad Kissingen. The bullet only grazed Bismarck's hand, but he did his best to get political profit from the attack. "The blow aimed at me was directed not at me personally," he said at a torchlight celebration of his escape from serious injury, "but at the cause for which I have dedicated my life: the unity, independence, and freedom of Germany." Though a Catholic, Kullmann was not even a member of the Center Party, and there was no evidence of any conspiracy, but Bismarck carried his campaigning into the Reichstag itself. "You may try to disown this assassin," he said to the Center delegates there, "but he is clinging to your coattails all the same." The Reichstag deputies shouted and stamped; ordinary citizens were not greatly impressed. Though Bismarck denounced the Center Party as *Reichsfeinde* or enemies of the empire, the Center nearly doubled its strength in the elections of 1874, from fifty-seven seats in 1870 to ninety-one, thus becoming the second strongest party in the legislature.

Bismarck's understandable fear of assassination led to another serious crisis with France. In December 1874, the *Norddeutsche Allgemeine Zeitung*, which was close to Bismarck, published a report attributed to the French police and claiming that a Belgian boilermaker named Duchesne had offered to kill Bismarck if the archbishop of Paris would pay him 60,000 marks. A diplomatic protest by Germany accused the Belgians of tolerating "ultramontane" agitation and demanded the prosecution of Duchesne. This controversy grew worse when Kaiser William announced in March a ban on the export of 10,000 military horses to France, a prospective purchase that was traditionally a sign of impending warfare. Later that same month, the French National Assembly suddenly approved a measure to add a fourth company to every battalion and a fourth battalion to every regiment in the French army. Moltke's staff officers immediately calculated that this would furtively add 144,000 men to the French army, and that by the fourteenth day of any future mobilization, the French would have "a great superiority over the German army."

Bismarck leaked a story to the *Kölnische Zeitung*, which reported on April 5 that an imminent meeting between Emperor Francis Joseph and King Victor Emmanuel of Italy, together with a possible restoration of monarchical rule in France, might lead to Bismarck's greatest nightmare: the creation of a "Catholic League" that would reverse the Prussian military triumphs of 1866 and 1870. A few days later, similar speculations appeared in a Berlin newspaper, *Die Post*, under an ominous headline: "Is war in sight?" Having sounded these alarms, Bismarck issued a formal denial, and the kaiser was reported to be "shocked" at such talk of war. Bismarck also let it be known, however, that Germany did feel threatened by the French military expansion and reorganization. French Foreign Minister Louis Descazes, on the other hand, told anyone who would listen that it was Bismarck who was threatening a new war.

He was not the only German official doing so. At a diplomatic dinner in Berlin in late March, War Minister Georg von Kameke argued that Germany had a right to attack France before the French completed their ominous rearmament program, and that "if war was not already unavoidable, the best course would be to begin it next year." In April, Bismarck himself told the Austrian ambassador, Count Aloys Karolyi, according to Karolyi's statement to the British ambassador, Odo Russell, that it was Germany's duty "to take the initiative and put a stop to war by energetic measures."

Unlike Bismarck, Moltke was genuinely worried about a French attempt at revenge, and he genuinely believed in both the efficacy and the propriety of preemptive warfare, which Bismarck emphatically did not. In May, therefore, Bismarck sent Moltke to see Odo Russell to argue the case for a preemptive German assault against aggressive France, which Moltke had actually been planning since 1873. The responsibility for such an attack, Moltke said, lay with the nation that provoked it. France's Descazes responded to Bismarck's threats by calling the world's attention to them. In a message to all his ambassadors on April 29, he asked them to warn the governments to which they were accredited of the Germans' "strange doctrine" of preemptive war. If this strange doctrine "should actually be adopted by Germany," he said, it would threaten the security of all Germany's neighbors.

The German threats had no effect in deterring French rearmament, but they did unite the other powers in resisting Berlin. The Russian ambassador to London, Peter Shuvalov, reported that Bismarck was in a "morbid state of mind," and that "fatigue, anxiety, and other causes had produced . . . a state of nervous excitement that may explain many of his recent sayings and doings." So Tsar Alexander II of Russia came to Berlin on a state visit on May 10, with a note of support from Queen Victoria of England, for what he and his foreign minister, Alexander Gorchakov, regarded as a Russian peace initiative. The kaiser, who was uncle to the tsar, said he agreed with the Russians' views; Bismarck had to sit silent and apparently humiliated while the visitors told him that Europe would not sit idle if France were attacked. "The emperor is leaving Berlin convinced of the pacific dispositions that reign here," Gorchakov later telegraphed all Russian ambassadors. Bismarck never forgave him for posing as a mediator and "angel of peace." But the great war scare of 1875 soon passed into history.

What ended the *Kulturkampf* was not only Bismarck's accurate assessment of the political realities but the death of the first "infallible" pope, Pius IX. He was succeeded in 1878 by Leo X, whose chief mission was peace and reconciliation, even with the apostate ogre of Berlin. And so the *Kulturkampf* gradually faded away. Some of Bismarck's punitive laws were rescinded, some not enforced. By 1887, the struggle was generally considered finished, though its renewal of the conflicts of the Reformation left some scars and suspicions that never healed.

Slightly more realistic, among Bismarck's paranoid fears, was his dread of the Socialists. Among admirers of cutthroat capitalism, the early 1870s became known as the *Gründerjahre,* or founding years, when the Prussian economy and the *Zollverein* reached what economists call the takeoff phase. German coal production soared from 34 million tons in 1870 to 59 million in 1880; pig iron from 1.4 million tons to 2.7 million. The founding of the Reichsbank in 1875 assisted a great concentration and consolidation of financial power. As in many such periods, of course, a lot of profits came from financial deals that could not bear too close an examination (Bismarck himself, with the help of his personal banker, Gerson Bleichroeder, engaged in shady transactions that ranged from speculating on the nationalization of Prussian railroads to putting pressure on local officials for preferential treatment of his taxes). Almost inevitably, there was a major stock market crash in 1873, followed by a prolonged recession. Unemployment spread. Workers in German mines, for example, declined from 289,000 to 275,000 between 1873 and 1879. Among the survivors, pay cuts followed. Average industrial wages dropped about 10 percent between 1873 and 1879, from 620 marks per year to 558. Workers struggling for the right to a ten-hour day contributed to the *Gründerjahre* with a series of bitter strikes. In 1873 alone, there were 222 walkouts in mining, smelting, textiles, and other industries.

The Social Democrats naturally tried to transform these dissatisfactions of the working class into votes for Reichstag seats, but Bismarck, who had been terrified by the uprisings of 1848, saw all these new conflicts as new threats of revolution. He responded with a draft law outlawing virtually all Socialist political activities, which he denounced as "an invitation to bestiality." The Reichstag rejected the bill. When two Socialists in succession attempted to assassinate the kaiser, the second inflicting a serious wound, Bismarck resubmitted his bill and waged a whole election campaign on the need to suppress socialism. The new law forbade all meetings and demonstrations that supported what Bismarck called "Social Democratic, Socialist, or Communist activities designed to subvert the existing political and social order in ways that threaten the public order and particularly the harmony of the social classes." In the wake of two successive attempts to assassinate the kaiser, the Reichstag felt it had no choice but to approve whatever restrictions Bismarck asked. He wanted not only to stop Socialist meetings but to shut down Socialist newspapers and publishers of Socialist books and pamphlets, Socialist unions, Socialist fundraising. And he left it to the police to decide what was Socialist, what should be silenced and suppressed. Within a few months, forty-five of the forty-seven main Socialist newspapers had been outlawed (in addition to police censorship and other forms of coercion against Socialists, Bismarck also spent freely to bribe the mainstream press from a secret fund of more than 1 million marks known as "the reptile fund"), and many of the Socialist leaders were driven into exile.

At the same time, Bismarck was determined to show the working classes that they could best look for help to the government, not the Socialists. And so he invented the welfare state. In 1883, his government insured workers against sickness. In 1884, it compelled employers to insure their workers against accidents. In 1887, it put limits on the labor of women and children and shortened the work hours in various industries. In 1889, workers were insured against the expenses of old age.

The results of this combination of coercion and charity might have been predicted. The Socialists, who had won nearly half a million votes in 1877, climbed to nearly three times that number by the time of Bismarck's downfall in 1890.

Though the German intellectual establishment fawned and groveled before its rulers—as intellectual establishments so often do—some German thinkers were sharply critical of Bismarck's triumphs. "Bismarck left behind as a political heritage a nation without any political education, far below the level which, in this respect, it had reached twenty years earlier," wrote the pioneering sociologist Max Weber. "Above all he left behind a nation without any political will, accustomed to allow the great statesman at its head to look after its policy for it. As a consequence of his misuse of the monarchy as a cover for his own interests in the struggle of political parties, he left a nation accustomed to submit, under the label of constitutional monarchy, to anything which was decided for it."

Crown Prince Frederick, the hero of Königgrätz and Sedan, held a similar view about the consequences of his own victories. "We are no longer looked upon as the innocent victims of wrong," he wrote in his diary, "but rather as arrogant victors, no longer content with the conquest of the foe, but determined to bring about his utter ruin." The world was beginning to fear and hate Germany, "this nation of thinkers and philosophers, poets and artists, idealists and enthusiasts; and see her only a nation of conquerors and destroyers, to which no pledged word, no treaty, is sacred, and which speaks with rude insolence of those who have done it no injury. . . . At the moment it must seem as though we are neither loved nor respected, but only feared." And again: "Bismarck has made us great and powerful, but he has robbed us of our friends, the sympathies of the world, and—our conscience."

One of those lamented "thinkers and philosophers," Friedrich Nietzsche, was equally embittered. "A great victory is a great danger," he wrote in *Thoughts Out of Season.* "It is more difficult for human nature to bear than a defeat. . . . Of all the evil consequences of the last war with France, perhaps the worst is the widespread error that German culture too has been victorious. . . . This illusion is highly pernicious, not only because it is an illusion—for there are healthy and blissful illusions—but because it can pervert our victory into a total defeat, nay even into the extirpation of the German spirit for the benefit of the German Reich."

Freya von Moltke, the widow of Helmuth James von Moltke, who was killed by the Nazis in 1945 for his part in the resistance to Hitler, does not blame the field marshal for the political consequences of his military victories but neither is she in awe of the celebrated ancestor. "The field marshal was a very interesting man and a very gifted person," she says, "and he lived out his gifts and his life and gave it all to building up what I would say was a *terrible* Germany. Helmuth never got to really living out his great gifts, and giving them to much more than Germany—to the new world. He wasn't allowed to do it, but he helped to at least close up that terrible chapter of German history . . . through his death. You know, his role is a much better role than the poor field marshal, who gave all his gifts to building up a *terrible* Germany, politically. I admit that in those years, the Germans also contributed other things except politics. But these two people were involved in German politics through their gifts. . . . The field marshal stands at the opening, and Helmuth stands at the end. And that's interesting. That's why it's an interesting family. Because it takes that whole course. And it's not over yet."

Not many Germans had dark premonitions about the future when they assembled to bid farewell to the field marshal's coffin and to bury it with all the honors they could bestow. The parade in Berlin was a great national ceremony, worthy of comparison to Siegfried's funeral in the last act of *Götterdämmerung,* but finally it had to end at the railroad station, the symbol of one of Moltke's decisive weapons in his lightning campaigns against Austria and France. Moltke's coffin was taken into the Kaiser Salon, the royal waiting room, until a special train could carry him back to Kreisau the following day. The ten-car train, laden with funeral wreaths, left at 7 A.M., and even in these last miles to the grave, the official protocols were elaborate. The train bore not only Moltke's relatives but the new chief of the general staff, Count Schlieffen, a pride of lesser generals, a deputation from the Reichstag, about sixty people in all. And when the train reached the little rural station in Kreisau, the official mourners found the road from the station to the Moltke estate lined not only with lilacs and cherry trees but with schoolchildren, members of veterans societies, and other local worthies. All the officers from the nearby garrison town of Schweidnitz joined the funeral cortege, as did a delegation from Breslau, of which Moltke had been an honorary citizen. After a brief funeral service at the mausoleum that Moltke had built for his wife and himself, the oaken coffin was finally laid to rest there.

The mausoleum still stands, empty now, on a little hill overlooking Kreisau. It can be reached only by a narrow dirt road up the side of the hill, then by an overgrown footpath. The trees around the mausoleum are also somewhat overgrown, so shadows dapple the monument. There are other family graves down the hill. The mausoleum stands alone, a modest brick building in the style of a Greek temple, with an iron gate in the front. On the back wall, in large letters, the field marshal inscribed a quotation from Romans that he wanted remembered as his judgment on his history as a warrior: *"Die Liebe ist des Gesetzes Erfüllung,"* which the King James Bible renders as "Love is the fulfilling of the law."

III

The Nervous Nephew

The Great European war could come out of
some damned foolish thing in the Balkans.
—BISMARCK

The lamps are going out all over Europe. We
shall not see them lit again in our time.
—SIR EDWARD GREY

Helmuth Johannes Ludwig von Moltke
(1848-1916)

Kaiser Wilhelm II (1859-1941)

Erich Ludendorff (1865-1937)

11

On the Brink of Armageddon

WHEN GENERAL HELMUTH VON MOLTKE, NEPHEW AND NAMESAKE OF the famous field marshal, heard that he was to be offered his late uncle's post as chief of the imperial general staff, he reacted in a way that was quite uncharacteristic of his family and his caste. He rejected the idea. He was out riding in the Tiergarten with Prince Bernhard von Bülow in January 1905 when the imperial chancellor asked him if he would soon be replacing Count Alfred von Schlieffen. Moltke answered, according to his memoirs, that he hoped "that this cup would pass me by."

That, at least, is Moltke's complete account of the exchange. Bülow, who was not the most reliable of witnesses either, left a much fuller version in his own memoirs. He portrayed Moltke as suffering a kind of crisis of self-doubt. Specifically, he quoted the general as saying, "I lack the power of rapid decision. I am too reflective, too scrupulous, and, if you like, too conscientious for such a post. I lack the capacity for risking all on a single throw, that capacity which made the greatness of such born commanders as Napoleon, or our own Frederick II, or my uncle."

Bülow diplomatically let the matter drop, according to Moltke's account, and then went off to consult further, presumably spreading his own report of Moltke's misgivings. "His majesty was extremely surprised and unsettled," Moltke's memoirs continued, "and now he

sent ____ to me to tell me that he had complete confidence in me."
Moltke and the anonymous intermediary soon agreed that it would be
best for the general to discuss the question of his future with the
emperor himself. Two days later, he was invited to dinner at the royal
palace, with the promise of a private interview beforehand. He dutifully appeared, of course, and the kaiser, also of course, kept him
waiting. While he waited, he pondered what he planned to say, telling
himself that he had a duty to inform the kaiser about "what was only
whispered in officers' circles."

When he tried to start on that, the kaiser interrupted to say that
he and Bülow had been discussing the danger of a war with Britain
and Bülow had observed that Schlieffen was getting old. (Schlieffen
was then seventy-one, Moltke fifty-six, the kaiser forty-five; mere children by the standards that had prevailed in 1870.) The kaiser said he
had answered that if Schlieffen could no longer do the job as chief of
staff, "then Moltke is there." Bülow had then informed him that
Moltke didn't want the job. The kaiser said that he had been amazed
at this news, that he had appointed Moltke to the general staff a year
earlier so that he could prepare himself to head it, that he had consulted Count Schlieffen about a successor, and that Schlieffen himself
had said he could think of no better choice than Moltke. His uncle,
the late field marshal, had once said that the essential element in a
chief of staff was not to be a genius but to have a character that could
stand up to all challenges. "I can tell you," the kaiser continued, "that
I have full confidence in you. You are a well known personality in the
army, everyone admires you and will trust you as I do." The kaiser
even confided that when he had been younger, he had thought that
the responsibilities of the crown were too great for his own abilities.
But in the difficult task of dismissing the aged Bismarck, he said, he
had done what he had to do. "So it will go for you too," he concluded. "When you confront the task, you will find in yourself the
strength to deal with it."

The kaiser's assumption that Bülow had been right in reporting
Moltke overwhelmed by modesty seemed flattering, but Moltke was
eager to deny it. He wanted instead to bring up a widespread criticism
of the monarch himself. It had been generally understood for years
that whatever unit the kaiser commanded in the annual war games
had to "win" those games. Always. It was like the gladiatorial games
in ancient Rome, when bloodthirsty emperors like Nero invariably
succeeded in slaughtering the gladiators chosen to oppose them. With
the most deferential apologies and self-criticisms, Moltke now
declared that these artfully arranged royal triumphs must stop. The

officer corps needed more realistic training. "It is very difficult, if not impossible, to picture what a modern European war would be like," he said. "We have now a period of more than thirty years of peace behind us, and I believe that we have become very unwarlike in our outlook. No man can tell in advance how or if we can lead as a unit the mass armies that we are now creating. Our enemies have also changed. We no longer have to deal with an enemy army that we can just overwhelm with superior numbers. We now have to confront a nation in arms. It will be a war between peoples, which will not be finished by one decisive battle but will become a long, exhausting struggle against a country that will not admit defeat until the whole strength of its people is broken, a war that will push our own people, even if we are the victors, to the brink of exhaustion."

To prepare for such a war, Moltke argued, the German army must stop treating its annual war games as a mere game. "When I now see how the strategic maneuvers that are prepared for your majesty every year regularly include the capture of five or six hundred thousand of the enemy forces, and even come to an end after a few days, I cannot avoid the perception that these will never in any way resemble the conditions of a war. Such war games I cannot perform." Having said all that, Moltke went on to argue that all his fellow officers felt the same. The kaiser must have noticed, he said, that nobody wanted to oppose him in the maneuvers. "Everyone has the impression that it doesn't matter what one does," he said, "because a higher destiny organizes things and arranges them this way or that to reach the desired end." Worse: "The officers say to themselves, 'The kaiser is much too smart not to notice how everything is prepared here so that he wins. He must have wanted it that way.'"

It is quite possible, of course, that Moltke never said more than part of this, perhaps none of it. Prussian generals were not celebrated for scolding their rulers—and Moltke less than most—so perhaps the whole discourse falls into that category of things one wishes one had said. But Moltke recalled the kaiser greeting his criticisms with an uncharacteristic graciousness. "Here the kaiser interrupted me," he wrote, "and protested that he had no idea of this, no idea that both sides did not fight with the same weapons. He spoke in completely good faith about this—I was to tell Schlieffen that in the next maneuvers he was not to be treated any better than his opponents. I answered him that Count Schlieffen said, 'When the kaiser plays, he must win; as kaiser, he cannot be beaten by one of his own generals.'"

Whether Moltke's show of independence ever actually took place, it did not prevent the kaiser from doing what he wanted, naming

Moltke as chief of staff. The whole army was "surprised," according to Erich Ludendorff, the thickset warrior who was to become a kind of protégé. Moltke was widely considered "soft," and he had no combat experience to counteract that impression. The War Ministry even sent the kaiser a memorandum listing five reasons for Moltke's inadequacy as a prospective chief of staff: (1) He showed no inclination for hard work; (2) his years at court deprived him of a familiarity with tactical problems; (3) he lacked self-confidence and a gift for leadership; (4) he was lethargic; and (5) he often became bogged down in details. To this indictment, Dietrich von Hülsen-Haeseler, the chief of the kaiser's military cabinet, added a sixth charge: "Above everything else, he is a religious phantast, [who] believes in guardian angels, faith-healing and such nonsense."

In the atmosphere of the time, when spiritualism was both widely practiced and widely feared, this last charge was perhaps the most damaging. The kaiser actually had a conference with Moltke on the subject and demanded as a condition of his promotion that Moltke give up spiritualism. Despite his proclaimed reluctance to become chief of staff, Moltke seems to have agreed. At least, he asked his wife to be more discreet about her similar views. Still, he had further talks on the subject with the kaiser and reported as late as 1911 that he was impressed with the emperor's "possibilities."

Moltke's interest in spiritualism may even have been one of the ties that bound the two men together, but there were other connections. The flabby general was artistic, which may have irritated other generals but charmed the kaiser. He played the cello and translated Maeterlinck, and even on maneuvers, he carried Goethe's *Faust* around with him. But there were differences too. Perhaps more important than any of his eccentricities, in the eyes of his military colleagues, he had a grotesque penchant for falling off his horse during maneuvers. A chief of staff who was regarded with snickers; this was something new in the military annals of Prussia. Ludendorff was reasonably typical in writing that Moltke "was a highly cultured and clever man of unimpeachable character . . . but was an irresolute man." The chief of the military cabinet, General Moritz von Lyncker, strongly opposed Moltke's appointment and won a promise from the kaiser that he would be relieved in case war actually broke out, a promise conveniently forgotten when the time for fulfillment arrived.

It was said that the kaiser chose Moltke because it made him feel secure to have someone named Moltke in command of the armies that he knew he was incompetent to lead himself. Or that Moltke's years of staff work had given him a mastery of court etiquette, which the kaiser regarded as the equivalent of a mastery of international diplomacy. Or perhaps the kaiser just liked the shy and self-effacing Moltke, so different from the arrogant Schlieffen and the other generals who swaggered around him. In any case, regardless of the views of the ambitious generals, regardless of Moltke's own views, the kaiser appointed him chief of staff at the start of 1906. If his career had not been interrupted by war, the same qualities that recommended him to the kaiser might have carried him still further. Chancellor Bülow, whose antennae were sharply tuned to any threats to his own position, heard rumors toward the end of 1906 "that a formidable intrigue was going on against me, and that Philip Eulenburg was in the center of it, since he wanted Moltke, the chief of the General Staff, to become Imperial Chancellor." This rumor was all the more sharply barbed because Bülow could remember that Eulenburg had been one of the first to support him as chancellor. Nothing was officially known, of course, but when Bülow attended the empress's birthday party at the Neues Palais, he was pained to be "asked by several different people if it were true that Moltke was going to replace me." Remembering his ride in the Tiergarten with Moltke, Bülow was able to adopt a tone of grand disdain. "I replied that, though I should be grateful to Moltke if he freed me from the cares of office, I very much doubted whether he wanted to."

This disdain almost certainly did not end Bülow's anxiety, nor, presumably, that of Moltke. "Next morning," Bülow's account continues, "one of the Berlin papers . . . announced . . . that intrigues were afoot to put Moltke in my place. That same evening Moltke came to see me and, with his usual honorable frankness, told me how painful he found such rumors. He said he had no idea of becoming chancellor, a post for which he considered himself entirely inadequate. . . . I am still entirely convinced that this upright but unfortunate man was speaking the truth, as he always did."

Moltke had quite enough to do, of course, in working out the strategic plan that he had inherited, the plan that would lead him and his country to ruin, the Schlieffen Plan.

This was Count Schlieffen's bold but risky alternative to what he himself might have called the Moltke Plan. Ever after smashing the French in the war of 1870, the old field marshal had worried about how to combat what he considered an inevitable French desire for revenge. What made the danger even worse was the possibility that the French would act in alliance with the Russians, forcing the Germans to defend themselves on two fronts at once. Bismarck had done his best to avert that danger by signing in 1887 the so-called reinsurance treaty with Russia by which both countries promised to stay neutral in almost any war involving the other. When Bismarck's successors foolishly let the treaty lapse in 1890, the Russians naturally turned to the French for support, and their new alliance of 1891 was reinforced by a military agreement the following year. Amid the diplomatic maneuvering, Moltke had been planning for a two-front war during the 1870s and 1880s. France's postwar recovery and its development of new fortifications in the northeast made him doubt that he could repeat his great triumph of 1870–1871. "If we must fight two wars . . ." he wrote in 1879, "then, in my opinion, we should exploit in the west the great advantages which the Rhine and our powerful fortifications offer to the defensive and should employ all the fighting forces which are not absolutely indispensable [in the west] for an imposing offensive against the east." He did not want, though, to be lured into any imitation of Napoleon's disastrous invasion. "To follow up a victory in the Kingdom of Poland by a pursuit into the Russian interior would be of no interest to us," he said. Moltke's cautious strategy obviously foresaw no overwhelming victory in either east or west but rather a kind of stalemate that could lead to a negotiated settlement. "If war, which has now for more than ten years been hanging like a sword of Damocles over our heads—if war breaks out, one cannot foresee how long it will last or how it will end," the field marshal said in 1890 in one of his last speeches to the Reichstag, almost exactly anticipating what his nephew would tell the kaiser fifteen years later. "It is the Great Powers of Europe, armed as they never were before, which are now entering the arena against each other. There is not one of these that can be so completely overcome in one, or even in two campaigns that it will be forced to declare itself vanquished or to conclude an onerous peace. . . . Gentlemen, it may be a Seven Years' War, it may be a Thirty Years' War; and woe be to him who sets Europe in flames."

Schlieffen, who became chief of staff in 1891, considered these the counsels of pessimism and old age. A generation younger than Moltke (he was born in 1833), he had served in the Uhlans and joined the general staff in 1865, in time to serve as a staff officer in both 1866 and 1870. He believed in Clausewitz's theory that a commander should primarily seek a decisive battle, but unlike Moltke, Schlieffen argued in a memo to the kaiser in 1892 that this kind of battle should not be fought in the east. As Moltke had been somewhat daunted by the new fortifications that the French had built in their northeast, Schlieffen was impressed by the Russians' new fortifications around Warsaw. And like every general who had grown up under the shadow of Napoleon, he was haunted by the Russians' ability to withdraw into their vast territory, there to entangle their enemies in an exhausting war of attrition. In case of a two-front war, Schlieffen argued, "the whole of Germany must throw itself upon *one* enemy, the strongest, most powerful, most dangerous enemy, and that can only be France." His solution was to organize an irresistible right wing and then smash through the French frontier to the north of Metz, through the lands that old Moltke had conquered in 1870. "It is essential to form a strong right wing," Schlieffen wrote, "to win the battles with its help, to pursue the enemy relentlessly with this strong wing, forcing him to retreat again and again. . . . By attacks on their left flank we must try at all costs to drive the French eastward against their Moselle fortresses, against the Jura and Switzerland. The French army must be annihilated." As he kept refining his plan, envisioning a vast encirclement that would roll all the way to Paris and then sweep around behind the capital, Schlieffen kept adding to the strength of his right wing until it totaled fifty-four divisions, leaving only eight to defend the upper Rhine and only ten to block any threat from Russia. If the French attempted to attack the weak defenses in southern Germany, they would be sucked into the great encirclement, much as Hannibal had surrounded and devoured the Roman center in his classic victory at Cannae. But Schlieffen soon saw that his gigantic right wing did not have enough room to carry out its assigned movements. His solution was simply to expand his field of maneuver. As early as 1897, he declared, "An offensive which seeks to wheel around Verdun must not shrink from violating the neutrality of Belgium as well as of Luxembourg."

This was a very serious political miscalculation, which was to play a major part in bringing Britain into the war. Though Schlieffen showed his plan not only to the kaiser but also to Chancellor Theobald von Bethmann-Hollweg, neither of them seems to have understood the implicit consequences any better than he did. In 1905, when he presented to the younger Moltke the "final" version of what now became known as the Schlieffen Plan, he dismissed the whole question of the Low Countries' neutrality. "The neutrality of Luxembourg, Belgium and the Netherlands must be violated," he wrote. "The violation of Luxembourg neutrality will have no important consequences other than protests. The Netherlands regard England allied to France no less as an enemy than does Germany. It will be possible to come to an agreement with them. Belgium will probably offer resistance." As for the military effect of any British intervention, Schlieffen expected that an expeditionary force of as many as 100,000 British troops might well land at Antwerp, but he added: "They will be shut up there, together with the Belgians." As the Germans swept westward, he said, "let the last man on the right brush the Channel with his sleeve." British naval power seems to have played no part whatever in his planning.

Schlieffen undoubtedly felt considerable misgivings about leaving his grand strategy to be carried out by someone else. His dying words were reported to be: "Remember: keep the right wing strong." Moltke undoubtedly felt the same at having to carry out a plan bearing the name of his predecessor. As early as 1904, he wrote to his wife: "From time to time Schlieffen asks for my opinion, and this is almost never in accordance with his own. One could not imagine a greater contrast than in our two ways of looking at things." Schlieffen's plan, as they both knew, was that of a gambler, not a reckless adventurer but someone who carefully calculates all the risks, and then, having made his calculations, stakes everything on his chosen course. Moltke was too thoughtful and too anxious for such hazards. He could not shut his eyes to all the things that might go wrong; he could not escape the sense that it was his duty to foresee all the dangers and to forestall them. "I lack the capacity," as Bülow had quoted him, "for risking all on a single throw."

It was all very well for Schlieffen to predict that any French offensive in Lorraine would be swallowed in the German trap, but suppose the trap didn't hold? Suppose the French broke through and seized the wealth of the Ruhr? Suppose they curved northward and cut off the supply lines to Schlieffen's advancing right wing? Suppose they swept all the way to Berlin while the Germans were marching to Paris? Haunted by specters like these, Moltke began subverting the Schlieffen Plan, diluting and weakening its essential idea of committing everything to a smashing blow by the right wing. When more troops became available, Moltke added them not to the right wing but to the left, to the defense of Lorraine and the upper Rhine. According to Schlieffen's influential disciples and admirers, Moltke betrayed the Schlieffen Plan, which ultimately failed because Moltke lacked the courage and determination to carry it out. This widespread condemnation may be too harsh, however. An Israeli military analyst named Jehuda L. Wallach has demonstrated that Schlieffen's array of forces in 1905 included a number of units that existed only on paper, and that when Moltke acquired new units in 1914, he increased his left wing from eight divisions to sixteen but kept his right wing at Schlieffen's strength, with fifty-four divisions deployed between Metz and Aachen. To do that, he weakened his eastern force from ten divisions to nine. More generally, Moltke's son Adam announced long afterward (in 1958) that his father had decided, on taking office, to carry out Schlieffen's plan. "But while judging the different circumstances brought on by the course of time," Adam Moltke wrote, "he changed his mind on the steps to be taken, and was therefore compelled to create a 'Moltke Plan' corresponding to his strategic considerations."

Moltke was somewhat more perceptive than Schlieffen in seeing the dangers of attacking the Low Countries. "I cannot agree that the envelopment demands the violation of Dutch neutrality in addition to Belgian," he wrote. "A hostile Holland at our back could have disastrous consequences for the advance of the German Army to the West, particularly if England should use the violation of Belgian neutrality as a pretext for entering the war against us. A neutral Holland secures our rear. . . . Furthermore, it will be very important to have in Holland a country whose neutrality allows us to have imports and supplies. She must be the windpipe that enables us to breathe. However awkward it may be, the advance through Belgium must therefore take place without violation of Dutch territory."

In sparing Holland, though, Moltke committed himself to the invasion of Belgium. He was convinced that the Germans needed to control the Belgian railroad centers of Liège and Namur. "It is of the greatest importance," he wrote, "to take at least Liège at an early stage, in order to have the railway in one's hands." So important was this that he wanted troops assigned to seize Liège by a coup de main "immediately war is declared." German diplomats had hoped to justify the invasion of Belgium on the ground that the French planned a similar invasion, but Moltke's belief in the need for a surprise attack against Liège committed Germany to the dangerous mistake of invading neutral Belgium regardless of what the French did.

Moltke's greatest miscalculation in all this was, not unlike the miscalculation of his uncle before 1870, his assumption about the inevitability of war. As early as 1912, when fighting broke out in the Balkans and the great powers lined up in much the same way they would array themselves in 1914, Moltke told a meeting of the kaiser's war council: "I believe war to be unavoidable and the sooner and the better." When even the pugnacious Admiral Tirpitz argued for delay, Moltke offered the interventionist's traditional justification: that the army faced "an increasingly unfavorable position" because "the enemies are arming more strongly than we."

The kaiser shared this gloomy prognosis and saw it as a great tribal conflict. "There is about to be a *racial struggle* between the Teutons and the Slavs . . ." he wrote to a friend in 1912. "In it the future of the

Habsburg monarchy and the *existence* of our country . . . are at stake."
Moltke dutifully echoed his master's hallucinations in a letter to General Franz Conrad von Hötzendorf, chief of the Austro-Hungarian general staff, in 1913: "I continue to think that a European war must come in the end and that this will essentially be a struggle between the Germanic and the Slav races. It is the duty of all states which are the standard bearers of German culture to prepare for this. . . ."

By the following May, however, Moltke had shifted from preparing for war to provoking it. After a state luncheon in Potsdam, the general drove back to Berlin with Foreign Minister Gottlieb von Jagow and presented his dark premonitions. "The prospects of the future oppressed him heavily," Jagow recalled in a memoir written several years later. "In two–three years Russia would have completed her armaments. The military superiority of our enemies would then be so great that he did not know how we could overcome them. Today we would still be a match for them. In his opinion there was no alternative to making preventive war in order to defeat the enemy while we still had a chance of victory. The chief of general staff therefore proposed that I should conduct a policy with the aim of provoking a war in the near future. Moltke was not a man who lusted after the laurels of war. In our first conversation, at the beginning of 1913, I had been able to observe that he regarded the possibility of war with great gravity but without desiring a conflict. His present position was therefore all the more thought-provoking."

Jagow responded rather like a maiden hearing an improper proposal: "I countered that I was not prepared to cause a preventive war, and I reminded him of Bismarck's words, that one could not see what cards were held by Providence." Neither of them could know that the cards held by Providence would soon trump all of theirs.

• • •

To anyone trying to understand the affairs of mankind, it must seem absurd—ludicrous—that a major war could be started by an eighteen-year-old Serbian student. Gavrilo Princip did not actually start the war, of course. For fully a month after he murdered Archduke Franz Ferdinand, the heir to the Austro-Hungarian empire, the world remained quite at peace—enjoying one of the softest and most beautiful summers that anyone could remember—but the absurdity began to reverberate, creating new absurdities. The complicated diplomatic arrangements that Bismarck had designed to keep the peace now evolved into complicated diplomatic arrangements that made peace almost impossible. The younger Moltke, who had played an important part in that evolution, knew that the German army's commitment to the Schlieffen Plan committed Germany, once mobilized, to an invasion of Belgium and France. "Two mobilized armies like the German and the French will not be able to stand side by side without resorting to war . . ." he told the kaiser. "Germany, when it mobilizes against Russia, must also reckon on a war with France." And this, he had warned, would be a prolonged war of nations, exhausting even to the winner.

Princip presumably had none of that in mind that morning when he saw the archduke's limousine, which had taken a wrong turn, stop to turn around just at the corner of the Appel Quay where Princip himself was waiting and wondering what to do next. Acting almost automatically once the long-planned moment appeared so close before him, he pulled out his Browning pistol and fired two shots at the archduke and his wife, Sophie. She slumped over the archduke's knees, blood gushing from a wound in her abdomen, blood soaking through her white silk dress and onto the bouquet of red and white roses in her hand. "*Sopherl, Sopherl, stirb nicht!* [Don't die, little Sophie!]" the archduke gasped. "*Bleib am Leben für unsere Kinder.* [Stay alive for our children.]" A bodyguard clinging to the running board noticed that the archduke himself was slumping forward as the car leaped ahead. He asked if the archduke was in pain. "It's nothing," the archduke muttered again and again as his mouth filled with blood. By the time the church clocks of Sarajevo struck 11 A.M. the two victims were both dead.

Princip, who could probably imagine the fate that awaited him at the hands of the Austrian police, put his pistol to his head, but someone in the crowd on the Appel Quay snatched it away from him. He bit into a cyanide pill, but a policeman clubbed him on the head and knocked the poison out of his mouth. He was beaten unconscious then and hauled off to the police station, where he was tied to an overhead beam so that only his toes touched the ground. Then the interrogation began, of Princip and a half-dozen accomplices. And they talked, of course, trying to keep a few details secret but spilling enough so that their interrogators knew that the operation had been directed, armed, and financed by Colonel Dragutin Dimitrijević, who was director of the Intelligence Bureau of the Serbian general staff and also leader of a sinister organization called Ujedinjeje ili Smrt (Union or Death) and widely known as the Black Hand. The Serbian government's exact connection with this terrorist network is still murky, as is usual in such operations, but the Austrian police learned enough to persuade General Conrad that Vienna should inflict a very severe punishment on the Serbian regime. A handsome and elegant figure, widely admired as a military technician, Conrad had wanted for years to demolish Serbia and all its dreams of creating a greater Serbia. "We must take the first opportunity of settling accounts with our most vulnerable enemy," he said in a memo to Emperor Francis Joseph in 1907; and to Foreign Minister Leopold von Berchtold in 1912: "The way out of our difficulties is to lay Serbia low without fear of consequences." His chief opponent in this strategy had been the late Franz Ferdinand, who resolutely opposed all talk of war against Serbia. At one point, he remarked that if Austria-Hungary annexed Serbia, it would acquire nothing but some plum orchards, pastures filled with goat droppings, and a lot of ruthless killers. From the Serbian point of view, of course, Austria had already provoked the hatred of its Slavic subjects by annexing Bosnia-Herzegovina in 1908; and Vienna administered its Slavic territories with the mixture of brutality and incompetence that had become the trademark of the Habsburgs. The site of Franz Ferdinand's murder is still marked by a black plaque that says: "Here, in this historical place, Gavrilo Princip was the initiator of liberty, on the day of St. Vitus, the 28th of June, 1914."[1]

The act of assassination tends to shift history's judgments—an ugly crime with ugly consequences. No matter how idealistic Princip may have appeared, no matter how oppressed the Serbs, their plaque to Princip, in Winston Churchill's words, "records his infamy and their own." Nobody really mourned the archduke as a man. He was a choleric figure, subject to blind rages. He seems to have loved his Sophie, but their marriage was marked mainly by endless quarrels with the court protocol officials who constantly tried to humiliate the morganatic wife by insisting on her lack of a royal pedigree. Even at their funeral, she was placed in a smaller coffin, which lay at a lower level than that of her husband.

The one man probably most responsible for turning this assassination into an international bloodbath was the Austrian chief of staff, Conrad von Hötzendorf. The day after the killing, while Croatian and Muslim mobs plundered Serbian shops and homes throughout Bosnia,

---

[1] Like many of the millions killed in the war inspired by his "initiation of liberty," Princip died a slow and agonizing death. Locked up in the Theresienstadt prison that was later to become a Nazi concentration camp, he never got proper medical attention for the broken rib and crushed arm he had suffered at the time of the assassination. The arm became tuberculous and infected. He tried three times to commit suicide. His arm was finally amputated in 1917. Though handcuffs could no longer be used, he was kept in heavy leg irons in a windowless cell where he died in the spring of 1918, just as Ludendorff was organizing his "final" offensive on the western front.

under the benevolent surveillance of the Austrian police, the Serbian government sent Vienna its less-than-grief-stricken condolences, promising that it would "most loyally do everything to prove that it would not tolerate within its borders the fostering of any agitation . . . calculated to disturb our already delicate relations with Austria-Hungary." This was hardly enough for General Conrad, who understandably feared a loss of control over the restive Slavs within the Austro-Hungarian empire. At a cabinet meeting on June 29, he spoke fiercely of crushing the skull of the Serbian serpent that was hissing at Austria's heels. The Austrian ministers trembled at the prospects. How would Conrad defend them from the hordes of Russians who stood pledged to protect their Slavic brothers in Belgrade? Conrad still had his Berlin card to play. He had long been in regular consultation on this very question with his counterpart at the head of the general staff in Berlin, General von Moltke. As long ago as 1909, Conrad had written to Moltke to say that as a result of Serbian agitation against the recent Austrian annexation of Bosnia-Herzegovina, Austria might have to invade Serbia, and this might lead to Russian intervention on behalf of the Serbs. Conrad said he assumed that Germany would support Austria "in conformity with the treaty of 1879," but since France might also join the fighting on the Russian side, he needed to know how much military force Germany planned to devote to its Austrian alliance. Bismarck had planned the 1879 treaty as a purely defensive agreement, and he had specifically warned: "We must not encourage the tendencies to which the Austrians are prone by pledging the armed forces of Germany for the sake of . . . Catholic ambitions in the Balkans. . . . For us Balkan questions can in no case constitute a motive for war." Moltke's answer to Conrad unwisely ignored Bismarck's warning and just as unwisely accepted Conrad's assertion that Austria might soon fight Serbia and expected German military support in any such conflict. If Russia intervened, Moltke said, "that would constitute the *casus foederis* for Germany." This was a major and dangerous change in German policy, arming the Austrians for any Balkan adventures they might undertake, but Moltke was trying once again to carry out the commitment to the Schlieffen Plan which left the defense of the east largely up to the Austrians. Schlieffen himself, concentrating on the invasion of France, had treated the Austrians with his customary arrogance. An Austrian commander who met him at the funeral of the elder Moltke in 1891 found him "taciturn" and "hardly forthcoming." Military staff talks between the two countries deteriorated accordingly. Schlieffen at one point urged that the Austrians send troops to defend Prussian Silesia against any Russian offensive. The Austrians, already stretched thin in the defense of their own extensive territories, angrily refused, and the German-Austrian military talks were thereupon suspended in 1896. "Austria need not worry," Schlieffen airily remarked, "for . . . the fate of Austria will be decided not on the Bug but on the Seine."

When Conrad wrote to Moltke in 1909 to inquire about German military planning, however, Moltke quickly saw that while Austria was asking for German reinforcements in the east, Germany was even more in need of an Austrian commitment to help in keeping the Russians out of Prussia. While the Germans worried about a two-front war, so did the Austrians. To the south, they confronted Serbia, which could field an army of 400,000 men, while any intervention by Russia would threaten them from the Polish frontier in the northeast. Unlike the Germans, the Austrians had only a crude railway system to shift troops from one front to the other. Conrad's main ambition was to strike fiercely at the Serbs; his main worry was that he would not know the Russians' intentions until he had already committed most of his troops to the Balkans. Conrad's provisional solution was to divide his forces in three, keeping one group of twelve divisions, known as B-Staffel, as a reserve that could be committed to either front. While prudently precautionary, though, Conrad's provisional solution obviously weakened his striking power on both fronts. So he wanted Moltke to promise a German offensive against Russia. Moltke, on the other hand, wanted Conrad to promise an offensive in southern Poland so that the Russians could not march into Prussia.

In the course of their correspondence, each general somewhat rashly promised to deliver what the other wanted. "I will not hesitate to make the attack to support the simultaneous Austrian offensive," Moltke wrote somewhat ambiguously in March 1909, grandly assuming that there would actually be an Austrian offensive. "Your excellency can count absolutely upon this assurance." Conrad also wanted to know how long Moltke thought he would need to crush the French and then start sending German reinforcements east. In a giddy state of prewar euphoria, Moltke first said he could do the job in three weeks, then in four; finally, as in Schlieffen's own timetable, Moltke said six weeks. In saying so, he forgot the warning by Shakespeare's King Henry V to the herald Mountjoy: "The man that once did sell the lion's skin / While the beast liv'd was kill'd with hunting him."

Moltke was cautious enough not to make these rash promises entirely on his own. His letters to Conrad noted that copies were going to both the kaiser and Chancellor von Bülow. The kaiser characteristically took up Moltke's new policy as his own creation and trumpeted his promise to support the Austrians in any crisis. "You may rest assured that I stand behind you and am ready to draw the sword," the kaiser told Foreign Minister Berchtold in 1913, ostentatiously placing a hand on his stage-prop sword. Some lesser officials tried to mute these trumpetings. During the first days after the assassination of Franz Ferdinand, the German ambassador to Vienna, Count Heinrich von Tschirschky, took pains to warn the Habsburg authorities "with great emphasis and seriousness against hasty measures in settling accounts with Serbia."

The ministers agreed that there should be no hasty measures. Berchtold carried that message to the eighty-four-year-old Emperor Francis Joseph when he went to propose a course of action. Nothing hasty. Austria must appear moderate and reasonable in all its moves, and it must coordinate those moves closely with Berlin. Fine, said the emperor, he himself would write to Kaiser William to make sure that they agreed on everything. Berchtold himself drafted the letter, which spoke cautiously of the need to "neutralize Serbia as a political power factor." Berchtold's own chef du cabinet, Count Alexander Hoyos, a young conservative of strongly anti-Serb views, volunteered to carry the letter to Berlin himself, and there he explained at the German foreign ministry that the "neutralization" of Serbia meant its destruction by military force. When informed of this, the kaiser renewed his vow that he would not fail the Austrians. "His Majesty," according to the next day's cable from the Austrian Embassy in Berlin to the foreign ministry in Vienna, "authorized me to convey to our august sovereign . . . that we may count on the full support of the German Reich. He quite understands that . . . if we really recognize the necessity of military measures against Serbia, he would deplore our not taking advantage of the present moment, which is so favorable to us."

The kaiser then boarded his yacht *Hohenzollern* and set sail for a cruise off Norway. This fitted neatly into the Austrian strategy of feigning moderation and reasonable restraint, of making no warlike noises while preparing for war. After assigning a team of assistants to draft the diplomatic note that would set forth Austria's terms to Serbia, Foreign Minister Berchtold began his diplomatic rounds to spread soothing messages. He assured the French ambassador that Austria's note to Serbia would be "reasonable." The British ambassador was quite persuaded of Austrian moderation. "Not a word was let drop that a crisis impended," he reported. Berchtold also requested General Conrad to join in the game. "I recommend," he said to the chief of staff, "that you and the minister of war leave Vienna for your vacation so as to keep up an appearance that nothing is going on." Conrad dutifully took himself to Innichen, a small village high in the Dolomites, and diligently kept up an appearance that nothing was going on. Prominent Germans did much the same. General Moltke repaired once again to his favorite spa, Carlsbad. Foreign Minister Jagow went honeymooning on Lake Lucerne, and Admiral Tirpitz took his family to the Engadine.

Led on by the leaders of the Central Powers, other European statesmen took advantage of the beautiful summer. Like the kaiser, French President Raymond Poincaré went cruising in the North Sea. At home, the Parisian newspapers were primarily concerned with the opening of the trial of Henriette Caillaux, wife of the finance minister and former premier, who had fired six bullets into the editor of *Le Figaro*, Gaston Calmette, because he had published love letters from Caillaux to her when they were both married to other people.

On July 21, after nearly two weeks of secret meetings at the foreign ministry on the Ballhausplatz, Foreign Minister Berchtold rode to the holiday resort of Bad Ischl to discuss his note to Serbia with his emperor.

"The note is pretty sharp," the emperor said, according to Berchtold's memoirs.

"It has to be, Your Majesty," the minister replied.

"It has to be indeed," said the emperor. "You will join us for lunch."

The note had actually been read and royally initialed and sent to Belgrade the previous day. It quickly ended the peaceful tone of all those official vacations. It was, in the words of the British foreign secretary, Sir Edward Grey, "the most formidable document ever addressed by one state to another," or in Winston Churchill's account, "an ultimatum such as had never been penned in modern times before." The Austrian note demanded that Serbia, as penance for the murder of Franz Ferdinand, abandon the very essence of its sovereignty and independence. Specifically, it insisted that Serbia, first, publish an official apology for all Serbian acts, official and unofficial, against Austria; second, eliminate all anti-Austrian materials from Serbian schools and newspapers; third, dismiss all army officers and government officials guilty of anti-Austrian acts, including a number of such officials to be named by Austria, and fourth, accept the participation of the Austrian police in the suppression and apprehension of all anti-Austrian subversives. And finally, all these measures must be undertaken within forty-eight hours.

The Serbian premier, Nikola Pašić, was out campaigning for reelection when this official death threat arrived at 6 P.M. on July 23, and it was 8 P.M before he heard the details over the telephone. He returned immediately to Belgrade and immersed himself in meetings on how to answer the Austrian note. There was, of course, no reasonable way to answer. The Austrians hadn't really expected their terms to be accepted, didn't even want them accepted; they wanted war. But this immediately raised the question of Russian and German reactions, and the Germans immediately began to worry about their perilous commitment to Austrian belligerence. Foreign Minister Jagow said he told the Austrian ambassador "that the contents of the Austrian note to Serbia seemed pretty stiff and going beyond its purpose. . . . I expressed my pained surprise . . . that the decisions of the Austrian government had been communicated to us so tardily that we were deprived of the possibility of giving our views on them. The Chancellor, too, to whom I at once submitted the text of the ultimatum, thought it was too harsh." Jagow also tried to spread this disavowal by cabling Germany's main foreign embassies that "we have had no influence of any kind on the wording of Austria's note to Serbia, and no more opportunities to take sides in any way before its publication."

Though the Austrian note was deliberately written so as to be unacceptable—and carefully timed just after Poincaré's meeting with Tsar Alexander ended, so that Serbia's two main supporters could not coordinate their responses—Serbia surprised everyone by virtually accepting the unacceptable. Just fifteen minutes after the expiration of the Austrian deadline, Serbia's white-bearded Premier Pašić marched up to the Austrian embassy and handed in Serbia's official answer, a document covered with inked alterations and corrections. The Austrian ambassador, Baron von Giesl, who had already packed his bags to return home, had to go through the motions of studying the Serbian reply. Without even asking his visitor to sit down, he hastily read through the document, noting with surprise that the Serbians agreed to one Austrian demand after another. They agreed to apologize, to suppress anti-Austrian newspapers, to dismiss suspected officials. On only one point did they resist—the Austrian demand that Austrian police take part in the investigations. That, said the Serbs, would be "a violation of the Serbian constitution and of the law of criminal procedure." On the other hand, the Serbs offered to submit all differences to arbitration by either the Great Powers or the International Court at the Hague. But the one rejection of one demand was all that Baron Giesl needed or wanted. That made the groveling response "unsatisfactory," and so he announced that Austria was breaking off diplomatic relations with Serbia. Half an hour after he had received the Serbian note, he boarded a train for Vienna.

In the capitals of Europe, the Serbian reply was read with at least as much surprise as the original Austrian note. Perhaps the most surprised reader of all was Kaiser William, newly home from the Scandinavian seas. "A brilliant achievement in a time limit of only 24 hours!" he scrawled on the margin of his copy. "More than one could have expected! A great moral success for Vienna! All reason for war is gone!" No sooner had he written this than an aide handed him a cable announcing that the Austrians, declining the honor of a moral victory, had just declared war on Serbia. Feigning forgetfulness of his own involvement, the kaiser summoned his chancellor, Bethmann-Hollweg.

"How did all this happen?" he demanded. The chancellor gasped out that he had been deceived by the Viennese, those adventurers whom Winston Churchill called Germany's "idiot ally." He offered to resign. The kaiser forbade him any such escape. "You have cooked this broth," he said. "Now you are going to eat it." The kaiser's "exaggerations were mainly meant to ring in the ears of the Foreign Office . . ." according to ex-chancellor Bülow, who was a witness to this humiliation of his successor. "He did not trust his nerves under the strain of any really critical situation. The moment there was danger His Majesty became uncomfortably conscious that he would never lead an army in the field."

According to the original German scenario, that would not be necessary. The Austrians would punish the Serbs, and the threat of German support would keep the Russians at bay, just as it had in the similar crisis over the Austrian annexation of Bosnia-Herzegovina in 1908. Since this German scenario required another Russian humiliation, however, its success now depended on what Tsar Nicholas would actually do. Like most of his fellow monarchs, Nicholas was a man of very limited intelligence, reared to believe that he should act in the national interest but also reared to confuse the national interest with that of his own family. Like most monarchs, too, he was surrounded by mendacious courtiers and inept officials whose perception of the national interest was as cloudy as his own.

Because Russia had a very large army, it was widely thought to be extremely powerful, and so it was correspondingly humiliated by the smashing victories of the Japanese in the war of 1904–1905. Its failure to retrieve Bosnia-Herzegovina from the Austrians in 1908 added to its sense that it could not tolerate one more embarrassment, particularly not at the hands of anyone Germanic. The Austrian declaration against Serbia was just such an embarrassment, since the Russians like to consider themselves the protectors of all Slavs. When the Austrians began shelling Belgrade at 5 A.M. on July 29, therefore, the tsar ordered the mobilization of all military districts along the Austrian frontier. The launching of a military attack was so slow in those days that a mobilization decree was generally considered tantamount to a declaration of war, but both sides were frightened by the prospect they had created. Russia quickly told Germany that this was a limited and defensive mobilization, not in any way aimed against Germany. Kaiser William, presuming on his cousinship with the tsar, sent him a personal telegram to urge restraint. "I fully understand how difficult it is for you and your government to face the drift of public opinion," he said, quite aware that public opinion was virtually nonexistent in tsarist Russia, feebler even than in his own domain. "Therefore . . . I am exerting my utmost influence to induce the Austrians to deal straightly[2] to arrive at a satisfactory understanding with you. I confidently hope you will help me in my efforts to smooth over difficulties that may still arise."

This disingenuous message crossed with an equally disingenuous cable from the tsar: "In this most serious moment I appeal to you to help me. An ignoble war has been declared on a weak country. The indignation in Russia, shared fully by me, is enormous. I foresee that very soon I shall be overwhelmed by pressure brought upon me and forced to take extreme measures which will lead to war. . . . I beg you in the name of our old friendship to do what you can to stop your allies from going too far." The pressure on Nicholas was simply the demand by his generals to declare total mobilization, a demand now supported by Foreign Minister Serge Sazonov, who was nonetheless still trying to promote a mediation by Britain. In Berlin Moltke argued that the tsar might still be persuaded to remain neutral. Even though Austria had already declared war on Serbia, he wrote in a long memo to Bethmann-Hollweg, that was "a purely private quarrel" designed "to burn out with a glowing iron a cancer that has constantly threatened to poison the body of Europe." Austria had mobilized only eight army corps, Moltke wrote, while the Russians were mobilizing twelve. "It cannot be denied," Moltke wrote, "that the whole thing is a masterly piece of staging on the part of Russia." And because Russia had "placed herself at the side of this criminal nation," Serbia, mankind now faced a "war which will annihilate for decades the civilization of almost all Europe." On the afternoon of

---

[2]English, of a schoolboy sort, was the only language these two monarchs had in common, so they both used it, as best they could, in this exchange of messages between "Willy" and "Nicky."

July 29, War Minister Erich von Falkenhayn urged the kaiser to declare a state of *Kriegsgefahr*, or danger of war, a preliminary to mobilization. Bethmann-Hollweg appealed for delay, and so the kaiser delayed. Moltke angrily cabled Conrad in Vienna to urge immediate mobilization and promising that Germany would soon follow. This inspired Foreign Minister Berchtold to ask a sardonic question that bothered many officials during those tense days. "Who rules in Berlin? Moltke or Bethmann?" After posing that question to the Imperial War Council, Berchtold added, "I now have the most reassuring pronouncement from responsible military quarters." Moltke's message thus inspired the council to submit the order for general mobilization to Emperor Francis Joseph for his signature.

Kaiser William, however, was still pursuing Moltke's view that the Austro-Serbian war might be kept local if only Russia would stay out of it. "It would be quite possible for Russia to remain a spectator of the Austro-Serbian conflict . . ." William suggested to the tsar. "I think a direct understanding between your government and Vienna possible and desirable and as I already telegraphed you, my government is continuing its exertions to promote it. Of course, military measures on the part of Russia which would be looked upon by Austria as threatening would precipitate a calamity we both wish to avoid." The tsar thanked the kaiser "for your conciliatory and friendly telegram" but complained that the German ambassador had been speaking "in a very different tone" and proposed that "the Austro-Serbian problem must be submitted to the Hague." Russia was already mobilizing, though, and the tsar now explained that this was "for reasons of defense on account of Austria's preparations. I hope with all my heart that these measures won't interfere with your part as mediator. . . ." That same afternoon, July 30, Foreign Minister Sazonov asked for a meeting and then told the tsar that his generals were right in demanding full mobilization because Germany and Austria were both "determined to increase their power by enslaving our natural allies in the Balkans." So the argument for preventive war triumphed once again. "You are right," the tsar said, after what Sazonov called "a terrible inner struggle." "There is nothing left for us to do but get ready for an attack upon us. . . . Give . . . my order for mobilization."

The tsar hastened to inform the kaiser that his preparations for war meant no harm. "It is technically impossible for me to suspend my military preparations," he cabled Berlin. "But as long as conversations with Austria are not broken off, my troops will refrain from taking the offensive." The kaiser was infuriated by these Russian pirouettes. "And these measures are for defense against Austria which is in no way attacking him!!!" he scribbled in the margins of the tsar's explanation. Part of his anger, of course, came from the sight of his own bluff being called. Now he would really have to support the reckless Austrians with more than trumpet calls. "I have gone to the utmost limits of the possible in my efforts to save peace," he cabled the tsar. "It is not I who will bear the responsibility for the terrible disaster which now threatens the civilized world. You and you alone can still avert it. . . ." More specifically, at Moltke's urging, he sent his aged ambassador in St. Petersburg, Count Friedrich von Pourtalès, to deliver an ultimatum demanding cancellation of the Russian mobilization within twelve hours or the kaiser would "consider himself in a state of war with Russia." Moltke strongly urged Austria to take similar action against the Russians. "It is necessary for Austria-Hungary to take counter-measures," he cabled Conrad.

Step by step, Moltke and the kaiser were now approaching the day that old Field Marshal Moltke and Bismarck had dreaded, the day when Germany would find itself fighting enemies on both its eastern and western frontiers. The French, of course, were equally pugnacious and equally complacent. For nearly half a century, the generals had been dreaming of vengeance for 1870. Marshal Joffre's celebrated Plan XVII envisioned an irresistible French invasion through the Ardennes toward Aachen and Berlin. Asked by an aide whether he thought war would come soon, Joffre calmly said that it would. "I shall fight it and I shall win," he said. "I have always succeeded in whatever I do. . . . It will be that way again."

With so many generals so eager for war—or so convinced of its inevitability—it remained for the statesmen to shrug their shoulders and talk of honor. Once the tsar had ordered full mobilization and the kaiser had sent an ultimatum demanding a halt in this mobilization, it remained only for the German ambassador to burst into tears. Just after noon on August 1, Count Pourtalès had gone to the foreign ministry to announce that the expiration of the German ultimatum meant that the two nations were at war. At 7 P.M., he returned to hand Sazonov the formal declaration of war.

"The curses of the nations will be upon you," said Sazonov.

"We are defending our honor," said Pourtalès. Then he began weeping. "Who could have thought I should be leaving St. Petersburg under such circumstances?" he said. Sazonov patted him kindly on the shoulder as he ushered him out.

Even after the kaiser had declared war, another one of his cables arrived in St. Petersburg with new demands for concessions as "the sole way to avoid endless misery." The tsar professed bewilderment. "What on earth does William mean, I thought, pretending that it still depends on me whether war is averted or not?" he recalled wondering as he prepared for a bath and bed. He went to the Empress Alexandra's room and read the kaiser's latest outburst to her. "You're not going to answer it, are you?" she asked. "Certainly not," he said.

Returning home from a visit to Belgium, Stefan Zweig found Vienna in a state of happy hysteria. "In every station placards had been put up announcing general mobilization," he wrote. "The trains were filled with fresh recruits, banners were flying, music sounded. The first shock at the news of war—the war that no one, people or government, had wanted—the war which had slipped . . . out of the clumsy hands of the diplomats who had been bluffing and toying with it, had suddenly been transformed into enthusiasm. There were parades in the street, flags, ribbons, and music burst forth everywhere, young recruits were marching triumphantly, their faces lighting up at the cheering. . . . And to be truthful, I must acknowledge that there was a majestic, rapturous, and even seductive something in this first outbreak of the people from which one could escape only with difficulty. And in spite of all my hatred and aversion for war, I should not like to have missed the memory of those first days. As never before, thousands and hundreds of thousands felt what they should have felt in peacetime, that they belonged together. . . . All differences of class, rank, and language were swamped at that moment by the rushing feeling of fraternity. . . . Each individual experienced an exaltation of his ego, he was no longer the isolated person of former times, he had been incorporated into the mass, he was part of the people, and his person, his hitherto unnoticed person, had been given meaning. . . ."

Leon Trotsky, who clung to the idea that the people wanted peace, was amazed at the fervor that animated the working classes of Vienna as they marched through the streets, shouting, "*Alle Serben müssen sterben!* [All Serbs must die!]" (His youngest son, Seryozha, "prompted, as usual, by an instinct for being contradictory," shouted, "*Hoch Serbien!* [Long live Serbia!]," which duly brought him "a black eye and experience in international politics.") Trotsky himself quietly "watched the most amazing crowd fill the fashionable Ring, a crowd in which hopes had been awakened. . . . Would it have been possible at any other time for porters, laundresses, shoemakers, apprentices . . . to feel themselves masters of the Ring?"

Ludwig Wittgenstein would have had difficulty in answering Trotsky's questions. The philosopher's father had tried to shield his family from the foreseeable calamities by transferring many of his investments to the supposed safety of the U.S. Steel Corporation, but Ludwig was in the process of giving away his share of the inheritance when war broke out. He promptly enlisted as a volunteer in the artillery, not to support the Habsburgs' charges against Serbia but to "turn into a different person." He did feel a sense of satisfaction that "things will come to an eruption once and for all," but when the authorities assigned him to operate the searchlight on a patrol boat cruising pointlessly along the Vistula, he found his fellow crewmen "unbelievably crude, stupid, and malicious," so he spent much of his time immersed in Tolstoy's *Gospel in Brief*.

Another young Austrian with intellectual ambitions felt passionate joy at what he considered the end of the old order. "To me those hours seemed like a release from the painful feelings of my youth . . ." Adolf Hitler wrote in *Mein Kampf*. "Overpowered by stormy enthusiasm, I fell down on my knees and thanked Heaven from an overflowing heart for granting me the good fortune of being permitted to live at this time. A fight for freedom had begun, mightier than the earth had ever seen; for once destiny had begun its course, the conviction dawned on even the broad masses that this time not the fate of Serbia or Austria was involved, but whether the German nation was to be or not to be."

A similar hysteria, a similar sense of emotional relief, erupted in many capitals on the start of war. A character in Alexander Solzhenitsyn's novel *August 1914* recalled that she had "seen the patriotic mob wrecking the German embassy in St. Isaac's Square [in St. Petersburg], breaking windows and throwing furniture, marbles and slashed pictures out into the street, toppling the enormous bronze horses and the bronze giants leading them from the roof to the pavement, while all the onlookers rejoiced as though what had come to them was not war but a long-awaited happiness."

The next capital to be swept by the Viennese exhilaration was almost inevitably that of the Austrians' main ally. Berlin too erupted in flag-waving parades, and the historian Friedrich Meinecke overheard one newly commissioned lieutenant cry out: "War is like Christmas!" Older Germans saw it as a catalyst for the restoration of traditional values. "At last life had regained an ideal significance," Ernst Gläser wrote in his novel *Jahrgang 1902*. "The great virtues of humanity . . . fidelity, patriotism, readiness to die for an ideal . . . were triumphing over the trading and shopkeeping spirit. . . . This was the providential lightning flash that would clear the air. . . . the war would cleanse mankind from all its impurities."

Mixed in with this ominous "idealism," however, was an element of paranoia that had long been characteristic of the Germans' view of the surrounding world. It was best summarized by their paranoid kaiser, who now felt that the war begun by Austria was all a plot against him by the uncle who had never liked him, the late King Edward VII of England. "I no longer have any doubt," he wrote on the night of July 30–31, when nobody except Austria had declared war on anyone, "that England, Russia and France have *agreed* among themselves—knowing that our treaty obligations compel us to support Austria—to use the Austro-Serb conflict as a *pretext* for waging a war of *annihilation* against us ... That is ... the situation, slowly but surely brought about by Edward VII. ... So the celebrated *encirclement* of Germany has finally become an accomplished fact, in spite of all the efforts by our politicians to prevent it. The net has suddenly been closed over our head, and the purely *anti-German policy* which England has been scornfully pursuing all over the world has won the most spectacular victory. . . . Even after his death Edward VII is stronger than I, though I am still alive!"

Britain actually was deeply divided about entering the war at all. Many felt sympathy for the Austrians on the murder of their archduke, but the Balkans were far away, mysterious, and the idea of fighting a war over Serbia seemed almost inconceivable. With France, there was an *entente cordial,* but that was far less than a military alliance. The threat of an attack on Belgium did raise some British hackles, for London had formally guaranteed Belgian neutrality (as had Berlin) ever since 1839, and there were some geopolitical theorists who argued that Belgium represented Britain's frontier on the European mainland. The Liberal prime minister, Herbert Henry Asquith, was inclined to be cautious. A Yorkshire lawyer, he was once described as "excruciatingly moderate," or, in another version, "moderately imperialist, moderately humorous, moderately progressive, and, being the most fastidious of Liberal politicians, only moderately evasive."

"Happily," he wrote to King George V of the ominous developments on the continent, "there seems to be no reason why we should be anything more than spectators." And in his diary on July 31: "Are we to go in or stand aside? Of course everybody longs to stand aside." The Tory press, notably the *Daily Mail* and the rest of the Northcliffe Group, disagreed vehemently, preaching sternly on the demands of honor. The Liberal *Daily News,* by contrast, denounced this warlike preaching as "madness" and "infamy." Such worthies as Thomas Hardy, G. M. Trevelyan, Norman Angell, Keir Hardie, the lord mayor of Manchester, and the bishops of Lincoln and Hereford all issued pronouncements urging that Britain remain neutral. "No such crime is ever committed without an appeal to honor," the Labor Party leader Ramsay MacDonald protested in Parliament. "It was so with the Crimean War, it was so with the South African War; it is so today."

The talk of honor was indeed something of a pretext. In 1887, when there was talk of a war between France and Germany, the British government told the Belgians not to expect any help from Britain if either neighbor violated Belgian neutrality. Asquith's cabinet was no less divided than the country as a whole. Winston Churchill, who reveled in the post of first lord of the Admiralty, did not actually insist that Britain enter the conflict ("It would be a wicked war," he wrote to his wife), but he was determined to keep the navy in a very pugnacious state of readiness. When the cabinet rejected his request to order a full naval mobilization, he ordered it on his own, "against cabinet decision," as Churchill later put it, "and without legal authority." The cabinet similarly opposed Grey's plan to promise the French ambassador that the German navy would not be allowed to pass through the Straits of Dover to attack the French coast; Grey made the promise anyway. Two ministers promptly resigned.

Grey was clearly on Churchill's side of the scales, and he indicated that he would resign as foreign secretary if Britain abandoned France at the critical moment. But as Britain's chief diplomat, he felt obliged to carry out Asquith's cautious views. One of his first moves was to ask the Austrians to extend the forty-eight-hour deadline in their ultimatum to Serbia. The Austrians refused. Then he tried to organize a conference of the great powers to mediate the dispute. The Germans and Austrians raised objections. He asked both the French and Germans to promise that they would respect Belgian neutrality. The French agreed; the Germans didn't answer. And time was running out.

Despite the Hohenzollerns' delight in trying on the costume of "supreme warlord," there were certain constitutional restrictions on the kaiser's ability to wage war. The most important, probably, was the requirement of Reichstag approval for military spending. It is not easy, as Americans learned at the time of the Tonkin Gulf resolution and again at the start of the Persian Gulf war, for legislators to stand up and cast their votes against a chief of state who wants to go to war. And so it was that Germany's Social Democrats, who had become the largest party in the Reichstag by winning almost 35 percent of the votes and 110 seats in the 1912 elections, now confronted the opportunity to stop the national war machine from going into action. It was a challenge that they failed miserably.

As late as July 25, the Socialists were staging large antiwar demonstrations throughout Germany. The party had traditionally opposed war, since the working classes traditionally provided most of the casualties, but it had always claimed to support the nation's right to defend itself. This was a central issue now since the kaiser and his ministers insisted that Germany was being threatened by an encircling ring of hostile neighbors. Watching the nationalist fervor sweeping the country, including the working classes, the Socialist leaders gathered to plan their strategy. They resented the Conservatives' taunt that they were *regierungsunfähig* or unfit to govern. Most of them frankly favored the preparations for war, but the party's executive committee decided on July 30 to send their chief foreign-policy expert, Hermann Müller, to Paris and Brussels to see if an antiwar coalition could be formed. Any prospects of such a coalition received a shattering blow the very next day when a deranged Parisian art student named Vilain climbed onto a windowsill of the Café du Croissant on the Rue Mont-martre and fired two shots into the neck of the Socialist leader Jean Jaurès. Jaurès had just returned from making a speech in Brussels where he had urged Russia to follow "counsels of prudence and patience," adding: "If Russia should take no notice, then it is our duty to declare: We know only one treaty—the treaty that binds us to humanity." It seems hard to believe that Vilain acted entirely on his own—he claimed that he shot Jaurès for opposing the extension of military service to three years—but the French Socialists were in no mood to negotiate with the Germans when they had the opportunity for a great symbolic ceremony. So they staged a mammoth funeral procession for Jaurès—carrying thousands of red banners through the streets—while the government lurched on toward mobilization.

The German government formally asked the French what they would do about the Russo-German war that had just been declared. The French carefully postponed an answer. Russian Ambassador Alexander Isvolsky called on President Poincaré at 2 A.M. on August 1 to ask the same question. France and Russia had a formal alliance, but the French legislature had neither seen nor approved the actual text, which promised that an attack on either would require both to mobilize immediately and take action "so that Germany will have to fight at the same time in the East and in the West." Poincaré promised that the legislature would follow his government; to the Germans, he sent word only that "France will act in accordance with her inter-ests." At nine o'clock that morning, August 1, General Joseph Joffre went to the War Ministry to argue that France's interests required an immediate mobilization order. He had to wait for the cabinet to approve, but the cabinet did approve, and at three-thirty the mobilization order was turned over to the post office. At 4 P.M., the first mobilization poster appeared on the Place de la Concorde. Since the French were also playing the victims-of-aggression game, though, the mobilization order was accompanied by a presidential order withdrawing all troops to a line ten kilometers behind the German and Belgian frontiers.

Within an hour of the French mobilization, the Germans ordered full mobilization, too, and formally declared war on Russia. The next day, August 2, without any declaration of war, the Germans marched into Luxembourg and delivered an ultimatum to Belgium, demanding the right to march across Belgian territory (on the way to France). That same day, with war virtually at hand, the German Socialists met once again to argue about their policy. The government had done its bit by promising them that although the kaiser had just proclaimed a "state of siege," which suspended many civil rights and imposed censorship, there would be no repression, as in Bismarck's time, if nobody interfered with the war effort. The labor unions, which always tend to keep a close eye on material considerations, thereupon called off all current strikes. Still, the Reichstag was to meet on August 4, and the 110 Socialist deputies had to decide whether to cast their votes for war. A majority of them favored that course, including the twenty-five or so who represented the unions. Only fourteen opposed it. One of them was cochairman Hugo Haase, but even he finally decided that party unity required him to support the majority. Virtually the only holdout was young Karl Liebknecht, who lived to organize the unsuccessful Spartacus revolution of 1918–1919 and to be murdered by soldiers at the end of it.

So the Social Democrats sat docilely in their places when the kaiser told the Reichstag that Germany was being attacked by its encircling enemies. They felt a warm glow of patriotic subservience when he exonerated them of partisanship, declaring, "I do not know parties any longer, I know only Germans." Thus praised for their prudent submissiveness, the heirs of Karl Marx joined in the unanimous approval for a war credit of 5 billion marks.

The generals were getting impatient. Just after 5 P.M. on August 1, Undersecretary Arthur Zimmermann received a phone call at the Foreign Ministry in Berlin, then turned to the nearby editor of the *Berliner Tageblatt* and said, "Moltke wants to know whether things can start." Even while they felt themselves hurried along by the generals, though, the diplomats continued their efforts to find some kind of settlement.

During one of Sir Edward Grey's last maneuvers, he somehow persuaded the German ambassador that there was a way to avoid war. The ambassador, Prince Karl Max Lichnowsky, was an ardent Anglophile who may have prided himself too highly on his mastery of English. Possibly Grey in turn prided himself too highly on his mastery of the subtle language of diplomacy. Or perhaps this was simply a demonstration that delicate international maneuvers should never be conducted by telephone.

In any case, after his phone conversation with Grey, Lichnowsky cabled Berlin that Grey had said "that in case we did not attack France, England would remain neutral and would guarantee France's neutrality." This naturally caused amazement in Berlin. The orders had already gone out for German troops to seize a railroad station in Luxembourg, the first step to the invasion of Belgium and then of France. The time set for this attack was now only an hour off, and here the British were promising to keep France out of the war entirely if . . . But this required that Moltke call off his invasion. Moltke had already left the royal palace, and nobody seemed to know where he was. An officer was sent racing off to find him. Almost miraculously, he succeeded in bringing the general back to the palace. Moltke found the kaiser in a state of great excitement—he had already called for champagne—at the prospect of going to war only against Russia. "'So we simply march with the entire army to the East,' the kaiser said to me," Moltke wrote in recalling this extraordinary scene. For once in his life, the general refused to obey. "I replied to his majesty that this was impossible. The deployment of a million troops cannot be improvised. It is the product of a full year's hard work, and once set in motion, it cannot be altered. If your majesty insists on leading the entire army to the east, it will not be a combat-ready army but rather a confused crowd of armed men without organization or supplies."

Moltke's argument was quite justified, for the German deployment, once it got under way, was a truly awesome project. Along four main trunk lines from the interior of Germany, a steady stream of trains clanked toward the French and Belgian frontiers at a rate of about one train every ten minutes, day and night. Each army corps, and there were forty of them, required 170 railroad cars for its officers, nearly 1,000 for infantry troops, and as many again for supplies, guns, ammunition, food, tents, medical wagons. When it was all done, a million and a half men had been mobilized for combat within thirteen days. But the kaiser, accustomed to governing by whim, was "very displeased" by his objections, Moltke said. Then he lashed out with an accusation exquisitely calculated to unnerve and humiliate his chief of staff. "Your uncle," he said, "would have given me a different answer."

In recalling the scene, Moltke immediately began trying to defend and excuse himself. "I have never made any pretense of being the equal of the field marshal," he wrote. "But nobody seemed to realize that it would cause a catastrophe for us if we were to march off to Russia with our entire army, with a mobilized France at our rear. How could England—assuming its goodwill—ever prevent France from falling on our backs ...? The atmosphere became more and more excited, and I stood there all alone. Finally, I succeeded in convincing his majesty that our deployment, with the main strength against France, with a weak defensive force against Russia, had been thought out and must systematically run its course if he wanted to avoid the most disastrous confusion. I said to the kaiser that after a completed deployment, it would be possible to convey a strong part of the army to the east so long as the deployment itself was not altered. Otherwise, I could not accept the responsibility."

Reluctantly accepting Moltke's reasoning—which was surely correct—the kaiser now tried to gain credit from his "restraint." He sent a telegram to King George V of England saying that because of "technical reasons" the German mobilization could not be canceled, but he added: "If France offers me neutrality, which must be guaranteed by the British fleet and army, I shall of course refrain from attacking France and employ my troops elsewhere. I hope France will not become nervous."

Prince Lichnowsky, during all this, had not neglected to have further conversations with Sir Edward Grey, in the course of which he realized that he had misunderstood the foreign secretary's position. Britain proposed to guarantee French neutrality not just if Germany refrained from attacking France but if it refrained from attacking either France or Russia. In other words, if the war were limited to the Balkans, France would stay out of it. Even that, Lichnowsky surrounded with diplomatic fog. "A positive proposal by England," he cabled Berlin later that evening, "is, on the whole, not in prospect."

Moltke was utterly crushed by the kaiser's contempt for his judgment. *"Fast verzweifelt"* is his term, meaning almost despairing, almost hopeless. According to the German plan, the 16th Division was to seize the Luxembourg railroad on the first day of the offensive because, in Moltke's words, "we had to secure the Luxembourg railroad against a French surprise attack." But now Chancellor Bethmann-Hollweg argued that no such seizure of the Luxembourg railroad could be attempted because it would "make the proposed British guarantee [of French neutrality] illusory." The kaiser agreed without even consulting his chief of staff. "While I stood by," Moltke wrote, "the kaiser, without asking me, walked over to an adjutant and ordered him to telegraph immediately to the 16th Division to command it not to enter Luxembourg." Moltke said of this snub: "I was overwhelmed, as if my heart were breaking."

Once again, he saw all his laboriously organized plans swept into chaos. "Again we faced the danger that our deployment would be reduced to confusion," he wrote. "What that means can only be judged in full by those who know what a complicated labor, organized down to its smallest detail, a deployment is. Where each train must be scheduled to the minute, every alteration must have a disastrous effect. I tried respectfully to convince his majesty of this, that we needed the Luxembourg railroads and had to secure them. I was dismissed with the remark that I could use other railroads. The orders stood. With that I was dismissed. It is impossible to describe the mood in which I came home. I was broken and burst into tears of despair. When the orders to the 16th Division were laid before me, confirming the orders that had been given by telephone, I threw down the pen on the table and said, 'I am not signing these. . . .' 'Do what you want with them,' I said to Lieutenant Colonel von Tappen. 'I am not signing them.'"

Moltke sat idly in his room until 11 P.M., when he was suddenly recalled to the royal palace. The kaiser received him in a nightshirt. Having now learned of Lichnowsky's misunderstanding, which had made the previous scene with Moltke meaningless, the kaiser had prepared a new humiliation for his chief of staff. "Now," he grandly declared, "you can do what you like." Moltke promptly telegraphed the 16th Division, telling it to ignore all previous orders and seize the Luxembourg railroad. He did not realize until later that the 16th had not received the kaiser's previous cancellation of its orders and therefore had already seized the railroad, as originally ordered.

Moltke could not get over it, the whole sequence of mixups and embarrassments. "That was my first experience in this war," he wrote. "I am convinced that the kaiser would not have signed the mobilization order if the dispatch from Prince Lichnowsky had come a half hour earlier. And I have not been able to overcome the impression made by this experience. Something in me was destroyed, something that could not be rebuilt again. Confidence and trust were shattered."

Other confidences were no more secure. When the first Germans crossed the Belgian frontier on the morning of August 4, the Belgians opened fire. That afternoon, the German ambassador to Paris, Baron

Wilhelm von Schoen, arrived at the office of Premier René Viviani with a long list of false charges of French border violations, air raids on Nuremberg and Karlsruhe, and "organized hostility." As a result, he said, "the German Empire considers itself in a state of war with France." Thus did Moltke's predictions of the inevitable come true.

In one last message from Vienna, though, Conrad raised a question about Moltke's confidence that the French army would be erased from the battlefields of France within six weeks. Suppose the French actually won, he asked. What would Moltke do then? "Well," said Moltke, "I'll do what I can."

12

Defeat on the Marne

IF MOLTKE'S LONG-PLANNED COUP DE MAIN AGAINST LIÈGE COULD NO longer remain secret, it could at least be sudden, sharp, and violent, which made it a natural assignment for Erich Ludendorff. Now a beefy and bull-necked figure of forty-nine, he had been too young for the great wars of 1866 and 1870, but the army was nonetheless his destiny. Enrolled in cadet school in Holstein at twelve, he excelled in mathematics, geography, and military history and won a lieutenant's commission at seventeen. Then came the military academy in Berlin and the general staff, where he caught the attention of Count Schlieffen. "He was a man of iron principles," Margarethe Ludendorff said of the man she married in 1909. "Time was not reckoned in our house by hours but by minutes."

Named chief of the *Aufmarschabteilung* or deployment office in 1908, Ludendorff played an important part in preparing the mobilization for war. His chief demand was for more troops. "Our political and military situation makes it our duty to assemble all our available manpower," he said, "for a struggle which will decide the existence or destruction of the German Empire." In France, by comparison, a population of 40 million supported an army of 750,000 men while Germany's 65 million produced only 600,000 soldiers. France required 82 percent of its youths to undergo military training, Germany only 52 percent. Moltke was suitably impressed, but he knew that the cost of providing the troops that Ludendorff requested would be greater than the Reichstag would accept. And Ludendorff wanted not only more troops. He wanted more aircraft and Zeppelins, better wireless equipment, better field kitchens, more of everything that an army might need.

"To achieve his ends," Walter Goerlitz has written in his history of the German general staff, "Ludendorff put his demands through the mouth of Moltke, for in this matter Moltke gave him his most complete confidence. Indeed . . . Ludendorff was operating as a sort of secret Chief of Staff himself, the remainder of the hierarchy being short-circuited." Ludendorff can probably be blamed or credited for some of Moltke's more extreme statements of this prewar period. Such as: "We must again become a nation in arms. . . . For Germany there can be no going backward, only forward." Ludendorff can be similarly credited or blamed for an increase of nearly 120,000 in military manpower. "The army bill which is coming is my work," Ludendorff wrote to a friend, "although I wanted even more."

Ludendorff's maneuvering made him some powerful enemies, though, and even Moltke had difficulties with his hard-driving subordinate. "I have had to make Moltke stand his ground by gripping him like a vise," Ludendorff said to his wife after one turbulent day of conferences. "Otherwise I think his weakness would bring him to utter ruin." When even gripping Moltke like a vise failed to bring him what he wanted, Ludendorff joined forces with the former general August Keim and other warriors of the Pan-German League, a nationalist organization financed by ultraconservative bankers and manufacturers. This league organized a "defense fund" of 1 billion marks to help finance Ludendorff's ambitions. His enemies triumphed, though, as is often the way in military politics. Ludendorff was removed from the general staff as "inconvenient" early in 1913 and rusticated to the command of a regiment in Dusseldorf.

On the outbreak of the war, when he had hoped and expected to become chief of operations, and thus second in command to Moltke, Ludendorff was named deputy chief of staff to the Second Army under General Karl von Bülow. On August 2, the day after Germany declared war on Russia, Ludendorff rode all day long—"thirsting for action," as one account has it—to get from Strassburg to his new assignment in Aachen, where the Second Army had already begun its march into Belgium.

Liège was not a very large city, numbering perhaps 150,000 souls, but its history was one of violent conflicts ever since St. Monulph, bishop of Tongres, first built a chapel near the confluence of the

Meuse and the Legia in 558. The town acquired so much territory under the rule of Bishop Notger in the tenth century that it was recognized as an independent principality of the Holy Roman Empire. Annexed by France during the revolution, it became known as the department of the Ourthe. Joining the Belgian revolt of 1830, it naturally became a citadel of the new nation of Belgium. The Belgians took advantage of its site atop the cliffs overlooking the Meuse to create a thirty-mile ring of a dozen forts, built of concrete, buried in the cliffs, linked by a network of tunnels, and guarded by 400 guns and some 40,000 troops.

General Otto von Emmich reached Liège on the morning of August 4, after an eighteen-mile march over torn-up and blockaded roads, and issued a call for the city's surrender. The garrison commander, a doughty old general named Gérard Matthieu Leman, refused. King Albert had ordered him "hold to the end." Emmich opened fire with his artillery the next morning, then launched repeated infantry assaults. Leman beat them back and inflicted so many casualties that Emmich had to ask Bülow for reinforcements. The fighting raged back and forth all the next day, August 6, until the Belgians withdrew to the nearby Gette River. This happened at just about the time that Ludendorff arrived on the scene as an observer. One of the first things he observed was the death of General von Wussow, commander of the 14th Brigade. Ludendorff persuaded Emmich to let him replace Wussow. Then he commandeered a Belgian car and led a squad of Wussow's men up to the main fort of the citadel. He said later that he thought a Colonel von Oven had taken over the citadel, but "when I arrived no German soldier was to be seen and the citadel was still in the hands of the enemy." Clambering out of his car, Ludendorff marched up to the gate of the fort and banged on it with the hilt of his sword. When the gate opened, Ludendorff bellowed a new demand for surrender. He must have been an awesome sight, that burly, heavy-shouldered figure with the bristling moustache and the blazing eyes. Or perhaps the defenders were chilled by the fact that the regular army troops had all withdrawn. In any case, they offered no resistance. "The few hundred Belgians who were there surrendered at my summons," Ludendorff nonchalantly observed. Emmich promptly informed General Bülow of Ludendorff's feat, and Bülow promptly sent word of the "great victory" to Berlin. There the commanders reacted with delirious joy. The kaiser embraced Moltke and, as the general recalled, "rapturously kissed" him.

There apparently was in Ludendorff some quality of imperious command that inspired obedience. Nearly a decade after this first triumph, after he had risen to become the de facto commander of the whole German army and the virtual dictator of Germany, and after he had finally seen all this end in defeat and disgrace, the former commander joined forces with a former corporal, Adolf Hitler, in the farcical adventure known as the Beerhall Putsch of 1923. As the putschists attempted to march across the Odeonsplatz in Munich, armed police ordered them to halt, then enforced their orders with gunfire. Hitler, marching arm in arm with an aide named Max Scheubner-Richter, fell to the ground when Scheubner-Richter was killed by a bullet to the heart; Hermann Goering, wounded in the groin, took refuge in the nearby home of a Jewish doctor. Ludendorff, apparently unable to believe that any German policeman would dare to shoot at him, continued resolutely marching straight ahead, all alone, until a young police lieutenant said, "Excellency, I have to take you into custody."

"If those are your orders, Lieutenant, I will follow you," said Ludendorff. He followed the lieutenant into custody, but when put on trial, he was acquitted. Elected to the Reichstag as a Nazi deputy, he broke with the Nazis after Hitler came to power and finally died in 1937, unmourned.

Not until the day after Ludendorff's bluff in Liège did it become clear that the news had been somewhat exaggerated. Although Ludendorff had captured the central fort, the city and its remaining forts had not surrendered. Indeed, Ludendorff and Emmich were now surrounded and besieged themselves. Bülow threw in more reinforcements, which reestablished contact with the trapped Germans but failed to rescue them. Only after three days of maneuvering did Emmich succeed in capturing another fort from behind and thus clearing the way for his liberation.

That also cleared the way for a German secret weapon, the first big tactical surprise of the war. This was the so-called Big Bertha, a ninety-eight-ton, 420-millimeter howitzer that could fling a yard-long shell a mile into the air. It was August 9 before the first of these monsters could be hauled onto specially built railroad cars at the Krupp works in Essen and started on the journey to Belgium. The journey ended at Herbesthal, twenty miles beyond the border, where the retreating Belgians had blown up the railroad tunnel. A team of 200 technicians had to take the giant cannon apart and load it onto horse-drawn wagons. On August 12, the terrifying thing finally arrived at Liège, where the technicians reassembled it and fired at Fort Pontisse. A swirling cloud of debris, of the fort and its defenders, soared a thousand feet into the air. Then they fired the weapon at Fort Loncin with the same result. "A number of dazed and blackened Belgian soldiers crawled out of the ruins . . ." Ludendorff observed with satisfaction. "All bleeding, they came toward us with their hands up, stammering, '*Ne pas tuer, ne pas tuer* [Don't kill, don't kill].'"

"*Wir waren keine Hunnen,*" Ludendorff added, meaning "We were no Huns," meaning that he had no intention of killing his prisoners.

There was no need to do so, of course, for once the giant howitzers were in position, they could demolish all the forts, one by one. General Leman, obeying the royal orders to "hold to the end," doggedly refused to surrender, but the Krupp guns finally silenced him too. He was found unconscious under a collapsed wall of brick and masonry. When he awoke, he still protested his refusal to surrender, but he protested in captivity.

Once Liège was overwhelmed on August 16, the gateway to France lay open, and the 320,000 men of Kluck's First Army marched through, followed by the 280,000 men of Bülow's Second Army. The only thing more extraordinary than Moltke's ability to push 600,000 men through this gap in Belgium was the French army's steadfast refusal to believe it was happening. If Moltke was rather blindly committed to the Schlieffen Plan, the French commander, Joseph Joffre, was just as committed to his own Plan XVII (which originally included an invasion of Belgium). This called for an immediate French offensive into the Ardennes Forest, and Joffre would allow nothing to prevent his attack from proceeding according to plan. During an early meeting on the offensive, one of Joffre's generals ventured to point out some serious flaws, and Joffre responded by saying, "That may be your plan; it is not mine." Baffled by Joffre's sphinxlike answer, the general repeated his criticism. Joffre imperturbably repeated his reply. At sixty-two, Joffre was a mighty presence, with a mighty white moustache and a mighty paunch. As the paunch testified, he was devoted to his dinner table, where he appeared at regular hours, regardless of confusion or crisis, and indulged his appetite with the relentless gusto of that beast he rather resembled, Lewis Carroll's walrus. Oldest of eleven children of a wine-barrel maker in the Pyrenees, Joffre had none of the characteristics associated with aristocracy—and bloodlines were considered almost as important in the French army as in the German. He had none of the intellectual interests of Moltke or the strategic imagination of Schlieffen. He had learned his profession in engineering school and earned his promotions in the colonial wars of Asia and Africa. He waddled around in his black tunic and baggy red trousers (*"le pantalon rouge, c'est la France,"* he

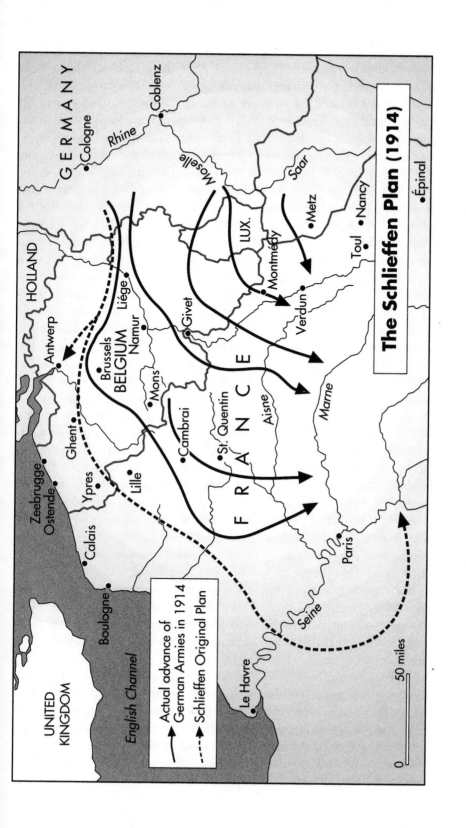

The Schlieffen Plan (1914)

UNITED KINGDOM

English Channel

GERMANY

HOLLAND

BELGIUM

LUX.

FRANCE

Cologne

Coblenz

Rhine

Moselle

Saar

Metz

Nancy

Toul

Épinal

Montmédy

Verdun

Liége

Namur

Givet

Brussels

Mons

Cambrai

St. Quentin

Aisne

Marne

Seine

Paris

Antwerp

Ghent

Ypres

Lille

Zeebrugge

Ostende

Calais

Boulogne

Le Havre

Actual advance of German Armies in 1914

Schlieffen Original Plan

0   50 miles

once said in response to a proposal that the ridiculous uniform be abolished), but he watched everything out of those serene blue eyes and listened laconically to every opinion, then announced one of his monumental decisions. In his very monumentality, Joffre possessed a quality of calm confidence that France would desperately need in the coming days. This immunity to panic was indeed a quality that would save France from defeat. It was also a quality that could lead to disastrous miscalculations. Like most French generals of his generation, Joffre had been trained to believe in the supreme value of élan and the offensive spirit, so now he dismissed all reports of a huge German buildup on his left as signs that the Germans must be weakening their center, where Joffre's own offensive would theoretically destroy them.

The only French commander who seemed to have some foresight about the threat of the German right wing was General Charles Lanrezac, the scholarly chief of the Fifth Army, which stood right in the path of Kluck's advancing First Army. Joffre had once called Lanrezac "a veritable lion" and "the best commander in the French army," but now the lion was afflicted by doubts and misgivings. If he advanced into the Ardennes, as called for by Joffre's invasion plan, he would dangerously expose his left wing, which was supposed to be covered by the arriving British, whom Lanrezac had not yet seen and did not really expect to see. Lanrezac even put his anxieties in a letter to Joffre, criticizing Joffre's whole strategy. "Once the 5th Army is committed to an offensive in the direction of Neufchâteau," he wrote, "it will be unable to parry a German offensive further north." Joffre was not impressed; he declined to change his plan. Lanrezac sent his chief of staff to Joffre's headquarters to explain the menace in more detail. A headquarters official calmly answered that Lanrezac's anxiety was "premature" because such a German flank movement would be "out of proportion to the means at the enemy's disposal." It never occurred to the French that the Germans could increase their strength by the unorthodox tactic of using reserve divisions in their front lines. And so the official French verdict was that the Germans couldn't have as many troops on the field as Lanrezac feared—and as they actually did have.

If French intelligence was disastrously inaccurate, German intelligence seemed correspondingly unaware of the British arrival. The British themselves were badly divided on how many troops to send, where and when to send them. Britain had only six divisions (plus four more overseas) and a cavalry division to protect the sceptered isle from invasion, not to mention a worsening rebellion in Ireland. In prewar staff talks with the French, the British planned on sending four divisions as soon as war began, to concentrate at Maubeuge, near the Belgian frontier, as the left flank of the French front line. When the declaration of war brought fierce old Lord Kitchener out of retirement to become minister of war, however, one of his first moves was to argue against risking the British Expeditionary Force so far forward so soon. He wanted it to concentrate back in Amiens so that it could be preserved as the core of a much larger conscript army that he saw would be needed for the long war ahead. Overruled in the cabinet, Kitchener warned the departing BEF commander, Sir John French, that he must cooperate with the French but avoid letting Joffre use the British as cannon fodder, exercising "the greatest care towards a minimum of loss and wastage."

Moltke could know nothing of all that, of course. On August 16, when the bulk of the BEF disembarked in France and headed toward Maubeuge, he was occupied in moving his headquarters from Berlin to Coblenz, about fifty miles from the front and about as close to the action as Moltke's headquarters would ever get. As for the British, he heard only that an advance guard had arrived far down the coast at Boulogne. He had other concerns. Not only were the French pressing forward in Alsace but the Russians were streaming across the frontier of East Prussia. Instead of wallowing around in their mobilization preparations, as everyone had expected, they won a quick victory at Stallupönen. This was a violation of the sacred Prussian homeland, and members of distinguished Junker families soon began appearing at court to wail of barbarian threats to their estates.

Still, since the Schlieffen Plan called for a massive sweep across Belgium, Moltke gave orders on August 18 for the sweep to begin. The small but plucky Belgian army resisted as best it could, then began withdrawing toward the fortified city of Antwerp. Kluck's First Army tried to cut the Belgians off but failed; he therefore detached two reserve corps to guard Antwerp. It was the first erosion of the Schlieffen Plan. Unaware that this lost strength would never be regained, Kluck's gray columns of troops marched on through the dusty streets and red-brick cottages of Belgium, still and serene under the blazing August sun. Although they seemed an irresistible force as they paraded through Brussels, they were already plagued by dithering at Moltke's headquarters. Fretting about the possibility of a gap appearing between Kluck's First Army and Bülow's Second, which was supposed to proceed up the Meuse valley toward Namur, Moltke suddenly put Bülow in command of both armies. This absolutely infuriated Kluck, an easily infuriated officer who had been wounded in 1870 and, though only recently ennobled, considered himself in no way inferior to the somewhat more sedentary Bülow. At this point, a concerted attack by the First and Second armies, supported by General Max Klemens von Hausen's nearby Third Army, might have enveloped and destroyed the French Fifth Army, perched at the juncture of the Meuse and the Sambre, but Bülow was not the man to undertake such a complex offensive. When Kluck wanted to move westward to outflank the British forces that were appearing straight ahead of him, Bülow refused on the ground that by such a move "the 1st Army might get too far away and not be able to support the 2nd Army at the right moment." Kluck despairingly asked Moltke's supreme headquarters if he had to remain under Bülow's command; it answered that he did.

Moltke was now besieged by such questions on all sides; and on all sides, he proved deplorably indecisive. In Lorraine, the German Sixth Army under Crown Prince Rupprecht of Bavaria had been carrying out its assignment to fall back before the advancing French, keeping them away from the fighting on the Belgian frontier and leading them into a giant trap. After three days of this, Rupprecht wanted to counterattack, but Moltke's headquarters could not come to a decision. Rupprecht's chief of staff, General Krafft von Dellmen-singen, demanded to know whether headquarters was forbidding a counterattack. "Oh, no," said Moltke's aide, General von Stein, "we won't oblige you by forbidding an attack. You must take the responsibility. Make your decision as your conscience tells you."

"It's already made," said Krafft. "We attack!"

"*Na!*" said Stein, "then strike, and God be with you."

The prospect of a victory in Lorraine helped to keep Moltke from advancing his headquarters from Coblenz into Belgium, where he might have straightened out the squabbles between Kluck and Bülow. Instead, he issued a vague directive: "The Supreme Command needs to be intelligently helped by the initiative of army commanders. The latter, on their side, should always think in terms of the general situation and try unceasingly to conform to it."

Moltke was also distracted, during these critical days, by the news from East Prussia. The Russians were not only invading the holy soil of East Prussia but defeating every German attempt to stop them. At 8:30 P.M. on August 20, there came a phone call from General Max von Prittwitz und Gaffron, commander of the Eighth Army in East Prussia, to say that he was ordering a general retreat behind the Vistula, thus abandoning virtually his entire territory to the despised Slavs. "General von Moltke was deeply shattered when the order to retreat was announced," said one of his aides in Coblenz, "but he did not think of giving a resolute counter-order." What he did do was to remove Prittwitz. As his replacement, he dragged out of retirement a stolid but undistinguished veteran (wounded at Königgrätz) named Paul von Beneckendorf und von Hindenburg. Assigned to him as chief of staff, however, was the hero of Liège, Ludendorff.

Since Ludendorff was already engaged in the important siege of Namur, the Belgian fortress at the juncture of the Meuse and the Sambre, he could not be expected to depart for the east with any great enthusiasm. "You are being given a new and difficult task, perhaps even more difficult than the assault on Liège . . ." urged the message from Moltke's headquarters. "I know no other man in whom I would have such absolute trust as yourself. Perhaps you can salvage the situation in the east. Naturally you cannot be held responsible for what has happened, but with your energy you can still prevent the worst. Accept then this new call, which is the greatest honor a soldier can receive. . . ." Starting out immediately, Ludendorff met Hindenburg for the first time in the railroad station at Hannover, shortly after 3 A.M., and the two proceeded to East Prussia. There they soon smashed the Russians at the Battle of Tannenberg and started the process that eventually led to Lenin's rise to power on the slogan of "Bread and peace."

Back in Belgium, the British finally arrived to take their stand on General Lanrezac's left flank. The French greeted them with a snarl. "At last you are here," Lanrezac's chief of staff said at his first meeting with British officers on August 17. "It's not a moment too soon. If we are beaten, we shall owe it to you." The startled British had no sooner taken up their positions than they found themselves dangerously out in front of the French forces on their right. Sir John French expected his allies to advance accordingly, but a British liaison officer warned him that Lanrezac had no intention of advancing. The Germans' intelligence was no less murky. As late as the evening of August 21, when British cavalry patrols had already made contact with the Germans, Moltke's headquarters warned vaguely that "a landing of British troops and their advance from about Lille must be reckoned with," but it added that "no landing of British troops on a large scale has yet taken place." On the scene, intelligence reported some British around Maubeuge, suggesting that Kluck might advance southward toward the Mons-Condé canal.

August 23 was a Sunday. Kluck's troops awakened to a drizzle, but as they marched southward toward Mons, the sun burst through the clouds, and church bells summoned the citizens to Mass. Miners in black suits led their wives and daughters in starched dresses through the cobblestoned streets—some gawking, some doing their best to ignore the soldiers wrestling cannons into position. German cavalry blundered into British cavalry, then called for reinforcements. Artillery opened fire on both sides. Great billows of black smoke rose above the brick cottages, and shrapnel rained down. Kluck's Ninth Corps infantry charged against a British salient north of Mons. The British Second Corps responded with devastating rifle fire, so rapid that the Germans thought they were charging machine guns.

Neither side knew that the Germans outnumbered the British by about two to one. Stopped cold, the Germans regrouped, then charged again. "Well entrenched and completely hidden, the enemy opened a murderous fire . . ." one German survivor recalled. "The casualties increased . . . the rushes became shorter, and finally the whole advance stopped." The outnumbered British slowly withdrew to a fallback position two miles south of the canal, but it was the German buglers who signaled cease-fire at the end of the day. One German captain whose regiment had lost 500 men that day recalled his troops gathering in the darkness and singing *"Deutschland Über Alles,"* recalled his superior officer telling him: "You are the only company commander left in the battalion. . . . The battalion is a mere wreck, my proud, beautiful battalion."

The British had suffered too—some 1,600 casualties—and they had been pushed back, but their two divisions had stopped six German divisions for a full day, and since this was the first battle the British had fought in northern Europe since Waterloo, it soon acquired the legends and ornaments traditional to British victories, including even sightings of an "angel of Mons," which magically halted the German advance. Some of the Germans felt their own weakness. "If the English have the slightest suspicion of our condition, and counter-attack, they will simply run over us," one colonel predicted. The battered British did not suspect and did not counterattack, however, and since many German commanders had already learned that Moltke's headquarters hungered for news of victory, they hastened to oblige. "News of victories in the west including the repulse of the English cavalry by General von Bülow," a court official wrote in his diary. "Great jubilation." And the next day, August 25: "Bülow is driving the enemy before him. The 1st Army is already turning the French and English flanks and a great debacle is expected. The Kaiser is radiant!"

"The entirely favorable news that arrived every day from the right wing and which was still arriving at O.H.L. [German supreme headquarters] on August 25 created the belief that, together with the great victory in Lorraine of August 20–23, the great decisive battle of the western front had taken place and had been favorable to us," wrote Moltke's aide, Colonel Adolf von Tappen. Under the euphoric influence of this delusion of victory in the west, Moltke made another mistake, one that he later called his greatest. It was part of Ludendorff's nature to confront any challenge by calling for more troops, and now that he faced "the greatest honor that any soldier can receive," he was already demanding reinforcements. And the Schlieffen Plan promised just that, the rapid transfer to the east of troops no longer needed by the victorious armies of the west.

As soon as Namur surrendered on August 25, Bülow notified headquarters that two corps were "available for other duties." The very next day, Moltke snatched them up "for the earliest possible transportation to the East," though he later claimed that it was the threatening Russian advances in the east that had "obliged us to send reinforcements to this front before a definite decision could be reached over the Franco-English army." What particularly rankled in Moltke's assessment of his error was that the troops sent east arrived too late to be of any significant use. Ludendorff, characteristically, said later that he didn't want them or need them. This transfer, however, was part of the Schlieffen Plan in all its prewar trials; its actual effect on the crumbling German right wing in Belgium has remained a matter for speculation and debate among military theorists.

On the battlefield at Mons, though, Sir John French was dismayed to hear that Lanrezac, far from advancing to the line held by his British allies, was, without any advance warning, retreating. French felt betrayed—and furious. He ordered an immediate British withdrawal, but while Lanrezac came to a halt after a few miles, French kept retreating and talked darkly of reorganizing his forces in Le Havre, some 150 miles to the rear.

This retreat was a dark time not only for the French and British forces but for the civilians trying to escape from the shifting front lines. "A typical day's fighting often consisted in being smothered all day by heavy shells from invisible German batteries . . ." one British officer recalled. "There was always a generous interval for lunch, then the shelling would start again. It was maddening, all the more so that whenever any of our batteries did open fire they seemed to be located immediately by one of the ubiquitous *Taubes* [a German airplane used for aerial observation]." So the long day wore on, the constant shelling slowly exhausting the men's nerves. And all the time no sign of a single German. It was only when the long shades of evening lengthened on the plain that there seemed to be a movement as of hardly discernible shadows: far away along hedges and beneath trees, the field grays, almost invisible in the fading light, were creeping forward.

To both the retreating and the advancing, the accompanying army of refugees was an annoying nuisance, blocking roads and slowing serious traffic. A British officer irritably described the scene: "A very sick woman, who looked as if she were dying, balanced somehow on a perambulator; a paralytic old man in a wheelbarrow, pushed by his sturdy daughter; a very old, very respectable couple, who for years had probably done no more than walk arm in arm around a small garden, now, still arm in arm, were helping each other in utter bewilderment of mind and exhaustion of body down the long meaningless road. . . . And none might stop: the gendarmes pounced on any who tarried and shoved them forward. The mass of refugees must be kept on the move. If they halted they would hopelessly block the communications they were already so seriously encumbering. . . . So on they had to stagger, men and tired cattle together, with here and there a huge cart drawn by oxen, packed with children . . ."

From a French perspective, these refugees were an even more dispiriting sight. "Men, women, children, furniture, bundles of linen . . . were piled on their wagons," wrote Marc Bloch, then twenty-eight and just beginning his distinguished career as a teacher of history. "These French peasants fleeing before an enemy against whom we could not protect them left a bitter impression, possibly the most maddening that the war has inflicted on us. We were to see them often during the retreat, poor refugees crowding the roads and village squares with their wagons. Wrenched from their homes, disoriented, dazed, and bullied by the gendarmes, they were troublesome but pathetic figures. . . ."

On the German side, of course, there was jubilation, for the flight of the enemy seemed to herald the quick victory that the Schlieffen Plan had promised. So euphoric was Moltke that he scrapped Schlieffen's doctrine of the right-wing offensive and ordered an advance on all fronts. "The French . . . are in full retreat . . ." he announced in a general directive dated August 27. "It is the task of the German army, by advancing rapidly on Paris, to deny the French army the time to reorganize itself . . . and to take away from France all possible means of resistance." He then outlined the marching routes for each army, the First to the lower Seine, the Second toward Paris, the Third toward Château-Thierry, the Fourth toward Epernay, and so on.

In ordering this general advance, Moltke not only ignored the Schlieffen Plan but overlooked some of the "frictions" that Clausewitz had warned of: the Germans were outmarching their own supply lines, running short even of food. "The men stagger forward," one officer wrote of the twenty-five-mile daily advance, "their faces coated with dust, their uniforms in rags, looking like living scarecrows. They march with their eyes closed, singing in chorus so that they will not fall asleep." Another reported bitterly on his men's boots: "Scarcely a single pair didn't have a nail sticking through the soles, which were thin as paper. A few more days and my grenadiers would be marching barefoot." The First Army officially notified O.H.L. on September 4 that it had "reached the limit of its endurance." Not uninfluenced by all this, probably, Kluck began thinking of a shortcut. On August 28, before the increasingly unreliable German communication system delivered Moltke's directive for a general advance, Kluck proposed to Bülow that both their armies should wheel to the south before reaching Paris, thus abandoning as beyond their capacities Schlieffen's plan for a great march around the west side of the capital. Bülow raised no objection. Moltke, who was never consulted on the change of direction, tamely acquiesced. "The movements carried out by the 1st Army conform to the intentions of O.H.L.," he said.

Quite apart from the exhaustion of his men, Kluck had plausible reasons for his shift. Judging by the speed of the British retreat, he believed the B.E.F. was no longer a serious opponent (Sir John French was indeed doing his best to remove his troops from the front lines). As for the French, Kluck felt confident that they had no more forces with which to outflank him on the west. His only apparent opponent, then, was Lanrezac's battered Fifth Army, which had also been retreating for more than a week. If Kluck could now demolish Lanrezac, the war would be virtually over, so the sooner he attacked, the better. "The general fears nothing from the direction of Paris," one of Kluck's aides noted. "After we have destroyed the remains of the Franco-British army, he will return to Paris and give the Fourth Reserve the honor of leading the entry into the French capital."

Kluck's shift was to prove a bad mistake, though Papa Joffre did not at first realize it. He was still trying to organize new forces to halt the great retreat. The man who saw and seized the new opportunity was General Joseph Galliéni, sixty-four, ill with prostatis but still sharp and peppery. Joffre's commanding officer during the subjugation of Madagascar at the turn of the century, Galliéni had been a rival candidate for Joffre's supreme command, and Joffre had resisted any effort by Galliéni to assert influence at his headquarters. As commandant of Paris, though, Galliéni did have a post at the edge of the battlefield, and the new Sixth Army being formed under General

Michel-Joseph Maunoury did come under his command. When Joffre's intelligence officers learned of Kluck's turn from a bloodstained map found on the body of a slain German cavalry officer, they neither understood its implications nor informed Galliéni of the discovery. Galliéni had his own sources of information. A Parisian reconnaissance pilot spotted the Germans "gliding from west to east" toward the Ourcq Valley on the morning of September 2. Galliéni's chief of staff entered the office of his *Deuxième Bureau* just as another pilot's report confirmed the Germans' altered line of march. Instantly seeing the meaning of it, he cried out: "They offer us their flank!"

Though Galliéni still had to obtain Joffre's approval for a counterattack against Kluck's exposed flank, he ordered Maunoury to get ready to move. He found Joffre still preoccupied with other things. Now that Kluck had reached the Marne on the evening of September 3, Joffre wanted to retreat to the Seine, southeast of Paris, which implicitly meant a military abandonment of the capital. He accordingly urged President Poincaré to move the government to Bordeaux. And he had decided that Lanrezac had to be fired. ("My friend," he told Lanrezac when they were alone together, "you are used up and undecided. You will have to give up command of the 5th Army. I hate to tell you this, but I have to." "General, you are right," said Lanrezac, who knew that his greatest sin had been to be right about the menace of the German right wing.) To Galliéni, though, Joffre said he needed more time to decide on his strategy. His troops were exhausted; reinforcements were on the way. He could begin a counterattack on the Seine in a few days. Galliéni moved on to Melun, the headquarters of the British, who also had not yet agreed to take part in any counterattack. Sir John French could not be found; he was said to be inspecting his troops; nobody knew when he would return and nobody could make a decision without him. Back at his own headquarters, Galliéni found that he had converted Joffre, who had ordered the counterattack to start, but only on September 7. And the usually confident Maunoury was starting to worry. "In case we are overwhelmed," he asked, "our line of retreat will be—?" Galliéni's answer was curt: "Nowhere." Galliéni turned to the telephone to reach Joffre, who hated talking on the phone ("The real battle of the Marne was fought on the telephone," Galliéni later remarked) and argued him into advancing the counterattack from September 7 to September 6. Joffre's General Order No. 6, issued that night, almost echoed Galliéni's passionate arguments. "The time has come," it said, "to profit by the adventurous position of the German First Army and concentrate against that army all efforts of the Allied Armies of the extreme left. . . ."

For Moltke, September 1 was a notable date, the forty-fourth anniversary of the day that his uncle had crushed the Emperor Napoleon III at Sedan. He could hardly help drawing comparisons with his own situation; he was still able only to hope for a similar devastation of Joffre's forces. "By my wish," he wrote to his wife of the Sedan anniversary, "the kaiser was out in the field, at headquarters of the 5th Army, with the crown prince, and spent the night there. It is good for him to come to the troops for once, and also for them to see him. . . ." The kaiser returned the next day in what Moltke glumly called a *"Hurrastimmung,"* or "hurrah mood."

Though the French forces still eluded Moltke's grasp, Kluck's advance on Paris forced French leaders to confront a dark choice: battling over the city or fleeing it. Joffre had warned them on August 30 that Paris was "seriously menaced," and that the government should depart to some safer place. President Poincaré, painfully aware of the siege of 1870, asked Galliéni how long the capital could hold out, and whether the government should leave. "Paris cannot hold out," was Galliéni's chilling reply, "and you should make ready to leave as soon as possible."

By this time, the Germans were sending one or two *Taubes* over Paris every day, usually at about the cocktail hour of 6 P.M., to drop a few small bombs and some leaflets demanding surrender. The Parisians affected nonchalance, but on September 2, with the Germans only twenty miles outside Paris and actually in sight of the Eiffel Tower, Poincaré decided that "the hateful moment had come." For the second time in a half century, the French authorities fled their capital to escape an advancing German army. It was a miserable spectacle. The Grands Boulevards were deserted, buses had vanished, stores were shuttered. On the outskirts of the city, swarms of conscripted citizens dug trenches. Just as in 1870, thousands of cattle were herded into the Bois de Boulogne to await a German siege. Flocks of sheep wandered across the Place de la Concorde on their way to being shipped east to the front. The War Ministry in the Rue St. Dominique was dark and deserted, its courtyard filled with trucks loading up archives to be carried away to Bordeaux; what could not be moved was being burned. Galliéni found War Minister Étienne-Alexandre Millerand sitting alone in an empty office, and Millerand gave Galliéni his orders to defend Paris *"à outrance."*

Galliéni was eager to fight, but he was shocked at the implications of such a scorched-earth policy in the heart of Paris.

"Do you understand, *M. le Ministre,* the significance of the words, *à outrance?*" he asked. "They mean destructions, ruins, dynamiting bridges in the center of the city."

"*À outrance,*" Millerand doggedly repeated, wishing Galliéni farewell.

Galliéni did his best to add a little élan to the ominous orders. In a proclamation to the soldiers and citizens of Paris, pasted on walls all over the city on the morning of September 3, he declared that the government had left "to give a new impulse to the national defense." He added: "I have received a mandate to defend Paris against the invader. This mandate I shall carry out to the end."

Paris could not be defended, as Galliéni well knew, against a siege like that of 1870. The giant guns that had destroyed Liège could easily do the same for Paris. The only alternatives were to declare it an open city, offering no defense, or to defend it in combat outside the city. The latter choice, which was Galliéni's choice, required him to mobilize forces that he did not really control. Joffre had sent him three corps from the eastern front, explaining that Galliéni had "attacked prematurely," but there was still a large gap where the retreating British had to be persuaded to stand and fight. "If I could give orders to the English army as I could to the French army," Joffre told War Minister Millerand, "I would pass immediately to the attack." Sir John French, however, remained bitterly distrustful of his allies. To Kitchener's attempt to cajole him back into battle, he blamed the gap in the French lines on Lanrezac's penchant for retreating, "usually without notice," and he petulantly added: "I do not see why I should be called upon to run the risk of absolute disaster in order a second time to save them." To rally Sir John back into the war, Joffre drove 115 miles to the British headquarters at Melun and launched into a passionate appeal. It was all the more impressive because it was so uncharacteristic of the laconic Joffre. In this "supreme moment," he said, he had already ordered his own forces to launch an attack for the "lives of all French people, the soil of France, the future of Europe." In such a "supreme crisis," he added, "I cannot believe the British army will refuse to do its share. . . . History would severely judge your absence." Having evoked history, the soil of France, and the future of Europe, Joffre somehow sensed that still more was needed. He banged his fist on the table and declared to Field Marshal French: "*Monsieur le Maréchal,* the honor of England is at stake!"

French reddened at Joffre's challenge, and tears started to his eyes. He struggled in vain to reply in French, then said to an aide, "Damn it, I can't explain. Tell him we will do all we possibly can." An English officer translated: "The field marshal says, 'Yes.'" The English then served tea.

Closing in for the kill, Moltke should have felt jubilant, but a cabinet minister visiting his headquarters on September 4 found him "serious and depressed." Perhaps he was remembering that the seizure of Paris had been his uncle's final triumph; perhaps he felt, as he had all his life, unworthy to walk in the old field marshal's boots. "We must not deceive ourselves," he told the visiting minister. "We have had success but not victory. Victory means annihilation of the enemy's power of resistance. When armies of millions of men oppose each other in battle, the victor has prisoners. Where are our prisoners? There were some 20,000 taken in the Lorraine fighting, another 10,000 here and another 10,000 there. Besides, the relatively small number of captured guns shows that the French are conducting a planned and orderly retreat. The hardest work is still to be done."

In this spirit of disappointment, anxious about Joffre's westward troop movements and with only an uncertain knowledge of where his own forces actually were, Moltke suddenly decreed a halt to the German advance. "The enemy has evaded the enveloping attack of the 1st and 2nd armies, and a part of his forces has joined up with those about Paris. . . ." he said in a general order issued in the evening of September 4. "It appears that the enemy is moving troops westwards from the Toul-Belfort front, and is also taking them from the front of the 3rd, 4th and 5th armies. The attempt to force the whole French army back in a southeasterly direction is thus rendered impracticable, and the new situation to be appreciated shows that the enemy is bringing up new formations and concentrating superior forces in the neighborhood of Paris, to protect the capital and threaten the right flank of the German army. The 1st and 2nd armies must therefore remain facing the east front of Paris . . ."

This, according to British analyst Corelli Barnett, was "the directive that lost the Germans the campaign." It did so by surrendering the strategic initiative to the French, by halting the offensive of the right wing and putting it on the defensive. "As the German armies marched into the supreme battle crisis," Barnett argues, "they needed an inflexible driving will—moral courage amounting to faith. This is the core of generalship. Instead, far behind them lay an old and desperately tired man, his physical and mental powers spent by a month of crisis and responsibility heavier than that of any other soldier, shattered in his innermost confidence by that terrible interview in the Star Hall on the day before mobilisation. His plump features pallid with fatigue and unstrung nerves, Moltke could barely drive his own body through the daily round of duty, let alone drive his armies through catastrophic danger into victory. This, even more than alterations to

Schlieffen's plan, Kluck's vagaries, and the brilliance of Joffre and Galliéni, was the essential cause of the German failure in 1914." That may well be true, but no more so than ascribing the older Moltke's victories at Königgrätz and Sedan to the weak wills and general incompetence of Benedek and MacMahon. Kluck, who grievously underestimated the French and British forces on his flank, was more magnanimous in his tribute to their fighting spirit. "The reason that transcends all others," he said in 1918, "was the extraordinary . . . aptitude of the French soldier to recover quickly. That men will let themselves be killed where they stand—that is well known and counted on in every plan of battle. But that men who have retreated for ten days, sleeping on the ground and half dead with fatigue, should be able to take up their rifles and attack when the bugle sounds, is a thing upon which we never counted. It was a possibility not studied in our war academy."

Until the last moment, Kluck and Bülow remained confident that victory was within their grasp. Kluck declared in the evening of September 3 that he saw "the beginnings of great disorder among the retreating enemy columns," and Bülow reported on September 4 that the "decisively beaten" French were hastening back, utterly disorganized, to the south of the Marne." Small wonder, then, that they were both amazed to find Maunoury's makeshift Sixth Army attacking Kluck on the north bank of the Marne, where Kluck had advanced in defiance of Moltke's order to turn west. Turning west now under fire, Kluck's forces let a gap open between themselves and Bülow's Second Army. Into this gap plunged the revived British, alongside the French Fifth Army, now commanded by General Louis Franchet d'Esperey. "Gentlemen, we will fight on the Marne," Joffre had told them, adding with flinty intransigence: "No failure will be tolerated." But the Germans struck hard in the east, forcing back Ferdinand Foch's Ninth Army, which inspired Foch to send Joffre his deathless message: "Mon centre cède, ma droite recule, situation excellente, j'attaque."

It was at this point, when hundreds of thousands of soldiers were grappling for advantage along a front of some 300 miles from Paris to Alsace, that Moltke's chronic indecision became incarnate in the figure of Lieutenant Colonel Richard Hentsch. Dismayed by his inability to get accurate and up-to-date information from Kluck and Bülow, Moltke had spent the last few days staring numbly at maps in his new headquarters in a girls' school in Luxembourg. To ease his frustration, he had decided to send Hentsch to the front as his personal emissary, his eyes and ears, to gather information and assess the situation. This was a very questionable move, delegating to Hentsch a responsibility

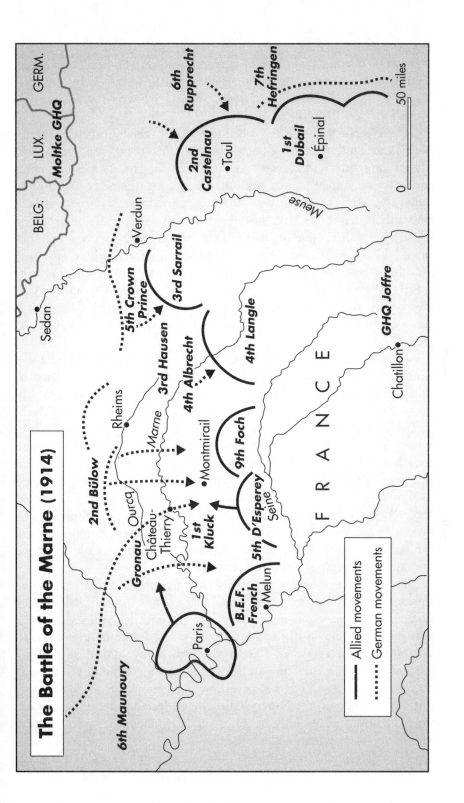

The Battle of the Marne (1914)

GERM.

LUX.

BELG.

Moltke GHQ

6th Rupprecht

7th Hefringen

2nd Castelnau

•Toul

1st Dubail

•Épinal

Meuse

50 miles

•Verdun

5th Crown Prince

3rd Sarrail

•Sedan

4th Langle

3rd Hausen

4th Albrecht

•Rheims

Marne

2nd Bülow

9th Foch

•Montmirail

F R A N C E

•Chatillon

GHQ Joffre

Gronau Ourcq

Château-Thierry

1st Kluck

5th D'Esperey

Seine

•Melun

B.E.F. French

•Paris

6th Maunoury

Allied movements

German movements

somewhat beyond his capabilities, but Hentsch was head of the foreign armies section of Moltke's general staff, described by one colleague as "a very clever, conscientious man, hard-working, well versed in his job." And Moltke trusted him.

Hentsch arrived at Kluck's headquarters in the evening of September 5 and handed Kluck a complete set of Moltke's orders, of which only a summary had so far been sent over the rickety German communications system. Kluck and his top aides gathered to discuss the situation with Hentsch. It was all a little unreal, since, in the words of one aide, "neither O.H.L. nor the 1st Army staff had the remotest idea that an immediate offensive of the whole French army was imminent." Hentsch offered only the judgment that the whole situation was "dubious." Kluck promised to carry out Moltke's wishes but with a little delay; the movements ordered for September 5 would be carried out September 6. Hentsch professed himself satisfied. "The movement could be made at leisure," he said, "no special haste was necessary."

Late that day, Maunoury's Sixth Army launched Joffre's offensive north of Paris, but the German Fourth Reserve Corps, assigned to defend Kluck's right flank, checked the French advance near St. Soupplets. So began the Battle of the Marne, in a lumbering, ungainly fashion, with huge forces flailing at enemies only vaguely perceived somewhere in the distance. "Many bodies still lay on the ground where they had fallen in complete exhaustion," Marc Bloch reported from one small corner of the gigantic battlefield, "their muscles contracted as if making a final effort. Those who die in great battles do not know the majesty of eternal rest. The stench turns one's stomach. The ground was strewn with all sorts of debris, weapons, equipment and human fragments. I saw a severed leg that lay far from its body, alone and almost ridiculous amid the horror. . . ."

The next day, September 6, was one of confused and inconclusive fighting from the Forest of Compiègne to the Argonne. Maunoury renewed his attack but was stopped again, with heavy losses. Kluck was mainly occupied in turning his army, as Moltke had ordered, to face Maunoury. Franchet d'Esperey's Fifth Army lunged at Bülow's Second, then dug itself in rather than advancing. The next day was more of the same. Kluck regained some more ground from Maunoury, but as he turned on the Ourcq Valley, he neglected to tell Bülow of his move. Bülow learned only by accident that the gap between the two armies was now twenty miles wide.

Schlieffen had once imagined the modern commander as a mastermind sitting at the center of a vast network of controls. "The modern commander-in-chief is no Napoleon who stands with his brilliant suite on a hill," Schlieffen wrote, describing rather accurately the position of Moltke at Sedan. "Even with the best binoculars he would be unlikely to see much, and his white horse would be an easy target for innumerable batteries. The commander is farther to the rear in a house with roomy offices, where telegraph and wireless, telephone and signaling instruments are at hand, while a fleet of automobiles and motorcycles, ready for the longest trips, wait for orders. Here, in a comfortable chair before a large table, the modern Alexander over-looks the whole battlefield on a map. From here he telephones inspiring words, and here he receives the reports from army and corps commanders. . . ."

Moltke received very few such reports, however, and he had no inspiring words to offer. In these first few days of staring at his maps and waiting in vain for news, Moltke issued no orders at all. Instead, feeling isolated and helpless, he wrote to his wife strange (for a German general) outpourings of anxiety and guilt. "Today destiny will deliver a great decision," he wrote her from Luxembourg on September 7. "Since yesterday the whole German Army from Paris to Upper Alsace is at grips with the enemy. If I could give my life to achieve victory, I should do it with infinite joy, following the example of thousands of our brothers who have already fallen. What torrents of blood have flowed! And how much misery has come upon innumerable innocent people whose houses and farms have been burned and devastated. I shudder sometimes at the thought. I have the impression that I am responsible for all these horrors, and yet I could not do otherwise."

One of his staff officers was shocked to find the chief of staff in a kind of collapse, "sitting hunched up over his table, his face buried in both hands." Moltke looked up, this officer reported, "and turned a pale and tear-stained face [on us]." Again, Moltke could only try to explain to his wife. "The weight of responsibility has borne me down in the last few days," he wrote. "For still our army is struggling on and there has been no decision. It would be frightful if there is nothing to show for the blood that has been spilled. The suspense, with the absence of news from the far distant armies, almost goes beyond what human strength can stand. . . ."

Once again, Moltke fell back on Hentsch. At a meeting with his top aides on September 8, Moltke decided to send the colonel back to the front, not only to survey the situation but to decide what to do about it. This was such an astonishing delegation of authority that the participants later disputed exactly what authority Hentsch had been given. Colonel von Tappen claimed later that "the officer sent on this mission had not . . . received any kind of full powers to order or approve retreats on the parts of these armies," since supreme headquarters "had not given any orders laying down rearward movements." Under official questioning three years later, shortly before his death, Hentsch insisted that since First and Second army headquarters could be reached only by radio, which involved a twelve-hour delay, both Moltke and Tappen "formally gave me full powers to act on my own initiative." Specifically, Moltke told Hentsch that if he found either Kluck or Bülow in retreat, he should see to it that the two withdrew together so that no gap could open between them.

A pessimist by nature, Hentsch now saw the front lines under particularly depressing conditions. It was a sweltering hot day for a 400-mile drive, and Hentsch's car had to make its way past supply convoys and trucks loaded with wounded soldiers. When he reached Bülow's headquarters in the Château de Montmort, near Montmirail, he settled into long conferences with Bülow, who was also gloomy by nature, and Bülow's staff aides, who were consumed with anxiety about the gap separating them from Kluck. Next morning, Hentsch set out to find Kluck and again saw dispiriting sights along the way. "Groups of wounded flowed in the same direction; they were afraid of being cut off," one officer recalled. "Different columns were bottled up in a jam: an air attack had caused a complete panic. I had to get out of my car several times to clear a way by force."

While Hentsch was absorbing this atmosphere of disarray, Kluck's battle against Maunoury's Sixth Army was actually going rather well. Pushed back all along the front, Maunoury pleaded with Galliéni to send him reinforcements. Galliéni had just acquired the Fourth Corps, which Joffre had removed from the eastern front, but he had no way of shipping these reinforcements to the battlefield. Galliéni was not a man to be daunted by obstacles like that. If there were no railroad trains available, there were always taxis, so Galliéni simply ordered the police to requisition all the taxis that could be found on the streets of Paris. They rounded up 600 of them, and into each one Galliéni crammed ten soldiers. "*Voilà au moins qui n'est pas banal,*" Galliéni remarked with satisfaction as he reviewed the bizarre armada of 600 taxis and sent them honking onward for the thirty-five-mile journey to the front. A miracle it seemed at the time, and in later years "the taxis of the Marne" became a poignant symbol of a time when Parisians would try anything rather than surrendering their beautiful capital.

But Bülow, probably anticipating Hentsch's decision, had already made his own decision to order a cautious withdrawal. "To support the 1st Army north of the Marne," as Bülow said, diplomatically putting the blame on Kluck, "the 2nd Army . . . found itself obliged to retreat to avoid being completely outflanked on its right." This news had its due effect on the overawed Hentsch, confirming his own decision to recommend a general retreat, ascribing to Bülow's Second Army the dangers that Bülow had ascribed to the First. "As there was no possibility of giving immediate help to the 2nd Army," Hentsch said, "I therefore gave the 1st Army the order to retreat, basing my action on the full powers given me. . . ."

So, just twenty miles from Paris, the mighty force that Moltke had sent in the footsteps of his uncle ground to a halt, on the orders of a mere colonel, halted and then turned back toward safer positions along the Aisne. To the exhausted French, it seemed like a kind of liberation. "On Sept. 12, at a quarter past four in the morning, when it was still dark, we set out on a terrible day's march," Marc Bloch wrote. "We were, in fact, in full pursuit of the Germans. Along the side of the road their fires were still warm. During our short halts we ransacked their campsites, and . . . turned up a mass of odds and ends. In one place I recall finding a violin. . . ." There seems to be a remarkable tradition in French literature, dating back at least to *The Charterhouse of Parma*, of heroes remaining unaware of what battles they are fighting in, and so Bloch contributed his share: "It was the victory of the Marne, but I would not have known what to call it. What matter, it was victory."

Or, for the Germans, defeat; for Moltke, failure, shame, and ruin. "For my part I preserve only a confused and burning recollection . . ." one lieutenant of Dragoons remembered. "The heat was suffocating. The exhausted troopers, covered with a layer of black dust sticking to their sweat, looked like devils. The tired horses . . . had large open sores on their backs. The heat was burning, thirst intolerable. . . . We kept advancing without knowing why or where. . . ." Sometimes the fighting was ferocious, as when the British Ninth Lancers charged a Berlin Guards regiment. "A non-commissioned officer of the 9th," said an American witness of the scene, "ran his lance full through a German officer who, thus impaled, struck at the lancer and severed his hand at the wrist." But more often things went as the lieutenant of Dragoons reported: "We knew nothing, and we continued our march as in a dream, under the scorching sun, gnawed by hunger, parched with thirst. . . ."

Back at headquarters, Moltke could only imagine what was happening, but what he imagined filled him with dread. "Things are going badly," he wrote to his wife on the night of September 9. "The battles east of Paris will not be decided in our favor. . . . The war which began with such good hopes will in the end go against us. . . . We shall be crushed in the fight against East and West. . . . Our campaign is a cruel delusion. And we shall have to pay for all the destruction which we have done."

When Hentsch returned to Luxembourg the next day, Moltke conferred with him at length, then finally decided—at long last—to emerge from the shelter of his headquarters and inspect the front. He not only approved the withdrawal of Kluck and Bülow but ordered a retreat by the Third, Fourth, and Fifth armies as well. So ended, or rather faded away, the Battle of the Marne. If victory in war can ever be credited to the will of one man, a Napoleon or a Wellington, that man of unbreakable will at the Marne was Joffre; the man who lacked such a will was Moltke.

Like General Meade after Gettysburg, though, the victors on the Marne were simply too exhausted to exploit their victory fully. The British advanced only ten miles a day behind the retreating Germans, as compared to the twenty-five-mile daily gains that Kluck's men had made at the height of their advance on Paris. And though both sides kept their losses secret, in order not to discourage their civilian populations, those losses were severe. French casualties have been estimated at 250,000, German casualties about the same, British casualties about 5 percent of that. Hentsch reported Bülow's Second Army "burnt out to a cinder," and the same could have been said of the French Fifth Army. General Franchet d'Esperey, who inherited the Fifth from the faltering Lanrezac, promised Joffre that it would fight but admitted that "its condition is far from brilliant."

But if the Battle of the Marne was a storm of blood, it came to seem almost an idyll compared to what followed. As both sides settled down into the hell of trench warfare, barbed wire, and poison gas, the Germans concentrated their attacks on the stronghold of Verdun until about a million men died in the wreckage. Few survivors could even remember the widespread belief in August 1914 that the war would surely be over by Christmas. It endured for another four terrible years, ending, as it had begun, with a German defeat along the Marne. In that beginning, then, was the whole. "The measured silent drawing together of gigantic forces, the uncertainty of their movements and positions, the number of unknown and unknowable facts made the first collision a drama never surpassed," Winston Churchill wrote. "Nor was there any other period in the war when the general battle was waged on so great a scale, when the slaughter was so swift or the stakes so high. Moreover in the beginning our faculties of wonder, horror and excitement had not been cauterized or deadened by the furnace fires of years. In fact the war was decided in the first twenty days of fighting, and all that happened afterwards consisted in battles which, however formidable and devastating, were but desperate and vain appeals against the decision of fate."

. . .

From the very first days of the war, Moltke's physical and mental condition began to worry even those accustomed to his various peculiarities. "On Sept. 14, in the afternoon, General von Lyncker appeared before me in the office," Moltke wrote later, "and said that the Kaiser had the impression that I was too sick to be able to lead operations any further. His majesty had ordered that I should declare myself ill . . . and return to Berlin. General von Falkenhayn should take over operations."

Moltke unquestionably seemed sick. He had suffered from heart trouble and shortness of breath since 1911. His doctor then attributed this not to his being overweight but to an infection from inflamed tonsils. In 1913, his doctor told him that his heart had increased in width and that his heart murmur was louder. Moltke clung to his sense of military duty at a time of impending danger to the Reich.

"I am not so sick as you think," he said.

"Your excellency," said the physician, Dr. Hermann, "is nevertheless much more seriously ill than *you* think."

"According to your view, doctor, I cannot continue as chief of the general staff," Moltke complained. The doctor felt unwilling to confirm that, and so the dialogue ended. Moltke treated himself by taking the cure in Carlsbad, which was convenient for his strategy meetings with the Austrian chief of staff, General Conrad. But once the fighting actually started, the pressures on Moltke became intense, the fear of invasions from both France and Russia, the fear that he had done something wrong and that his misjudgment would lead not only to terrible bloodshed but to national disaster, fear that he was distrusted by both his fellow generals and his temperamental emperor, fear that nothing but his illustrious name held him in place. Fear, fear, fear. His colleagues often noticed that he sat staring into space, and they could only wonder what demons were raging inside his head.

"There are also some very strange stories," says Veronica von Moltke, the pianist, "that he lost the Battle of the Marne because he fell into trances and had visions. This is in a book called *The Spear of Destiny* which somebody gave me, which I hated to read and then I did read because it was—Trevor Ravenscroft, that's the name of the man who wrote it. It's a weird story, but apparently a lot of it is true insofar as Hitler had quite a belief in occult things and thought that whoever owned the spear—that's the *Parsifal* spear—! And then there's this amazing story that—"

She snatches up the book from a nearby table and begins laughing as she reads aloud its account of Moltke's mysterious collapse, when aides found him "slumped across his desk in what outwardly appeared to be a stroke or heart attack." Moltke was thought to be dying, Ravenscroft asserts, with his breathing "barely audible" and "only the slightest trace of heartbeat. The open eyes had a vacant, lifeless look as though all consciousness had been extinguished." Moltke was not suffering from "any immediately diagnosable illness," Ravenscroft declares. "He was experiencing a new-born awareness so concentrated, sharp and vivid that it took him to the edge of pain as his soul was transported on a journey back through Time across a thousand years." In this trance or vision, the fallen general supposedly saw himself incarnated as Pope Nicholas I, an assertive advocate of papal authority during the confusion that followed the division of the Carolingian empire in 843 A.D. Not only that, but Moltke also saw his military colleagues as other figures of the ninth century. Thus Schlieffen appeared as the scheming Pope Benedict II, and even Moltke's late uncle, the field marshal, came back to life in his vision as the soldierly Pope Leo IV, who repaired the damages of the Saracen raids of 846, built new walls around St. Peter's, organized a fleet, and defeated the Muslims in a major naval engagement off Ostia. It puzzled Moltke that a series of ninth-century popes should now be chiefs of the German general staff, but according to Ravenscroft, he solved this puzzle by ignoring "the 'religion' of the Popes" and concentrating on "such things as customs, habits, the quality of personal relationships, bearing and gestures." It impressed him that the officers of the general staff "lived almost totally sequestered lives . . . as withdrawn as the Roman Cia . . ." He concluded that the basic mission of both groups was "the balancing of power between East and West in which the very existence of the Roman See was perpetually at stake." On a visit to Vienna, General Conrad had taken Moltke to see the holy spear in the treasury of the Hofburg, talking all the while of the imminence and inevitability of a war with the encircling powers of France and Russia. "And now, in the transcendent awareness in which he was reliving the life of Pope Nicholas I," Ravenscroft wrote, "[Moltke] was astonished to discover that just this very question of the conflicting factors of fate and free will had tormented the medieval Pontiff. . . . At the zenith of his transcendent vision, General von Moltke grasped the true significance of the Spear of Destiny which now appeared to him in the form of a mighty apocalyptic symbol."

This all sounds bizarre even if one recalls that Moltke and many of his contemporaries believed in the doctrines of anthroposophy, that it was the age of Madame Blavatsky and various Indian swamis, of table rappings and transmigration of the soul and Scriabin's "mystic chord." Moltke reported some of his visions to his wife, Eliza, who believed in them as devoutly as he did. To his military colleagues, he remained a strange and enigmatic figure. Stripped of authority just as his great invasion was beginning to falter, Moltke could only plead for a face-saving delay in his removal. "I went immediately to General von Falkenhayn," he wrote, "and informed him of his majesty's order. He was taken completely by surprise. We went together to the kaiser, who explained to me that he had the impression that I had been weakened by my two cures in Carlsbad and must rest. I said to the kaiser that I thought it would not make a good impression in the army and abroad if I should be sent away immediately after the retreat of the army. General von Falkenhayn joined in this view. The kaiser thereupon explained that Falkenhayn should act as chief quartermaster[1] and I should remain 'pro forma.' Falkenhayn said that he could take charge of operations only if he had a completely free hand. I could only acknowledge this. So I remained at headquarters while everything was taken out of my hands and I remained a bystander without any influence."

Though Moltke later received various assignments, he never recovered his command or his health. The kaiser finally sent him to a castle in Homburg for further rest, and it was there that he learned on November 3 that Falkenhayn had officially taken over—Falkenhayn, who ignored the Schlieffen-Moltke delusion of a quick and decisive victory and replaced it with the no less costly delusion of myriad "limited" attacks; Falkenhayn who then decided to launch an offensive against Verdun so that he could make the French army "bleed to death"; Falkenhayn who presided over the beginning of that horror known as trench warfare. While the months of fighting for Verdun still raged on, Moltke died.

"It was not until *after* his death in 1916," according to Ravenscroft, "that he gave the real explanation of everything which had happened, describing it from a higher vantage point from which he could see

---

[1]In German, *Oberquartiermeister.* The German title of *Quartiermeister* is much higher than in the U.S. army and is accordingly translated sometimes as deputy chief of staff.

without personal prejudice exactly why the Schlieffen Plan had been fated to fail. The close bond between the General and his wife was not severed at his death. Eliza von Moltke, who had by this time also awakened within herself higher faculties, remained in a deep communion of spirit with him. And it was through the faculty of 'Inspiration,' that which St. Paul calls 'speaking with tongues,' that the dead General was able to speak through her from higher levels of time and consciousness. Many of the closest friends of the Moltke family assembled regularly and in secret to hear descriptions of what he could behold in the 'Cosmic Chronicle,' the eternal tapestry of world destiny in which past, present and future are inseparably woven."

By this peculiar technique of conjugal glossolalia, Moltke was said to have predicted the downfall of the Romanov, Hohenzollern, and Habsburg dynasties, which was perhaps not so strange since these dynasties had already fallen at the time of these seances in the 1920s. A little stranger was the late general's naming of the obscure Adolf Hitler as the future Führer of a Third Reich, but that, of course, may have been the basic reason why these seances were held in the first place. Both Hitler and Ludendorff featured in various shadowy political movements of the 1920s, movements that needed all the support they could get from the ghosts of dead generals, heroes, and gods.

"The Moltke 'Mitteilungen' [communications] are very extensive," Ravenscroft writes, "and amount to several hundred pages of typescript, photostats of which are still circulating secretly among hidden Grail groups in Germany today." Freya von Moltke, who probably knows more than anyone else about the Moltke family history, says she knows nothing about these transcripts or about the seances that led to their existence.

IV

The Martyr

The world is divided into those who, willingly or unwillingly, fight for Bonaparte's ambition, and those who oppose him.

—FIELD MARSHAL GNEISENAU

Just as God once promised Abraham that he would spare Sodom if only ten just men could be found in the city, I also have reason to hope that, for our sake, he will not destroy Germany.

—GENERAL HENNING VON TRESCKOW
ON JULY 21, 1944

Helmuth James von Moltke with Caspar, Kreisau, Christmas 1938

Freya with Caspar at Kreisau, 1938

On Trial: January 10, 1945

13

"A Wild National Jubilation"

S<small>INCE</small> M<small>ARIE VON</small> M<small>OLTKE HAD DIED CHILDLESS, AND THE FIELD MARSHAL</small> never remarried in the twenty-three years of life that remained to him, the estate at Kreisau, together with all the orchards and gardens that he had planted, and the family vault where he and Marie lay in their coffins, passed on not to a son but to the oldest of his nephews, Wilhelm, son of Adolf and older brother of the general blamed for the defeat on the Marne. Wilhelm, who was forty-five at the time of his uncle's death, also became a general, though not so exalted in rank as the chief of staff, a failing that the family liked to attribute to personal prejudice on the part of the kaiser. Relatives also liked to deride the music-loving Wilhelm as "the dwarf violinist," though he stood more than six feet tall, a sign of dwarfism among the more elevated Moltkes.

The dwarf violinist's wife spent a lot of time and effort in expanding the *Schloss* at Kreisau, but she was said to be bored by her summers in the remoteness of Silesia, and that was why she put ads in newspapers announcing that an aristocratic family living in the country would be happy to welcome paying guests who could play bridge. The ads attracted an answer from a South African lady who had come to Europe for the enlightenment of her eighteen-year-old daughter. Thus was the Moltke family introduced to that of Sir James Rose Innes, the attorney general under Cecil Rhodes and the future chief justice of South Africa. Sir James was a liberal of renowned probity, and his views on justice were to have a marked influence on his future grandson. "We look forward to a union of races in this country," he rather optimistically prophesied in 1905. "They were meant to be joined together and no body of men will in the long run keep them asunder."

Some fortune-teller had informed Wilhelm von Moltke's bridge-playing wife that good luck would be brought to Kreisau by a girl from abroad wearing a white dress and a blue necklace, so she was pleased to note that young Dorothy Rose Innes was wearing a white dress and a string of turquoise beads when she sat down to dinner on her first evening in Kreisau in 1904. It was probably just as inevitable that during the long evenings of bridge, the young visitor from South Africa should fall in love with the heir to the estate, Helmuth von Moltke, who was nine years older than she. When the young people began talking of marriage, though, Lady Rose Innes took her daughter to London and booked passage back to South Africa. The providential death of Wilhelm von Moltke in 1905 brought Helmuth into his inheritance, and so he rushed to London to dissuade Dorothy from departing, and the two of them were married that October.

The new lord of Kreisau was something of an eccentric. After recovering from a serious illness in his youth, he not only became a Christian Scientist but traveled to Boston to undertake a German translation of Mary Baker Eddy's *Science and Health*. He raised all his children as Lutherans, however. Having inherited his great uncle's title of count, he held a seat in the Prussian Herrenhaus, or House of Lords, but politics did not cut deeply into his leisure time. Kreisau was made for the nineteenth-century tradition of family readings and theatricals, and Count Helmuth liked to join his children and visiting relatives in ambitious projects like *Faust, Hamlet,* and various plays by Molière. Music also played its part in German domestic culture. Helmuth sang to his captive audiences the lieder of Schubert, Brahms, and Strauss. His oldest son, Helmuth James Ludwig Eugen Heinrich, who was born in the Kreisau *Schloss* in 1907, described him as "easy-going, good-natured and when he chose full of consideration for others. But at times he would insist on pursuing some objective which he chose to regard as important without paying attention to the interests of anyone else, including his wife." If Helmuth James's passionate opposition to Nazism drew on the courageous idealism of his grandfather, it also had roots in his father's stubborn fixity of purpose.

But the most direct and powerful family influence on young Helmuth James, according to those who knew him, probably came from his mother, not only as a vehicle for her father's progressive views but as a forceful personality in her own right. Countess Dorothy was warm and encouraging both to her family and to her neighbors. She used her own money to enlarge the village kindergarten that the field marshal had created; she found and hired a woman to serve as village nurse. She was also a conciliator, keenly aware of the unspoken differences that separated an outsider from her adopted land. "Driving home . . . last night in the clear calm moonlight . . ." she wrote her mother, "I was thinking how different in many ways my married and unmarried years are and I could not help being thankful that I have had so much rich experience of several sides of life, several points of view, several sorts of ideals, for it has enriched me very much." The sense of that still continues. "We are a Central European family," says Helmuth James's older son Helmuth Caspar, now a business executive in New York, "but I think I've been changed by my own wife and by the wives my ancestors married. . . . I do think that what sets the Moltkes apart is that they've married well. I think we've just been good about it, clever about it. It has made us much more open to the world."

Helmuth James watched his father drive off to war in his gray Mercedes, with all the servants assembled on the stairway to bid him farewell, but this was the war that no Moltke could win. The boy remembered asking his great uncle, who lived in the red-brick headquarters of the general staff in Berlin, "Uncle Helmuth, when are we going to win the war?" The old general's answer remains unrecorded, perhaps nothing more than a grunt.

The boy had started private lessons with the village schoolmaster, then with a doting governess, but in 1916, he had to begin going to school in the nearby town of Schweidnitz. At the age of nine, he harnessed a gray horse to its wagon for the four-mile trip. In the last years of the war, though, the main fact in the child's life was hunger. When Sir James Rose Innes arranged a postwar visit to Holland to see his daughter and the children, he observed that the British blockade "had left its mark upon them. The children were peaked and sallow and their mother declared that she never wanted to look at . . . potatoes again." The children were restricted in their eating during the first days in Holland, so one of Helmuth James's most vivid memories was being finally allowed to eat chocolate and whipped cream to celebrate the birthday of his younger brother Wilhelm (Willo).

When Helmuth was fifteen, his parents decided that he was getting too confined in Kreisau and Schweidnitz, so they sent him to a boarding school on the Ammersee, a lake southwest of Munich. This was an institution that tried to model itself on the famous public schools of England, but Helmuth, being fifteen, and away from home for the first time, and full of the communal spirit of Kreisau, resisted the imposition of "school spirit." He won election to the school council to oppose it, which involved him in fights with other boys, who invaded his room and beat him up. When his father learned of his troubles, he wearily sent him a map of Germany and asked him where he would like to go to school next. Berlin was then the greatest magnet in central Europe, so Helmuth James picked a *Gymnasium* (high school) in Potsdam, where he could live with a Baron von Mirbach whose wife was one of the boy's many cousins. One of his schoolmates in Potsdam was the kaiser's grandson, Prince Louis Ferdinand of Prussia, who was quite impressed by the newcomer. "He could talk very effectively and spiced his remarks with witty anecdotes which amused the masters," the prince wrote. "Although they must have noticed that he had no respect for them, and may have suspected that he knew more than they did, they appreciated his intelligence. . . . I used to cycle home with him and liked him for his lively and rather cynical manner." A fledgling democrat, Helmuth James actually disapproved of the royal family. When someone took him to meet the dethroned kaiser in exile in the Dutch town of Doorn, the monarch monarchically deigned to ask his chief of staff's great nephew, "What was your father's regiment?" Moltke impertinently replied, "No idea, Your Majesty." That was the end of the interview.

Moltke plunged into the study of history, politics, and law—later exploring all these at the universities of Berlin, Breslau, and Vienna—but the central subject to be studied in the Berlin of the 1920s was Berlin itself, not only a laboratory of political morphology and social transformation but a theatre of the avant-garde, of atonalism and Surrealism. Through his father's connections with Christian Science, Moltke established contact with the Berlin office of the *Christian Science Monitor.* He could not only serve as an interpreter for American correspondents lost in the alien metropolis, he could tell them what plays to see, what concerts to attend. Thus he came to know Dorothy Thompson, the imperious correspondent for the New York *Evening Post,* who was in the process of divorcing a Hungarian intellectual named Joseph Bard and starting her tempestuous marriage to Sinclair Lewis. Miss Thompson later did Moltke the dubious honor of addressing him as her pseudonymous friend Hans in a series of wartime propaganda broadcasts published under the hectoring title, *Listen, Hans.* Though she claimed to be a close friend of "Hans," privy to his supposedly typical German thoughts, there is something grotesque about the contrast between Moltke risking his life to organize resistance to

Hitler and Miss Thompson sitting behind her typewriter in Vermont and exhorting him to take action. "I said that one day you would have to demonstrate by deeds, drastic deeds, where you stood. . . ." she wrote. "And I remember that I asked you whether you and your friends would ever have the courage to act. . . ."

The 1920s in Germany were a time of activism and experimentation, of an almost absurd confidence in the possibility of changing and improving the world, particularly by teaching. One who thought so was an energetic woman from the Romanian province of Bukovina named Eugenia Schwarzwald, one of the first women in Europe to get a Ph.D. She had started a progressive coeducational school in Vienna, where she hired people like Oskar Kokoschka to teach art. Her specialty was talk, though, and in the home designed by Adolf Loos, and in a converted country hotel on the Austrian Grundlsee, she loved to entertain such visitors as Bertolt Brecht, Karl Kraus, and Arnold Schoenberg. Good works were also high on her agenda, and her husband, Hermann, was a prosperous banker who could afford to indulge her, so she organized several country homes for poor children and several soup kitchens in both Vienna and Berlin. There she met young Helmuth von Moltke, and doted on him. He was so bright, so handsome and confident. She liked to predict a great political career for him. She urged him to come and study in Vienna, and he did. He was impressed by Dr. Schwarzwald, too, with her bustling, motherly involvement in everything, but he always remained a little aloof. They addressed each other by the formal *"Sie,"* rather than the *"du"* that is standard among good friends, relatives, and professional colleagues.

Another major influence on Moltke in these years was Eugen Rosenstock, a professor of the history of law at the University of Breslau. Then in his late thirties, Rosenstock was a stocky and energetic man whose interests reached far beyond the law, including economics, sociology, theology, and philosophy. He and Moltke were both interested in doing something about the impoverished textile and mining areas around Waldenburg, west of Kreisau. Rosenstock, an ardent believer in adult education, favored a program that would bring together workers, peasants, and students. He and Moltke decided to start an *Arbeitslager,* or work camp, in the town of Löwenberg. At the invitation of Moltke and others, about one hundred representatives of the three groups gathered there in March 1928 for three weeks of manual labor interspersed by lectures, discussions, and communal whatnot. Moltke pitched in with everything from fundraising to kitchen chores—his mother reported to his grandparents that he excelled at scraping carrots. Back in Berlin, he called on the Reichstag representative for the region, Heinrich Bruening, who would soon become chancellor, and persuaded him to get government financing for the project. The camps reassembled in 1929 and 1930, and similar operations opened in other areas, but Moltke gradually dropped out, not because he lost faith in the method, which Rosenstock later imported to Vermont as part of the New Deal's Civilian Conservation Corps, but because other things demanded his time and attention.

One was a romance with a handsome young student named Freya Deichmann, daughter of a prominent banker in Cologne. Their paths had been approaching each other for many years. Freya's oldest brother, Carl, was one of the boys whom Moltke recruited to his side in his campaign against the authorities at the school on the Ammersee. Her other brother, Hans, had been a protégé of the all-seeing Dr. Schwarzwald. So when Moltke met Freya at the Schwarzwald establishment on the Grundlsee in the summer of 1929, it was almost like encountering a high-spirited sister. Moltke liked to announce, in the manner of adolescents, that he would never marry, but it was only a matter of time until he realized that the Moltke family traditions dictated otherwise. He foolishly protested to the end. "I have suddenly become afraid that you expect too much from me . . ." he wrote in the summer of 1931. "Marriage is such a high-sounding word which calls up a grandiose idea—at the very least, a more settled way of life. Dear Freya, will you . . . be content for us to be just two students who would rather live together than alone?"

She would, and so they were married in October 1931. It was a modest affair—Freya's father was already in the process of going bankrupt and died not long afterward—but these were hard times, and everybody was having troubles. The Kreisau estate was also on the brink of bankruptcy, afflicted by a wide variety of vexations. To begin with, the capital bequeathed by the field marshal had been largely invested in bonds, and these had become worthless during the great inflation of 1923, when the mark fell to 4.3 trillion per dollar. Count Helmuth cut back somewhat by renting out the adjoining estate of Nieder-Gräditz, but an attempt to sell Wierischau failed because of a slump in real estate. A barn full of corn burned down; a crop of grain was flattened by hail. To cut down on expenses, the family moved out of the *Schloss* and into the modest *Berghaus* in 1928. Still the misfortunes continued. The estate manager suffered a stroke that nobody recognized. He began ordering supplies that he didn't need and contracting to sell crops that he didn't have. When he died of a second stroke in 1929, his accounts were in a shambles. By now, the estate's debts amounted to 700,000 marks (about $175,000).

Many east German aristocrats were in similar difficulties during these years, and many of them, including the sanctimonious President Hindenburg, turned to the government for help; Count Helmuth turned to his oldest son, who had just received his law degree at Breslau and who agreed to spend a year straightening out the mess.

Moltke had no real experience at either business or farming, but after many long days of work, he was able to offer a rescue plan to the *Allgemeine Kredit Anstalt* and lesser creditors. He would reorganize the estate as a corporation, with himself in control as agent for the creditors. The Moltke family would keep their home but get no income out of it for twenty years. In addition, they had to sell silver, jewelry, and furniture for the benefit of the creditors. "Things are going better than I expected," Helmuth wrote after the creditors accepted his plan in November 1929, "but it is a strain on the nerves." The national government even helped out by buying some of the field marshal's papers and mementos and leaving them in the *Schloss* on condition that several rooms remain open to the public.

There were still serious bumps ahead. "Today I've seen for certain that I shall be able to resolve the unpleasantest part of this business . . ." Moltke wrote to Freya in March 1930. "In the spring of last year the manager sold plots of land to small peasants, took the money from them and spent it. Now when land is sold, the rule is that ownership does not pass to the purchaser until the plot is struck off the register of the vendor's holdings. This can only be done with the consent of the mortgagers who will only give that consent if some of the money owing to them is paid . . . But the manager had spent all the money and when I got here in October it looked as though the peasants were bound to lose their money. At any rate the mortgagors were demanding 35,000 marks. By endless negotiating . . . I have succeeded in bringing down the amount of hard cash needed . . . to 7,000 marks and that I can find. You can have no idea what that means to me, for what is going to happen even if everything else goes wrong is that small peasants aren't going to lose the money which they handed over on the strength of our good name."

Millions of other Germans did not have a Moltke to shelter them from the storms caused by the Wall Street crash of 1929. Companies failed; mortgages were called in. Unemployment rapidly climbed to 5 million and stayed there all through 1932. This was not just a statistic but an army of men reduced to bitterness and despair. One place where they could find help was in the ranks of the SA, Hitler's brown-shirted Storm Troopers, on whom the Nazis were now spending 2.5 million marks per week. Street fights between the SA and rival bands of Communists and Socialists left some 500 dead or seriously injured that summer. Elections simply mirrored the appalling situation. Running for president against the incumbent President Hindenburg, who agreed to run only to stop the Nazi tide, Hitler collected an ominous 36.8 percent of the votes in April 1932 against 53 percent for Hindenburg and 10.2 percent for the Communist Ernst Thälmann. The Nazis lost 2 million votes in the Reichstag elections that summer, but they still held 196 seats, by far the largest bloc in the chamber.

Though Hitler was quite justified in declaring that his election victories entitled him, as the leader of the nation's largest party, to a chance at being chancellor, this decision rested with President Hindenburg, who had vowed that he would never appoint "that Austrian corporal." Hitler soon discovered ways of working on the aged field marshal, however. On January 22, 1933, he held a secret conference with Hindenburg's son Oskar and apparently threatened him with prosecution for graft and tax evasion unless he helped to change the president's mind. "Oskar von Hindenburg was extremely silent," according to an official who shared a taxi with him on leaving the meeting, "and the only remark which he made was that it could not be helped—the Nazis had to be taken into the government."

That was also the plan of the outgoing chancellor, General Kurt von Schleicher, who had undermined and overthrown two previous chancellors but then proved unable to win a Reichstag majority for his own regime. He had originally tried to split the Nazis by taking in the dissident Gregor Strasser, but now he favored a deal with Hitler. What Schleicher really wanted was for Hindenburg to let him govern by use of presidential decrees, without consulting the Reichstag, but Hindenburg refused. He was dismayed not only by Schleicher's failure to deliver on past promises of Nazi support and a Reichstag majority but by his new efforts to gain wider backing. In a broadcast just before Christmas, Schleicher had announced that he was ending the agricultural quotas that benefited large eastern landowners. He also declared that he was going to take 800,000 acres from bankrupt estates and distribute them to 25,000 peasant families. Hindenburg, whose estate was as bankrupt as any, told Schleicher that he no longer enjoyed the presidential confidence.

"I already have one foot in the grave," the aged field marshal sighed with a crocodile tear as he accepted Schleicher's resignation, "and I am not sure I shall not regret this action in heaven later on."

"After this breach of trust, sir," said the furious Schleicher, "I'm not sure that you will go to heaven."

Despite that insult—Hindenburg was, after all, a pious believer—

the president then assigned to Franz von Papen, an aristocratic dandy and intriguer with virtually no political support, the job of negotiating some kind of coalition. Papen, too, hoped to recruit Hitler into a partnership under his own rule. That night, January 29, an emissary from Schleicher warned Hitler that Papen and the army commander, Kurt von Hammerstein, had put the Potsdam garrison on alert and were planning to establish a military dictatorship. This was probably untrue, but Hitler reacted by organizing a countercoup. He alerted Count Wolf von Helldorf, the commander of the Berlin Storm Troopers, to prepare for a seizure of the main government offices on the Wilhelmstrasse. But he still had no way of knowing what the army would actually do, or who actually controlled it. While Schleicher had been war minister as well as chancellor in the outgoing cabinet, nobody had consulted him when General Werner von Blomberg was chosen as war minister in a prospective Hitler cabinet. A large ox of a man, Blomberg was then serving as chief military adviser to the German delegation at a disarmament conference in Geneva. Summoned back to Berlin, he was met at the railroad station by General von Hammerstein's adjutant, Major von Kuntzen, who hoped to escort him to the war ministry on the Bendlerstrasse. But Oskar von Hindenburg also appeared at the station with orders for Blomberg to proceed directly to the president's office. The bewildered general hesitated barely a moment, then decided, knowing nothing of the choices or risks or issues that might be involved, to report to his president. He was promptly sworn in and given the responsibility for keeping the army in line.

One can only imagine what the high-minded press of London or Paris might have said if the German army had had the temerity to intervene against Hitler's rise to power. The sad fact is that it behaved just as a democratic army is supposed to behave: it did nothing. The beneficiary of its timidity was appropriately grateful. "If in the days of our revolution the Army had not stood on our side," Hitler told a Nazi Party rally later that year, "then we would not be standing here today."

In retrospect, it is easy to see that Hitler's rise to power launched an era of crime and shame for all of Germany, but in its first days, the coming of Nazism seemed to many people a rebirth of national vitality and national pride. The popular awakening that the Nazis had demanded—*Deutschland, erwache!*—was now proclaimed to be a reality. "In those first hopeful, intoxicated months of the new millennium . . ." a young lawyer named Hans Gisevius later wrote, "all misery of body was to be exchanged for work, bread, and a good livelihood. . . . Abruptly, men's spirits changed. A wild national jubilation broke out. Banners, garlands, testimonials, laudatory telegrams, worshipful orations, changes of street names became as commonplace as parades and demonstrations. . . . The glorious sensation of a new fraternity overwhelmed all groups and classes. Professor and waitress, laborer and industrialist, servant girl and trader, clerks, peasants, soldiers and government workers—all of them suddenly learned what seemed to be the greatest discovery of the century—that they were comrades of one race, 'Volksgenossen.' Above all, youth, youth was getting its due."

In such times, it is hard to see that the jubilation will lead to a police state and the triumph of crime over justice. It is hard to see and hard to say no. It is hard to realize that everyone will have to make a choice, to resist the new fraternity, to deny it and reject it in every way, or to collaborate in the coming crimes. To resist or collaborate— or, as a third choice, to leave the country that one considers home, to leave one's family and friends, one's profession, one's very language, and to start all over again as a beggar.

The first temptation is to wait and see how bad things really are. Even Hitler's most perceptive critics could hardly imagine the extent of his future atrocities and could not imagine that he would last long enough to carry them out. A few months, perhaps a year or two. Those staunch conservatives who had cooperated in his rise to power, most notably including Hindenburg, felt quite sure that they themselves retained the real power in the land. Hitler's new cabinet, installed on January 30, 1933, included only three Nazis in its eleven posts, while conservatives and independent experts ruled over the machinery of foreign affairs, defense, economics, agriculture.

They had no idea how suddenly and decisively the former Austrian corporal could strike. On February 27, less than a month after Hitler had been sworn in, the Reichstag went up in flames; the next day, the new chancellor prevailed on Hindenburg to sign a decree "for the protection of the people . . . against Communist acts of violence." The decree left no constitutional liberty unviolated. "Restrictions on personal liberty," it said, "on the right of free expression of opinion, including freedom of the press; on the rights of assembly and association; and violations of the privacy of postal, telegraphic and telephonic communications; and warrants for house searches, orders for confiscations as well as restrictions on property, are also permissible beyond the legal limits otherwise prescribed." A Reichstag majority for these measures was achieved by the simple device of expelling, also with President Hindenburg's approval, all eighty-one Communist legislators. Then came the last "free elections," on March 5, in which, with Goering in command of the Prussian police, the Nazis won 44 percent of the total vote. Then, on March 23, came the "Law for removing the distress of people and Reich," by which the Reichstag gave Hitler the authority to rule by decree.

Even then, it was tempting to wait and see how long the crisis would last. Not long, many supposed experts thought. On the day Hitler took power, which Moltke considered a disaster from the start, he was having lunch with a Socialist friend who argued that the new chancellor's appointment would soon demonstrate his inability to cope with the national crisis, that there was no point in delaying his attempt at governing because the sooner he came to power the sooner he would be out of power. A year and a half later, in the summer of 1934, Hermann Schwarzwald, who was a Jew, told Moltke that "good people" should stay where they were, keeping out of trouble, doing what they could to resist the inroads of Nazism, and waiting to see how things developed.

The choice was easier, in some ways, for those who could see that they had very little alternative to flight or imprisonment. Bertolt Brecht, for example, had learned as early as 1923 that he was number five on a Nazi list of people to be eliminated. His crime was to have written in 1918 a bitter ballad entitled *Legend of the Dead Soldier*, in which the slain hero is dug up, given a medical exam, pronounced fit for duty, fumigated, painted with the imperial colors, and marched back to the front to die another heroic death.

> *Die Sterne sind nicht immer da*
> *Es kommt ein Morgenrot.*
> *Doch der Soldat, so wie er's gelernt*
> *Zieht in den Heldentod.*[1]

When the Brecht-Weill opera *Mahagonny* received its premiere in Leipzig in 1930, Nazi Storm Troopers greeted it with boos and whistles ("By the time the last scene was reached, fist fights had broken out in the aisles," Lotte Lenya recalled, "panicky spectators were trying to claw their way out. . . ."). So when the Reichstag caught fire, Brecht interpreted that as a message for all of Hitler's opponents, to

---

[1]In *Manual of Piety*, his anthology of Brecht poems, Eric Bentley provided this translation of Brecht's lines: "and the stars aren't always in the sky/For lo! the dawn cometh!/But the soldier, just as he has been taught,/Marched to a hero's death."

which he responded by leaving for Vienna the very next day.

Heinrich Mann, now remembered primarily as the author of the novel that Josef von Sternberg used as the story of Marlene Dietrich in *The Blue Angel,* was already being threatened. He and the artist Käthe Kollwitz were among the signers of an appeal for Socialists and Communists to join forces in the March 5 election. The Nazi representative at the Prussian Ministry of Culture thereupon demanded that they both be expelled from the Prussian Academy of Arts (which meant the loss of all state support, such as Kollwitz's studio, or any teaching job), or the Ministry would shut down the Academy itself. The Academy reacted as academies generally do. A few days later, the *Völkische Beobachter,* the Nazi newspaper, denounced Mann as "national vermin." Like Brecht, he decided it was time to leave. He bought a ticket to safety across the French border in Strasbourg. (Be it noted that Käthe Kollwitz went on living and working alongside her husband in Berlin throughout the Nazi era until her death there in 1945.)

The case of Thomas Mann was, as usual, somewhat more complicated. Like Heinrich, Thomas Mann produced an anti-Nazi statement in the first month of Hitler's rule, but in contrast to Heinrich's work, Thomas's manifesto was ignored. The Berlin Convention of Socialist Culture, at which Thomas's *Avowal of Socialism* was to be read on February 19, was postponed indefinitely because of the threat of Nazi demonstrations. Mann published his unread text in the February issue of *Sozialistische Bildung,* but there too it remained largely unnoticed. In Munich, however, a band of forty-five pro-Nazi cultural enthusiasts, ranging from the lord mayor to such local musicians as Richard Strauss and Hans Pfitzner, denounced Mann for, of all things, a panegyric that he had just composed in praise of Richard Wagner. The Goethe Society of Munich had commissioned this effort, and so Mann had devoted much of that fateful January 1933 to writing the essay that he called *Sufferings and Greatness of Richard Wagner.* It resounded with Mannian trumpetings. "What is it," he wondered, "that raises the works of Wagner to a plane so high, intellectually speaking, above all older musical drama? Two forces contribute, forces and gifts of genius, which one thinks of in general as opposed; indeed, the present day takes pleasure in asserting their essential incompatibility. I mean psychology and myth. . . ."

Mann's reading received the customary applause at the University of Munich on February 10, and he pursued his frugal practice of repeating his performance in Amsterdam, Brussels, and Paris, but the forty-five protesters denounced Mann's musings as an "insult" to their own patriotism. Mann was vacationing from his lectures in Switzerland when he learned of the Reichstag fire. He too began to think of flight, but he also thought of returning to Munich to pack up his considerable belongings. His son Klaus and his daughter Erika, both more closely attuned to current politics than the aging author of *The Magic Mountain,* warned him on the telephone to stay in Switzerland. The Munich weather, they said in the kind of guarded language that was now becoming common, had taken a turn for the worse.

"How extraordinary!" Mann remarked to his friend René Schickele. "One leaves one's country to lecture on Richard Wagner in Amsterdam and Paris, and when one wishes to return, it has run away."

So Mann very quietly began metamorphosing from a vacationer into an exile. It was a very reluctant metamorphosis. "The question arises," he wrote to his Italian translator on March 13, "whether from now on there will be any room at all in Germany for the likes of me, whether I will be able to breathe that air at all. I am much too good a German, far too closely linked with the cultural traditions and the language of my country, for the thought of an exile lasting years, if not a lifetime, not to have a grave . . . significance to me."

Over and over again, individual Germans had to make the painful decision on what they would do, how much tyranny they would accept, how much they would resist. Adolf Busch, the eminent violinist, put aside his Stradivarius and took a new violin on tour so that he could break it over the head of any Nazi who created a disturbance. In Stuttgart, a man in the audience rose to his feet in the middle of Busch's concert and flung up his arm in the Hitler salute. Busch stopped playing and shouted, "Put your arm down!" Only when the Nazi complied did he resume his playing. In Hamburg, though, an official wrote to inform him that the Busch Quartet could not give a scheduled concert until it replaced its violist (a Jew) and cellist (married to a Jew). The letter ended, "Heil Hitler." Busch not only refused to change his quartet but added that he considered the words "Heil Hitler" an insult to any decent German. He became a Swiss citizen in 1935 and emigrated to the United States in 1939.

Walter Gropius, creator of the Bauhaus, had troubles with the authorities in Weimar as early as 1924, when the army searched his home on the ground that the Bauhaus was a nest of subversion. After moving his pioneering school of design to the Socialist-run city of Dessau, Gropius retired to private practice in 1928. When the Nazis won the elections in Dessau in 1932, one of their first demands was that the Bauhaus close. Mies van der Rohe managed to revive the school in Berlin, and the students even threw one last wild Bauhaus party in that February 1933—"Our party was wonderful . . ." wrote one of the 700 who were there, "and apparently it was something special even for Berlin"—but the Gestapo was soon heard from, issuing its own rules for instruction in the arts. "Ludwig Hilbersheimer and Vassily Kandinsky are no longer permitted to teach," the Gestapo announced. "Their places have to be taken by individuals who guarantee to support the principles of National Socialist ideology." And so on. Mies took the discreet course. "The economic situation," he diplomatically informed the Bauhaus students in August, "does not allow for a continuation of the Institute."

Individual lives cannot be so simply closed down. Gropius was all too willing to cooperate with the regime that despised his Bauhaus. He freely joined Propaganda Minister Joseph Goebbels's new *Reichskulturkammer* and submitted architectural plans for such Nazi projects as a Strength Through Joy education and recreation center; his plans were rejected. On the other hand, Gropius irritated Goebbels by accepting a lecture invitation in Leningrad, and when his office manager reported for work in a Nazi uniform, Gropius fired him. Such gestures could be risky—life in Berlin was terrifyingly ambiguous in those days—but Gropius relied on not only his eminence as an architect but his status as a wounded veteran of four years on the western front, proud holder of the Iron Cross First Class.

This was a time of personal troubles, too. Manon Gropius, the seventeen-year-old daughter of his turbulent first marriage to Alma Mahler, fell gravely ill with polio in Vienna. After visiting her there in June 1934, Gropius left for England the following month, but he took care to leave with official permission, by way of a Fascist-sponsored theatre conference in Rome. He also got official permission to remain and work in England, and he never criticized the Nazis ("Any criticizing remark about the present policy made by me would easily be taken as a hostile act . . . risking very unpleasant consequences"). He could not get another Austrian visa in time to see Manon again before she died (Alban Berg dedicated his new violin concerto "to the memory of an angel"), but he remained politically neutral. When Harvard invited him to become a professor there in 1937, he once again requested and received Berlin's official permission for the move, and he made no public criticisms of the man he referred to in private correspondence as "that horrible Hitler."

As for Mies, he stayed on until 1937—there were commissions to be had during the 1936 Berlin Olympics—before immigrating to Chicago. Very few refugees took flight immediately. It was not only a question of deciding when life in Germany had become literally unbearable but of searching out where and what might be bearable. Jobs were everywhere hard to find in the 1930s. The official rules decreed that nobody could leave Germany with more than 20 marks, and no other countries welcomed the indigent.

Thomas Mann's entangling professional problem in the early days of the Nazi regime was that he was just finishing *The Tales of Jacob,* the first volume of *Joseph and His Brothers,* which had occupied him for most of the past decade. The day on which the distinguished publishing firm of S. Fischer shipped the first 10,000 copies to the bookstores in October 1933 happened to be the day on which Alfred Rosenberg's Reich Office for the Furtherance of German Writing issued instructions to the German publishing industry to cancel all further business with refugee authors. Rosenberg's decree was at least partly inspired by an anti-Nazi article by Heinrich Mann. Entitled *L'Éducation morale* and originally written for the *Dépêche de Toulouse,* it was harsh in its condemnation: "Never yet has such an avalanche of lies descended on a nation, falsified its own recent history and brought about such total oblivion." In French, this was bad enough, but a German translation appeared in the September issue of a new refugee magazine in Amsterdam called *Die Sammlung,* sponsored by André Gide, Aldous Huxley, and Heinrich Mann, and edited by Thomas Mann's twenty-seven-year-old son, Klaus.

Did this mean that 10,000 copies of *The Tales of Jacob* would have to be consigned to the scrap heap? Not if the distinguished publishing firm of S. Fischer could help it. To repair the damage, Samuel Fischer's Gentile son-in-law, Gottfried Bermann, made his way to the Manns' temporary headquarters in the Riviera town of Sanary. There he persuaded Thomas Mann to repudiate the anti-Nazi criticisms in *Die Sammlung.* "CHARACTER OF FIRST NUMBER SAMMLUNG DOES NOT BEAR OUT ITS ORIGINAL AIMS," said the exculpatory telegram that Mann sent to Berlin, thus repudiating not only his own brother but his own son. (While Bermann was in Sanary, he collected an even stronger disavowal from another of his authors, Alfred Döblin, the author of *Berlin Alexanderplatz,* whose exile eventually ended in Hollywood. And another from Stefan Zweig, who ended a suicide in Brazil.) "I was faced . . ." Mann tried to explain, "by the question whether I wished to sacrifice the life of my work, whether I wished to disappoint and take my leave of those people in Germany who listen to me. . . ."

So *The Tales of Jacob* appeared in October, and its first edition sold out in a week, and then so did the second, third, and fourth printings, but the price that Mann paid was to remain silent about the Nazi regime. Though he did not dare return to Germany, he even accepted the formality of being enrolled in the Nazi writers' guild, the *Reichschrifttum-kammer.* Alfred A. Knopf invited him to New York in June 1934, and Mayor Fiorello La Guardia welcomed him at a testimonial dinner, and President Roosevelt chatted with him in Washington, but Mann remained silent. This was the month of the Röhm purge, the famous Night of the Long Knives, when Heinrich Himmler's SS troops butchered not only the leading Storm Troopers but such inconvenient figures of the recent past as ex-chancellor Schleicher, and Mann still remained silent. To a friend, he argued that he could only go on with his work, and "then one day people will say that during this period we were the real Germany."

Not until the following year did Mann begin to express "the real Germany" by joining his older brother's efforts to win the Nobel Peace Prize for Carl von Ossietzky, the crusading editor held in a Nazi prison camp. Only then did Mann's commercial tie to Nazi Germany fade because Bermann negotiated a deal to move the Fischer publishing operations to Switzerland, leaving only the name behind under "Aryan" ownership. The deal collapsed, however, when the Swiss authorities refused their permission to this newcomer. While Bermann trekked on to Vienna (the firm ended in New York, returning only after the war to Frankfurt) Eduard Korrodi, literary editor of Switzerland's main newspaper, the *Neue Zürcher Zeitung,* published an article supporting the Swiss policy of exclusion. In doing so, Korrodi denied that German literature had emigrated, claiming that the writers who had emigrated from the Third Reich were Jews. Many were, to be sure, but many were not. Mann, for one, was not, just as Brecht and Gropius and Mies and Busch were not. "Countless human, moral, and aesthetic observations," Mann now wrote, belatedly, in the *Neue Zürcher Zeitung,* "support my profound conviction that no good can possibly come of the present German regime, not for Germany and not for the world. This conviction has made me shun the country in whose spiritual traditions I am more deeply rooted than the present rulers. . . ."

By now it was 1936, and these present rulers seemed to be flourishing. The French had tamely acquiesced in Hitler's illegal remilitarization of the Rhineland; the British had signed a new naval agreement with the man whom Lloyd George called "a great German." Now it was time for the nations of the world to gather in Berlin for that festival of athletic excellence known as the Olympics. Many English and American visitors came, and many were impressed with

Hitler's success in rescuing Germany from the Depression that still afflicted Chicago and Birmingham. There were occasional reports of Nazi "excesses" in obscure prisons, but most Germans seemed to be prosperous and contented. And though the American press enjoyed making a fuss about the triumphs of the black star Jesse Owens, the overall team victory went to the Germans. And besides, what pride could Americans take in their own treatment of blacks when the so-called Scottsboro boys were now on trial for their lives in Alabama?

Helmuth James von Moltke, oldest son of the Christian Scientist who presided over the field marshal's estate at Kreisau, celebrated his twenty-sixth birthday during the turbulent first days of the Nazi regime. He was still uncertain what to do with his life. He had been tempted by social work during his university days. He had even been tempted by the chimera of journalism. In the spring of 1929, he told his grandfather that he had three choices: to get a job at I. G. Farben, the chemical firm that later became one of the Nazis' principal users of slave labor; to work part-time as Edgar Ansel Mowrer's assistant in the Berlin office of the Chicago *Daily News;* or to go to New York and work for the *Evening Post.* He innocently decided on thralldom to Dorothy Schiff at the *Post* but was dissuaded by friends. The attractions of the law were still strong. At the time of the Nazi takeover, he had just passed his exams to begin work as a referendar, roughly the equivalent of a court clerkship. The Nazis completed his education by requiring young lawyers to spend several weeks at an indoctrination camp. Like the others assigned to the camp at Jüter-bog, Moltke was supposed to sing Nazi songs, study Nazi texts, and attend seminars on the Nazi interpretation of legal principles. It was a horrid parody of the work camps he had helped to organize a few years earlier. Characteristically, Moltke argued vehemently with the instructors and organized concerts of Bach and Beethoven to disrupt the reading periods. Even before the Nazis, though, he had doubts about the legal profession. "I am sure that my life is not the law but politics . . ." he wrote as early as 1929. Nazism, of course, put both law and politics in considerable jeopardy. "I may well give up the law for the time being," Moltke wrote in 1933. "The old jurisprudence, which I have learned and which is inspired by the concept of abstract justice and humanity, is today only of historical interest because no matter how things develop in Germany there is absolutely no chance of bringing back these old ways of establishing what is just."

Moltke was now working in the Berlin law firm of Koch-Weser and Karlebach. Edgar Koch-Weser had been a minister of the interior and a minister of justice in the Weimar Republic, but as a half-Jew, he decided in 1933 that the Third Reich would not be a comfortable place for him, so he immigrated to Brazil. His partner, Alfred Karlebach, also a Jew, also decided to leave Germany that first year of Nazi rule. These were certainly examples for Moltke to consider, but when flight is not a matter of indisputable necessity, then the whole process of decision is slower, more complex, more difficult. How does one decide when one must go, or where, or under what circumstances? "I really wanted to write you a letter about the people in Germany who aren't persecuted," Moltke wrote to a friend with a rather strained jocularity. "They are the people whose patriotism is beyond question, who are above having socialist inclinations and who are for all that not outspoken monarchists. You will already have gathered from the description that I belong to this group. . . One has the following advantages: one can express a dissenting opinion without worrying, for the worst that people will think is that one is a bit injudicious. . . ."

There were unpleasantnesses, of course, but people in the Moltkes' position could always make arrangements. The Kreisau manager installed by the creditors was a Nazi Party member named Adolf Zeumer, and he provided a certain insulation between the Moltke family and the local party authorities. When everyone was ordered to fly a swastika banner to celebrate some Nazi occasion, for example, none flew over the Moltkes' *Schloss* or over the *Berghaus* but one hung from Zeumer's window, and there were no troubles. And while Helmuth claimed that he felt free to say what he pleased, his mother went through all his books and burned any that she thought might bring difficulties. "I have learned . . ." Moltke had written some years earlier, "that one must never get alarmed when things go wrong but learn to live through it."

Still, he kept fingering the bars of the cage. For Prussian aristocrats, the Moltkes were unusually international, and the international connections represented both a magnetic attraction and a means of escape. He applied for a Rhodes scholarship but failed to get it. In 1934, when Hitler struck down the Storm Troopers in the gory purge known as the Night of the Long Knives, Moltke and his wife were enjoying a long sojourn in South Africa, enjoying the contact with non-German relatives, and the freedom of a non-German society. Unlike the Mann brothers, Moltke returned to Germany and found it shivering in the aftermath of the great purge. Hindenburg died that summer, and Hitler coolly took over all the president's official duties.

Moltke tried finding work in the sanctuaries of international law, a somewhat dispiriting mission in the best of times. He visited the headquarters of the League of Nations in Geneva, and of the International Court in The Hague. He found nothing that challenged him. "There are a number of well-read people in the League Secretariat but nobody with any personality," he wrote. "Bureaucrats abound but men of weight are lacking. What is worst is that everyone regards himself as his country's representative rather than as the League's official. . . ." He went to London and was captivated by the venerable traditions of the Inns of Court. He applied for admission to the Inner Temple and began almost commuting between Berlin and London, seventeen trips in the next five years. Moltke's English connections brought him introductions to many notable people—E. M. Forster, for example, Lord Halifax, and Lord Lothian. Among these also were the members of Lord and Lady Astor's notorious Cliveden set, who were all too sympathetic to German political demands. Lord Lothian, who had recently interviewed Hitler and then written in the *Times* that the Führer wanted peace, told Moltke that the Nazis had risen to power largely because of the vindictive Versailles treaty and the French occupation of the Ruhr. Moltke replied that this was an exaggeration that the Germans liked to use as an excuse. He had a similar interview with Bishop Headlam of Gloucester, chairman of the Church of England Council on Foreign Relations, about Nazi persecution of both Christians and Jews, and the bishop brushed him aside. "Moltke seems to me to be a bitter opponent of the whole Hitler regime," the bishop wrote disapprovingly, "and to be determined to keep up the Church feud. . . ."

Moltke worked prodigiously to pass his British bar exams in 1937 and 1938. At one point, he had to read 7,000 pages and write ninety-five short essays in the course of a month. Still, he maintained a practice in Berlin, joining, in 1935, the office of Karl von Lewinsky, a former German consul general in New York, now engaged in private international law. In 1938, the year of the Austrian *Anschluss* and the Sudetenland crisis, Lewinsky warned him to make up his mind to emigrate. "Get out of this odd country," Lewinsky said. "You will never be able to make good in it. The pity is that I am too old to go." Instead, Moltke simply shifted in the summer of 1938 to another Berlin law office, that of Paul Leverkuehn.

The trouble was, probably, that Moltke was not only too cautious but too responsible simply to cut and run. He felt acutely in charge of his family and the family estate at Kreisau, and both were undergoing difficult times. His mother, to whom he was devoted, suddenly died in 1935. "He had always been a kind of father to his younger brothers and sister," Freya von Moltke recalls now, "especially after their mother's death." Moltke became a real father at the end of 1937, thus giving a hostage to fortune, with the birth of Helmuth Caspar von Moltke, whom a neighborhood gardener incorrectly designated as *"Barönchen,"* or "little baron." "Today is the baron's first birthday," Moltke wrote his wife the following year, "and accordingly a day to wish you happiness." The widowed count, meanwhile, had turned to a younger Christian Science practitioner and married her in 1937. Helmuth and the other children were openly hostile to this second marriage, referring to their divorced and penniless stepmother as "Pensioner Annie."

Despite all the ties to Kreisau, despite all the forces of doubt and inertia, Moltke eventually, and almost inevitably, came to find the Third Reich unbearable and decided to move to London. "I can't stand the inanity of this existence much longer," he wrote in August 1938. "Wouldn't it be better to be done with the false values and the pretenses here and live extremely humbly in some place where one isn't continually under pressure to conform? I have the feeling that I would far far rather starve in a free land than go on trying to keep up appearances. For that is what we are all doing. We let ourselves be a facade to cover up the atrocities which go on continually and the only reason for it is that we are left alone for a relatively long time before it's our turn to be got at. I've just no more stomach for it."

Pastor Martin Niemoeller, who was sent to Dachau at about this time for resisting the Nazi takeover of the Protestant churches, bitterly summed up the difficulties of such resistance: "They came first for the Communists, and I didn't speak up because I wasn't a Communist. Then they came for the Jews, and I didn't speak up because I wasn't a Jew. Then they came for the trade unionists, and I didn't speak up because I wasn't a trade unionist. Then they came for the Catholics, and I didn't speak up because I was a Protestant. Then they came for me, and by that time no one was left to speak up."

Even in the earliest days of Nazism, Moltke had said that "voting for Hitler means voting for war," but all through the crises of 1938, which ended with the Munich conference, he had convinced himself that there would be no war. Since nobody was really ready for war, the dangerous game of bluffing would have to end with somebody backing down, as the British eventually did. "In my view it is wrong to lose one's head over all this talk of war and rush out of the country," Moltke wrote. "In the last resort, the more that individuals can keep calm and cool and collected, the greater the chances of nothing happening." So Moltke was rather laggard in actually carrying out his move; it was as though the years of preparation had become a substitute for the actual departure. But he did take Freya to London in June

1939 to help in the arrangements for a temporary move. He rented an office and ordered furniture. "I even picked out the curtains," she says now.

But there were last-minute arrangements to be made in Berlin and Kreisau too, and by pure chance the Moltkes were back in Germany when Hitler attacked Poland by surprise at dawn on September 1.

"Then you were simply *caught* by the outbreak of the war," a questioner asks Freya von Moltke in the tranquillity of her Vermont home.

"Yes—caught." She sighs.

To avoid the draft, Moltke decided, he had to find some kind of official job. He consulted with his father's cousin, Hans Adolf von Moltke, who had been ambassador to Warsaw until the war, then tried to retire but was assigned to be ambassador to Madrid. Helmuth reported that Hans Adolf "was rather negative" but promised to "have a look around" at the foreign ministry for possible jobs. "His opinion seems to be," Moltke added, "that anti-aircraft gunnery is the right activity for me." When Hans Adolf found no openings, Helmuth was drafted into the foreign department of the Abwehr, the German military intelligence service.

"The catastrophe is rushing toward us," Moltke wrote Freya on October 13, as the Wehrmacht was sweeping to victory in Poland. "I've reached the point where I can no longer see anything standing between us and this catastrophe. . . ."

Of Helmuth's younger brothers, the army swallowed up Joachim Wolfgang (Jowo), then thirty, and Carl Bernd, twenty-six. Jowo survived the war and became an art historian. C. B. disappeared in 1941, when he was twenty-eight, lost somewhere over North Africa. "The search for C. B. has so far been without result," Helmuth wrote to Freya in January 1942. "It seems, however, that the British broadcast names by wireless telegraphy; one military station, at any rate, already had names of men killed on Dec. 30 and buried by the British. The chief danger is that he may not have been found and died of thirst somewhere. This waiting is ghastly."

"C. B. was a happy person, by inclination and character," Freya von Moltke recalls now, "but he had a difficult early life because he was not very interested in studying. He wanted to become—he was very much interested in sports, and it was not done that a son of his family would go into sports only and not finish school. So he was pressed and pressed to finish school, which he didn't do in the end. He wasn't stupid, but he could not make it in school. So in the end, he gave up and took an apprenticeship in a firm. He was sent to Paris and had an interesting semester there. But on the whole things didn't develop that well for him. Then he had to join the army, and he hated the Nazis. He had loved the Nazis as a youngster, but when he was sent to Paris, he saw the thing from the outside, and he understood and changed. There was never any discussion about politics with him, but he changed. He refused to be an officer because he hated the Nazis so much. So he flew, as he had to be in the war, and he was shot down."

After two weeks of "ghastly waiting," Helmuth heard a report. "Bad news about C. B. . . ." he wrote. "The British airman who shot down the plane is reported to have said that two airmen bailed out but that one of them was caught by the falling plane and died. This story doesn't quite fit into the picture given by other reports. . . ."

After a visit to the family cemetery in Kreisau that March, Helmuth had a strange vision.

"I was a very old man and had outlived you all," he wrote to Freya about the vision. "I was walking slowly but steadily. It was the anniversary of your death and I was coming from your grave. You'd been dead 20 years. . . . Walking along—as an old man—I thought of the day when I had put a memorial stone for C. B. in the new cemetery and how painful it had been. . . . I had achieved all I wanted; the world looked the way I'd wanted it but it had cost a terrible effort, and you had not lived to see the result. That was the worst pain: I had not been able to tell you that all the sacrifice and renunciation and effort were rewarded. . . ."

14

Willo's Escape

THE ONLY ONE OF HELMUTH'S THREE YOUNGER BROTHERS WHO ESCAPED from the German military machine—at Helmuth's urging—was Wilhelm Viggo von Moltke, known in the family as Willo. "Helmuth had really educated him politically," says Willo's widow, Veronica, the pianist. Determined to become an architect, Willo studied under Hans Poelzig at the Technische Hochschule in Berlin. Just a month after he got his degree, in the spring of 1937, at the age of nearly twenty-seven, he set off for England "partly to broaden my education but mainly because I was thoroughly opposed to the Nazi regime in Germany." It was not easy for refugee architects (or anyone else) to find work in the middle of the Depression, but Willo had more than enough talent to get by. He found a place in the London architectural firm of Hening & Chitty, working, as he put it, "on the design of housing developments, schools, airports, farms and other projects."

"I didn't really escape—that's too dramatic—I simply left," Willo recalled in a subsequent interview with Judith Pearlman, an American engaged in making a TV documentary about the Bauhaus. "I had English friends, architects, who said, 'Whenever you're ready, you can come and start work on Monday.' So I came on a Friday and I started on Monday. And that made it very easy for me, because I couldn't take any money out of Germany but I could borrow from friends until my first paycheck. Since I was not Jewish—the Nazis wanted to have all Germans under their control. They wouldn't have allowed it when I said I wanted to leave the country. So I was under subterfuge. When I went to get a new passport, the man said, 'Go back to Germany, that is where you should be.' Then fortunately I remembered that I knew somebody in the diplomatic service in London who was anti-Nazi, and so the next day I had a passport."

History has been so colored by the horror of the Holocaust that we misremember much of its evolution. It is widely assumed, for example, that the Nazis devoted much of their energy to rounding up and killing Jews throughout the 1930s. In actual fact, the main targets of political persecution during the early years of Nazism were political opponents, particularly Communists and Socialists, labor union leaders, and dissident intellectuals. Toward the Jews, who represented a very small minority of the population, the Nazis' early policy was to remove them from positions of influence, to terrorize and humiliate them, to strip them of their possessions, and to drive them into exile. Only after the war began did the basic policy shift to the mass murder that may have been implicit all along, starting with shootings by the *Einsatzkommandos* who suddenly appeared in Poland; only in January 1942, however, was the "final solution" proclaimed at a conference in the Berlin suburb of Wannsee.

All policies in this field involved hypocrisy and deception. While the Nazis encouraged Jews to emigrate (after being reduced to poverty), Willo von Moltke was finding how strongly they opposed the emigration of "true Germans," for such departures represented not only a powerful criticism of the Nazi regime but a rejection of the Nazis' efforts to speak for ethnic German minorities in neighboring countries. Conversely, neighboring countries were not free of hypocrisy and deception either. They regarded Jewish refugees as a natural result of Nazi persecution, but they did their best to avoid letting Jews settle in new homes. But while they felt no ethnic objections to German Gentiles in search of safety, they regarded such emigrants as politically suspicious, either troublesome radicals or covert Nazi agitators.

London proved, in any case, not to be the ultimate political sanctuary for Willo von Moltke. After a year there, he encountered what his widow, Veronica, calls "difficulties with working permits," so he decided to explore Scandinavia. "I went to Sweden, at that time one of the leading countries in modern architecture," Willo stated on a later job application. Once again, he found work in an architectural office and "designed housing projects, offices, a city hall and community center . . . as well as furniture." But this was not the ultimate sanctuary either, particularly after war had broken out in Poland. "I got a message from my eldest brother that I had better leave for America," Willo later recalled. "I had planned the same idea. Because I was too close to Germany. And I didn't want the Nazis to put my family in a concentration camp to cause me to come back." This was a tactic known as *Sippenhaft,* literally family imprisonment, by which the relatives of any opponent of Nazism became hostages to the goodwill of the Gestapo. "You stay out," Helmuth wrote to him. "One of us has to survive."

Getting to America was not easy even for people with money and connections. This was the time of the celebrated voyage of the S.S. *St. Louis,* which sailed from Hamburg to Havana with 907 Jewish passengers who thought they had all the documents needed to escape the impending Holocaust, who then found that the Cuban authorities required an impossible quantity of additional bribes before they would let any refugees land, who then tried without success to negotiate their way ashore in Miami, New York, or anywhere else in the United States, and who finally had to sail back to the embrace of Nazi Germany.

"I went to the American Consulate," Willo recalled, "and they said, 'Sorry, but we are full for three years. We won't even take your name.' Then I went systematically to all consulates in Stockholm, and I got visas for Guatemala, Honduras, and Panama. But the shipping lines between Stockholm and Central America were all freighters, and they took only two passengers, and they did *not* take any passengers of belligerent nations. I found I could go by way of New York, so I went to the Norwegian-American Line, but to get an American transit visa was a very difficult thing. The first time I went to the American Consulate, they said, 'All you want to do is go to America. Guatemala is just an excuse. Goodbye.'"

Being a von Moltke had its advantages. Willo had met the American ambassador at a party, so now he asked him to use his good offices. "The ambassador was not very friendly," Willo recalled. "He said, 'You have to join your own country.' But I told him I can't exist there, it's such a terrible regime." The ambassador agreed to give the question "consideration." At about the same time, the South African ambassador received notification that Willo's South African grandparents were making South African money available.

After a certain amount of haggling produced a U.S. transit visa for Central America, Willo packed up and headed for the waterfront in Oslo. He sold his camera "because a German with a camera would be suspicious, but I kept my sketch book and started sketching. I was arrested." After some argument, Willo managed to convince the suspicious Oslo police that he was an artist rather than a spy, and there remains in his Cambridge studio a sketchbook neatly recording his last day in Europe. It includes a slightly absurd series of pictures of the voyaging artist's sandaled feet, as seen from the artist's eye some six feet above.

> *You who will emerge from the flood*
> *In which we have gone under,*

wrote Brecht, who was also dodging through Scandinavia in these last prewar days, first to Denmark, then to Sweden, then to Finland. . . .

> *Remember*
> *When you speak of our failings*
> *The dark time too*
> *Which you have escaped.*
> *For we went, changing countries oftener than our shoes. . . .*

While Moltke was sailing from Oslo to New York (and Brecht trekking from Stockholm to Helsinki, then to the officially neutral Soviet Union), the Germans invaded Denmark and Norway. When Moltke docked in New York, he found that "all Latin American republics [had] developed a fear of Germans, so all my three visas were cancelled and I was stranded. I was without a place to go."

"We happened to arrive on a Friday night, and all the officials were away for the weekend," says Moltke's voice from a tape recorder. This is another version of the story. Willo used to like telling tales of his coming to America in the dark times, and Veronica once put a tape recorder next to the dinner table at the house in Cambridge, where Willo ended as a professor of architecture at Harvard. So even though Willo died in 1987, Veronica still has his voice on tape, and now he is posthumously recounting to a visitor in that same sunny Cambridge dining room the story of his flight from the Nazi police state. "So I had to wait until Monday, in prison on Ellis Island, my welcome to the United States by the Statue of Liberty. We slept in dormitories with about two meters between beds. There was a small light on all night so the guards could look at people. Males and females were separated, even if you were married. And we marched to get our meals. But in between, in the lounge, we could talk a bit, and there were some Chinese who had been sitting there for six months.

"So finally on Monday, I got out, and here I was in New York.

Once I was here, I got a permit to stay sixty days in New York.

"I knew a Canadian architect who introduced me to Alvar Aalto, who was working on the remodeling of the Finnish Pavilion at the New York World's Fair. He spoke English quite well, but it was an effort. I talked Swedish to him, and he was so delighted. He said, 'Oh, you speak Swedish and you're an architect. Can you work for me?' So I was delighted to work for that famous architect, for about a month, which, however, I must also confess was illegal because I was on a transit visa."

Like any other would-be immigrant, Willo found himself conferring with lawyers, who recommended legal appeals for some kind of residence permit. One obvious route was to apply for student status. "The best thing was to try to get to Harvard. I knew about Harvard. I knew about Gropius. So I got a letter saying they would admit me, but all the answers from Washington were negative. I went to Washington, to the Justice Department, and visited the person who had the decision in this matter. Incredible. He was sitting there in his shirtsleeves with his feet in the drawer, the bottom drawer of his desk, and a big cigar, and he said, 'What can I do for you?' The next question he asked me was, 'Are you Jewish?' When I said no, he became naturally suspicious. Also somebody with a military name. He cross-examined me, and finally I convinced him that I was honest, and he said at the end, 'Very soon, you will hear from me.'"

In two weeks, Willo received his student visa. In the traditional manner of the wandering German student, however, he didn't immediately go to Harvard. Somebody told him about the free-form improvisations newly beginning at Black Mountain, where Josef Albers had already established one of the first Bauhaus refugee outposts, so he headed for North Carolina. Feininger, Léger, Huxley, Cage and Cunningham, Buckminster Fuller, De Kooning and Motherwell—who was not at Black Mountain in those days?

"I arrived there without knowing anybody," Willo told Miss Pearlman, "but I had an introduction from Xanti Schawinsky, the painter, not even a letter but just hello and greetings. And they said, 'We could use somebody with your training. We need an assistant to our architecture instructor.' I had never taught before, but it was easy because I was assisting somebody who had teaching experience.

"But then I had to leave. I had met in New York Oscar Stanoroff, the architect, and the Museum of Modern Art was having at that time a competition for designers of modern furniture. So we did this competition together, and we won the first prize in bedroom furniture, which gave people the opportunity to call us 'the bedroom experts.'

"It was the beginning of a new era in furniture design. That was the same competition where Charlie Eames and Eero Saarinen entered living-room furniture, and the first time that the molded chair designed by this team appeared.

"But anyhow, that gave me a certain glory when I finally came to Harvard in the spring of '41. 'Oh, here's the man who won first prize in the bedroom category in the Museum of Modern Art competition.' And I met Gropius. He was a very quiet man who loved to smoke cigars. And always spoke German to me, unless somebody would approach his desk, and then he would switch to English. He didn't want to give the impression that there were secrets.

"I always had the feeling that Gropius was terribly German, much more German than I am. He was very successful, of course, and he was very honored, but his great work was done before he came to America.

"But he loved to build. I remember where he said, at the age of seventy or something, 'Well, I'm going to lay some more eggs.' He enjoyed it so much that he probably forgot what must have been a terrible ordeal for him in leaving Germany.

"I had a really very pleasant time. He suggested that I build a school which could be prefabricated and shipped to different parts of the country, and that was one of my projects. He also organized the so-called Collaborative Studio, where we worked with city planners and architects together on the development of a new town in the outskirts of Boston.

"I had quite a pleasant existence. Of course, I also realized, after America got into the war, that I was somewhat of a problem. I had to register as an enemy alien, and I was barred from going to certain places. And I had to get permission if I moved more than a three-mile radius from my house.

"Then I suddenly got a letter from the Department of Justice saying, 'You are still on a student visa here. Would you be interested to become an immigrant?' And I quickly wrote back, 'I would be delighted.' The German quota had opened up because refugees from Germany couldn't get across the Atlantic—they were in Lisbon or in London or other places, waiting for transportation—so nobody was applying for the German quota.

"So I filled in all the forms they sent me—questions like whether my grandmother had a house of prostitution and so on—and then it took about eight months to process this. And finally, I got a letter saying that I would have to leave the country to become an immigrant, but they said I could do this in Montreal. So I took a girlfriend along and went skiing and then came back to Cambridge.

"And very soon after my return, I received a letter from President Roosevelt, saying, Greetings, and your neighbors have selected you to have the great honor to serve in the American army. You could refuse to serve, and nothing would happen to you, but you would lose your right ever to become an American citizen. And since I left Berlin for political reasons, it was not a difficult decision for me. I knew better than many people why this war was fought."

Willo must have been richly conscious of the irony of his situation. Here was a von Moltke, great-great nephew of Germany's most honored and admired professional soldier, taking the oath in the army of another country, a country that was now at war against Germany, or against the criminal regime that had seized control of Germany.

"So I was inducted at Fort Devens," Willo recalled. "This was my first encounter with a certain class of Americans who had a very limited vocabulary full of four-letter words, some of which I just didn't understand. The only person I knew was Philip Johnson, the architect, who had been in Germany and knew German, and who was inducted with me. He was a nice person and an interesting person to talk to. Then we got separated. I was sent to Fort McClellan, Alabama, and I finished my basic training there. But I remained a German citizen. After ninety days, I was entitled to become a naturalized American, but ninety days later—two times ninety days—three times ninety days—I didn't get naturalized. It wasn't too bad, but I was annoyed.

"I had some good friends who were officers, and they told me I should find out what was in my files. Of course, in America, you can always find out things, so I went to a sergeant in Intelligence and I said, 'What does it mean that I'm still a German citizen?' He said, 'You can't be naturalized. You'll only be naturalized after the war.' I was outraged, of course, but nobody could understand that. They said, 'You should be happy, you don't have to go to the front.' But I left Germany for political reasons, I knew what I fought for, and so on.

"On my next leave, I went to Washington and talked to friends who knew something about the government, and they said, 'Why don't you write to Mrs. Roosevelt, and she'll send your letter to the secretary of war, and then an investigation will start from there?' So I came back to the camp and threatened to do that, and the major who was in charge of intelligence was horrified at the idea of an investigation from Washington, so he cross-examined me for two days. What had happened—but I didn't find this out until after the war—was that when I lived in New York, I was invited to a lot of cocktail parties and met a lot of people, and somebody—I don't even remember his name—said, 'I just came from Detroit and I met a very charming professor of history at Wayne University, and his name is Heinrich von Moltke, and he must be a relative of yours.' So he wrote out this professor's address in my address book. I lost the address book on the train between Boston and New York—it slipped down behind the seat or something, and somebody found it and gave it to the FBI. And the FBI thought that the wife of this Professor von Moltke—whom I never met—was some kind of a Nazi agent, so—but the major who was cross-examining me apparently got the impression that I was an honorable man. So he recommended that I be naturalized. And the moment I was naturalized, I was open for officer training.

"By that time, I was quite happy to be an enlisted man—you didn't have to make any decisions, and so on—but I felt it was my duty to be an officer because of my training and experience. So I became an officer and I went to Fort Knox, Kentucky, and trained for the armored forces. Lost fifteen pounds. I was just a skeleton because we went on the double between classes, running everywhere. And finally I was finished, and I was ready to be shipped to Europe, and I had my orders to go on May 8, 1945. Of course, this was V-E Day, the end of the war in Europe. So they sent me to the Pacific, as a tank unit commander, and I went to Manila. . . ."

15

Extraordinary Times

In one sense, Helmuth James von Moltke could be said to have started cooperating with the Third Reich on the day he went to work in its military intelligence headquarters, for he thus became part of what he himself had recently called "a facade to cover up the atrocities which go on continually." In a more important sense, however, joining the Abwehr meant joining not Hitler but the anti-Hitler resistance, for the Abwehr chief, Admiral Wilhelm Canaris, was one of the most important figures in that resistance.

Widely known as "the little Greek," Canaris belonged to a family that had actually come to Germany from northern Italy many years earlier; his father was chief engineer at a smelting plant in the Ruhr. Canaris was no democrat. A submarine captain in World War I, he later became involved in some of the dirtiest nationalist activities of the Weimar years—the murder of Rosa Luxemburg, the Freikorps violence, the Kapp Putsch, the secret rearmament. He was an enthusiastic supporter of Hitler when he took charge of the Abwehr in 1935, and he seems to have become disillusioned only in the late 1930s, largely because of the machinations of Reinhard Heydrich, whom Himmler had put in command of the malevolent *Sicherheitsdienst* (SD). Still, Canaris had created his own web of deception and intrigue. His agents were everywhere, and whatever they learned, Canaris learned. Some of this he fed to Himmler and Heydrich, but just enough to persuade them of his loyalty, which they often doubted, for good reason. Canaris took part in several of the military conspiracies to overthrow Hitler; he made several efforts to open secret peace talks with the Allies, but he was not really devoted to the Resistance. Though he repeatedly rescued Jews and other Gestapo victims by taking them under the protective mantle of the Abwehr, he remained one of those who believed that Hitler was a heroic leader, led astray by killers like Himmler and Heydrich. His chief role in the Resistance was to provide a sanctuary and a field of operations for more active dissidents like his chief of staff, Colonel Hans Oster, a minister's son who brought an almost religious ardor to his crusade against Nazism.

Moltke's entry into the Abwehr was not, in any case, entirely voluntary. "Helmuth was *drafted* into the Abwehr," says Freya von Moltke. "It was his war job. It happened because of his expertise in international law. It is true that he wanted to be drafted for this particular position because he hoped that he could do good there and would not be confronted with Nazi dogmas. But he had no idea that he was coming into a center of active anti-Nazis. Since everybody had to be very careful, it took him a long time to find out the depth of that opposition."

Moltke's job nonetheless gave him an opportunity for a fairly overt kind of resistance. He was a *Kriegsverwaltungsrat* (war administrative counselor) for the Abwehr's foreign countries division, a group that worked mainly in evaluating intelligence material and providing liaison between the foreign ministry and the military supreme command (OKW). This gave Moltke an opportunity to point out and criticize conflicts between German military activities and the body of international law, particularly the Hague Conventions of 1899 and 1907, which supposedly guaranteed certain protections to civilians and prisoners under "the laws of war." The very concept of such restraints was quite alien to most of the men commanding Hitler's war machine, but Moltke soon discovered that even the most ardent Nazi would hesitate when informed that something was "against the rules." Such hesitation could be increased by evidence that Germany was vulnerable to retaliation. So Moltke soon found himself embroiled in heated arguments over such questions as whether to fire on passenger ships. "This morning the draft of a new law landed on my desk for immediate comment . . ." he wrote to his wife that first October of the war, "I had to obstruct it massively, and the result so far is a meeting tomorrow of all the ministries concerned, at which I for my sins must play the leading role."

In the midst of these arguments, Moltke was continually harassed by doubts as to whether he was really accomplishing anything. "The worst is still to come," he wrote at one point. "Whether there will be anything left then, heaven only knows." But something kept driving him to renew his efforts. "My new assignment has in fact brought me to grips with one of the basic questions about the whole conduct of the war," he wrote in November, "and perhaps put me in a position where I can in minor respects set limits to the misery." Like any man in such a position, he was tempted all too often to wash his hands of the whole problem. "How thankful I am that my purely technical work in all these fields involves me in no responsibility!" he wrote at one point. But all the perfumes of Arabia would not sweeten any military official's hands for long. "I have been sleeping badly lately because I've been too worked up about my jobs," he wrote. "Fighting for human lives is gratifying but also terribly agitating." And then: "When I survey these four months, I find that I've never before prevented so much evil and achieved so much good."

In the midst of these debates, Moltke learned of another kind of resistance that cast a long shadow over his efforts. A carpenter named Georg Elser, recently imprisoned in Dachau on suspicion of communism, had spent several nights breaking into the *Bürgerbräukeller* in Munich and planting a bomb in a pillar behind the dais where Hitler spoke every year on the anniversary of his 1923 Beerhall Putsch. The bomb went off with a great crash on the night of November 8, 1939, killing eight people in the audience and injuring sixty-three, but Hitler had left the hall ahead of schedule. The Gestapo was so quick to blame the explosion on British intelligence agents that historians have suspected Himmler of arranging the event for that purpose,[1] but all that Hitler's enemies could know at the time was that although the Führer was heavily guarded and seemed to enjoy a charmed life, he was surprisingly vulnerable to attack, if only the attacker was sufficiently determined. That was the challenge that now confronted the only men who actually controlled enough force to end the Nazi dictatorship—the generals. They prided themselves on their sense of honor and their aristocratic traditions, on the army's historic claim to be a virtually autonomous state within the state; they grumbled endlessly about the vulgarities and pretensions of "that man," the ex-corporal and his private army of street-fighters. Now, over and over again, the

---

[1]Interestingly enough, Elser was never prosecuted but held as a "special prisoner" in various concentration camps until the last weeks of the war, when he was murdered in a way that was meant to look as though he had been killed in an air raid.

generals had to face the question of whether they were tough enough, brave enough, and smart enough to fight back. Over and over again, they faced it and failed. Hitler simply knew how to fight better than they did. Often, in fact, he won his way before the generals even realized that there was anything to fight about. The key element in *Blitzkrieg,* Hitler knew, was not just speed but surprise, not just force but deception and guile in using it.

In truth, the army had been gradually surrendering to Hitler ever since that day in 1933 when General Blomberg, returning from Geneva to Berlin, had proceeded directly to Hindenburg's office to be sworn in as war minister, thus signaling that the army would not interfere in Hitler's becoming chancellor. Blomberg had been Hindenburg's own choice for the war ministry, and as he led the officer corps in bowing down to Hitler, he did so with the pretense that it was the venerated Field Marshal Hindenburg who was really in command, the field marshal to whom the generals bowed down. The only general who briefly disputed that surrender was the commander in chief, Kurt von Hammerstein-Equord. He had discussed with outgoing Chancellor Schleicher the possibility of an anti-Hitler putsch, but they had decided to do nothing. Hammerstein was notorious for his indolence; he preferred aimless horseback riding to the rigors of his official duties. He and Schleicher found it convenient to believe that Hammerstein would retain the power to change his mind and to expel Hitler from the chancellery. They were mistaken. When it became clear, after nearly a year of bickering between Blomberg and Hammerstein, that one of them would have to go, Hindenburg saw to it that it was Hammerstein who went. Hindenburg also chose his successor, Baron Werner von Fritsch. A Rhinelander brought up by extremely strict middle-class parents, Fritsch was not remarkably intelligent but had done brilliantly at the *Kriegsakademie,* where he not only graduated first in his class but received superlative grades of nine in both tactics and military history, the two chief subjects. He served mainly as a staff officer in the war but received a head wound from a grenade at the front. Introverted, reclusive, a lifelong bachelor and a devout Christian, Fritsch professed to be completely "nonpolitical"; he concentrated on his work, won the highest praises, and despised all lesser mortals. Even after the Nazis came to power, an American journalist who stood next to Fritsch at a parade noted that he "poured out a running fire of sarcastic remarks about the SS, the Party, and various Nazi leaders from Hitler on down. He did not disguise his contempt for them all."

The internal conflicts brought on by the first year of the Nazi dictatorship disturbed old Hindenburg, who may not have known the full extent of Hitler's crimes but did know that he had come to power as a result of Hindenburg's acquiescence. And now there were dark reports about people being dragged off to a concentration camp called Dachau. One of Hindenburg's protégés, Vice Chancellor Papen, even drafted a speech calling for an end to Nazi terror. Hitler ordered it canceled. Papen promised to "advise Hindenburg of this immediately." When Hitler flew to see Hindenburg at the president's country estate, he was received by the ordinarily obsequious Blomberg, who coolly announced that President Hindenburg had authorized him to say that the present state of tension in the Reich was intolerable, and unless Hitler could quickly end it, Hindenburg would declare martial law and put the army in charge of the government. Hitler demanded to see Hindenburg face to face, and the old man repeated his warning. Hitler was aghast; this was the one retaliation that could still checkmate him. He nonetheless had one strong move to try.

One of the army's chief grievances against Hitler was the size and power of the SA, the private militia of brown-shirted street-fighters known as Storm Troopers. Now that there were no more street-fights to fight, SA chief Ernst Röhm wanted to bring his 2 million Storm Troopers into the much smaller regular army, with the strong implication that he himself should command the combined force ("I am the nucleus of the new army," Röhm said). The generals fiercely opposed any such move, but not to the extent of acting on their own. Hitler, who felt that he now needed the generals more than the SA, took counsel with Goering and Himmler, and they convinced him, without too much difficulty, that Röhm was plotting a coup against him. At this delicate moment, Blomberg published an article declaring that "the Army . . . stands behind Adolf Hitler . . . who remains one of ours." Taking that as his cue, Hitler told Himmler and Goering to smash Röhm's supposed coup. The main SS raiding party found the SA chief and his top aides fast asleep, several with male companions, at a lakeside hotel near Munich. Then followed what soon became known as the Night of the Long Knives. Röhm, hauled off to a prison in Munich, was left with a pistol and told to do the honorable thing. He refused. "If I am to be killed," he said, "let Adolf do it himself." Two official killers promptly marched into his cell and shot him down.

The slaughter went on all that night, eliminating not just SA leaders but anybody Hitler wanted dead. A gang of SS men went to the villa of General Schleicher, who had resisted surrendering the chancellor's office, and shot him down in his doorway. Another SS gang ransacked Papen's office but failed to find him—he had gone into hiding. They butchered three of his aides. Estimates of the total number of murders have ranged from the official 61 to more than 1,000. When it was over, the SA was virtually destroyed, and Hindenburg thanked Hitler for his "determined action and gallant personal intervention which have . . . rescued the German people from great danger." The army won no victory here, though, for the slaughter spattered it with disgrace, not least for its acquiescence in the murder of General Schleicher; the only real winners, other than Hitler, were Himmler and the SS for they had displayed a ruthlessness that now filled their opponents with fear.

Just a month later, on August 1, Hindenburg's long life scraped to an end. He had hoped, as did many traditionalists in the officer corps, that this would provide the occasion for a restoration of the Hohenzollern monarchy. Hitler announced instead that he was merging the vacant presidency with his own position as chancellor and Führer. As chief of state, he demanded the very next day that all officers swear a new oath of loyalty, not to the constitution, as under the Weimar Republic, but to him personally, as they had once sworn loyalty to the Hohenzollern kaisers. "I swear before God," the oath said, "to give my unconditional obedience to Adolf Hitler, Führer of the Reich and of the German people, Supreme Commander of the *Wehrmacht*, and I pledge my word as a brave soldier to obey this oath always, even at peril to my life." Such oaths may not mean a great deal anymore, and many of the generals who swore fealty to their Führer may have known that Hitler never felt the slightest qualms about breaking any pledge or promise, but this oath had a paralyzing effect on the officers who took it. "This is one of the most disastrous moments [*verhängnisvollsten Augenblicke*] of my life," Chief of Staff Ludwig Beck said to a friend at the conclusion of the torch-lit ceremony in Berlin. Whenever the generals were subsequently asked to join in stopping Hitler from leading Germany to war and ruin, whenever they were shown that his course could only lead to catastrophe, they remembered the oath they had sworn on that summer day in 1934, remembered and quailed.

And though they reveled in the illegal rearmament that Hitler had ordered, in violation of the Versailles Treaty, they quailed, too, at some of the consequences. One was that the new army, increasing from 100,000 to 300,000 men, was rapidly filling up with young Nazis, products of the Nazi-dominated schools and the Hitler Youth movement, who actually believed in Hitler's promises of a German rebirth. If the generals ever ordered these young zealots to march against their Führer, whose orders would they obey?

The other consequence that frightened the generals was that Hitler seemed determined to actually use his enlarged forces for the reestablishment of German power. They began to get nervous when he announced a boycott of the Geneva disarmament conference in the fall of 1933 and said he would fight any punitive sanctions by the League of Nations against German rearmament. They became even more nervous in 1936, when Hitler sent troops to reoccupy the supposedly demilitarized Rhineland. War Minister Blomberg, who had signed the orders for the troops to march, had also issued orders for them to withdraw if the French resisted. Hitler himself later admitted that he would have had to resign if the French had fought. The French did nothing. Sending forces to aid the Fascist uprising in Spain in 1936 was yet another of Hitler's dangerous gambles, and yet another of his victories over the doubting generals.

In November 1937, the Führer called his highest commanders together and told them his plans for taking over Austria and Czechoslovakia. The Germans, he said, had "the right to a greater living space than other peoples." Germany's future was therefore "wholly conditional upon the solving of the need for space," and Germany's problem could be "solved only by means of force." Although he predicted that this "solution" must come before 1943–1945, he told the generals that they should be ready for war within a year. "Our first objective . . . must be to overthrow Czechoslovakia and Austria." That was too much for Blomberg and Fritsch. Germany was not ready to fight a major war, they said, so it must not take such risks. Hitler scowled. He did not believe Himmler's persistent warnings that the generals were conspiring to overthrow him, but he did begin to realize that his daring ideas of conquest would never be achieved by men like these.

Blomberg, whom Hitler had rather capriciously made a field marshal as a reward for his having helped the Nazis to gain power, was known behind his capacious back as "the rubber lion." Now nearly sixty and a widower with five grown children, he confided to Goering one day that he wanted to marry a War Department secretary named Erna Gruhn. She was, he admitted, "a lady with a past." Since such a marriage would be considered disreputable in the Prussian military caste, to which his late wife had belonged, Blomberg asked Goering whether it would be acceptable to the new leadership of Germany. Goering, who may well have known more about Fräulein Gruhn than he let on, checked with Hitler and then gave Blomberg the official blessing. The new Wehrmacht was not bound by antiquated Junker prejudices against the common people, he said. Not only did Hitler approve but he and Goering would act as witnesses. And so, in a quiet but much-noted civil wedding in January 1938, they did.

Some police officials, meanwhile, just happened to be going through some dossiers when they just happened to discover one dealing with Fräulein Gruhn, including some pornographic pictures and a record of her arrest for prostitution. The dossier worked its way fairly quickly to the office of Count Wolf Heinrich von Helldorf, the Berlin chief of police, who was horrified by the political possibilities of what he had learned. Instead of sending the dossier to his superior, Himmler, who he knew would use it to blackmail and thus control Blomberg, he went to the head of the military administration, General Wilhelm Keitel, who also happened to be Blomberg's son-in-law. Keitel, even more horrified, went to Goering. Goering, not at all horrified, since he yearned for Blomberg's job, went to Hitler and told him that the disgraced field marshal must resign to preserve the honor of the officer corps. So did Commander in Chief Fritsch, who had heard rumors of the scandal and hurried to Hitler's office to join in the stoning of the war minister. He found the authorities already discussing Blomberg's successor, who should rightly be Fritsch himself, but Goering and Himmler blocked that. Hitler took the question under advisement.

While he was thinking, Himmler provided him with a new dossier containing testimony against Fritsch by a petty hoodlum named Otto Schmidt. This Schmidt, then in his late twenties, with a long record of convictions for larceny, embezzlement, and blackmail, made a practice of hanging around near the men's room of the Wannsee railroad station in Berlin. There, in November 1933, he had spotted a rather elderly gentleman, sporting a monocle and a silver-handled cane, who went into the men's room and soon emerged in the company of a notorious homosexual named Martin Weingaertner and known as Bavaria Joe.

Schmidt followed the pair as they retreated into a dark alley, then watched as the elderly gentleman paid some money to Bavaria Joe. Schmidt accosted his victim, identified himself as a detective, said he had seen the couple's vile activities, a violation of Paragraph 175 of the criminal code, and he wanted money. The elderly gentleman offered several hundred marks from his wallet, but Schmidt said that was not enough, so the two went to the victim's apartment in the suburb of East Lichterfelde, and Schmidt collected 1,000 marks. This soon became a regular practice, Schmidt always demanding and getting more money from a man he identified as "Von Frisch or Von

Fritsch," until Schmidt was finally arrested and imprisoned for an unrelated crime. Once the Gestapo had him in its clutches, it soon persuaded him to be more specific in his recollections. He was ready to swear that his victim had been Baron Werner von Fritsch, commander in chief of the German army.

Curiously enough, Hitler had seen this dossier when Schmidt's testimony was first taken in 1935, but he had dismissed it as "filth" and ordered it destroyed. Now that Himmler presented it again, the Führer was more receptive. He summoned Fritsch to his office, then went to a door and dramatically flung it open to reveal the disreputable figure of Schmidt. The shabby blackmailer pointed at the bemedaled general and declared, "That's the man." Fritsch, who had heard rumors of machinations against him, flushed scarlet and became quite speechless with rage. That such a thug should appear in the office of the chancellor of the German Reich to accuse him, the commander of the German army, of—it was unspeakable. When he finally was able to control his fury, Fritsch managed to say that his accuser "must be mistaken." He swore on his word of honor that the accusation was a lie. Hitler, who had no honor and therefore believed no man's word, interpreted Fritsch's agitation as evidence of guilt. The general demanded a military trial to clear his name. Hitler refused, since the case seemed so clear to him, and ordered Fritsch to go on indefinite leave.

Fritsch did finally get a military trial, which demonstrated not only that the charges against him were false—Schmidt's real victim had been a Captain von Frisch, now dead—but that the Gestapo knew they were false. But the news of the trial was virtually obliterated when Hitler marched into Austria that same week, and Fritsch never won the reinstatement that he and his friends thought he deserved. Hitler had seen and seized his great opportunity to humble the army. "From now on," said the decree that was read over the radio on February 4, 1938, "I take over personally the command of the whole armed forces." In the great reshuffle—sixteen generals were relieved and forty-four transferred—Hitler abolished the war ministry. All its administrative functions were assigned to the new *Oberkommando der Wehrmacht*, or OKW, under the servile General Keitel, who was given ministerial rank. Goering was placated by being promoted to field marshal. And Fritsch's position of army commander was given to Walther von Brauchitsch.

A cultivated and rather elegant figure, Brauchitsch was by no means a Nazi, but he lacked the courage to recapture the political territory that Fritsch had lost. And he, too, had a marital problem. Separated from his wife for five years, he needed money to pay the divorce settlement that she demanded for herself and their four children. The woman he now wanted to marry was a divorcée named Charlotte Schmid-Rüffer, also generally described as "a woman with a past," but unlike the new Frau von Blomberg, she made up for her past by being what one diplomat called "a two hundred percent rabid Nazi." Hitler cemented Brauchitsch's obedience by not only approving this second marriage but providing 80,000 marks to make it possible. The new wife often reminded the general of "how much we owe to the Führer."

Fritsch, after his downfall, saw little hope of a change. "This man, Hitler, is Germany's destiny for good and for evil . . ." a visitor quoted him as saying. "If he now goes over into the abyss—which Fritsch believes he will—he will drag us all down with him. There is nothing we can do." Fritsch asked and obtained the command of a combat unit assigned to the impending invasion of Poland, and there he was killed in action. Blomberg lived on, safely out of combat, through the war and the defeat. Imprisoned by the victorious Allies, he was waiting to testify at the Nuremberg war-crimes trials when he died in 1946, an emaciated and nearly forgotten figure.

The one general who seemed ready and willing to take action against Hitler during the crises of 1938 was Ludwig Beck, who now held Field Marshal Moltke's old position of chief of the general staff. Son of a metallurgical engineer, Beck had trained in the Prussian field artillery before serving on the General Staff during the war. Like Moltke, he was something of an intellectual, an amateur violinist and the author of a celebrated manual on tactics. Widowed after a brief marriage and the birth of a daughter, Beck accustomed himself to fifteen-hour work days, his only recreation being early-morning rides in the Tiergarten. It was perhaps a consequence of his intellectuality that he mistakenly thought he could get his way by writing memoranda and arguing with his opponents, starting with the army's commander in chief, Brauchitsch. When Beck realized in the spring of 1938 that Hitler planned to attack Czechoslovakia, he began sending memo after memo to Brauchitsch, arguing that Britain and France would not permit such a conquest, that the attack would lead to another world war, that Germany could not win it, and that Brauchitsch must prevent Hitler from attempting it. "I now feel in duty bound . . ." Beck wrote to Brauchitsch, "to ask insistently that [Hitler] should be compelled to abandon the preparations he has ordered for war, and to postpone his intention of solving the Czech problem by force. . . . This view is shared by all my Quartermasters-General and the departmental chiefs of the General Staff." Brauchitsch stammered and stalled and finally refused. "Why, in heaven's name, should I, of all men in the world, have taken action against Hitler?" Brauchitsch later protested to a colleague. "The German people had elected him, and the workers, like all other Germans, were perfectly satisfied with his successful policy."

There was some justification for this argument, even if it was mainly a justification for doing nothing, but Beck would not be silenced. He formally requested a meeting of all the leading generals, at which they should decide on a joint demand to Hitler to halt his war plans or else they would all resign—a kind of generals' strike. Brauchitsch agreed only to call the meeting, which was held in the first week of August. Most of the generals supported Beck's views, but when it came time for Brauchitsch to read out the ultimatum that Beck had written for him—"You must support me and follow me unconditionally along the path which I must tread for the welfare of our German Fatherland"—Brauchitsch could not do it. Instead of leading the generals to Hitler, as Beck had expected, Brauchitsch would only tell them that he had taken note of their views. On August 10, however, Hitler summoned the nervous generals to a state dinner at the Berghof in Berchtesgaden. There he harangued them for three hours on his future and theirs. When a few of the generals ventured to express some of their doubts, Hitler angrily scolded them. One of them nonetheless dared to express the view that the western defenses against France could not be held for more than three weeks. Hitler exploded. "That position can be held not only for three weeks but for . . . three years," he cried. "The man who doesn't hold these fortifications is a *Hundsfott* [an extremely vulgar term for the sexual organs of a female dog]."

The generals docilely dispersed. Hitler sent Brauchitsch an order that military interference in political affairs was henceforth forbidden. When Hitler's order reached Beck, the chief of staff rejected it and demanded that Brauchitsch join him in resigning. Brauchitsch refused. Beck requested another interview with Hitler and once again argued that Germany could not risk another world war. He demanded a promise that Hitler would not go to war. Hitler refused. "The army is an instrument of politics," he said. "I shall assign the army its task when the moment arrives, and the army will have to carry out this task without arguing whether it is right or wrong."

Beck said he could not be responsible for orders that he did not approve. That was tantamount to resigning, but Beck did not quite resign, not quite yet. Following protocol, he notified Brauchitsch of his resignation on August 18. Brauchitsch refused to accept it. Beck refused to accept the refusal. He stopped coming to his office, he stopped doing his job. Hitler finally acceded to Beck's resignation but insisted that it be kept secret until October—his deadline for the seizure of the Czech Sudetenland being October 1—and so Beck not only resigned alone but resigned in silence and obscurity.

He nonetheless refused to give up. He resolved to organize a coup against Hitler. As former chief of staff, he had lost all authority except that of his own personality, but that he used to the full. "What are at stake here are decisions that affect the existence of the nation," he declared in a memo to Brauchitsch. "History will brand the military leaders with blood guilt if they do not act according to their professional and political knowledge and conscience. Their soldierly duty of obedience has its limit at that point where their knowledge, their conscience and their responsibility forbid the execution of a command. If, in such a case, their advice and warnings are not listened to, then they have the right and the duty before their people and before history to resign their commands. If they all act with a determined will, the execution of an act of war becomes impossible. In this way, they save the fatherland from the worst possible fate, from destruction. Any soldier who holds a leading position and at the same time limits his duty to his military charge, without being conscious of his supreme responsibility to the nation, shows lack of greatness and of understanding of his task. Extraordinary times demand extraordinary methods."

The German commanders were not extraordinary men, or not extraordinary enough. Supreme Commander Brauchitsch responded to Beck's appeal, according to one colleague, by tightening his collar another notch and saying, "I am a soldier; it is my duty to obey." Beck did a little better with his own successor, Franz Halder, who agreed to lead a coup against the Nazi regime but only after Hitler finally ordered the invasion of Czechoslovakia. The man who actually agreed to carry out the coup was General Erwin von Witzleben, commander of the Third Military District, which included Berlin. One of his subordinates, Major General Count Eric von Brockdorff-Ahlefeldt, would lead his 23rd Infantry Division from Potsdam into Berlin and seize the Gestapo headquarters on the Prince Albrecht Strasse. His troops would arrest Himmler, Heydrich, and other top police officials. Hitler would then be confronted with this event and told that all the chiefs of the SS must be dismissed. When Hitler refused, as the conspirators expected, he would then be arrested and spirited away to some secret hiding place. "Witzleben was optimistic about this plan . . ." according to one of the conspirators, Fabian von Schlabrendorff.

"Proclamations charging that Hitler planned to drag Germany into a world war, and revealing the crimes committed by his regime would be issued, thus justifying the coup d'état to the German people."

How simple it all sounds! The generals never actually agreed on whether Hitler should be shot; most of them thought he should be confined in an insane asylum or brought to trial. It apparently never occurred to them that the dictator might be judged perfectly sane, or that a trial might lead to his acquittal by acclamation. In any case, Halder was about to give the orders to march—or so he later said—when Neville Chamberlain surrendered to Hitler at the Munich conference, abandoning the Czech Sudetenland in exchange for a mendacious promise of "peace in our time." At that point, according to Halder's subsequent testimony, the generals gave up, and the coup was never attempted. And the war that Beck had dreaded finally burst upon them all.

Halder still felt, or was told that he should feel, that he must do something. He said to an aide in 1939 that he took a pistol every time he went to see Hitler, in order "finally to shoot him down." Instead of shooting, though, he looked for help. As chief of staff, he had no troops under his direct command, so he tried to lure Brauchitsch into leading a new coup. Brauchitsch repeatedly refused. In mid-October, with Poland crushed and Hitler planning a new offensive in the West, some generals again talked of stopping him by force. Halder then suffered what one aide called "a complete nervous collapse," which reminded this aide of what had happened to the younger General Moltke. "A chief of the General Staff has no business breaking down," he wrote in his diary. "Just like 1914."

By the following month, with new plans for a coup well advanced, Halder had recovered enough to renew his appeals to Brauchitsch, but all Brauchitsch would agree to do was to tell Hitler of the generals' worries. The two of them drove to the Reich Chancellery on November 5, and Brauchitsch strode into Hitler's office armed with folders full of military memoranda criticizing the impending invasion of the Low Countries. When Hitler rejected the memoranda, Brauchitsch tried every argument he could summon. He even said that the Wehrmacht's morale was not up to a new offensive. Hitler responded with one of his characteristic tantrums against defeatism. "In what units," he demanded, "have there been any cases of lack of discipline? What action has been taken by the Army Command? How many death sentences have been carried out?" After twenty minutes of the Führer's shouting, Halder observed in the safety of an anteroom, Brauchitsch staggered out "chalk white . . . with a twisted countenance."

Driving back to military headquarters in the suburb of Zossen, the shaken Brauchitsch could barely manage to describe what had just happened to him. He knew that Halder had been involved in planning some kind of coup, and he wanted to give it a Brauchitschian blessing. Although he himself would do nothing, Brauchitsch said, he would "also do nothing if someone else did something." He said that Hitler had ranted against the "spirit of Zossen" and vowed to destroy it. (Hitler was even more blunt about his army commanders at a subsequent meeting with Luftwaffe officers. "Here comes my Coward Number One," he remarked when Brauchitsch entered the room, and when Halder followed, he added: "Number Two.") Not understanding that the "spirit of Zossen" was sitting right next to him, Halder took Hitler's threat to mean that the generals' latest conspiracy had been discovered. When he actually arrived at Zossen, he gave no signal for any coup to start but instead ordered the plotters to begin immediately destroying all incriminating papers, maps, and code words. Once again, there was to be no attempt at a coup.

One of the Resistance leaders, Colonel Hans Oster of the Abwehr, did go so far as to tell a friend in the Dutch embassy the date of the planned invasion, November 12, but then it was postponed because of bad weather. Oster continued to report each subsequent invasion date, until, when Hitler finally struck in May 1941, Oster's warnings had lost so much credibility that the British and French were taken by surprise.

Moltke doggedly continued his arguments at OKW, trying to impose on the triumphant Nazis the restraints of international law. Thus in November 1939: "I slept miserably because I'm too excited about the possibility of averting the catastrophe that seems imminent. . . ." And: "Today I won my case. But it was like winning a victory over a hydra. No sooner have I chopped off one of the monster's heads than ten new ones have grown in its place. . . ." And in February 1940: "One is waiting for the spring and the troubles it will bring. . . ." And in March: "There has been a big row today and I wonder whether they won't finally decide to throw me out. I was outvoted again in the big committee . . . over a question which in my opinion will have a quite decisive opinion on Germany's position in the postwar world. . . . After the meeting was over, I . . . said I . . . remained unconvinced and would like the right of every official to have my dissenting opinion recorded in the minutes. A big row. I was an officer and . . . must simply obey. I said I was sorry but in this case a question of responsibility to history was involved and for me that had priority over the duty to obey orders. The matter was referred to the admiral [Vice Admiral Karlgeorg Schuster, Moltke's immediate superior at the time] and after listening for five minutes he said he agreed with me. He obviously had felt like that all along but had been hesitating and my intransigence had given him courage. . . . Result: the Admiral will certainly put the office's point of view forward officially but will have his own personal dissent recorded in the minutes and speak to these minutes in front of the Führer. That naturally removes the need for my disagreement to be put on record and I escape from the firing line. . . ." And the next day: "Today I celebrated a great triumph. Yesterday's battle was joined again with all the top military brass mobilized. In the end Schuster succeeded in getting Keitel [chief of the OKW] on my side and Keitel in turn succeeded in getting the Führer on my side[2] and at 6:30 there arrived the Führer's order containing my conclusions and my arguments."

To have provided the arguments for one of Hitler's orders may seem a questionable victory, but contemporary accounts of even the most important wartime conferences tend to smell of office politics. Who will be assigned the responsibility for building a new branch office, and should it be located in East Nowhere or West Nowhere? These are the kinds of questions over which powerful men tell lies and threaten resignations. Yet Moltke always remembered that lives depended on his maneuverings. "A terrible tragedy has been averted," he wrote to his wife about this occasion when he won Hitler's approval, "and in spite of everything I get satisfaction in thinking that many non-German wives have your husband to thank for the continued existence of their husbands. For this decision is in the last resort simply and solely that of your husband against all other ministries and against my own superiors! Isn't that pleasing?"

Unfortunately, the rules of the Third Reich forbade the Abwehr from intervening in "political affairs." And when Hitler put Himmler's police forces in charge of slaughtering Poles by the thousands—priests, Jews, aristocrats, professors, anyone suspected of opposition to the New Order—that became a political affair. A few generals offered grumpy protests, but neither they nor the police took them very seriously. So the slaughter went on. One must ask—Moltke must have asked—how much it matters to save one man from being killed when thousands of others continue being killed. The only rational

[2]The wartime destruction of the Abwehr's files has prevented historians from determining exactly what this controversy was about, but it seems to have involved the economic consequences of the impending German invasion of Denmark and Norway, which Moltke naturally opposed.

answer is that it matters quite a lot to the man who was saved, to his wife and children. Every life is worth something to somebody, even when deaths are counted on a scale of thousands, or go uncounted.

The "catastrophe" that Moltke had been dreading since the autumn of 1939 seems to have been the start of a serious offensive against France. His feelings were fairly widespread. The generals who remembered the trench warfare of 1916 could not believe that the French were not a powerful enemy. They could not believe the French still had not learned the lessons that old Moltke had taught in 1870; instead, the French had built the Maginot Line.

The original German plan of attack was a rather unimaginative repetition of the Schlieffen Plan, a massive attack through Belgium—the "old Schlieffen twaddle," as Hitler himself described it. Field Marshal Brauchitsch unhappily told the Führer that German forces were not strong enough to win such a campaign (numerically both sides were about even, with 135 divisions each). Hitler himself described the prospect as "a gamble" but ordered Brauchitsch to plan on invading Belgium in November. The one man who both disliked the invasion plan and had an idea for improving it was a relatively junior staff officer, General Erich von Manstein, chief of staff to Gerd von Rundstedt's army group south in the recent Polish campaign. Manstein, a fervent admirer of the elder Moltke, said the planned invasion was exactly what the Allies would expect, and plan on repelling. On the other hand, the Ardennes Forest, which the French repeatedly described as "impassable," might be just the place for a tank offensive that could sweep right to the English Channel. OKW rejected Manstein's plan as too risky, but when he talked of his ideas to Hitler at a dinner party, the Führer was fascinated, all the more so because of the OKW disapproval. Tank commander Heinz Guderian felt confident that he could push his armor through the Ardennes, and it was near the legendary battlefield of Sedan that his panzers churned across the swiftly flowing Meuse. The milestones of the last two wars—milestones of Moltke family history—Arras, St. Quentin, Amiens, the Meuse, the Somme—now became milestones on Hitler's march to Paris.

To Helmuth James von Moltke, Hitler's great victories were profoundly discouraging. Even before the attack on France, the clawmarks of Nazi rule could be seen in Scandinavia. "Today was another terrible day because we are now starting to behave in Norway as we did in Poland," he wrote his wife in April. "It is terrible. The SS have been sent in and . . . the soldiers agree to it all. I am terribly depressed." The attack on France made everything worse, of course, both Hitler's victories and the overwhelming of his opponents. "Everything that I could have been doing has been overtaken by events . . . ," Moltke wrote in May. "For the moment I prefer to do nothing because I see nothing useful to do. Everything is in flux and in a few days, weeks, months all one's basic assumptions will be turned upside down." And a few days later: "I have never before known myself to be made physically ill by merely having to look on at an external situation. . . . At times I am unable to eat, at times I feel about to be sick. . . ."

At this low ebb, Moltke called on two sources. One was music, particularly Bach, who is, among other things, the most consoling and reassuring of composers. Moltke's letters of this period are speckled with citations of recordings he was playing: Beethoven's *Eroica*, Bach's Suite in B minor, the Fifth Brandenburg Concerto.

The other resource was the Bible, which he described as "an activity I pursue with more enjoyment now than ever before." But he noticed a change. "It used to be all stories to me, at least the Old Testament, but now it is all contemporary. . . . I find it much more gripping than ever before. I used to be annoyed by the long-drawn-out inessentials and the brevity of the essentials, but now I have learned that what matters can be expressed in one sentence or not at all. Therefore, when anyone tries to stretch out something essential, it's a sure sign that he can't say it at all. . . ."

Moltke also took advantage of this period to visit some of the areas of France that had been so important in the history of his family. He concentrated, oddly enough, not on the field marshal's victories of 1870 but on the failures of 1914. Like the field marshal, though, he regarded the defeated French with an antipathy bordering on contempt. "The attitude of the population . . . is reserved, but obviously on the whole sickeningly friendly. . . . Everybody confirms unanimously that the women, for instance, were positively queuing up to get a German soldier into bed, evidently from a feeling that he was the stronger. . . ." He collected tales of French troops fleeing in panic, seeing them as evidence of "a moral debacle." He was dismayed in Paris by the spectacle of German plundering—"a general who bought fur coats for himself and his wife"—but he blamed that mainly on Nazi Party bureaucrats. "Control of the troops is very strict," he commented. "You don't see soldiers driving with girls, and the few who misbehave receive incredibly harsh punishments." After a visit to Fontainebleau, which "looks like Potsdam with a little more money," he proceeded eastward to the battlefields of the last war, a haunted region where a traveling companion named Otto Kiep had once served, and where he had even encountered the famous Colonel Hentsch, General Moltke's emissary.

"Shortly before reaching Montmirail," the younger Moltke now wrote to his wife, "we came to the most westerly point of the German advance of 1914. Kiep had a horse patrol in that area. One evening after dark he came from such a patrol and was asked to report to his army chief, Bülow, in a barn at Vauxchamps near Montmirail, where Bülow was deliberating with Hentsch about a retreat. Kiep had to report and then fell asleep. When he woke in the morning, the order to retreat had been given in that barn, the order that may have decided the last world war. We got out at Vauxchamps and inspected the barn. The farmer came and spoke to us. But he was a new owner who had taken over in 1925 and knew nothing of former days. From Vauxchamps to Verdun and on to Pont-à-Mousson, we followed the front of 1914. War graves right and left; tens of thousands here, more tens of thousands there. . . ."

Back in Berlin again, Moltke found himself embroiled in a bizarre struggle with Hermann Goering. "I spent the whole day fighting like a lion for a French officer's life which the Reich Marshal wants to have at all costs," he wrote his wife. "The fight is not over yet; but the result so far at least is that the execution will be put off. It was dramatic and I not only fought here in Berlin but was also driven to the nearby Führer headquarters—without Führer at the moment—to see what I could do on my own. Now I have just come from there . . ." Only the next day did Moltke learn that the struggle for the French officer's life had all been a game, the kind of game that would amuse a man like Goering. "Today I fought once more for the life of that officer, like a lion," Moltke wrote. "The matter received the attention of Göring, Keitel, and probably the Führer; but at 1:15 it turned out that this officer does not exist, that we had all got excited about a hypothetical case. . . ."

At some point, if a dictatorship is sufficiently evil, its opponents shift from merely opposing it to resisting it, some point at which people start to say, "This cannot go on." It is difficult to define that point, though, or to say what brought it about. "He opposed Nazism from the first day," Freya von Moltke recalls, "and was looking from the beginning for ways to resist it. There was no special event. He had read *Mein Kampf* and expected that Hitler, once in power, would carry out everything—which he did. As Nazism arose in Germany, he saw its dangers, its threat to everything that made Europe precious, and Hitler meant war too. But it is very difficult to resist in an authoritarian state without being immediately killed."

It is particularly difficult when the ruling powers have everything—guns, blackjacks, broadcasting stations, prisons—and the opponents have nothing. What can possibly be done? It is a question that has periodically confronted obscure rebels. It was a question that confronted Mao Tse-tung, for example, when he and a few comrades were scrambling through the barren hills of western China on the 6,000-mile Long March from defeat to failure. Organize, was Mao's answer and Mao's teaching, organize and keep organizing.

In very different circumstances, a similar question confronted Adolf Hitler when he lay in a hospital bed outside Berlin in 1918, temporarily blinded by poison gas and maddened by rage at the German surrender. "And so it had all been in vain," he later wrote. "In vain all the sacrifices and privations; in vain the hunger and thirst of months which were often endless. . . ." That description of rage ended in one of the most pregnant sentences ever written: "I, for my part, decided to go into politics."

Drifting back to Munich, where he had lived before the war, Hitler received a postcard inviting him to attend a meeting of a little group that called itself the Committee of the German Workers Party. With some misgivings, he went to an obscure beerhall called the Alte Rosenbad. "I went through the badly lighted guest-room, where not a single guest was to be seen," he later wrote, "and searched for the door which led to the side room; and there I was face to face with the committee. Under the dim light shed by a grimy gas-lamp I could see four people sitting around a table. . . ." The minutes of the last meeting were read and approved, the party's funds were counted and found to total 7.5 marks, three letters were received and answered. Hitler decided to join this shabby little party and received membership card number seven.

Hitler's answer too was to organize and organize, which he did, and now so did Moltke. In the desperate summer of 1940, when even Churchill expected the aerial Battle of Britain to end in a German invasion, Moltke began meeting with like-minded friends and acquaintances simply to discuss where things stood and what might be done. He was not yet planning any real resistance at this point; that was almost beyond imagining. But when his wife wrote him from the calm of Kreisau to say that her mother accused her of sticking her head in the sand, and to ask what he thought, he offered a heartfelt answer. "Peace is not the same thing as *complacency*," he wrote. "Anyone who for the sake of peace and quiet calls black white and evil good certainly doesn't deserve peace and really is sticking his head in the sand. But someone who never for an instant forgets what good and evil are, no matter how complete the triumph of the evil may seem to be, has taken the first step towards overcoming the evil. . . ."

Not a very large step, to be sure, and one that would require many more steps to follow, but still a step. "We must today reckon with having to live through a triumph of evil," he had written to another young lawyer that June 17, within a week of the conquest of Paris. "And, whereas we had steeled ourselves to face any amount of pain and misery, must now prepare to do something which is far worse, namely keep our heads above water amid a flood of public good-fortune, self-satisfaction." The other lawyer was Peter Yorck von Wartenburg, a direct descendant of that famous General Yorck who had defected from his king's alliance with Napoleon and led his Prussian troops over to the side of the Russians. Despite his antipathy to the Nazis, Peter Yorck had gone to work as a civil servant in 1935, first in Breslau and then at the Reich Price Commissariat in Berlin. He had even served as a lieutenant in the invasion of Poland. He was a cousin of Count Claus von Stauffenberg, whose attempt to assassinate Hitler would be the zenith of the German resistance. Ever since the late 1930s, Yorck had been trying to establish contact with men who shared his opposition to the Nazis, and now that Moltke had begun to do the same, the two of them naturally found each other. Theirs was a friendship that would endure until they were both executed.

"This makes it more important than ever," Moltke's letter continued, "to be clear in our minds about the basic principles of a positive doctrine of politics. I want to use this letter as a contribution to that process of clarification—in my head rather than yours!—and to link it to a conversation which I had with you and Schulenberg not quite a fortnight ago. You will perhaps recollect the wager. Schulenberg was ready to bet that within ten years a state would have come into existence of which we could fully approve. I was ready to maintain the opposite of this proposition. We went on to the question of defining such a state and I proposed as a criterion that of justice . . . That left us with the problem of defining justice and we agreed that justice consisted in the ability of the individual to expand and develop himself within the framework of the state as a whole. . . ."

By this time, a shadowy resistance movement already existed, based on nothing more than the common feeling that Hitler was leading Germany to ruin, and that there were men in the army who seemed determined to stop him. General Beck was the focal point of this movement, a man whom others admired and were ready to follow. This was not the only resistance, of course. By the time of his arrest in 1937, Pastor Martin Niemoeller led a vocal opposition movement within the Protestant Church. And though the Concordat of 1933 forbade Catholic priests to take part in political activities, some bishops—notably Preysing of Berlin, and von Galen of Muenster—were bold in protesting the manifest sins of the Nazi regime. The Communists, too, organized a resistance movement known as the *Rote Kapelle,* which concentrated on sabotaging the Nazi war effort. The *Rote Kapelle* efforts were seriously undermined, however, by the Communist policy of collaborating with the Nazis from 1939 until Hitler's invasion of Russia in 1941, and thereafter by the Communists' goal of creating a Communist Germany. Amid this profusion of opponents to Nazism, it was the military resistance movement around Beck that seemed to have the best chance of really halting the Hitler revolution and the Hitler march toward war. By resigning as chief of staff, Beck lost all official power of command within the armed forces but gained a political and moral leadership that remained with him until his death. The military conspirators also needed an experienced political leader, though, and so they joined forces with Carl Goerdeler, onetime lord mayor of Leipzig. An immensely energetic and optimistic man, whom Chancellor Bruening had unsuccessfully proposed to Hindenburg as his successor, Goerdeler had clashed with the Nazis in Leipzig over their demand for the removal of a statue of Felix Mendelssohn from the Gewandhaus concert hall. When a Nazi official unceremoniously removed the Mendelssohn statue during one of Goerdeler's absences from the city, the lord mayor abruptly resigned at the end of 1936. Hired as a foreign representative by the automotive firm of Bosch, Goerdeler was officially supposed to report on foreign opinions of the Nazi regime but actually spent much of his time in Western capitals warning of the Nazi menace.

One of the basic tasks confronting any resistance movement is to convince the outside world that a resistance movement does indeed exist. Dictatorships like the Third Reich devote a good deal of effort to portraying themselves as the representatives of a contented populace, undisturbed by any opposition, so the resistance must see to it that an occasional cry of protest can be heard. This is not easy, since most governments prefer to remain deaf to cries of protest, whatever the source. In the late 1930s, the main target for such protests from Germany was the government of Great Britain, which, under the hidebound rule of Neville Chamberlain, was as deaf as any.

Goerdeler visited Britain in July 1937, then the Netherlands, France, Canada, and the United States, and back to Britain in the spring of 1938. A Conservative of moderately nationalistic tendencies, Goerdeler got into difficulties in his talks with Sir Robert Vansittart at the foreign office because Goerdeler, like many opposition figures, found at least some of Hitler's territorial demands quite reasonable.

When Vansittart said that Britain was "prepared to see the Sudeten Germans obtain a degree of autonomy," Goerdeler recalled, "I answered that the area was German . . . and must be incorporated in the Reich." Vansittart was not persuaded. As the Sudeten crisis intensified that summer, though, the German opposition leaders decided to send another envoy to London to warn that Hitler planned to attack Czechoslovakia toward the end of September but could be stopped if the Western allies stood firm. This envoy was Ewald von Kleist-Schmenzin, a distinguished Prussian landowner, publisher of a Conservative magazine, and an open anti-Nazi from the start. He brought Beck's message to Vansittart, to whom he spoke as a man who had "come out of Germany with a rope round his neck to stake his last chance of life," and Vansittart forwarded his account to Halifax and Chamberlain. The prime minister was not unduly impressed. "We must discount a good deal of what he says," he observed, adding that the German visitor reminded him of past exiles, specifically "of the Jacobites at the Court of France in King William's time." This did not mean that Chamberlain was totally against responding to Kleist's warnings. "I confess to some feeling of uneasiness," he wrote to Halifax, with a vigor worthy of Brauchitsch, "and I am not sure that we ought not to do something."

Kleist did a little better with Churchill, who, being a fiercely anti-Nazi independent, felt quite free to support Kleist with a fervor that implied no official commitments. "The spectacle of an armed attack by Germany upon a small neighbor and the bloody fighting that will follow will rouse the whole British Empire and compel the gravest decisions," Churchill wrote in a letter for Kleist. "Do not, I pray you, be misled upon this point. Such a war, once started, would be fought out like the last to the bitter end. . . ."

Despite these warlike words, Kleist's mission had as little effect as those of Goerdeler or Moltke or anyone else. Chamberlain was determined to appease Hitler—appeasement had not yet become a term of scorn, was indeed a proudly advocated policy for maintaining the peace. Besides, the British had little reason to trust anyone claiming to oppose Hitler. At about the time of Elser's bomb attack in Munich, two British officers who had been negotiating with Gestapo agents claiming to be members of an anti-Nazi underground were suddenly kidnapped in the Dutch frontier town of Venlo and spirited off to a German concentration camp. From then on, the British attitude toward anyone who predicted a coup against Hitler was to express nothing more than a polite interest in seeing the coup actually take place. Understandable though this British skepticism might be, it meant that the German underground movement was the only one in all of Europe that got no outside support of any kind. While French and Yugoslav resistance groups were showered with British guns, bombs, and radio messages of guidance and encouragement, the German resistance was denied even the mild moral support of being acknowledged to exist.

Spurned by the Allies, the Germans finally turned to one last channel that proved stronger than they had expected. Pope Pius XII had served as papal nuncio to Germany in the 1920s and was all too sympathetic to the German government. God knows he did little enough to defend the Jews or publicize their plight. But when it came to peace-making between nations, Pius stood ready to help in any way he could. Colonel Hans Oster of the Abwehr discovered a Munich lawyer named Josef Müller, known both for his temperament and for his native town of Ochsenfurt as *Ochsensepp* or Joe the Ox. A long-time anti-Nazi, Müller had developed a remarkable skill for keeping Catholic people and property out of the hands of the Gestapo. Müller had many contacts in the Vatican, not the least of whom was Monsignor Ludwig Kaas, former chairman of the German Center Party and now an adviser to the pope. Taken into the Abwehr as a lieutenant, Müller went to see Kaas in Rome, and Kaas took his message to the pope's summer residence in Castel Gandolfo. The pope declined to meet directly with Müller, but he did agree to have Müller meet regularly with a papal private secretary, Robert Leiber, a Jesuit priest from Baden, in Leiber's private quarters at the Papal University. And so a channel was finally opened from General Beck to Müller to Leiber to the pope, who could then forward any messages he chose to the British ambassador, Sir Francis d'Arcy Osborne.

Once Britain and Germany were at war, this kind of communication amounted to virtual treason, but the German military conspirators were obsessed with the fear that the overthrow of Hitler would leave Germany's frontiers open to an Allied invasion. They wanted guarantees of a cease-fire. The British, of course, remained as skeptical as ever, suggesting once again that post-Hitler planning must begin with the removal of Hitler.

Still, after months of maneuvering, the anti-Nazi resistance had finally acquired a pipeline into the Allied camp—if only they could figure out what use to make of it, if only they could organize the revolt that might give it some purpose. If only—

16

Fundamental Principles

WHATEVER THE GENERALS MIGHT FINALLY DECIDE, MOLTKE BELIEVED even before the war that the anti-Nazi forces should think not just about deposing Hitler but also about planning the kind of Germany that should replace the Nazi Third Reich. In a sense, he was returning to 1848, when Germany's liberals had tried so hard—and so notably failed—to design a post-feudal society. In a sense, he was going back even farther, to 1789, when the makers of America gathered in Philadelphia to draft a constitution.

George Kennan was surprised, after meeting Moltke at the American embassy in 1940, to find him "immersed in a study of the *Federalist Papers* to get ideas for the constitution of a future democratic Germany." Kennan was greatly impressed. "The picture," he wrote, "of this scion of a famous Prussian military family, himself employed by the German general staff in the midst of a great world war, hiding himself away and turning, in all humility, to the works of some of the founding fathers of our own democracy for ideas as to how Germany might be led out of its existing corruption and bewilderment has never left me."

Moltke never believed, however, that he and his friends could organize a popular revolution. For one thing, Hitler's popularity among ordinary citizens was dismayingly strong. For another, the Gestapo spied on everyone and tore apart any signs of opposition with every tool of state terrorism. "Can you imagine what it is like," Moltke wrote to a friend in London early in 1943, "if you

"a. cannot use the telephone,

"b. cannot use the post,

"c. cannot send a messenger, because you probably have no one to send, and if you have you cannot give him a written message as the police sometimes search people in trains, trams etc. for documents,

"d. cannot even speak with those with whom you are completely *d'accord,* because the secret police have methods of questioning where they first break the will but leave the intelligence awake, thereby inducing the victim to speak out all he knows; therefore you must limit information to those who absolutely need it. . . .

"In Germany people do not know what is happening. I believe that at least 9 tenths of the population do not know that we have killed hundreds of thousands of Jews. They go on believing that they just have been segregated and lead an existence pretty much like the one they led, only farther to the east, where they came from. Perhaps with a little more squalor but without air raids. If you told these people what has really happened they would answer: you are just a victim of British propaganda. . . .

"A third fact: We now have 19 guillotines working at considerable speed without most people even knowing this fact, and practically nobody knows how many are beheaded per day. In my estimation there are about 50 daily, not counting those who die in concentration camps. Nobody knows the exact number of concentration camps or of their inhabitants. . . . Calculations on the number of inhabitants vary between 150,000 and 350,000. Nobody knows how many die per day. By chance I have ascertained that in one single month 160 persons died in the concentration camp of Dachau. . . . We only know for certain that scores, probably many hundreds of Germans are killed daily. . . ."

In such circumstances, Moltke felt it was totally unrealistic to expect or hope for a popular rebellion against Nazi rule. So if rebellion was impossible, and if the generals could not be persuaded to act, that appeared to mean that only an Allied military victory could free Germany from its dictator. It seems a morally questionable judgment, leaving it up to the Allies to shed the blood that the Germans were unwilling to shed for their own liberty, but it was a judgment that Moltke regarded as unavoidable, a matter of historic inevitability. And history, of course, was to prove him right.

If it would be the responsibility of the Allies to overthrow Hitler, though, it might still be the responsibility of the Germans to design the kind of Germany that would follow the Third Reich. This, too, would actually become an Allied responsibility, and the Allies were already making plans accordingly, but Moltke had no way of knowing that. He only knew that he felt a duty to begin the planning. He did not want simply a restoration of the Weimar Republic of 1918–1933. Like many Germans, he felt that the republic had been deeply flawed, that it shared some of the responsibility for its own collapse under the hammer blows of Nazism. But he did not want to restore the Wilhelmian Reich either; that unhappy creation of Bismarck's wizardry undoubtedly shared in the responsibility for its own collapse in the last days of World War I. That was how, as Moltke explored further and further back in German history, he inevitably reached the thwarted idealists of 1848. He would make the same fundamental mistake that they did, the mistake of leaving aside the crucial question of how political power should be mobilized to carry out political ideas, but he did realize that he needed to confront some of the basic problems that they had failed to solve in 1848, problems that had remained unsolved ever since.

Moltke's original plans had been largely political. Inspired by the fall of France, he wrote to Peter Yorck von Wartenburg in mid-June of 1940 that they now had to confront the triumph of evil. "Instead of the suffering and misfortunes for which we had prepared ourselves, we will have to endure a much nastier mixture of external fortune, comfort and prosperity. This makes it more important than ever to be clear in our minds about the basic principles of a positive doctrine in politics. I want to use this letter as a contribution to that process of clarification—in my head rather than yours!—and to link it to a conversation I had with you. . . ."

Moltke knew his man. Yorck was three years older than Moltke and distantly related. When Moltke met him for lunch in January 1940, he described him to his wife as "Davy's brother," referring to Davida von Yorck, who had married Moltke's cousin, Hans Adolf von Moltke, the former German ambassador to Poland. "He lives near the botanical gardens, in a tiny house which is furnished very nicely," Moltke wrote. "I think we found ourselves very much in agreement and I'll be seeing more of him." Out of this friendship, out of this correspondence, grew the whole group known as the Kreisau circle.

"The foundation of all political science," Moltke wrote to Yorck that June, "seems to me to consist of the following fundamental principles:

"1. It is not the purpose of the state to control men and to restrain them by force ... but rather to bring men into such a relationship with each other ... that the individual can live and act in complete security without at the same time harming his neighbor.

"2. It is not the purpose of the state to turn men into wild animals or machines, but rather to provide the individual with the support that enables him to develop and use his body, spirit and intelligence.

"3. It is not the purpose of the state to demand unconditional obedience and blind faith in itself ... but rather to guide individual men so that they live according to the dictates of reason. ...

"I am far from believing that these principles can be fully realized. I believe them, however, to be standards against which we must judge all constitution-making." When Yorck chided him about his "three negative definitions," however, Moltke saw that he would have to probe still deeper into the beginnings of beginnings and the fundamentals of his "fundamental principles."

Writing letters was not enough. Moltke felt that he had to meet face-to-face with Yorck and a few like-minded friends to argue through their various differences and work out the details of what they could agree on. In August, he invited Yorck and his wife, Marion; Horst von Einsiedel, whom he had known since his days in the Silesian work camps; and a lawyer named Eduard Waetjen to spend a weekend at his estate in Kreisau. The main topic was the educational system, but the six friends often wandered off into various byways. Then came more correspondence and lots more meetings, sometimes in Kreisau, more often in Berlin, sometimes at Yorck's Silesian estate at Kleinöls.

Finally, when Moltke realized that a shadowy organization had been born, he decided to expand both its scope and its agenda. One of the most important problems that had afflicted Germany for many years was the problem known as "particularism," the fact that the Germans, despite their reputation as a herd of conformists, had never succeeded in healing the myriad divisions of the medieval Holy Roman Empire. They might sing *"Deutschland Über Alles,"* that anthem of the illusions of 1848, but they remained Prussians or Bavarians or Swabians, still remembering the bruises that resulted from Bismarck's campaign to bring them all together. And if Germans were divided by regions, they were no less divided by classes; the Social Democrats, whom Bismarck had reviled as unfit to take part in the government, had founded the Weimar Republic, and there were many judges, generals, professors, and others who never forgave them that. And by religion. Germany was the birthplace of the Reformation and the battleground of the Thirty Years War. Bismarck had revived the old conflicts in his *Kulturkampf* against the Catholics, and Hitler had given them a new twist with the campaign known as *Gleichschaltung*. This untranslatable term has been variously translated as standardization, coordination, and conformity. It literally means making things the same, so it served as a convenient pretext for expelling Jews from official and professional positions.

Moltke's response to the various divisions of Germany was partly a matter of process. He felt strongly that Germany needed spiritual revival, and he felt this could be achieved only by bringing Protestants and Catholics together again. Since he himself was of Protestant origins (despite his father's involvement with Christian Science), he considered it particularly important to recruit significant representatives of the Catholic Church. One of these was Augustin Rösch, the Jesuits' provincial for the Upper German Province and in many ways the most important Catholic official in Germany. A winner of the Iron Cross during the World War, Rösch led the Jesuits' spirited resistance to Nazi persecution and harassment. "A peasant's son with a first-rate brain, clever, educated, solid," Moltke wrote after his first meeting with Rösch, "—I liked him very much."

With him, Rösch brought his chief aide, Father Lothar König, S.J., a onetime engineering student who had been led to religion by his passionate involvement in the Catholic youth movement. A professor of cosmology at the Jesuit school in Pullach, König once summed up his views by declaring, "There is no such thing as I cannot." Another Jesuit and one of the intellectual leaders at Kreisau was Alfred Delp, a philosopher and sociologist who had written several pioneering studies on existentialism, notably *Tragic Destiny: On the Philosophy of Martin Heidegger*. The Catholic representatives at Kreisau included experienced administrators too. Hans Lukaschek, for example, had been the president of Upper Silesia and had worked for conciliation between Germans and Poles. Hans Peters had served eight years as a Prussian civil servant as well as three in lecturing at the University of Breslau.

The Protestants were ably represented by Carl Dietrich von Trotha, one of Moltke's cousins, who had actually been born at Kreisau; Adolf Reichwein, a youth-movement leader who had directed the adult-education program at Jena; Theodor Steltzer, a district magistrate in Schleswig-Holstein; Otto Heinrich von der Gablentz, a chemist who had been a pupil of the liberal theologian Paul Tillich; and Harald Poelchau, another Tillich pupil.

Moltke's idea now was to invite a dozen of these friends and colleagues, both Protestant and Catholic, to gather in Kreisau at Whitsun of 1942, May 22–25. It was an ominous time. The German army was advancing toward the Volga, just north of Stalingrad. General Rommel was preparing an offensive in Libya to seize the British stronghold of Tobruk. And on the seventh Sunday after Easter, a day devoted to commemorating the descent of the Holy Spirit, it was almost unworldly for this tiny band of idealists to gather on a remote country estate for a series of discussions on what should follow the coming defeat of Nazism. Even the most idealistic of thinkers have to be fed, though, so Freya von Moltke had been saving ration coupons for months to stockpile the necessary supplies, and even today, when the bare-chested young Dutch volunteers assemble for lunch in the midst of their efforts at rebuilding Kreisau, one adjoining room is still reverently referred to as "Freya's kitchen" in "those days."

The meetings at Kreisau were those of a most unorganized organization. Its model, if it had one, was the "Round Table," a little group led by one of Moltke's South African friends, Lionel Curtis, which met in a series of English country houses during the 1920s and 1930s to discuss ways and means of transforming the British empire into a commonwealth of nations. The members of the Round Table were hardly in danger of being hanged for their efforts, of course, but that danger was one of the main justifications for the free-form structure of the Kreisauer Kreis. (The Kreisauers never even gave themselves that name; it was concocted by police officials trying to sort out suspects after the attempt to kill Hitler on July 20, 1944.) People came and went; some attended some meetings; others, other meetings; some close associates of Moltke's never came to any Kreisau meetings at all.

To the extent that the Kreisau meetings were organized at all, they were organized rather like academic conferences. An expert was selected to outline the subject for discussion—Rösch explained the Catholic view on relations between church and state, for example, while Peters explained the 1933 concordat between Germany and the Vatican; Moltke himself read a paper on the reform of higher education—and then the others raised questions or offered their views. But sometimes the visitors simply went for long walks through the sunny meadows around Kreisau; sometimes they discussed weighty matters on these walks, and sometimes they simply enjoyed the warm Silesian sunshine.

At the end of the extended Whitsun weekend of 1942, Moltke gathered together everyone's notes and wrote his summary of what had been agreed. Though Moltke believed in the idea of separating church and state, his summary was almost medieval in its assertions of religious authority. "We see in Christianity the most valuable source of strength for the religious-ethical renewal of the nation, for the conquest of hatred and deception, for the construction of the western world and for the peaceful cooperation of nations. . . . Freedom of belief and conscience and the public practice of the Christian religion are guaranteed. . . . The Christian heritage is to be granted its proper place in the whole of education as well as in films and broadcasting."

This sounds like an admirable statement of Christian unity, all the more admirable for Germany's long history of Christian fratricide, but it startles a modern reader by its calm assumption that no other religions exist. Particularly remarkable is the absence of any reference to the Jews, who at that very moment were being hauled off by the thousands to the death camps of Poland. Moltke does not really need any outsider's defense for this omission, but it would probably be useful to recall the popular perceptions of 1942 in a bit more detail. For one thing, the current American dogma that everyone belongs to one of three equal religions—Catholic, Protestant, and Jewish—was a dogma not yet born. Even without considering the diminution of German Jewry through Nazi persecution, the number of Jews was so small— less than 1 percent of the population—as to be statistically insignificant. Furthermore, when Germans considered the Jews, they inclined to think of them as an ethnic rather than a religious group. If one thought of Albert Einstein, for example, did one think of him attending a synagogue? Did anyone imagine Artur Schnabel or Bruno Walter fasting on Yom Kippur? Moltke had helped a number of Jewish friends get to England or America in the 1930s, but as Freya von Moltke looks back on those years, the meanings of things change. "We didn't know any Jews at all who were of 'Mosesian' belief," she told a recent interviewer. "We didn't see at all it was a religious matter, not like the role the Jewish religion plays today. We weren't anti-Semitic, but we considered the Jews basically as if they were us."

Moltke had a rather exalted notion of the role of education. "The formation and sustenance of a Christian statesman are functions of education," he wrote to Gablentz in 1940. Hitler had already destroyed many German institutions, but his destruction of traditional education was perhaps the most ruinous and the most poisonous. The corruption of Nazism extended—as Allied reformers were soon to discover—from university professors of philosophy to village schoolteachers and throughout most of the available textbooks. "The present textbooks must . . . be banned," Moltke wrote in one of his most sweeping prescriptions, "even before the new ones are ready."

For young children, Moltke limited himself to a general exhortation to both churches and state: "The school ought to satisfy the right of every child to receive an education that is suitable for him. It ought to arouse and strengthen his moral powers. . . . Character training produces an upright man of religious conviction. . . . The state school is a Christian school in which religious instruction of both confessions is a compulsory subject. The lessons are the responsibility of the churches and, where possible, will be taken by clergymen."

In higher education, Moltke wanted to reorganize all institutions into two categories: "colleges of further education" and "Reich universities." The colleges of further education were to provide specialized training in a wide variety of disciplines, ranging from law and medicine to natural sciences, forestry and engineering to the arts. The Reich universities were to be "centers of universal scholarship." They were not only to "develop" the specialized research of the colleges but to "secure its relationship with the rest of scholarship." Its "intellectually distinguished" professors must "combine specialized competence with a universal vision." Moltke warned several times against the pedantic overspecialization for which German universities had long been notorious, insisting that his Reich universities must provide "easy integration into the totality of scholarship." The reward for this breadth of vision would be that a master's degree from a Reich university would be an "essential qualification for appointment to leading positions in public service."

It is easy to imagine Moltke's assembly of Catholic and Protestant churchmen subscribing to all these general principles—and Moltke considered it a major part of his mission to get such traditional antagonists to discuss and agree on anything—but as a practical blueprint for postwar German education, the Kreisau summary left a lot to be desired, or settled later. How teachers would be trained for the new Utopia was "left open." The creation of a new history textbook was simply "considered feasible." To settle such matters, it was suggested that the post-Nazi Reich chancellor would undertake "negotiations with the two bishops."

Despite the shortcomings of his summary, Moltke was so pleased with the first meeting at Kreisau—"What I aimed at at Whitsun has been achieved," he said—that he decided to have another one in the autumn. In fact, he proposed two meetings. The first, in September, would deal with the state. Then, in October, the participants would discuss the economic system. Moltke soon decided, however, that he was risking a visit from the Gestapo. One such meeting could certainly be passed off as a gathering of friends for a weekend in the country, but two such meetings in successive months might alarm even

the most somnolent police. "The whole thing is too dangerous . . ."
Moltke told Yorck. "I intend to suggest to Peters that we drop the
September meeting and instead defer the discussion of that topic until
October when, preferably, we should discuss both together. That must
be possible. Security considerations argue very strongly in favor of an
amalgamation of the two."

Yorck agreed, and so the second Kreisau meeting was scheduled
for October 16 to 18 on "the structure of the state and the economy."
Having devoted the first meeting largely to building a coalition with
Catholic and Protestant church leaders, Moltke now wanted to
expand his coalition to include another important group, the Socialists and labor unions. Both Protestant and Catholic leaders had long
viewed them with fear and suspicion, and all too many Germans had
approved when Hitler placed them among his first targets for persecution. The union leaders, for their part, had responded with equal suspicion and distrust, taking a perverse pride in their isolation. Moltke
was determined to end that.

Perhaps his most important recruit was Carlo Mierendorf, an
ardent and experienced politician who had devoted much of his life to
socialism. "A prophet who was strong, simple and convincing," the
dramatist Gerhard Hauptmann said of him. "In the ancient world he
would have been acclaimed leader."

A Saxon by birth, Mierendorf grew up in the Hessian city of
Darmstadt, where his father worked as a textile salesman. Mierendorf
was still a schoolboy when he volunteered for the war, was wounded
and decorated for bravery. Like many of his fellow veterans, he
returned home a revolutionary. He started his postwar life as editor of
a radical journal but consistently opposed the growing power of the
Communists. He studied at Frankfurt, Heidelberg, Munich, and
Freiburg, under such teachers as Max Weber and Alfred Weber, and
took an active part in student protests against the right-wing Kapp
Putsch of 1920 and the assassination of Foreign Minister Walter
Rathenau in 1922.

Working his way up through the Socialist Party ranks, he became
secretary of the transport workers union, editor of a Hessian Socialist
newspaper, and a member of the Reichstag party secretariat. In 1930,
he was elected to the Reichstag, where he became an ardent opponent
of the growing Nazi faction. He was a shrewd imitator of some Nazi
psychological tactics, however, inventing "freedom symbols" and a
"freedom greeting" to answer the Nazi swastika and the Hitler salute.
"Whoever has seen the masses that we have been able to mobilize
with the help of new techniques will be bound to agree that they will

not voluntarily submit to a Nazi dictatorship," said Mierendorf. Time was running out, though, and when a Nazi dictatorship became reality, he rejected all talk of flight. "What are the workers to make of us if we leave them in the lurch?" he asked. "They can't all go off to the Riviera."

Mierendorf went under cover in Berlin, but the Gestapo managed to tap one of his telephone calls, and so he had the painful honor of being one of the first resistance figures to be taken to a concentration camp. After five years of incarceration, including a stay at Buchenwald, he was turned loose in 1938. The Nazis placed strict restrictions on his work and his associations, but Mierendorf soon reestablished contact with many old friends. One of these was Adolf Reichwein, who led him to Moltke.

Mierendorf brought with him to the Kreisau circle one of his best friends, Theo Haubach. A gifted writer and speaker, whose mother was a Jew, Haubach went to school with Mierendorf, followed him into the army at the start of the war, and also emerged covered with medals for heroism. Haubach was studying under Karl Jaspers at Heidelberg when he learned that Mierendorf faced academic punishment for his part in the demonstrations against Rathenau's murder. Haubach successfully defended his friend before the university senate as a "militant representative of socialism, distinguished for his soldierliness, intelligence and sense of responsibility. . . ."

Like Mierendorf, Haubach gravitated toward journalism, becoming foreign editor of the Socialist *Hamburger Echo*. He also was one of the founders of the *Reichsbanner,* the street-fighting organization that the Socialists created to combat Hitler's Storm Troopers. In the late 1920s, he became press officer to Interior Minister Karl Severing, then to the Prussian interior ministry. "As long as I have an opportunity to use my sword, I will stay in Berlin like a soldier," he said. Even after Hitler came to power, Haubach urged resisting the Nazis by force and offered his *Reichsbanner* troops to the cause, but the Socialist leaders declined. Haubach was arrested soon afterwards, and he was confined in concentration camps until 1936.

"He was of a slender build, almost gaunt . . ." the playwright Carl Zuckmayer later said of him, "with a narrow face shaped by divergent tensions, and a manner that concealed the soft and gentle side of his personality behind a deliberately stressed vigor. Intellectual distinction was united in his features, his language and his bearing with soldierly discipline, a readiness to serve and to command—a rare combination."

Another leftist brought into the Kreisau circle by Mierendorf was

Wilhelm Leuschner, an experienced trade union leader, former deputy chairman of the German Labor Unions Association, a former Socialist interior minister of the state of Hesse, and also a veteran of two years in the Nazi concentration camps. Moltke called him "The Uncle." It was Leuschner who defended the traditional labor union view in opposition to some of Moltke's most cherished plans. "The aim of Helmuth and his friends was to build society from the bottom upwards . . . by creating a strong sense of community at the local level," according to an analysis by Michael Balfour and Julian Frisby. "They therefore regarded with mistrust all central organizations which might make claims on the individual's loyalty and thereby impede his willingness to work together with his immediate neighbor. Leuschner had been brought up in the tradition of German trade unionism and thought that the ability of the Nazis to gain power had been largely due to the failure of the workers to stand together. . . . The emphasis on the locality, and even on the individual factory, made him nervous lest it should result in a weakening of loyalty to the center. . . . It was not easy for even a moderate Socialist like Leuschner to think of doing away with the class struggle (except by the victory of the proletariat). But this was precisely what the Kreisau group was aiming at. . . . What is more, Helmuth actually talked of doing away with trade unions, on the ground that his other changes would give the workers so much say in society as to make them unnecessary. To convince a trade union leader that this was not visionary was bound to take some doing."

This fundamental argument flickered through all the remaining Kreisau meetings. Mierendorf "was in absolutely splendid form—clear, resolute, clever, tactful and witty," Moltke wrote after one meeting in late summer of 1942. "The result of the night session, which lasted till 5 o'clock, was that the gap which the Uncle [Leuschner] created has been filled, in that M will see to it that the comrades come over to us with him and leave the Uncle isolated. An enormous step forward has been achieved. . . ." Moltke's optimism was premature. In mid-November, he wrote that "considerable dangers" had arisen. "Mierendorf and Leber have gone off on lines which are not dissimilar to those of the Uncle. Great efforts will be needed to get them back again on the old track." Those efforts had hardly begun when Moltke's movement suffered a grievous loss. On the night of December 4, an Allied air raid struck Leipzig, where Mierendorf had gone to visit an aunt, and the passionate peacemaker was killed. His last spoken word was "Madness!"

The Uncle remained in place, doggedly pursuing his own views.

He was not without supporters. In the later days of the resistance, when Count von Stauffenberg was organizing his bomb plot against Hitler, he became convinced that the plotters should abandon the widely held assumption that Carl Goerdeler would be the acknowledged chancellor of a post-Hitler government. He even arranged to have the position offered to Leuschner, who had been designated as prospective vice chancellor, only to have Leuschner decline on the ground that he wanted to concentrate on the rebuilding of labor unions. Stauffenberg's attention then turned, just as fruitlessly, to another Kreisauer, Julius Leber.

An Alsatian by birth, Leber was studying economics and history at the University of Strasbourg and had already joined the Socialist Party when he enrolled in the German army. He soon became an officer and received many decorations, but the war embittered him. "The lies and frivolity, passions and fears of diplomats, princes and generals transformed millions of peaceful people into murderers, robbers and incendiaries for four years . . . ," he wrote, "only to leave behind at the end a continent brutalized, contaminated and impoverished. No nation made any lasting gains. . . ."

After the war, Leber moved to Lübeck, where he joined the staff of the *Lübecker Volksbote* and soon rose to be editor-in-chief. He also became the leader of Lübeck's Social Democrats, and in 1924 he won election to the Reichstag, specializing in defense and foreign policy. Leber's popularity in Lübeck kept both Nazi and Communist leaders out of the city, but the night after Hitler became chancellor, five Nazi thugs attacked Leber and beat him up. Though *Reichsbanner* militants tried to defend him, he was severely injured—and then arrested. Only a general protest strike won his release two weeks later. Urged to take refuge abroad, he refused, like Mierendorf, to abandon his followers. Returning to his seat in the Reichstag on March 23, he was promptly arrested again and spent the next four years in concentration camps.

Men like these brought a distinctly leftist emphasis to the discussions at Kreisau and helped to widen the differences between Moltke and the generals who supported Goerdeler as political leader of the resistance but between Moltke and his Socialist colleagues, the arguments were also long and wearisome. One labor union official named Herman Maass once talked for more than an hour about his network of anti-Nazi cells. "The rest of us slept through long stretches of the lecture," Moltke observed, "Peter and I shamelessly, while Friedrich's extinct cigar kept dropping out of his mouth, at which he woke up, looked at me, smiled, put it back in his mouth and went to sleep again. But these ninety minutes made us realize that here was a man talking who really had something to say about the position of the workers, and the ninety minutes included high points where we all listened with fascination while several pearls were concealed among the banalities."

They did not finish, of course, during the scheduled weekend of October 16 to 18. They talked, sometimes all night, they ate, they went to church, but they did not finish. How could they? They were trying to settle, all in one weekend, issues that had confounded Bismarck, Hegel, Marx, and quite a few others. Impossible. Whitsun seemed to have been an auspicious occasion, so they decided to meet again on the following Whitsun, June 2 to 14, 1943 when the Holy Spirit might again be among them. Not only would they settle all outstanding questions about the state and the economy but they would try to outline a postwar foreign policy, which meant healing Germany's relations with its neighbors and building a new Europe, and they would take up the touchy question of punishing those who had actually committed the Nazis' myriad crimes. And so they did.

It was all very worthy to discuss the future of education or the relations between church and state, but the disaster of Nazism was a political disaster. The failure of the Weimar Republic had been a political failure of the worst kind—a failure to stop its children from murdering their parents. One could blame the criminal personality of Hitler or the weakness of Hindenburg or various psychological defects of the German people, but Nazism was nonetheless a political pathology, requiring a political cure. It was to attempt this that Moltke secluded himself in August 1943 and tried to distill all the discussions at Kreisau into a blueprint for a new Germany.

He began on a characteristically lofty note, recapitulating his summary of the first Kreisau meeting. "The government of the German Reich," he wrote, assuming that there would still be a government of the German Reich, and that it would have some connection to his views, "sees in Christianity the foundation for the moral and religious renewing of our people, for the surmounting of hatred and lies, for the rebuilding of the European Community of peoples." This might sound like mere preaching, but its implications were as practical as those of a medieval pope preaching a new Crusade. "The main task now facing mankind in Europe . . ." he wrote, "is . . . the recognition by men of the divine order of things. . . . The solution lies in the resolute and vigorous realization of Christian values."

This meant, first of all, the reestablishment of law as "supreme throughout human affairs." Secondly, it meant an end to "totalitarian interference with the individual conscience." The new government would guarantee "the inviolable dignity of human life" and "the right to work and to own property." It would recognize the family as "the basic unit of a peaceful life," and it would guarantee every family "food, clothing, housing, a garden and health." It would promise every worker "a genuine share of responsibility for the conduct of his work." These guarantees and promises were not to be simply handed down from on high, however. "Every individual's personal political responsibility," Moltke wrote, "requires that he should make his voice heard in the self-government which is to be resuscitated in the small face-to-face communities."

Reluctantly, Moltke accepted the strong view of his Kreisau associates that "the *Reich* remains the supreme political authority of the German people," but everything in his blueprint worked toward the decentralization of that *Reich,* and toward its eventual incorporation into a European community. Both of these tendencies were fulfilled by the Bonn constitution of 1949 and by the government that it brought into being, but Moltke's only real role in this was the role of a prophet, not without honor save in his own country. The essential step in Moltke's "face-to-face communities" would be the election of town and county (*Kreis*) councils. Everybody over twenty-one would vote; a head of family would get an extra vote for each child. These councils would then elect the representatives to speak for them in the legislature of a larger area, a *Land* or province numbering 3 to 5 million inhabitants. The *Land* legislators, in turn, would elect their representatives in the national Reichstag.

The administrative hierarchy would be similarly organized. Each *Land* would be supervised by a *Verweser* or commissioner, elected by the regional legislature for a term of twelve years. These commissioners would elect a national upper chamber, the *Reichsrat,* which would elect a chief of state, the *Reichsverweser* (Moltke and his associates did not share the conservative yearning for a restoration of the monarchy). This *Reichsverweser* would nominate a chancellor to run the national government, subject to the approval of the Reichstag. The Reichstag could vote to overthrow the chancellor, but only if it first agreed on a successor (thus avoiding the dangerous stalemates caused by Nazi and Communist minorities in the last years of Weimar).

Before any such new government could be established, though, the debris of the Third Reich would have to be cleared away. Moltke's blueprint rather optimistically assumed that the arrival of the Allied armies would enable the Kreisauers' state commissioners to assume power and that the commissioners would be able to prevent the Allied armies from taking full power themselves. The commissioners were to cooperate with the Allies and to follow the Kreisau guidelines on the nature of the new Germany but to accept no Allied encroachment on their own authority. They were to bar all Nazi officials from office and to arrest anyone suspected of crimes. These suspects were not to be punished by the victorious Allies but turned over to the International Court of Justice at The Hague. As for who should be punished, Moltke's document quoted a passage from Macaulay's *History of England*: "The ringleaders, the men of rank, fortune and education, whose power and whose artifices have led the multitude into error, are the proper objects of severity. The deluded population, when once the slaughter on the field of battle is over, can scarcely be treated too leniently."

A nice distinction, which both Allied and German jurists would take a half century trying to carry out fairly. But though all such principles can be defined and refined with meticulous care, the key to any political program lies not just in the worthiness of its principles but also in the character of the people chosen to enact it. Ultimately, that choice would have to be made by the German people, but Moltke was dealing now with an anticipated postwar period of crisis and transition. For the commissioners to be able to do the jobs he assigned to them, he believed they should be selected in advance and ready for the onrushing moment when they would be needed.

So there began a long and complex process of singling out men in every region of Germany who could be relied on to step forward and grasp the power being given up by the Gauleiters and magistrates of the disintegrating Third Reich. This process had to be highly secret (much of it remains so to this day), because it was here, in this selection of post-Nazi officials, that Moltke's planning entered a new phase. Here, the Nazis could argue, his ideal evolved from daydreaming theories into outright treason. Any man who actually accepted the honor of being named a regional commissioner might have to accept at the same time a summons to the guillotine.

Moltke's efforts were not universally appreciated within the anti-Nazi opposition. Hans Gisevius, for example, was a former Gestapo official who became an ardent and quite outspoken advocate of a military coup. After the war, which Gisevius survived unscathed, he scornfully described Moltke as "the most prominent advocate of inaction." "Profoundly skeptical of any action on the part of the military," he added, "Moltke had in mind something like a 'directed defeat.' Because of Moltke's personality and political weight, his leadership was trusted by many oppositionists who were not at all prone to fold their hands in their laps and who, in another situation, might have enlisted their minds and wills under the banner of those who favored 'action' rather than 'politics.'"

The same charge of inaction echoes through William Shirer's *Rise and Fall of the Third Reich*. Moltke and his friends represented merely "a discussion group," Shirer wrote sarcastically. "Their ideals were noble, high in the white clouds, and to them was added a touch of German mysticism." Shirer quoted Dorothy Thompson's silly question broadcast to her pseudonymous friend "Hans," whether he and his friends "would ever have the courage to act." Shirer solemnly judged that frivolous insult to be "a penetrating question" and then provided his own answer that "Moltke and his friends had the courage to talk . . . but not to act."

Courage was never at issue in Kreisau, of course; if it had been, Moltke repeatedly demonstrated far more of it than either Shirer or Miss Thompson ever did. The real question was whether Moltke's meetings at Kreisau had any relevance to the future of Germany or were mere woolgathering. People who have difficulty comprehending the power of ideas like to ridicule them as unrealistic. President Eisenhower, for example, bequeathed to us his definition of research as the effort to find out why the sky is blue, and Stalin never did find the answer to his famous question of how many divisions the pope had. It is easy enough to answer that Moltke was simply a few years ahead of his time. His ideas on the decentralization of political power, on the workers' right to a share in corporate policymaking, on the need for European unification, and for a spiritual rebirth of Germany—all these are now matters of public policy in the Germany that did eventually succeed Hitler's Third Reich.

The Nazis recognized the power of Moltke's ideas, and they validated them by paying him the only kind of recognition that they knew: they killed him.

17

"Every Honest German Is Ashamed"

WHEN THE ANTI-HITLER CONSPIRATORS WERE TRYING TO PERSUADE General Halder to lead a coup against the invasion of Czechoslovakia in 1938, they kept encountering what one of them called "Halder's setback theory." According to the chief of staff's theory, Hans Gisevius later wrote, "Hitler still had such strong support among the common people that there was little prospect of overthrowing him successfully. . . . The soldiers, Halder argued, were as unreliable for our purposes as any other group in the population. They owed everything to the dictator; they constantly cheered him as their hero. It would take a succession of bad experiences to enlighten the army. What was needed was a setback, such as no propaganda tricks could dissimulate, to induce the army to co-operate with an uprising against Hitler."

Halder proved able to survive the entire war without ever witnessing a setback of sufficient magnitude to convince him to order a revolt. But to the soldiers whom Hitler had sent to invade Russia in June 1941, the whole campaign soon looked like one setback after another. Despite enormous advances, enormous seizures of Soviet territory, the quick victory that Hitler had promised at the start never seemed to arrive. In December 1941, a few days after a German reconnaissance unit reached the Moscow suburb of Khimki, where they could actually see the spires of the Kremlin, the Russians launched a counteroffensive with some one hundred divisions that the Germans had not known to exist. The snow and ice paralyzed Guderian's tank forces and reduced the general himself to despair. "The cold made the telescopic sights useless," he later recalled. "In order to start the engines of the tanks fires had to be lit beneath them. Fuel was freezing . . . and the oil became viscous. . . . Only he who saw the endless expanse of Russian snow during this winter of our misery and felt the icy wind that blew across it, burying in snow every object in its path . . . can truly judge the events which now occurred."

What now occurred was that the Russian counterattacks kept moving forward, and Hitler frantically tried to stop the German retreat by simply ordering his generals to stand fast. When Field Marshal Gerd von Rundstedt had to withdraw from Rostov, which had been conquered with great fanfare less than a month earlier, Hitler wired him to "retreat no further." Rundstedt retorted that it was "madness to attempt to hold," and that Hitler should rescind his order or find another commander. To that old-fashioned flourish, Hitler's response was blunt: "Give up your command." General Guderian, similarly, was fired for ordering a retreat; so was General Erich Hoepner of the Fourth Armored Group. Even Brauchitsch returned from a tour of the crumbling front and asked to be relieved. Hitler agreed, describing his top commander to Goebbels as "a vain, cowardly wretch . . . and a nincompoop." To Halder, he announced: "I have decided to take over command of the army myself."

Having declared Russia "finished," Hitler ordered ambitious advances in the summer of 1942. The Wehrmacht conquered the Maikop oil fields in early August, and a swastika flag was unfurled atop Mount Elbrus (18,510 feet), the highest mountain in the Caucasus. On August 23, the Sixth Army reached the Volga just north of Stalingrad. At the apex of German power, Halder's search for a setback ended with his dismissal. "We need National Socialist ardor now, not professional ability," Hitler told him on September 24. "I cannot expect this of an officer of the old school such as you." "So spoke not a responsible warlord but a political fanatic," Halder observed.

New reverses began almost immediately. Far to the south, Erwin Rommel launched a new offensive at El Alamein in the Libyan desert, hoping to push the British all the way back to Alexandria and the Nile, sixty miles to the east. Outgunned and outmaneuvered by Bernard Montgomery's Eighth Army, Rommel soon found himself in full flight, the most decisive defeat the Germans had yet suffered in the entire war. Worse was to come. On November 8, 1942, American and British troops swept ashore in Morocco and Algeria, and within a few months, they cleared Rommel's Afrika Korps out of Africa. They next invaded Sicily, then the toe of Italy. On the night of July 24, 1943, the Fascist Grand Council convened in Rome, denounced Mussolini, and demanded the restoration of a constitutional monarchy. The Fascist Grand Council, which had not met since 1939, was not a body that anyone took very seriously, but King Victor Emmanuel summoned Il Duce to the royal palace the following night, summarily dismissed him, and had him arrested. Hitler could only wonder if he might descry a similar future ahead of him. Like Belshazzar of Babylon, he did his best to decipher the ominous writing on the wall but could only decide to rescue the captive Mussolini by a commando raid.

On the Volga, too, Soviet reinforcements soon reached the river both north and south of embattled Stalingrad. As usual, Hitler's generals counseled withdrawal, and the Führer refused. "I won't leave the Volga!" he shouted. "I won't go back from the Volga!"

If Halder could not see the necessary setback, some of his fellow generals could. The man they assigned to organize a coup was General Henning von Tresckow, a former staff officer under Beck who now served on the staff of Field Marshal Günther von Kluge, commander of Army Group Center on the Moscow Front. Tresckow did his best to recruit Kluge for the cause, so that Kluge's troops could seize Hitler the next time he came to inspect them. Though sympathetic, Kluge would not agree to go that far. Tresckow decided that the only solution was to assassinate Hitler. So many others had tried and failed so often that he decided to do the job himself. That meant he had to make the plans himself, test them, refine them. It took months, all through the winter of 1942–1943.

Moltke, who lost a cousin killed at Stalingrad, disliked the idea of assassinating Hitler, but he could only wait to see what happened. "The most irritating part," he wrote in early January 1943, "is that I consider all the work being done now as having no chance. But it has to be done with all due care all the same, so that others, and we ourselves, can't blame ourselves for having missed any chance." And two weeks later: "I can do nothing but wait. I am too firmly convinced that there is nothing else to be done to have any faith in the busyness of the others. Waiting is, of course, much more difficult than action. . . ."

• • •

Not everyone was willing to wait for the perfect opportunity. Among the young, there were some who lacked the timorous patience of Halder and Brauchitsch. Hans Scholl, a medical student at the University of Munich, had served as a medic on the Russian front, and he had a younger brother still serving there when Hitler committed the entire Sixth Army to the battle for Stalingrad. While Hitler repeatedly spoke of how the death of these soldiers would be a heroic sacrifice, Scholl and some of his fellow students decided that they had to do something.

"Nothing is so unworthy of a civilized nation as allowing itself to be 'governed' without opposition by an irresponsible clique . . ." began the first of a series of bold, brave, and ultimately futile pamphlets that Scholl and his friends wrote, printed, and distributed in 1942 and 1943 in the name of an organization that they called the White Rose. "It is certain that today every honest German is ashamed of his government. Who among us has any conception of the dimensions of shame that will befall us and our children when one day the . . . crimes that infinitely outdistance every human measure reach the light of day?"

Within a year of this flowering, the White Rose had died. Scholl was arrested by the Gestapo on February 18, 1943, rushed before the "People's Court," and sent to the guillotine four days later. So was his sister and fellow conspirator, Sophie. She was twenty-two when she died, her brother twenty-five. Both were devout Christians. With them died a friend, Christoph Probst, twenty-four. By all the standards of the more organized resistance, the White Rose was a foolish protest, naive, romantic, and therefore pointless. But in accomplishing nothing, they accomplished exactly as much as anyone else did.

Like many members of the Resistance—like Goerdeler and Canaris—the Scholls had once been seduced by Nazism; both Hans and Sophie had been members of the Hitler Youth movement, despite the grumbling disapproval of their father, former mayor of the small Bavarian town of Kochertal. What turned them into rebels was their youthful opposition to two basic aspects of Nazism: its brutal violence and its insistence on intellectual conformity. Against this, they could only offer, with increasing passion, the doctrine of passive resistance. "The goal of passive resistance is to topple National Socialism," they declared in their third leaflet, "and in this struggle we must not recoil from any course, any action, whatever its nature. At *all* points we must oppose National Socialism, wherever it is open to attack. We must soon bring this monster of a state to an end."

As to exactly how this might be achieved, the Scholls were not very specific, but specific enough to be highly subversive:

"We cannot provide each man with the blueprint for his acts, we can only suggest them in general terms, and he alone will find the way of achieving this end: *Sabotage* in armament plants and war industries, sabotage at all gatherings, rallies, public ceremonies, and organizations of the National Socialist Party. Obstruction of the smooth functioning of the war machine. . . . Sabotage in all the areas of science and scholarship which further the continuation of the war. . . . *Sabotage* in all cultural institutions which could potentially enhance the 'prestige' of the fascists among the people. . . . *Sabotage* in all publications, all newspapers, that are in the pay of the 'government' and that defend its ideology and aid in disseminating the brown lie. . . ." After listing all these avenues of attack, the Scholls reverted to their university origins by concluding their leaflet with a long quotation from Aristotle (elsewhere, they repeatedly quote Goethe, Schiller, even Lao Tse). Like students, too, the Scholls called on other students to help spread the message. Several dozens of their friends and followers were soon carrying suitcases full of their leaflets on railroad trains all over southern Germany, to Frankfurt, Stuttgart, Karlsruhe, Mannheim, Vienna. Students there spread them far and wide. Their most audacious taunting of the authorities, however, came during the closing days of the Battle of Stalingrad, when they roamed through Munich with pots of paint.

"We have a tremendous surprise for you," Hans said to Sophie when he returned late one night. "When you go down the Ludwigstrasse tomorrow, you'll pass signs saying 'Down with Hitler' about seventy times."

"And written in peacetime paint," added one of his friends. "They won't find it so easy to get it off."

Pride goeth before a fall, as usual. The next time the Scholls went to the university with a suitcase of pamphlets, they arrived shortly before the classrooms were to open. Recklessly discarding their usual secrecy, they decided to climb to the top of the main staircase and send their messages fluttering down on the assembling students. They were spotted, of course, by the building superintendent, who promptly locked all the doors of the building and then notified the Gestapo.

The Scholls' protests sometimes had the quality of schoolyard pranks, but after half a century, their pitiful leaflets still seem not only a moving cry of pain but remarkably accurate, on target, and the Nazis were quite right to take them very seriously indeed. Roland Freisler, the president of the Nazi "People's Court," who will reappear soon in these pages, came from Berlin to sentence the Scholls and their friend Probst to death. The defendants all remained calm. "What we said and wrote is what many people are thinking," said Sophie. "Only they don't dare to say it."

The prison guards broke the rules to let the three prisoners have a cigarette together before their execution.

"I didn't know that dying could be so easy," said Probst, whose wife was still in the hospital after the birth of their third child. "In a few minutes we will meet in eternity."

"Then they were led off, the girl first," one of the guards later recalled. "She went without the flicker of an eyelash. None of us understood how this was possible. The executioner said he had never seen anyone meet his end as she did."

As Hans placed his head under the guillotine, he cried out, "Long live freedom!"

• • •

The Gestapo kept hunting. Three of the Scholls' friends were executed later that spring, and more than thirty were imprisoned, and so ended the White Rose. Moltke brought word of all this to Bishop Eivind Berggrav of Oslo when he went to Denmark and Norway in April 1943. The whole Protestant church of Norway was in revolt because of interference by the Nazi occupation authorities. The Abwehr sent Moltke and Dietrich Bonhoeffer to Oslo to pacify the Norwegians, but their real purpose was to encourage the Norwegians' resistance. Moltke not only told Berggrav about the White Rose but brought him one of the Scholls' leaflets, hoping that Berggrav would be inspired to spread the Scholls' message through church circles. So it duly reached Britain. BBC broadcasts and RAF leaflets then brought back to the Germans the news of what had been done in their name.

• • •

If waiting for the assassination attempt was difficult for Moltke, it must have been much harder for the would-be assassins, General Tresckow and one of his aides, Fabian von Schlabrendorff. They had decided that shooting would be too risky because Hitler was always surrounded by armed guards. A bomb would be more reliable. When they started to test various explosives, they found that all the German models used a fuse that made an audible hiss, easy to detect. They soon discovered, however, that the British made a plastic bomb that was small but powerful—"a package not bigger than a thick book was capable of tearing apart everything within . . . a fair-sized room"—and its fuse made no noise whatever. "Simply by pressing down on the head of the fuse," Schlabrendorff recalled, one could break a small bottle containing a corrosive chemical, which ate through the wire holding down the firing pin, "which, on being released, struck the detonator and set off the explosion."

Tresckow thought up a disguise for the bomb. "Taking two packets of explosive . . . we fashioned them into a parcel which looked like two bottles of Cointreau—the only brandy that comes in square bottles." Schlabrendorff then took the bomb back to his quarters while Tresckow and Kluge drove off to welcome the Führer on the morning of March 13, 1943. Schlabrendorff noted that it would have been easy to kill Hitler during his conference with Kluge, but that would have killed many army leaders, including Kluge, whom, as he cold-bloodedly observed, "we needed for the success of the coup." The conspirators' plan, instead, was to get the bomb aboard Hitler's plane.

Before one can kill someone, even a Hitler, one apparently needs to loathe and despise the victim, and so Schlabrendorff attended lunch with the Führer and found it "a revolting spectacle." Every dish had to be cooked by Hitler's personal cook and then tasted by his private physician, but it was only then that the "revolting spectacle" began. "His left hand was placed firmly on his thigh; with his right hand he shoveled his food, which consisted of various vegetables, into his mouth. He did this without lifting his right arm, which he kept flat on the table throughout the entire meal; instead, he brought his mouth down to the food. He also drank a number of nonalcoholic beverages which had been lined up beside his plate. . . ."

While this spectacle was going on, Tresckow approached a colonel in Hitler's entourage and casually asked if he would be kind enough to take a small package of Cointreau to a general back at headquarters. The colonel agreed. Schlabrendorff drove back to his quarters, retrieved the bomb, and then rejoined Hitler's party at the airport. At a signal from Tresckow, he pressed his thumb hard on the two-hour fuse, thus breaking the bottle of the corrosive chemical, and then handed the lethal package to the unsuspecting colonel. Following at his master's heels, the colonel boarded Hitler's plane, which soon took off for East Prussia. Now the worst waiting began for the assassins. They knew that Hitler's compartment was armored and his seat had a special parachute attached, but they figured that their bomb would tear the whole plane apart. All they had to do was to wait for the announcement that Hitler's plane had crashed. And wait. After more than two hours of expectation, they were amazed and horrified to receive a report that Hitler's plane had landed safely at Rastenburg in East Prussia, and that Hitler had returned safely to his headquarters. "We were in a state of indescribable agitation,"

Schlabrendorff recalled later. "The failure of our attempt was bad enough, but the thought of what discovery of the bomb would mean to us and our fellow conspirators, friends, and families, was infinitely worse."

So they decided, knowing that every move was a step deeper into a minefield, that they had to retrieve the bomb. For one thing, the general to whom they had sent the pseudo-Cointreau was not part of the plot so they could not rely on him for help. Tresckow telephoned the colonel who had carried the bomb onto Hitler's plane and coolly asked him whether he had delivered the package. The colonel said he hadn't yet had time. Ah, said Tresckow, still as cool as a slab of ice, there had been a mistake, the wrong package had been sent, so the gift should be kept in some safe place until a replacement arrived the next day. Then Schlabrendorff, with no way of knowing whether the bomb was now in the hands of the Gestapo, had to talk himself onto a courier plane to Rastenburg with a package containing two real bottles of Cointreau for the colonel to give the general. "As I exchanged parcels with him . . ." Schlabrendorff recalled, "I felt my blood running cold, for Hitler's aide, serenely unaware of what he was holding, handed me the bomb with a grin, juggling it back and forth in a way that made me fear a belated explosion."

Retrieving the bomb, Schlabrendorff boarded a train to Berlin, locked himself in a sleeping compartment, and began, very gingerly, to open up the lethal package with a razor blade. When he removed the wrapping, he could see that the explosives were all in place. Then he had to take the bomb apart and examine the fuse. Almost everything seemed to have worked just as it should. The bottle with the corrosive chemical had broken, and the chemical had eaten through the wire. The firing pin had struck. But the detonator had not detonated. "One of the few duds that had slipped past a British inspection," Schlabrendorff concluded, "was responsible for the fact that Hitler did not die on March 13, 1943."

• • •

The erosion of Nazi power during 1943 brought an increase in anti-Nazi resistance all across Europe, even in peaceful Denmark, which had offered only about two hours of military opposition when the Germans invaded in April 1940. During the first years of the German occupation, too, the Danes continued their quiet lives. The Danish king and parliament remained in place; Danish milk and butter continued to flow south. In 1943, however, the explosions of sabotage multiplied to such an extent that General Hermann von Hannecken, the German occupation commander, proclaimed a state of emergency on August 28. His decree forbade public gatherings, or strikes; it ordered press censorship, imposed a curfew at nightfall, and established new courts to prosecute violators. "Sabotage and any incitement thereto, attacks on units of the Wehrmacht . . . possession of firearms or explosives . . . shall be immediately punishable by death," the proclamation said.

The subject of Jews was not mentioned in this edict, but the German authorities suddenly decided that the period of "emergency" would be a good time to get rid of them. There were about 8,000, and they had lived harmoniously in Denmark for many years, as integrated as they wanted to be, a situation largely unchanged during the first three years of the German occupation. Now, at Hitler's prodding, the Gestapo made plans to round up all the Danish Jews and ship them to the concentration camp in Theresienstadt, Czechoslovakia.

Rumors about this decision spread quickly in Berlin, and so they soon reached the ears of Helmuth James von Moltke. There were already legal conflicts over the punishment of Danes taken prisoner under the state of emergency. The head of the judicial division of the OKH, Karl Sack, told everyone involved in these conflicts to consult Moltke, and so he had reason enough to visit the land of his ancestors. Once finished with his official business in Copenhagen, he sought out an old friend and fellow protégé of Eugenia Schwarzwald, Merite Bonnesen, who worked for the newspaper *Politiken*, and her brother Kim, an official at the Ministry of Social Affairs. To them he told the Gestapo's plans for Denmark's Jews so that they could spread the warning.

Happily, the alarm had already been sounded. One of the first men in Copenhagen to hear this same news was Georg Ferdinand Duckwitz, the German head of all shipping operations in Copenhagen harbor. Duckwitz had migrated to Copenhagen in 1928, when he was fresh out of law school. He had found a job with a German coffee firm and also worked for the German embassy as a shipping official. That was how he had learned on September 11 that the Germans would need three ships to take all the Jews to Stettin for shipment to Theresienstadt. Duckwitz first argued and protested, then checked with Berlin to confirm that the unthinkable was really being thought. Until then, there had been no restrictions on the Jews of Denmark; they enjoyed full equality with all other citizens. A German threat to impose anti-Semitic measures inspired Premier Erik Scavenius to declare that his government would immediately resign in protest. When a German official mentioned "the Jewish question" to King Christian X, the king is supposed to have retorted: "There is no Jewish question in this country. There is only my people."[1]

When Duckwitz was convinced that the Germans really did plan to stage a huge roundup of Denmark's Jews on the night of September 30, he resolved to do something about it. On the night of September 29, he attended a meeting of the Social Democratic Party and accosted the party leader, Hans Hedtoft. Hedtoft consulted with other Socialist leaders and then went himself to the home of C. B. Henriques, the leader of Denmark's Jewish community. "Mr. Henriques," Hedtoft said, "the thing we have feared so long has come. . . . Tomorrow night the Gestapo will raid all Jewish homes to arrest the Jews and take them to boats in the harbor. . . ."

Henriques was shocked, and his reaction was symptomatic. To his would-be savior, he said: "You're lying."

When Hedtoft began arguing, Henriques finally gave his reason for disbelief: He had just recently conferred with the Danish foreign minister, Niels Svenningsen, and Svenningsen had recently conferred with Werner Best, a former Gestapo official who now served as Germany's minister plenipotentiary in Denmark. Best, who had actually proposed the roundup himself, had assured Svenningsen that no such thing would happen. "Do you think Svenningsen would try to fool me?" Henriques demanded.

"Of course not . . ." Hedtoft said. "But he's only repeating what the Germans told him, what they want him to believe."

Nothing could persuade Henriques that the fate of the Jews of Poland and Germany and Russia and Holland and France awaited the Jews of Denmark too, so Hedtoft returned to the meeting of Socialists, and they decided to warn as many individual Jews as they could. One of them, Alsing Andersen, had a secretary, Inge Barfeldt, who was married to a German Jewish refugee. Andersen called Mrs. Barfeldt, and Mrs. Barfeldt called a friend named Julius Margolinsky, and Margolinsky was a friend of Marcus Melchior, the rabbi of the Copenhagen synagogue. On the morning of September 30, Rabbi Melchior stood before the Holy Ark in his synagogue and made an announcement to about 150 members of his congregation.

---

[1]Contemporary folklore spread many such tales of the king's right-mindedness. Another favorite: When the Germans threatened to make the Jews wear a yellow star, as was standard throughout Nazi-occupied Europe, the king supposedly said: "If the Germans want to introduce the yellow Jewish star in Denmark, I and my whole family will wear it as a sign of the highest distinction." While the king may well have held all these commendable views, most historians insist that he never publicly expressed any of them, that the tales reflect primarily what the Danes wanted to believe of their monarch.

"There will be no service this morning," the rabbi said. "Instead, I have very important news to tell you. Last night I received word that tomorrow the Germans plan to raid Jewish homes throughout Copenhagen to arrest all the Danish Jews for shipment to concentration camps. They know that tomorrow is Rosh Hashanah and our families will be home. The situation is very serious. We must take action immediately. You must leave the synagogue now and contact all relatives, friends, and neighbors you know are Jewish and tell them what I have told you. . . . By nightfall tonight we must all be in hiding."

And what the rabbi said must be done was done. Jews called other Jews, and Gentiles joined in the alarm. Shopkeepers warned their customers, doctors their patients, and students roamed through the streets, searching out Jews. The Gentiles did not just warn the Jews but took them in, hid them, and sheltered them. When the Gestapo banged on Danish doors all that night, they found nothing but sleeping Christians. When Kim Bonnesen answered his doorbell the next morning, he found Moltke smiling happily. "Hitler wanted to get six thousand," Moltke said, "but he hasn't even got two hundred."

There were indeed about 200 Danish Jews who refused to believe the warnings, or perhaps simply refused to hide, and they were taken down to the harbor for shipment to Theresienstadt. And the rescue operation was not finished by any means. It took weeks for a Danish underground, much of it improvised on the spur of the moment, to funnel the Jews from their hiding places onto fishing boats that could take them across the Kattegat to safety in Sweden. Though a few more were lost in this process, the vast majority were saved. Exact statistics are difficult to come by, but one of the most painstaking surveys, in Lucy Dawidowicz's *The War Against the Jews*, concludes that there were 8,000 Jews in Denmark at the time of the German occupation. "Some 6,500 were Danish Jews (including 1,300 offspring of mixed marriages). . . . About 1,500 were recent refugees from Germany, Austria, and Czechoslovakia." Martin Gilbert reports in *The Holocaust* that the Danes took to Sweden "5,919 Jews, 1,301 part-Jews . . . and 686 Christians married to Jews. . . . The Germans found only 500 Jews still in Denmark. All were sent to Theresienstadt; 423 survived the war."

Theresienstadt was an ambiguous destination. The Nazis long maintained it as a "showplace" camp where Red Cross inspectors were invited to see the comfortable accommodations provided by the Third Reich. Here is where many of the Gypsies were kept, until they were shipped to Auschwitz for extermination. Many inmates were killed in Theresienstadt, too, of course, but the odds of survival were higher here, particularly if outsiders made some effort to exert a protective influence. The Danish government was quite diligent in inquiring about the welfare of the missing 500, and in seeing that food packages got delivered. When the Theresienstadt prisoners were finally liberated, a fleet of Swedish Red Cross buses conveyed them back to Copenhagen, where thousands of Danes lined the streets and cheered and waved placards saying *Velkommen til Danmark*. The prisoners found their old homes waiting for them, not only scrubbed and swept by their neighbors but filled with flowers.

It is one of the few bright stories in the whole dark saga of the Holocaust, and it is a lasting testimonial to the character of the Danish people. It is also, of course, a remarkable demonstration of what might have happened elsewhere in Europe if the Christians of France and Poland and the Netherlands—not to mention Germany—had behaved more like Christians. For Moltke, who had put his neck in jeopardy to bring the warning, it was no great personal victory, since Duckwitz had already sounded the alarm, but after so many failures and defeats, it must have seemed wonderful to see the Nazi death machine thwarted for once—in the land of his ancestors—and to have played any part at all in that outcome.

• • •

In contrast to Moltke's sensitivity to the Jews of Denmark, he seems to have been surprisingly indifferent to the Warsaw Ghetto. He happened to be passing through Warsaw in the first week of May 1943, and observed that the city "doesn't look much worse than Cologne or Mainz. . . . The bulk of the population doesn't look worse fed than ours." He noted, though, that "a big cloud of smoke stood above the city."

"It was caused by a fight which had been raging for some days in the ghetto," Moltke wrote to his wife on May 4. "The remaining Jews—30,000—reinforced by airborne Russians, German deserters, and Polish Communists, had turned part of it into an underground fortress. It is said that they have made passages between the cellars of houses while the Germans were patrolling the streets. . . . Something like partisan fighting had been directed from these headquarters, so that it was decided to clear out the ghetto. . . ."

In actual fact, the Nazis had already deported nearly 60,000 "nonproductive persons" from the ghetto to the death camp at Treblinka during 1942; then Himmler ordered another 8,000 deportations in January 1943. Jewish resistance, quite unaided by "airborne Russians," led Himmler to order that the entire ghetto be destroyed. On April 19, some 3,000 Waffen-SS troops under General Juergen

Stroop surrounded and then invaded the ghetto. The Jews fought back with pistols, rifles, Molotov cocktails. Some tried to escape through the sewers, but the SS troops dynamited and flooded them.

On the same day that Moltke casually wrote to his wife about seeing a cloud of smoke over Warsaw, Stroop reported to his superiors a few details of what had caused it: "Our main forces were dispatched at about 1100 hours to sweep, purge, and destroy two large housing blocks of the former firms of Toebbens, Schulz & Co., and others. After these blocks were completely cordoned off, the Jews who were still in the buildings were first ordered to come forward voluntarily. 456 Jews were thereby apprehended for transfer. Only when the housing blocks were engulfed by fire and headed for destruction did a considerable number of Jews emerge, forced to flee the flames and smoke. Repeatedly the Jews tried to pass through burning buildings. Countless Jews who had been visible on the roofs during the conflagration perished in the flames. Others came into view on the uppermost floors at the very last moment and could have saved themselves from being cremated alive only by jumping. Today, a total of 2,283 Jews was apprehended, of whom 204 were shot; countless Jews were destroyed in fires and in bunkers. The sum total of Jews apprehended to date has risen to 44,089. . . ."

Moltke's account was somewhat more distant. "The resistance was so strong that a real assault with guns and flame-throwers was needed," he wrote his wife. "And that is why the ghetto is still burning. It had already been going on for several days when I got there. . . ."

It actually took another week for the firing to die down, and only on May 16 did Stroop blow up the Tlomacki synagogue as a signal that the Battle of the Warsaw Ghetto was over. "The Jewish quarter of Warsaw is no more," Stroop announced. Some 2,500 concentration camp inmates worked for more than a year to clear away nearly 450 acres of ruins and rubble so that the ghetto where about 500,000 people had once lived could be turned into a park. For this work by the concentration-camp laborers, Himmler sent the Finance Ministry a bill for 150 million Reichsmarks.

• • •

Amid great events, small efforts also have their effect. During a visit to the Netherlands in June 1943, Moltke consulted with General Alexander von Falkenhausen's chief of staff, Harry Craushaar, in an effort to win the release of all hostages. "I . . . arranged with Craushaar that he will release the 300 hostages he still has in custody," Moltke wrote his wife. "In these days, I have secured the liberty of more than 1,000 people, if all promises are kept."

• • •

As Nazi power weakened throughout 1943, many members of the German resistance—like many members of the government—began worrying about how the war might be cut short, brought to an end. One of these would-be peacemakers was Admiral Canaris, who dreaded the advance of the Red army and hoped to arrange a settlement in the West so that the Western Allies could join in defending the East. Though Roosevelt and Churchill had announced at their conference in Casablanca that January that they would accept no German peace terms except unconditional surrender, Canaris suspected that there were Western officials who shared his ideas for a negotiated peace, specifically Stewart Menzies, the chief of British Intelligence, and William Donovan, the head of the American Office of Strategic Services.

Canaris's chief operative in Istanbul was Paul Leverkuehn, that international lawyer who had taken Moltke into his Berlin office just before the war. Leverkuehn arranged a meeting in January 1943 between Canaris and a friend of Roosevelt's, Commander George H. Earle, a conservative ex-governor of Pennsylvania who was now serving as naval attaché and Balkans observer at the U.S. embassy in Istanbul. Earle did share Canaris's ideas for joining forces against the Soviets, but when he forwarded the proposal to the White House, Roosevelt vetoed it. The Cold War was still a few years in the future, and this was the era of supposed Allied solidarity. Ever since Stalin himself had been Hitler's partner, from 1939 to 1941, the Soviet dictator suspected his new allies in the west of planning a separate peace; those allies, who suspected the same of Stalin, were eager to reassure him of their good faith.

Canaris did not give up. He knew that Moltke was involved in litigation involving a fleet of Danube River steamers belonging to a French company. One of the company's directors had fled to Britain in 1940 and ordered the steamers to go to Turkey and be interned there. Now the pro-German directors running the company had sued for the ships' return. What could seem more natural than for Canaris to send Moltke to Istanbul in July 1943 to survey the scene? Moltke was well connected in the area. He was a friend not only of Leverkuehn but of Alexander Kirk, onetime U.S. chargé d'affaires in Berlin and now ambassador in Cairo. Once in Istanbul, Moltke soon made contact with a Dr. Alexander Rüstow, a German emigré sociologist who had mysterious connections with the OSS. Moltke asked Rüstow to ask Ambassador Kirk to meet him in either Cairo or Istanbul. Rüstow did so, but Kirk refused, thinking such a meeting too risky.

By this time, Canaris had arranged on his own a meeting with Menzies and Donovan that summer in Santander, Spain. The three intelligence chiefs, who seem to have shared a concern about the spread of Soviet power into central Europe, agreed with Canaris's proposal for a separate peace, but once again, the plan went to the White House and was quashed there. Roosevelt was determined to maintain the alliance with the Soviets, who were doing most of the fighting against the Germans.

Canaris still refused to give up. Moltke returned to Istanbul shortly before Christmas 1943. He found that Kirk had made no move toward a meeting. He even received a letter, falsely attributed to Kirk, saying that there was no good purpose in such a meeting since "nothing short of unconditional surrender of the German armed forces will terminate the war."

Underlying Moltke's maneuverings was a curious document headed "Exposé on the readiness of a powerful German group to prepare and assist Allied military operations against Nazi Germany." The origins and authorship of this curious document are all disputed. According to Anthony Cave-Brown's biography of Donovan, Moltke brought the document with him to Istanbul. This suggests that Moltke either wrote or endorsed the paper, which the Americans called the Herman Plan. It reached Ambassador Kirk, who rejected it on his own authority. According to the biography of Moltke by Michael Balfour and Julian Frisby, the report was a secondhand summary of Moltke's views, written by Rüstow and another German after Moltke's departure. The only surviving copy is an English translation by another German in Istanbul.

The most startling aspect of this document is that it proposed "military cooperation with the Allies on the largest possible scale." At a time when the Western Allies were still mobilizing their forces in Britain for an invasion of France, the German group proposed "to dispatch a high officer to a specified Allied territory by plane as their . . . plenipotentiary charged with coordinating the plans of collaboration with the Allied Command."

The document said that the anti-Nazi opposition was divided into pro-Western and pro-Soviet factions. It said it spoke for the Western group, which, though numerically weaker, is represented by many key men in the military and civil service hierarchy, including officers of all ranks and key members of the OKW. "Furthermore, it is in close touch with the Catholic bishops, the Protestant Confessional Church, leading circles of the former labor unions . . . as well as influential men of industry and intellectuals." This group, it said, in a paragraph guaranteed to interest the Allies, "is convinced of the justification of the Allied demand for unconditional surrender." In accepting this surrender in the west, though, the group insisted on "the continuance of an unbroken Eastern front . . . such as the line from Tilsit to Lemberg." If the Western Allies would thus promise to keep the Soviets out of Poland, "The Group would see to it that simultaneously with the Allied landing a provisional anti-Nazi government would be formed which would take over all non-military tasks. . . ."

This does indeed sound rather like a reformulation of the Kreisau plans, suggesting that the members of the *Kreisauer Kreis* were not idle dreamers, as is so often charged, but real revolutionaries eager to take control of the shattered remnants of Hitler's Third Reich. The most striking aspect of these proposals, though, is that they were false. There is no evidence that this group could produce military units ready to cooperate with the Allies, or an anti-Nazi government with any real authority. It was tempting, of course, to believe that the invasion of France would not be necessary, but the Allied leaders were not being merely cynical when they decided that this appeal for a separate peace was based largely on fantasy.

18

July 20, 1944

IT WAS PROBABLY INEVITABLE THAT MOLTKE WOULD EVENTUALLY BE arrested. The Gestapo was full of bunglers, like any secret police force, but they were not all complete simpletons. And Moltke had not been sufficiently secretive about his ideas, his friends, his travels, his activities. But if his arrest was almost inevitable, it was nonetheless absurd that he was arrested because of a relative triviality.

This involved a Fräulein Elisabeth von Thadden, who had been dismissed by the Nazis from her position as headmistress of a progressive boarding school for girls near Heidelberg. She was giving a birthday party for her sister. To this party she invited a friend named Henna Solf, the widow of Wilhelm Solf, who had been the last foreign minister of imperial Germany in the short-lived cabinet of Prince Max of Baden. Solf had also been ambassador to Japan under the Weimar Republic but opposed the Nazis from their takeover in 1933 until his death in 1936. It was Solf who recruited Goerdeler into the opposition. Frau Solf maintained a salon for diplomatic friends from the old days, like Countess Hanna von Bredow, granddaughter of Bismarck, where people enjoyed exchanging barbed remarks about the crudities of the Third Reich. One regular at her salon was Otto Kiep, former German consul-general in New York, with whom Moltke had recently toured the battlefields of France, so he was also invited to Fräulein von Thadden's birthday party for her sister. As was Moltke. As was a doctor named Paul Reckzeh, who appears to have been a police spy.

"Helmuth was always a little nervous about the Kiep group," Freya von Moltke recalls. "Because they talked. They were talkative people, and they talked small-talk about the Nazis, and that wasn't worth it. You know what I mean. To talk about one's annoyance about the Nazis may have relieved these people, but it was a very dangerous thing to do. And that's what they did."

So there was talk at Fräulein von Thadden's birthday party for her sister, talk in the presence of a police spy. "Reckzeh . . . in the brief space of an hour," according to one account, "appears to have provoked Otto Kiep into a series of indiscreet remarks." A few days after the party, an official named Plaas received an order from the Sicherheitsdienst (Security Service) or SD to listen in on the telephones of Frau Solf and her friends, including Kiep. Plaas, who sympathized with the resistance, told a friend in the Abwehr named Captain Gehre about these new wiretaps, and Gehre told his Abwehr colleague, Moltke, and Moltke warned his old friend Kiep. The SD arrested Kiep, Frau Solf, Fräulein von Thadden, and various others between January 10 and 12 and found that they had been forewarned. It did not take the SD long to learn that this collection of aging grumblers was not a major threat to the Third Reich, but they were intensely interested in the revelation that the suspects had been forewarned of the SD suspicions. When they intensified their interrogation of their prisoners, somebody mentioned Moltke. The SD had long suspected Moltke, but they had nothing specific for which to arrest him. Now they did. Tipping off a suspected subversive was a serious offense. On January 19, 1944, SD officials appeared at Moltke's door and arrested him.

"They came in the evening, not very late, seven-thirty or something like that," Freya von Moltke recalls. "They came to Peter Yorck's house in Berlin-Lichterfelde, where Helmuth lived after he had been bombed out of his apartment in Derfflingerstrasse. I was in Kreisau, of course, and knew nothing. Peter Yorck phoned me the next morning and said that Helmuth had gone for a sudden trip. I was so stupid that I did not immediately understand, so I asked when he would be back. Only when Peter said they did not know did I realize what it meant."

One consequence of Moltke's arrest was that it completely removed him from the conspiracy to assassinate Hitler. Moltke had always opposed the idea of killing the dictator, while the conspirators kept trying and failing and trying again. On Moltke's trip to Oslo with Dietrich Bonhoeffer in 1943, the two argued at length over this matter. It was a strange confrontation, the theologian insisting on the moral imperative to murder the chief of state while the heir to Germany's most celebrated military name upheld the Fourth Commandment against killing as higher than all reasons of state. They were not the only ones to engage in this argument; it divided the entire resistance movement. On the very night of Moltke's arrest, Peter Yorck was debating the same issue with a visitor, Count Claus Schenk von Stauffenberg.

This Stauffenberg was a newcomer who changed the whole equation in the resistance. Born in 1907 and thus still in his mid-thirties, he came from a venerable Swabian family that was deeply rooted in Catholicism. Athletic and energetic, he had joined a famous cavalry regiment, the Bamberger Reiter; indeed, he himself was nicknamed the Bamberger Reiter because of his resemblance to the famous thirteenth-century equestrian statue that still stands near the Bamberg cathedral. Transferred to the General Staff early in the war, he soon demonstrated outstanding ability as a planner and organizer. A soldier through and through, passionately dedicated to his calling, he returned to combat in the Afrika Korps, and there he suffered a mutilation about as destructive as a soldier can suffer without actually being killed: he lost an eye, his right hand, and two fingers of his left, plus sustaining injuries to his ears and knees. Such wounds might have turned any soldier against the dictator who had sent him into battle, but Stauffenberg had been against Hitler for years. Tresckow and Schlabrendorff had met him as a staff officer in 1941, and Stauffenberg was openly hostile to the Nazi regime. He liked to quote a poem by Stefan George entitled "The Antichrist," which seemed to him a vivid portrait of the Führer:

> Der Fürst des Geziefers verbreitet sein reich.
> Kein schatz der ihm mangelt; kein glück das ihm weicht.
> Zu grund mit dem rest der empörer![1]

When Stauffenberg had recovered from his wounds and returned to duty on the General Staff, he learned from an uncle, Count Nicholas von Uxkull, that there was a resistance movement within the army. Only after he had been assigned to be chief of staff to General Friedrich Olbricht, head of the General Army Office, did Stauffenberg

[1] Hilda Simon has translated these lines: "The Lord of all Vermin enlarges his realm; / No treasure he lacks; no luck ever fails. / And down with the rest of the rebels!"

learn from his uncle that Olbricht was a key figure in the resistance. The conspirators had meanwhile spotted Stauffenberg as a promising recruit. Olbricht asked him if he was willing to join the resistance, and Stauffenberg said he was. Olbricht assigned him to reorganize all plans for the coup that would follow Hitler's assassination. He had to update the orders telling various commanders where to move their troops to seize control of key installations and block any SS counter-coup. The official story was that the army was planning theoretical moves against a possible SS attempt to seize power. The sealed and secret orders were to be opened only on receipt of the code word "Walküre." This evocation of Brünhilde, the heroine of Wagner's *Ring of the Niebelungen,* was marvelously apt, for her great crime was to disobey Wotan, to do what he really wanted but could not do himself. For this transgression, she was condemned to lie unconscious within a circle of fire until a hero came to rescue her.

In planning this new version of the coup that his predecessors had repeatedly failed to carry out, Stauffenberg soon filled the enormous gap that had been left by the dismissal of Hans Oster in April 1943. Now it was Stauffenberg who served as "general manager" of the military resistance. This change was not without controversy. The concomitant to Stauffenberg's youth, energy, and courage was that he was abrasive; some considered him arrogant. And while the older generals like Beck and Witzleben had been content to leave all nonmilitary aspects of the coup to the civilian members of the resistance, Stauffenberg insisted on taking a strong hand in political matters. His critics considered this a deplorable intrusion into civilian affairs, and some considered him little better than a renegade Nazi. "Now that the Nazi leadership had failed and Hitler had been exposed as the bungling strategist he was," wrote one of them, Hans Bernd Gisevius, "the soldiers were to spring into the breach and save the lost cause. Stauffenberg wanted to retain all the totalitarian, militaristic, and socialistic elements of National Socialism." Both his views and his personality brought Stauffenberg into conflict with Goerdeler, who had long been the acknowledged civilian leader of the resistance. A stout believer in both democracy and free enterprise, Goerdeler impressed Stauffenberg as a "dinosaur" (a view that Moltke shared), and Stauffenberg openly campaigned to have him replaced by the Socialist leader Julius Leber. No less irritating was Stauffenberg's conviction that Goerdeler talked too much, and so he kept the older man out of his planning. When Gisevius asked Goerdeler in early July 1944 how he was getting along with Stauffenberg, Goerdeler first evaded the question, then paused and stared at the ceiling and finally said very carefully: "Well, you know, if he were not young and I were not much older, I would not be able to stand the way he cuts me off short."

Adding to the tension, of course, was the fact that Stauffenberg had decided that he himself would have to carry the bomb that would kill Hitler. This later proved to be a major mistake, for it removed Stauffenberg from Berlin during the crucial first hours after the bomb went off, but when Stauffenberg was appointed chief of staff to General Friedrich Fromm in June 1944, he decided that he had little choice. For Fromm, commander of the Home Army, was one of the few officers with regular access to the increasingly reclusive Hitler, and his chief of staff would share that access, a "privilege" that few members of the resistance possessed. The idea of murdering his supreme commander naturally troubled Stauffenberg, but he was convinced that only Hitler's death would free the vacillating generals from their oaths of loyalty and permit them to support the coup. At least six times during the last quarter of 1943, various assassins had attempted to kill Hitler, but every time, something had gone wrong. The "Lord of all Vermin" still bore a charmed life. The sixth time, Stauffenberg himself carried a bomb in his briefcase to a meeting at Hitler's headquarters in Rastenburg, East Prussia, only to have the meeting canceled on Hitler's whim.

If the Führer was lucky in his escapes, so was the resistance. The plotters seemed endlessly able to acquire illegal explosives and to carry them about wherever they chose. Hitler became more and more reclusive, but his famous secret police never seemed to catch the killers who haunted him. While they kept many suspects under surveillance, the surveillance seemed to do them no good. In his own way, though, Himmler was slowly closing in. His first great objective was to seize control of the Abwehr, and in February 1944, he finally achieved that. Hitler signed a decree creating a unified German intelligence with Himmler in command. Canaris was given a sinecure while the Gestapo men took over. Canaris had not escaped the net, though. In a last meeting with Himmler, the triumphant police chief told the fallen admiral that he knew all about the plans for a coup, and that his Gestapo would thwart them when the time was right. He knew how to deal with people like Beck and Goerdeler, he said. He was only waiting, he went on, to find out the names of everyone involved in the plot. This may have been true, though Himmler had his own daydreams of replacing Hitler and negotiating a peace, but it was probably mostly bluff.

On July 11, Stauffenberg once again brought a bomb to Hitler's headquarters, this time at Berchtesgaden, but when he saw that neither Himmler nor Goering was in attendance, he decided to delay the assassination until he could strike down more than just Hitler. That was an indulgence that the conspirators soon realized they could no longer afford. On July 17, an Abwehr spy within Himmler's empire reported that an order for Goerdeler's arrest had just been issued. Whatever Stauffenberg might think of Goerdeler, he could see that the secret police were threatening his whole operation.

Stauffenberg still had a few misgivings. When he asked Tresckow if he continued to favor a murder, Tresckow's answer was unequivocal: "The assassination must be attempted at all costs. . . . What matters now is not the practical purpose of the coup, but to prove to the world and for the records of history that the men of the resistance movement dared to take the decisive step. Compared to this objective, nothing else is of consequence." Stauffenberg's brother Berthold, a navy lawyer whom he deeply trusted, was even more inexorable. "The most frightful thing," said Berthold von Stauffenberg, "is to know that we cannot succeed, and yet that we must do it all the same, for our country and our children." Sharing an apartment with his brother, Claus von Stauffenberg practiced every night with a small pair of pliers so that his clawlike left hand could break the chemical bottle that would detonate the bomb. He was ready.

Stauffenberg's next encounter with Hitler was scheduled for July 20, when Stauffenberg was supposed to report on his progress in dredging fifteen new combat divisions out of the youths, wounded veterans, and assorted debris of Fromm's Home Army. Even early in the morning, it was blazing hot when Stauffenberg set off from Berlin with his aide, Lieutenant Werner von Haeften. "The heat was unbearable," one conspirator recalled. Stauffenberg and Haeften arrived at the Rastenburg airfield at about 10 A.M., breakfasted under an oak tree outside Mess Hall No. 2, and then went to a preliminary briefing presided over by Keitel. Only now did Stauffenberg learn that because of the heat, the conference with Hitler would take place not in the Führer's underground bunker but in a nearby wooden hut, in which, as it turned out, the force of the bomb would be seriously dissipated.

Stauffenberg and Haeften each had a two-pound bomb, and Stauffenberg now decided to combine both weapons in his own briefcase. He said to Keitel's adjutant that he wanted to wash up and change his shirt before the meeting with Hitler. The adjutant showed Stauffenberg and Haeften to a nearby lounge. Keitel, meanwhile, was waiting at the door of his hut and chafing at the delay in going to see Hitler. The adjutant sent a sergeant to go and get Stauffenberg. The sergeant happened to open the lounge door just as Stauffenberg was in the midst of rearranging his bombs, so he left Haeften's weapon alone rather than adding it to his own briefcase. But he did manage to use his pliers to start the fuse on his bomb. It was set to go off in exactly ten minutes. Keitel's adjutant called out to him to hurry, so Stauffenberg marched out, clutching his briefcase in his mangled left hand.

As soon as Stauffenberg saw the hut where Hitler's conference was being held, he began worrying whether his bomb would be powerful enough. The main room was about eighteen by forty feet, and it had ten windows that had been opened because of the heat. Hitler was standing at a large oak table, facing an open window. Stauffenberg asked a friend to get him a seat near Hitler because his hearing had suffered when he was wounded in Africa. The friend obliged, moving a naval officer to a more distant seat and shoving Stauffenberg's briefcase under the table, about six feet from where Hitler stood.

His heart pounding, Stauffenberg settled into his seat to make sure that everything was as it should be. General Adolf Heusinger, representing the ailing chief of staff, was briefing Hitler about the latest news from the Russian front. Hitler stared at an array of maps. Once Stauffenberg was confident that his briefcase was placed as close to Hitler as he could get it, he whispered to Keitel that he had to make an urgent telephone call to Berlin. Keitel nodded approval, and Stauffenberg slipped out. Nobody paid much attention, for people were always slipping in and out of these conferences, but one officer who did take note was a Colonel Heinz Brandt[2] who served as aide to General Heusinger. Brandt moved into Stauffenberg's vacant seat. He soon found that Stauffenberg's briefcase interfered with his leg room, so he edged it aside with his foot, moving it farther away from where Hitler was standing. And a thick oaken support under the table now stood between Hitler and the bomb.

It could be argued that Stauffenberg should have remained in the conference room, making sure that nothing went wrong. But to demand that someone who is risking his own life must go further and throw it away seems to be more than one can reasonably ask of even the most reckless adventurer. Besides, Stauffenberg knew that he was needed back in Berlin as soon as possible; he was the only conspirator with legal authority over the troops of Fromm's Home Army; he still had a coup to lead.

---

[2]This was the same colonel who had unwittingly carried Schlabrendorff's bomb aboard Hitler's plane the year before.

Heusinger was just finishing his report when, at 12:42 P.M., a tremendous explosion shattered Hitler's conference room. In the chaos of dust and flames, the voice of Keitel could be heard plaintively asking, "Where is the *Führer*? Where is the *Führer*?" The Führer was flat on his back, knocked unconscious, his trousers in tatters. Once revived, he was taken to a doctor, who found that his eardrum had been punctured, his right arm bruised, and his legs burned, but he was alive and otherwise well. Several of his aides were less fortunate. A secretary named Heinrich Berger had both legs blown off and soon died. A military adjutant also died of his wounds, as did a Luftwaffe general and the ill-fated Colonel Brandt. If only Stauffenberg's briefcase had not been moved . . . if only the conference itself had not been moved . . . if only Stauffenberg had stayed to watch over things . . .

Stauffenberg was a couple of hundred yards away when he heard the great explosion and saw bodies flying through the air. "There was an explosion like that of a fifteen-centimeter shell," he said later. "No one who was in that room can still be living."

Confident in that mistaken belief, Stauffenberg clambered into a waiting car and raced for the airfield. There were three security barriers to get through, but Stauffenberg bluffed, charmed, and threatened his way through all of them and onto a waiting Heinkel bomber.

In Berlin, of course, the conspirators were waiting with mounting anxiety for a call from General Erich Fellgiebel, the communications chief at Rastenburg, who was supposed to notify the plotters of the assassination and then cut off all communications to and from Rastenburg. In this he failed miserably. The first word that came to General Fromm, the wavering head of the Home Army, was an excited visit from his deputy, General Olbricht, one of the conspirators. When Olbricht told Fromm that Hitler had been assassinated, Fromm demanded to know how he knew. Olbricht said he had heard it by telephone from Fellgiebel. Since Fellgiebel had failed to shut down the communications center at Rastenburg, however, Fromm immediately telephoned Hitler's headquarters and got Keitel himself on the line.

"What in the world is going on at headquarters?" Fromm asked. "Here in Berlin the wildest rumors are afloat."

"What is supposed to be going on?" Keitel countered, just as though he had never noticed the bomb that had recently knocked him flat. "Everything is all right."

"I have just received a report that the *Führer* was killed by assassination," Fromm persisted.

"Nonsense," Keitel responded. "There was an attempted assassination, but fortunately it failed. The *Führer* is alive and received only superficial injuries. Where, by the way, is the chief of your staff, Colonel Stauffenberg?"

Stauffenberg was still airborne on his 350-mile trip from Rastenburg back to Berlin. When he arrived shortly before 4 P.M., he telephoned Olbricht to find out how the putsch was progressing. To his dismay and indignation, he learned that the putsch had barely begun. The generals were still milling around, waiting to hear from him. The police, who were supposed to move in the wake of the army, were lying low. Stauffenberg ordered the putsch to start at once, but this depended on General Fromm, who was supposed to order his Home Army into action but had never actually confirmed that he would do so. Stauffenberg and Olbricht went to Fromm's office to bring him into line by reassuring him that Hitler was dead.

"It is impossible," Fromm protested. "Keitel assured me that it was not so."

"Field Marshal Keitel is lying as usual," Stauffenberg retorted. "I myself saw Hitler being carried out dead."

"In view of this situation we have issued the code word," Olbricht added, meaning the signal "Walküre," intended to start the putsch.

"That is sheer disobedience," Fromm cried, pounding his fist on his desk. "What do you mean by 'we'? Who gave the order?"

Olbricht said that his chief of staff, Colonel Merz von Quirnheim, had issued the order. Fromm summoned Quirnheim and told him he was under arrest. Stauffenberg announced that he himself had set off the bomb and that nobody could have survived the explosion. Fromm was unimpressed. "Colonel Stauffenberg, the assassination failed," he said. "You must shoot yourself at once."

"I shall do nothing of the kind," Stauffenberg said.

Fromm then told his visitors that they were all under arrest. "You cannot arrest us," Olbricht replied. "You do not realize who holds the power. We arrest you."

There followed some frantic pushing and shoving, which ended when Fromm agreed to be confined in an adjoining room, but the question of "who holds the power" proved considerably more complicated. One of the few army units that seemed ready for action was the Grossdeutschland battalion of guards, which was sent to arrest Propaganda Minister Goebbels. As soon as the troops arrived at his office, Goebbels invoked a weapon more powerful than anything the rebels could command: the voice of the supposedly assassinated Hitler. Staring his own death in the face, Goebbels coolly telephoned Hitler's headquarters in Rastenburg and then handed the phone to the guards' commander, Major Otto Roemer.

"Do you recognize me, Major Roemer?" said the unmistakable voice at the other end of the wire. "Do you recognize my voice?"

"*Jawohl, mein Führer,*" said the major, paralyzed by the delights of obedience. Hitler not only told Roemer to spare Goebbels but canceled all the orders issued under "Walküre" and commanded Roemer to take charge of restoring order in Berlin. Roemer was thrilled at the opportunity. He marched his battalion to the War Ministry on the Bendlerstrasse. The ill-informed generals there thought Roemer had arrived to defend them from attack by Himmler's SS, but now they found themselves surrounded, trapped. Fromm was soon released from his room. He waved his pistol and ordered the conspirators to lay down their arms.

"None of us had any weapons," one of the rebels said later in describing this confrontation. But one did. "I have a pistol here," said General Beck, "but I should like to keep it for my private use." Fromm could hardly deny the aged general that traditional escape. "Very well, do so," he said. "But at once."

Beck loaded the pistol. Fromm nervously told Beck not to point the pistol at him—how very unmilitary these generals could become in moments of crisis!—but Beck paid little attention. "At this moment I am thinking of earlier days," he said. Fromm stopped him. "We do not wish to go into that now," he said. "Will you kindly go ahead!"

Beck put the gun to his head and fired. The bullet hit the top of his head and sent him reeling. "Did it fire properly?" he gasped.

"Help the old fellow," Fromm said vaguely.

Two officers standing near Beck approached him. "Take away his gun," Fromm told them. "No, no, I want to keep it," Beck protested. While the two disarmed Beck, Fromm turned to Stauffenberg and invited him to write down any last wishes he might want to make. Fromm then left the room. When he returned soon afterward, he announced that a court-martial had just been held and that it had condemned to death Stauffenberg, Olbricht, Colonel Merz von Quirnheim, and Stauffenberg's aide, Lieutenant Haeften. He then ordered a nearby lieutenant to lead the four condemned men down into the courtyard and "execute this sentence . . . at once." He then turned back to Beck, dazed and bleeding, and still convalescent from cancer surgery. "Well, what about it?" Fromm asked. "Give me another pistol," Beck said. Someone handed him a gun, but someone else fired the shot that killed him.

"I speak to you today . . ." Hitler declared in a radio broadcast that evening, "so that you may hear my voice and know that I myself am sound and uninjured; and in the second place, so that you may also hear the particulars about a crime that is without parallel in German history. An extremely small clique of ambitious, conscienceless, and criminal and stupid officers forged a plot to eliminate me. . . . The clique of usurpers . . . has nothing to do with the German armed forces. . . . It is an extremely small band of criminal elements who are now being mercilessly eliminated. . . ."

When Hitler spoke of merciless elimination, Himmler had the marching orders that he loved best. The entire Stauffenberg family, he promised, "will be exterminated down to its last member." And many were, including the assassin's prophetic younger brother Berthold. And so were many others, guilty and innocent alike.

Admiral Canaris, onetime chief of military intelligence, was hanged at the Flossenburg concentration camp. So was General Oster, once Canaris's chief of staff and the main planner of the military resistance. So was Dietrich Bonhoeffer, the theologian. Bonhoeffer's brother-in-law, Hans Dohnanyi, aide to Oster, was executed at the Sachsenhausen concentration camp.

Carl Goerdeler was executed. So was Field Marshal Erwin von Witzleben. And General Hoepner. And Peter Yorck von Wartenburg. And the labor union leaders Wilhelm Leuschner and Julius Leber. General Fellgiebel, who failed to shut down the communications center at Rastenburg, was hanged. General Henning von Tresckow walked off into the woods on the Russian front. When his body was found, he was reported killed in action and buried on his family estate. The Gestapo later exhumed and abused the body while his family was forced to watch; the remains were finally burned. General Friedrich Fromm, condemned to death for complicity in the July 20 plot that he had tried to stop, pledged his loyalty to Hitler shortly before being hanged. Field Marshal Hans von Kluge, who repeatedly promised to support the conspirators but finally abandoned them, was removed from his command in France and ordered to return to Berlin. He told his driver to go by way of the battlefield of Verdun, stopped there for lunch, then bit into a cyanide pill and died instantly.

This network of killing—an estimated 4,500 were slaughtered— would eventually reach Moltke, but not for a while. He had been in prison for more than six months, after all, by the time Stauffenberg set off his bomb. And he could say in all honesty that he had always been against the attempt. The first time that his wife went to visit him after July 20, the first thing he said was, "If I had been at liberty, this wouldn't have happened."

How can that be? How can a leader of the resistance movement have so totally condemned its most heroic hour? "Because it did what he had expected it would do," Freya von Moltke says now in the tranquillity of her living room in Vermont. "It did not get rid of Hitler, and it got rid of all the people who had worked against Hitler. That's what he thought would happen, and it did happen.

"He was a complex human being—I suppose we all are—but his complexity came out in the way that he had a big Anglo-Saxon strain in him through his mother, and then this mixture with the German side.

"As far as the plot of July 20 was concerned, there was an element of principle and there was an element of realism, where he said, 'They won't be able to carry it out, and then we'll all be killed, and there's nobody to rebuild Germany.' And that's what happened.

"The principle was that here we had been governed by a bunch of murderers for twelve years, and he wanted to start—help start—a new phase in German history—and he did not want to start that with another murder. That's a big principle, I think. But that was only part of Helmuth, because the other part of him said, 'You won't achieve it.' The principle and the realism both—you understand what I'm saying—were always trying to balance in Helmuth, and that made him complicated. . . .

"None of the resisters really did much in rebuilding Germany. I think democracy actually was introduced by the Allies, and it was the Allies that helped build democracy, and that's why it worked. It worked quite well, much better than one could expect."

19

Death and Transfiguration

WHEN HELMUTH VON MOLTKE WAS FIRST ARRESTED, HE WAS SIMPLY HELD at Gestapo headquarters in Prinz Albrecht Strasse, at the southern end of the Wilhelm Strasse, a site subsequently covered by the Berlin Wall. Freya von Moltke rushed there to see him. "I went to Berlin—I don't remember how soon, but pretty soon," she remembers now. "And I was allowed to meet Helmuth for a very short while at the Gestapo headquarters. My argument always was that I needed to see him because of our farm. Producing food was of great importance during the war. We were running *einen kriegswichtigen Betrieb* [an enterprise important to the war effort]. This argument mostly worked. To this day I am not sure that was the reason I got through to Helmuth sort of regularly." She is still troubled by another possible reason: her famous name, her social rank. "I never quite lost the unpleasant feeling," she says, "that those Gestapo people liked me as a type and therefore always treated me with deference. Maybe that was policy, too. I don't know but there it is."

By now, Berlin was enduring almost nightly air raids by British bombers, and it was not long before one of the bombs landed on the Prinz Albrecht Strasse. The Gestapo had to remain in the capital, of course, but it saw that there was no need to keep all its prisoners there. Moltke and a half-dozen others were transferred on February 6 to the concentration camp at Ravensbrück, forty-five miles north of Berlin.

Ravensbrück had opened in 1939 as the main German concentration camp for women, and about 115,000 of them passed through it. It was not a death camp, in the sense of Auschwitz or Treblinka, but executions were frequent and brutality commonplace. "Living conditions in 1943 were very harsh," the French anthropologist Germaine Tillion wrote in her passionate account of her own imprisonment there. "One could, with some difficulty, escape the obligatory labor duty of twelve hours a day, but there was no escape from the four interminable roll calls. . . . Windows and doors had to remain open day and night in temperatures often falling below zero. One had to eat standing, since there were no stools, and rise before the official reveille to be able to wash, etc. The death rate was high, of course, but the 'official' rate was reduced by the [fact that] from time to time groups of insane (or those declared to be), infirm and tuberculars simply disappeared. . . ."

In this grim institution, a new wing had been opened shortly before Moltke's arrest, and this was assigned to the confinement of political prisoners, male and female alike. Conditions here were somewhat milder than in the main camp, hardly pleasant but more bearable. Moltke was allowed to wear his own clothes rather than prison stripes. He could have his own books and papers, and he even continued to receive *Hansard,* the official account of debates in Parliament. Here he was pleased to find a British lord quoting Boswell's *Journal of a Tour to the Hebrides* to the effect that a man might find imprisonment much more pleasant than going to sea "because in gaol the quarters were much more comfortable, the food much better and the company more congenial, in addition to which he did not run the risk of being drowned."

Moltke was allowed to write to his wife twice a week, though letters in both directions were opened and censored by the Ravensbrück authorities. She was also allowed to visit him once a month, not in Ravensbrück but at a police training school in a town called Drögen, about twenty miles away. Ravensbrück officials drove Moltke there in a car while his wife made the day-long trek by train from Kreisau. She brought him food, especially tea and coffee, which were rare in those wartime days, plus the treasures of Kreisau: eggs, jellies, cakes.

"We met in the office room in a barrack," Freya von Moltke wrote later. "There was a bench and a table in one of the corners. The guard was sitting at his desk near the window, busy with his work. We could speak to each other quite freely. I brought a big ledger with me from the farm, pretending to talk business with Helmuth, and we did to some extent. But we were also able to fit in unsupervised exchanges. The guards knew me after some time, also through my letters, which they obviously enjoyed reading. One of them once said how sorry he felt that I had had such bad luck with my geese. When I told Helmuth this, saying that they seemed to be quite nice men, he said dryly, 'Except that they pull out fingernails when they interrogate.'"

Moltke was interrogated many times but never tortured. The interrogators finally gave up and just confined him. By March, he had recovered enough of his confidence to write to Gestapo headquarters, demanding, since no serious charge had been brought against him, that he be released. Challenged on this legality, the Gestapo coolly answered that a charge would be brought in due time, and that release was out of the question. Inspired to further audacity, Moltke wrote again, complaining about not being able to discuss his work with office colleagues. This time, the Gestapo did not answer. Moltke went on waiting. He really thought, apparently, that he might be released before long.

Among his fellow prisoners he discovered Isa Vermehren, the singer who had once been the great love of his brother Willo. Also a Princess Ruspoli, originally a Belgian marquise, and Elisabeth d'Arsche, known as Mary, with whom he had played cards when she was a close friend of General von Falkenhausen, the German commander in Belgium; Moltke now gave her a copy of Kipling's *If*. In the cell right next to his was a sculptor whom he already knew slightly, Marie Louise Sarré, nicknamed Puppi. "When I was allowed out for a walk in the morning of the 7th," Moltke wrote to his wife, "Puppi was looking out of her window, and her cell was so close to the exit that we were able to talk a bit. In the early days I was careful and guarded. . . . But every day I exchanged a few words with Puppi through the window. We then each walked separately. From the middle of March on we were allowed to walk with other prisoners."

Following the traditions of prison life, Moltke established a system by which he and his friends could signal each other by whistling various tunes. "In early June, we succeeded in getting Isa moved to cell No. 27, beside Puppi. I had strongly urged Isa to sing, and she started cautiously at first, and soon it was a regular habit that after everything had been closed down, that is, after 10 in the evening, she sang: first Italian folk songs or something cheerful and finally spiritual songs: Protestant hymns . . . the Gregorian *Te Deum*. The first time she sang it, an Austrian SS man in a cell obliquely below hers sighed loudly and said: 'I haven't heard that for 10 years.'"

After the July 20 plot, of course, prison life became harsher.

Moltke was interrogated repeatedly, as were many others. Most of his prison privileges were taken away. "On Aug. 19 I was put in prison uniform and locked up in a dark cell on the north side," he wrote his wife, "without a book, without writing paper, without my own things, except for socks and handkerchiefs, with bad food and no permission for walks for a week. Nevertheless I stayed in news contact with the others. Later, when I went outside again, Isa whistled my favorite songs, nothing but Mozart melodies." He did not mention that one of his neighboring cells held a newcomer, General Halder, who was finally reaping the reward for all his hesitations. The new neighbors chatted through a ventilator about the possibilities of Soviet strategy on the Eastern front.

Moltke's "news contact" with his friends kept him informed that other prisoners in Ravensbrück were faring much worse than he. "In all this existence terrible things would happen again and again," he wrote. "Almost every day some woman from the camp would get 25 lashes. . . . The women were strapped fast, naked, in the presence of the camp leader and doctor, and were beaten by two fellow prisoners. On one occasion a woman . . . had 75 lashes, in three installments. Her back was split open all over. . . . Then there were men who were suddenly asked in the morning 'to take a walk round the camp,' i.e. to be shot. It happened to Emil, a prisoner in my vicinity, who had an affair with one of the women guards and refused to divulge her name. . . ."

At the end of September, Freya von Moltke ventured to Drögen without a pass, taking along a clean suit in the hope that the "friendly" police would allow another meeting without official permission. It was not to be, but the authorities were understanding. "What a good thing you've come!" said one of them. "Your husband has just been taken to Berlin, and will need a suit." The man who had sympathized over her geese drove her back to the railroad station and helped put her suitcase on the train. "This transfer to Berlin," she said with a pretense at nonchalance, "it isn't serious, is it?" He still appeared sympathetic. "Well, yes," he said, "I'm afraid it is rather serious."

Once in Berlin, another sympathetic police official told her that her husband had been taken to the Tegel prison at the northwestern edge of the city. This was a stroke of relatively good luck because the Tegel prison chaplain was Harald Poelchau, one of the participants in the Kreisau meetings. Poelchau invited her to come to the prison the next day, and when she did, she caught a brief glimpse of her husband being bundled into a car. He saw her too, but neither of them gave any sign of recognition.

From now on, she commuted between Kreisau and Berlin, often staying with the Poelchaus in Tegel. The chaplain smuggled letters to and fro. Though she knew it would do little good, she wrote letters to Himmler in defense of her husband. She even obtained an interview with General Heinrich Müller, the chief of the Gestapo. Müller was polite, but he left little doubt that the authorities planned to execute Moltke. "We're not going to make the same mistake as in 1918 and leave our internal enemies alive," he said.

To be considered an internal enemy of the Gestapo was something the Moltkes could only acknowledge as an honor, but it was an honor that Moltke now had to defend before a Nazi court known as the "People's Court." This was run by a furious zealot named Roland Freisler. A war prisoner in Russia in 1915, he had returned from the East as an ardent Communist, but as early as 1925, he had transferred his allegiance to the Nazis. After some years in the ministry of justice, he took over the "People's Court" in 1942 and adopted as his model Andrei Vishinsky, the relentless prosecutor of Stalin's purges; among his victims in his pursuit of "treason," he counted the guillotined students of the White Rose movement. Now the July 20 plot had brought him new prey. Moltke's defense lawyer described the judge as "gifted, something of a genius, and not wise, and all this in the highest degree." The main charge against Moltke, conspiracy to overthrow the government, had faded because of lack of evidence, but there were plenty of other charges: knowing of such a conspiracy and failing to report it, hostility to National Socialism, discussing what might happen after the loss of the war. The war was virtually over when Moltke and seven other members of the Kreisau group went on trial on January 9, 1945. Hitler's last big counterattack in the West, the Battle of the Bulge, had just failed, and a new Soviet offensive was sweeping across Prussia. Still, Nazi justice creaked onward.

The trial "took place in a small hall which was filled to bursting," Moltke wrote. He made a point of reporting that the trial was secret, that Freisler had expressly forbidden everyone from making notes or recording the scene, which Moltke promptly proceeded to do. To anyone with a legal mind, Freisler's idea of a judicial process was bizarre. He read aloud the defendant's life history; the defendant was permitted and even encouraged to interrupt with comments and corrections, but if the interruptions seriously challenged Freisler's scenario, the judge lost his temper and began shouting accusations. In describing the meetings at Kreisau, Freisler feigned surprise that no Nazi official had been invited to join the discussions of Germany's future, and he displayed a perhaps more genuine indignation that the participants had included several clergymen. The meetings at Kreisau had expressed "the blackest defeatism," according to Moltke's summary of Freisler's charges, and the search for officials to run a post-Nazi regime represented "open preparation for high treason."

Since none of the Kreisau participants considered themselves engaged in treason, Freisler had to proclaim a series of theses that he declared to be "legal principles" governing the Moltke trial. Moltke's version of Freisler's principles: "The People's Court takes the view that the mere failure to report defeatist utterances like Moltke's, coming from a man of his reputation and position, already amounts to treason." "It is already tantamount to treason to discuss highly political questions with people who are in no way competent to deal with them, especially if they do not in any way actively belong to the party." And finally this absurdity: "It is already preparation for high treason to arrogate to oneself any judgment in a matter which it is for the Führer to decide." "And so it went on and on," Moltke wrote. "This only allows one conclusion: anyone who doesn't suit Herr Freisler commits high treason." Moltke's judgment of Freisler's "principles" was quite accurate, and so was his perception that "the name of Moltke kept being mentioned" in the questioning of other defendants. "It ran through everything like a red thread and . . . it was clear that I was to be done away with."

Moltke sat through all of this fairly tranquilly. A recent attack of sciatica made it painful for him to stand, so he was grateful that the authorities provided a chair for him. On the second day, Freisler began his direct questioning of Moltke. "It started off in quite a mild tone; very fast. . . . Thank God I am quick and found Freisler's speed child's play; which, incidentally, we both enjoyed. . . . Up to and including the discussion with Goerdeler and my position regarding it, everything went quite smoothly and without much ado. Then came my objection that the police and Abwehr had known about it. Now Freisler had paroxysm No. 1. . . . A hurricane was unleashed: he banged on the table, turned as red as his robe, and roared: 'I won't stand for that sort of thing. I won't listen to that kind of thing.' . . . Since I knew anyhow what the result would be, it all left me quite indifferent: I looked him icily in the eye, which he clearly didn't like, and suddenly I couldn't help smiling. This spread to the adjunct judges sitting on Freisler's right. . . ."

Freisler turned his questioning to the Kreisau meetings and "steered straight for two things: (a) defeatism, (b) the selection of regional commissioners [i.e., officials to take over after the collapse of the Third Reich]. Both led to paroxysms of the same quality, and when I submitted in defense that it all had its roots in official business, the third paroxysm: 'All Adolf Hitler's agencies base their work on the foundation of victory. . . . I simply won't listen to anything like that, and even if it were not so, every single man has the duty to spread the faith in victory on his own.' And so on in long tirades.

"But now," Moltke's account continued, "came the quintessence: 'And who was there? A Jesuit Father! Of all people, a Jesuit Father! A Protestant minister, three people who were later sentenced to death for taking part in the 20th of July! And not a single National Socialist! Not one! Well, all I can say is: now the fig leaf is off! A Jesuit Father, and with him of all people you discuss questions of civil disobedience! And you know the Jesuit Provincial too! He too was at Kreisau on one occasion! A Jesuit Provincial, one of the highest officials of Germany's most dangerous enemies, he visits Count Moltke in Kreisau! And you're not ashamed of it! No German would touch a Jesuit with a barge-pole! . . . If I know there is a Jesuit Provincial in a town, it is almost a reason for me not to go to that town! . . . What is your business with a bishop, with any bishop? Where do you get your orders from? You get your orders from the Führer and the NSDAP [Nazi Party]! That goes for you as well as for any other German, and whoever gets his orders, under whatever camouflage, from the guardians of the Beyond gets them from the enemy and will be treated accordingly.'"

From this, Moltke concluded, quite correctly, that all the meetings at Kreisau would be officially condemned as "preparation for high treason." And now the kangaroo court had nearly finished. Freisler asked Moltke whether he had anything further to say, and Moltke didn't know. All he wanted to say, he later recalled, was a quotation from Martin Luther:

> Nehmen Sie den Leib,
> Gut, Ehr, Kind und Weib,
> Lass fahren dahin, Sie haben's kein Gewinn,
> Das Reich muss uns doch bleiben![1]

He decided, though, that such a retort "would have harmed the others," so, after a slight hesitation, he replied only: "I don't intend to say anything more, *Herr Präsident.*" And so it was done. The verdict was guilty and the sentence death. Freisler still persisted in asking

---

[1] "And though they take our life, / Goods, honor, children, wife, / Yet is their profit small, / These things shall vanish all. / The city of God remaineth."

whether Moltke saw his own guilt, and Moltke said he did not. "If you still don't recognize it . . ." Freisler declared, "it shows that you think differently and have thereby excluded yourself from the fighting community of the people."

The accusation of thinking differently from the Nazi regime, and of excluding himself from the fighting community of the people, pleased and flattered Moltke so much that he seized upon it as a validation and vindication of everything he had done—more so, perhaps, than he would otherwise have thought. "The beauty of the judgment on these lines," he wrote, "is the following: It is established that we did not want to use any force; it is established that we did not take a single step toward organization. . . . We merely thought. . . . And in the face of the thoughts of these three solitary men, the mere thoughts, NS [National Socialism] is so scared that it wants to exterminate everything that is infected by it. If that isn't a compliment. After this trial we are out of the Goerdeler mess,[2] we are free from all practical action, we are to be hanged because we thought together. Freisler is right, a thousand times right; and if we are to die, I am in favor of dying on this issue."

In accepting so fervently the idea that his resistance movement had not actually provided any resistance, that "the spirit itself . . . is to be persecuted," and that "we are to die above all for St. Ignatius," Moltke was perhaps too eager for the crown of martyrdom, but it was natural that the imminence of a martyr's death should make him think along such lines. God now seemed very close at hand. "I always imagined that one would only feel shock," he wrote, "that one would say to oneself: now the sun sets for the last time for you, now the clock only goes to twelve twice more, now you go to bed for the last time. None of that is the case. I wonder if I am a bit high for I can't deny that my mood is positively elated. I only beg the Lord in Heaven that he will keep me in it, for it is surely easier for the flesh to die like that. How merciful the Lord has been to me! Even at the risk of sounding hysterical: I am so full of gratitude that there is hardly room for anything else. He guided me so firmly and clearly these two days. . . . It was truly as it says in Isaiah 43,2: When thou passest through the waters, I will be with thee; and through the rivers, they shall not overflow thee; when thou walkest through the fire, thou shalt not be burned. . . ."

Moltke could not know the day of his death, but he knew that he

---

[2]This is a polite translation of Moltke's actual term, *"Goerdeler Mist."* *"Mist"* refers to the manure that farmers spread on their fields.

did not have long to live, and he wanted to leave his two sons, then seven and three, a kind of testament. "Throughout my life . . ." he wrote them, "I have fought against a spirit of narrowness and subservience, of arrogance and intolerance, against the absolutely merciless consistency which is deeply ingrained in the Germans and has found its expression in the National Socialist state. I have made it my aim to get this spirit overcome with its evil accompaniments, such as excessive nationalism, racial persecution, lack of faith and materialism. In this sense and seen from their own standpoint the National Socialists are right in putting me to death."

In writing to his wife, though, Moltke was much preoccupied with religion. That is probably natural in the shadow of death—Moltke had less than two weeks to live—but he seemed remarkably unshadowed. "Now there is still a hard bit of road ahead of me," he wrote, "and I can only pray that the Lord will continue as gracious to me as he has been. . . . If I were to be reprieved now—which under God is no more likely or unlikely than a week ago—I must say that I should have to find my way all over again, so tremendous was the demonstration of God's presence and omnipotence. He can demonstrate them to us, and quite unmistakably, when he does precisely what doesn't suit us. Anything else is rubbish.

"Thus I can only say this, dear heart: may God be as gracious to you as to me, then even a dead husband doesn't matter at all. He can, after all, demonstrate his omnipotence even while you make pancakes for the boys or clean them up, though that is, I hope, a thing of the past. I should probably take leave of you—I cannot do it; I should probably deplore and lament your daily toil—I cannot do it. . . . I can only tell you one thing: if you get the feeling of absolute protectedness, if the Lord gives it to you, which you would not have without this time and its conclusion, then I bequeath to you a treasure that cannot be confiscated, and compared to which even my life weighs nothing. These Romans, these miserable creatures of . . . Freisler . . . they couldn't even grasp how little they can take away. . . ."

He continued the letter the next day, saying that he had "really nothing to say" but just felt "like chatting with you a little." And so his sense of his destiny swept over him once again. "I think with untroubled joy of you and the boys, of Kreisau and everybody there; the parting doesn't seem at all grievous at the moment." But he was still haunted by the trial, by the fact that specific charges of treason had proved unimportant. "What the Third Reich is so terrified of that it must kill . . . people is ultimately the following: a private individual, your husband . . . discussed . . . *without the intention of doing any-*

thing concrete . . . the practical, ethical demands of Christianity. Nothing else; for that alone we are condemned. In one of his tirades Freisler said to me: 'Only in one respect are we and Christianity alike: we demand the whole man!' . . . Of the whole gang Freisler was the only one who recognized me, and of the whole gang he is the only one who knows why he has to kill me. . . . [3]

"I wonder if he realized what he was saying? Just think how wonderfully God prepared this, his unworthy vessel. At the very moment when there was danger that I might be drawn into active preparations of a putsch—it was in the evening of the 19th that Stauffenberg came to Peter [Yorck]—I was taken away so that I should be and remain free from all connection with the use of violence. . . . And then your husband is chosen, as a Protestant, to be above all attacked and condemned for his friendship with Catholics, and therefore he stands before Freisler not as a Protestant, not as a big landowner, not as a nobleman, not as a Prussian, not as a German . . . but as a Christian and nothing else. . . . For what a mighty task your husband was chosen: all the trouble the Lord took with him, the infinite detours, the intricate zigzag curves, all suddenly find their explanation in one hour. . . . Everything acquires its meaning in retrospect, which was hidden. Mami and Papi, the brothers and sister, the little sons, Kreisau and its troubles. . . . it has all at last become comprehensible in a single hour. For this one hour the Lord took all that trouble. . . ."

He had to end this long letter, though, as a love letter. "You are not a means God employed to make me who I am, rather you are myself. You are my 13th chapter of the First Letter to the Corinthians. Without this chapter no human being is human. . . . Without you, my love, I would have 'had not charity.' I don't even say that I love you; that wouldn't be right. Rather, you are the part of me that, alone, I would lack. . . . Only together do we constitute a human being. We are . . . symbolically, created as one. That is true, literally true. Therefore, my love, I am certain that you will not lose me on this earth, not for a moment . . .

"One more thing: This letter in many respects complements the report I wrote yesterday. . . . Both together must be made into a leg-

[3]Freisler's odd link to Moltke held him like a judgment of the three Erinyes. The month after the Moltke trial, he was hearing the case against Fabian von Schlabrendorff, the young officer who had once smuggled a bomb onto Hitler's airplane, when an Allied air raid began. Everyone scurried to a bomb shelter in the basement of the courthouse, where, after a direct hit, a beam fell on the judge's head and killed him.

end. . . . I must remain the chief character in it, not because I am or want to be, but because otherwise the story lacks its center. For it is I who was the vessel for which God has taken such infinite trouble.

"Dear heart, my life is finished and I can say of myself: He died in the fullness of years and of life's experience. This doesn't alter the fact that I would gladly go on living and that I would gladly accompany you a bit further on this earth. But then I would need a new task from God. The task for which God made me is done. . . . But I end by saying to you by virtue of the treasure that spoke from me and filled this humble earthen vessel:

> "The Grace of our Lord Jesus Christ
> and the love of God and the fellowship
> of the Holy Spirit be with you all."

Being a practical woman, Freya von Moltke tried desperately to avert what her husband so calmly accepted as God's will. She went to Gestapo headquarters on the Prinz Albrecht Strasse and marched fearlessly into the lions' den. In vain. General Mueller and his lieutenants were as polite as ever, but clemency for Moltke was not part of their plans.

General Mueller "thought I knew nothing about what my husband was doing," she recalls. "He said, 'I am going to separate you from him.' Well, I didn't want that, so I said, 'I am going to raise my sons to honor their father and what he has done.' And he said, 'Of course.'" She also arranged an interview between Mueller and her husband, who apparently thought the authorities might be impressed by his many British contacts as a help to the various peace feelers that were vibrating during these last months of the war. "He didn't think that he had great success in these talks," she says now. She pauses. "It's funny how I tell you about all this with coolness," she says, "but I was not cool then."

She went to see Moltke in Tegel prison, bringing food and clothes and all the news of Kreisau. "Right to the end he was completely free in soul," according to Eugen Gerstenmaier, a fellow Kreisauer who was now a fellow prisoner in Tegel, "friendly, helpful, considerate, a truly free and noble man amid all the trappings of horror."

The trappings of horror did not include any announcement of Moltke's execution. Chaplain Poelchau, who had brought him some letters at about 11 A.M. on January 23, simply noticed at about 1 P.M. that his cell was empty. On making inquiries, he learned that Moltke had been taken to Plötzensee prison, about three miles away, in the north-central part of Berlin. It is a fearful place, preserved now as a kind of shrine to the victims of the July 20 plot, many of whom were executed there. A ticket permits entry to the execution chamber, a white-walled place that still contains rows of metal meat hooks where some of the victims were hanged from wires so that their twitching bodies could be filmed for the pleasure that such a spectacle gave to Adolf Hitler. Even now, one cannot view this slaughterhouse without a shudder of horror and disgust.

Here Moltke died, not yet having reached his thirty-eighth birthday. He was one of ten executed that day.

"They were all burned," Freya von Moltke says. "The ashes were put on the *Rieselfeld*. That is where you have your—the huge septic tanks of the city—what do you call them?—you don't have them here. They make the dirty water and sewage of the city run through obstacles—sand and clay and so forth—and that makes the water clean. And on these obstacles they put all the ashes. That was the dirtiest place they could think of. It shows how much they hated us."

A visitor can hardly resist asking her about her reactions to this blow. "We've talked about what you did but not about what you felt. Was it a feeling of great anger, or fear, or what?"

"It's very difficult to answer this," she says. "You are always influenced by the present, you know, so it is not quite clear anymore exactly what I felt at the time. Of course, it was the worst loss I could suffer, and I did suffer the loss. I have felt always tremendous *solidarity* with Helmuth. But this solidarity—it applies to the other women too—was something very supportive. That was an enormous struggle, and we lost—obviously—we *lost*. But it was still—it was so uplifting that we had fought for something—we thought it was worthwhile— that I didn't feel hatred. Anger was not what I felt. No. Not anger. Always I was sort of proud that the Nazis had realized that we were really their opponents, their true opponents. And it was much more bitter, in my opinion, to lose one's husband as a soldier *for* Hitler than losing him as a soldier *against* Hitler. That was always quite clear to me. Quite clear. . . .

"These people who died, killed by the Nazis—because they died, they sort of redeemed the German soul. I mean, it would be worse, the Germans would be worse off, if nobody had died *against* the Nazis. And I came to accept that this was what my husband was there for. And his friends. That some people have to stand up for principle, and if it comes to the worst, have to die for it. This is a redeeming factor. That in all the strata of its society, Germany did have a few people who resisted National Socialism or were against it or sabotaged it. It was a tiny minority, but I think it is a redeeming factor for the Germans that they existed. And in this respect I have come to accept my husband's fate."

V

Epilogue: Kreisau

TWO DAYS AFTER THE EXECUTION AT THE PLÖTZENSEE PRISON, FREYA VON Moltke took the train back to Kreisau, which represented, in a way, security and stability. These did not last long. "Everything was in confusion," she later wrote of the situation there. "The Russians were pressing westwards at high speed. For several weeks we had the Berghaus and the Schloss and the whole village full of refugees from across the Oder. . . . The whole farmyard was full of other people's vehicles. Something had to be done, but everyone was undecided."

Just after Easter, she decided to set out for the Riesengebirge mountains on the Czech frontier with a friend, Romai Reichwein, and the children of both families, with four horses hauling wagonloads of possessions. After trekking about sixty miles, they found a cottage just across the border, and there they settled down. There they learned that Hitler was dead and the war ending. It seemed hard to believe. "But I knew at once and for sure: That's how it is," Freya recalled. "The Third Reich was finished! Now the Russians would take over Kreisau. I had the feeling that in that case I must be there."

Leading her children back down the mountain, she returned to Kreisau just as the Russians were arriving—"an amazing spectacle, primitive-looking material, carts piled high with booty . . . the men defiant, healthy, strong—triumphant." The Soviet triumph meant violence and destruction, plunder, robbery, and rape. "Every man needs a woman—that's the way it goes," the Soviet commander amiably explained.

The Soviets had also redrawn the borders, seizing eastern Poland for themselves and transferring to the Poles a compensatory slice of eastern Germany, including Kreisau and the surrounding territory of Silesia. Into this territory drifted thousands of Poles from the lost lands to the east, claiming or simply taking over German farmlands and driving the German inhabitants farther west. Survival in those days meant bargaining and maneuvering, swapping, bluffing, scheming, dealing. Freya von Moltke proved a skillful negotiator, though a Polish militia officer once gave her a sharp box on the ear for ordering him out of her house. With a combination of luck and determination, she managed to make a trip to Berlin, where she established contact with Allen Dulles, the U.S. intelligence chief. She also sent messages to friends in Britain, one of whom wrote about her to Foreign Secretary Ernest Bevin. Wheels began to turn.

A few weeks later, help finally reached Kreisau in a large American touring car. It bore a German friend in an American colonel's uniform plus an American interpreter and a chauffeur. "The Poles and the Russians were simply pop-eyed to see an American officer in their midst." This happened just in time, for "the house was full of Poles poking into everything" in search of valuables supposedly hidden in the cellar. A certain amount of swaggering and shouting generally carried the day in that postwar period, and so the Poles were driven away. "It had become clear," Freya finally concluded, "that we could not in the long run stay in Silesia." For one thing, they were running out of coal, and another winter was threatening.

A week or two after the providential American appearance, another car arrived in Kreisau with two British officials from Warsaw. One of them provided some Polish zlotys and promised further help within a month. The survivors could only wait.

"They were very peaceful, lovely autumn days of calm, sunny October weather," Freya wrote. "I felt as though time were once more briefly at a standstill. Nothing disturbed us. . . ." Four weeks to the day after the British diplomats left, a British army truck arrived to carry away the three Moltkes and whatever possessions they could fit into the truck. "The house remained open and inhabited. We drove down the Berghaus hill on the slope facing the Eule. As the car moved forward I asked Caspar, 'When shall we come back again?' 'In a year,' he answered, happy and certain."

It was to be more than thirty years, but the only desire now was to find a sanctuary. "The Americans helped and gave me a passport so I could get out of Berlin to Frankfurt with my two children. I stayed with my brother in Frankfurt for a month, and then my other brother, Carl, got me into Switzerland. So I took the two boys and myself into Switzerland and the children went to Gstaad. My brother Karl had a friend there whom I also knew very well—a German who had left Germany because she disliked the Nazis, and her son had been with me because of the bombs. Always, you know, all human life is like a tapestry. We all interweave. And so through this interweaving, my sons came to Gstaad. And there they stayed for a whole year. But I was restless. . . ."

"My mother parked us, so to say, in Gstaad for a year," says Caspar, who now works in New York for an international investment firm as an executive for a large German chemical firm. He has the Moltke height, well over six feet, the handsomeness, and the easy Moltke charm. "And she traveled. She was touching bases in Western Europe basically, seeing people, speaking to some extent, and she was free to move, with us looked after by a family friend. So we lived with her in Gstaad for that year, and then the South African government said they would allow us to come to South Africa, which was hard in those days. (Germans couldn't move, essentially.)"

"I was very restless because of all that had happened," Freya resumes her story, "and I wanted to go back to Kreisau and warn the people there. . . . And I went back to Berlin and I visited all my friends. And in Berlin I found that my friends the Yorcks had been detained by the Poles when they tried to go to Kreisau. And so I was warned not to go back. And I didn't go back. But I traveled and I saw people, and then I returned to Switzerland. Then my English friends invited me to come to England, and the British advanced me money to pay for my passage to South Africa. Then I became a social worker in South Africa and my children went to school there. All my family followed me. Asta's family and Jowo's family all came to South Africa. And we all lived there rather well, happily. I mean, we all did things and worked hard and got settled, near Cape Town. But we didn't like the politics of South Africa. I didn't want to move my children back to Europe, I wanted to give them a steady childhood, so I stayed until my eldest son finished school. Then I went to Berlin with Konrad, and Caspar went to Oxford to study . . . Konrad didn't want to go to Oxford. He said, 'I want to go to the United States.' I had friends near here so I said, 'You can go to Dartmouth.' I came here in 1960, thirty-two years ago. . . ."

"I did my law degree at Oxford and was called to the bar," Caspar recalls. "Then I decided that I wasn't English enough to spend the rest of my life pleading in front of a British court, and that I didn't want to give up entirely my contacts with Germany, but really didn't feel I wanted to live in Germany. I'd lived too long outside it. But I didn't want to cut my ties to Germany, and I worked for a German company for nearly thirty years. I've done all sorts of things all over the world. I've worked only six of those years in Germany. I spent the rest of the years in other parts of the world, including Australia, where I met my wife. I spent a year in Italy, a couple of years in England. I spent twelve years in Canada and now the last five years in New York. But I still have a home in Montreal. I still feel myself to be German, though I've lived basically in an English environment for most of my life. And my wife is of course English-speaking—we speak English at home, though she's fluent in German. Both my sons are more Anglo-Saxon than they are German. That's almost a tradition of the Moltke family, though I still sense very much that we are a Central European family, Central European in character.

"What the European Community has done for Germany—and it's really a great gift—is that by blending the young, the next German generation, into Europe and making them Europeans, it has watered things down enormously. And therefore I think the present generation growing up—the postwar generation of young Germans—are a much more acceptable group of people to me, even though they still tend to have quirks in their character which make it difficult. . . . You're seeing in Europe now a resentment of foreigners which is frightening. Frightening.

"We have a friend of my younger son's, who's a Canadian and lives in Montreal but has been interested in Germany and has spent the last couple of summers in Germany. He speaks enough German to get by, and he's worked as a waiter on an island in the North Sea. He tells the story of a group of eighteen- or nineteen-year-old German teenagers coming in and, when he started to serve them, saying that they resented being served by a Pole in Germany. And they kept on getting nastier and nastier to him because they said, 'We don't need Polacks to work for us in Germany, we want Germans in there.' And he took it all—took it and said nothing—served them, and then when it was all done, he said to them, in English, 'Now I will tell you one thing. I am now going to the manager and I'm going to complain about your attitudes and if something isn't done, I'm going to the police.' As soon as these young men heard him speak English—North American English—they just walked out. They left the restaurant. But it shows the attitudes that—I think Europe is just at the beginning of the integration of all the other European countries into the community. The Cold War and the Iron Curtain allowed the cozy little European Community of the Treaty of Rome to thrive and to develop well. It's never been tested. And the tests are coming. Tests are going to come in this decade. And the tests are not going to be easy.

"I'm not a Socialist, I'm really a democrat. But I miss the decline of socialism. Though it didn't work, I think that we needed a left-radical alternative, and we haven't got it at present. And I think that's a disaster. We've got to find a humanist theory other than the one we've got at present. The capitalist victory is not good for us over the long run. And if it finds its counterpart on the right, which is a considerable risk, I think we're in for trouble. I think I see radicalization of the right—nationalist radicalization. Certainly in eastern Europe. And if the economy doesn't pull us out, it may leak into western Europe too. Yes. We're looking at a huge Europe of lots of nationalities competing with one another, competing for economic well-being. And I don't think they can all make it. The Serbs and Croats can't make it, Ukrainians, Romanians. . . . How are you going to keep them out? I don't think Europe can cope with all that. Will it all break down again? I'm fearful, yes. The Common Market was always an economic unit, never a political and emotional unit. People who hoped it would grow into that were mistaken. And I think that the larger it gets, the more mistaken they are.

"I feel at home where my family is. And they are everywhere, and I feel connected with their problems. . . ."

But Kreisau, now part of Poland and therefore outside the official boundaries of the European Community? What did it feel like to revisit the childhood home after more than thirty years of moving from country to country? Did he remember it clearly?

"I did, yes, because I was old enough—I was seven, going on eight—and I did remember places. I remembered them well. I said to my mother when I first went back, 'There's a clay pit there where I used to catch frogs.' She said, 'It should be here.' I said, 'No, it's a bit further down the road.' And so it was. It still had frogs in it. The *Berghaus* was much changed. They had taken parts of it out. In particular, they had taken away a very nice and extensive terrace that had collapsed. The family used to live a great deal on that terrace. And the old *Schloss* was in ruins. . . .

"Do I have a feeling of loss about it? Of course I do, but my life has gone on in other ways. I think it was a happy and important place for my family, and I am melancholy when I think of my relatives who are buried there, but my life has gone on in other ways and I live in a different time."

• • •

If Germany were still a monarchy, and if its boundaries extended to include Silesia, and if the aristocracy still owned its old estates, Kreisau and its surrounding lands would presumably belong to Helmuth Nicholas von Moltke, the oldest son of Helmuth Caspar. Since Germany is distinctly not a monarchy and its borders do not include Silesia, Nicholas von Moltke has been working in New York as a junior executive for the Philip Morris Company as an assistant manager in the field of promotions. "I put together a couple of sweepstakes a year—'Win a chance to go to the Indianapolis 500'—where we take consumers there. Before that I ran sponsorship of racing for

Marlboro, negotiating the contracts with the race car drivers. Handling the advertising, negotiating with the teams, organizing our sales force to entertain guests there. . . ." As his job suggests, he is cheerful and energetic. He is well over six feet, one of the tallest Moltkes, but rather stocky, with a full head of curly brown hair. He has been to Kreisau just once, in the early 1980s.

"It was a little bit shocking," he says. "I mean, it's not what you would expect. It was very, very run-down, and it just didn't seem to have any significance to it. Meaning that because it was so run-down it didn't look grand, or didn't look like it was an important place in history. And it really was. I was extremely moved."

"Did people tell you specific things about what Kreisau had been like in the old days?"

"A little bit. My father would tell stories about how they would chase chickens through the yard to catch dinner, or stories about getting in trouble for climbing on the roof, or things like that. But the things I remember most vividly were, you know, the gravesite of the field marshal, the steps of the main house, the fields, the beautiful fields—you know, fixed things, things that truly belong there and have always been there."

"What is your actual nationality, legally?"

"I'm Australian and German, dual citizenship. I was born in Australia when my father traveled there with his work and met my mother down there and got married. I lived in England for a while, in the States for a while, in Germany for a while. I got to Canada when I was about eleven and stayed there till about the age of seventeen. Then after Canada, I went to school in Germany for a year before coming back to the States. I went to Middlebury and studied film and economics. I've been in America since 1984, so seven years now."

"What is your sense of yourself in terms of nationality? Do you feel German?"

"My roommates always joke and say that I'm a citizen of the world. If I'm pressed, I'd be Australian first and foremost. A couple of things I like about Australia. Australians are more outgoing, less serious, and those are characteristics that I think my mother and I both have. Whereas my father is much more serious, much more, I think, much harder to read. I feel those are German characteristics, or maybe European."

"Is being a von Moltke important to you?"

"It is. It is. I'm proud of being a von Moltke, but I don't want to necessarily create my identity out of that. I want to create an identity for *Nicholas* von Moltke. I want to discover myself, discover what my strengths and weaknesses are as an individual before becoming too involved in what this whole von Moltke family is. That may be a reason why I'm comfortable here in the United States, because being a von Moltke doesn't have a lot of weight or pull or significance here."

"What does being a von Moltke stand for?"

"Well, it stands for great achievement. It stands for people who have gone as far as sacrificing their lives for something they truly and honestly believe in. It stands for individuality too. I mean, all the people of renown in the family are people who did things that were truly, truly unique, and they were recognized as individuals. That part of being a von Moltke I'm proud of. Because I certainly want to be known, I want to create—I would like to be significant in some aspect, some positive aspect, having done something good—I would like to be known for that. As a von Moltke that's done some good. But I would like to be known as Nicholas von Moltke who's done some good.

"I'm not sure what I want to do, you know, but I think I want to own and manage a consumer-products company myself. That's what appeals to me, running that company from the production through to the sale of the items. I'm just fascinated and intrigued by producing things and selling them."

"Is this all in an American context?"

"Not necessarily. I, like my father, am very intrigued by what's going on in eastern Europe right now, and I think there's a lot of potential over there. And I do want to be able to—you know, I speak four languages, English and German and French and Italian, in descending order of fluency. I would like to be able to use those languages, to be able to—sort of use what I know about the European culture to, you know, create something over there maybe for sale in the United States—if a global market allows that. That really interests me."

"Do you have any children?"

"No, I'm not married."

"But do you have any sense that you're going to get married and you're going to produce little von Moltkes—?"

"Yes. Yes. Yes, most definitely."

"And you're going to teach them—are you going to teach them your kind of individuality or are you going to—?"

"I do want them to understand that they are von Moltkes. I think there are certain responsibilities that I'm burdened with. Burdened is not the right word. That I have to do, but also want to perform. I think that I have to most definitely understand European history and the history of the von Moltke family and how we were involved in the shaping of European history. The significance of the sacrifice that my grandfather made. That I think is extremely important. That should not go unnoticed."

• • •

The Moltkes' feeling of political obligations became particularly clear in the fall of 1989, when West Germany's Chancellor Helmut Kohl was planning a state visit to Poland and decided that he would like to have one of Helmuth James Moltke's grandsons join him. This was actually the idea of a Dr. Reismuller, the publisher of a Bavarian newspaper, whose grandson was a friend of Nicholas von Moltke's younger brother, James, a student at Oxford.

"What happened," says James, a handsome youth with wavy dark hair, "was that when it had been announced that Kohl and the Polish premier were going to Kreisau, Dr. Reismuller rang the chancellor's office and said that he knew one descendant who was in Europe, and wouldn't it be a good idea for him to go along. Now I had taken a week off to go to France for some fun, and I came back to find my friends waiting for me in the quad at New College, saying that I must call Dr. Reismuller. So I did, and he told me what was going on, and said would I go? My first reaction was that I'd have to ask my grandmother because I know that decisions like that aren't made individually. So I rang my grandmother and told her what the news had been, and she said immediately, 'It's very clear, you can't go.' I spoke to Dr. Reismuller again and said that was my grandmother's position, and he said, 'Would that change if it were an official invitation as opposed to just an unofficial invitation?' I said I didn't think that would make a change, but I didn't know. I spoke to my grandmother again, and the day wore on, and it wasn't clear what was going to happen. . . ."

"It all happened in this room," says Freya von Moltke, sitting in the living room of her house in northern Vermont. "It would have been the normal thing for James to call his father—my grandchildren are all on very good terms with their parents—but somehow he couldn't get him that morning so he phoned me. He said, 'I have been told that I may be asked to go to Kreisau with Kohl. Am I supposed to do that?' And quite spontaneously, I said, 'James, don't do that. You know, you will have many opportunities of going to Kreisau later on, surely, and I don't think you should go with the German government because the Poles will think we still have claims on the property, and we have none.' That was what I said, and no more."

"In the evening, I was about to go to a class," James continues, "and a porter came and got me from my room and said that there was a telephone call. I went through the secretary to the secretary, and then the secretary, and then Kohl came on, and he explained what was going to happen. The bishop was going to be there, and the premier was going to be there, and they were going to hold a *Versöhnungsmesse,* a Mass of reconciliation, at Kreisau. He also explained what the content was going to be vis-à-vis Kreisau and the Oder-Neisse line. I repeated my grandmother's comments on why I wasn't to go, that our family held that the Oder-Neisse line was now the border of Germany, and we didn't want to give the impression of that not being the case. Secondly, we didn't want to create the impression in the Polish community that we had any claim to Kreisau. I said that if he wanted a clearer explanation of those reasons, he'd have to speak with my grandmother. So he said, could I get him in touch with my grandmother—they'd been trying. I then managed that—she was in the garden when he was trying to ring her—and they sorted it out. And very amicably."

"Poor James." Freya sighs. "It was a trial, and he stood up to it very well, because he said to Herr Bundeskanzler, 'My family says I shouldn't go with you.' I mean, it's quite brave, I think, to say that. Much braver than what I did. Then Kohl called me here and said, 'Why are you not letting your grandson go with me? The people will all wonder why I don't have a von Moltke with me.' And I said, 'I accept the fact that Kreisau is now Polish, and we do not have any claims for Kreisau anymore, and I don't want the Poles to think that we do.'

"And then he said—he was very nice; I really have a fond feeling for Kohl since that telephone conversation because he said, 'I understand you completely. Yes, I respect your view. But what shall I say to all the people who say, "Why don't you have a von Moltke with you?"'" Then I said, 'You must say that the von Moltkes only come when the Poles invite them.'

"And then comes the lucky stroke. Because when it was all over, I had a call here, and the man from New York, from one of those television stations, wanted to come and have an interview with me. But on the past, you know, not on the present. But I was still excited about the present. I said, 'Oh, you're coming because of Kohl talking to me.' He said, 'Kohl talking to you?' And he became interested, so he came here, and I told him the story, and he put it over the news, so it got into the German news. And of course they used it politically, and I was happy that it was used politically because I am of the opinion that the Germans have to accept what happened to them through making the war, the Hitler war."

"I think the Poles want the family to be in Kreisau and play a role in the building of the conference center," James says, "but I don't think they do that to a man, and I think they have a not-unambiguous position about it. So my grandmother plays that very quietly, and in an unassuming fashion, although she was named the honorary chairperson of the group. She doesn't impose any views of her own on what they do. She tries to be a guiding hand or a mediator."

When the word finally reached Poland that the von Moltke family would welcome an invitation from the Poles, an invitation eventually came in July 1990. "That was the trip that was organized for my great aunt Asta's birthday by her husband, Henssel," James says, referring to Helmuth James's only sister. "There were seventeen of us—only four Moltkes, or something, including Asta—the rest were Hülsens and . . . members of the sort of larger family. We went as a group and were there at the official handing-over of the Hof and four hectares to the Kreisau *Stiftung* [Foundation]. I was there subsequently two more times that year, always privately, and I went to one of the *Stiftung*'s conferences the following May.

"I don't really understand what draws people to territories, and what leads people to fight for them, but I did find that I liked the country around Kreisau. I think the countryside—the rolling hills of that area—I found that very beautiful and appealing, yes. And I found the upstairs in the *Schloss*, the heights of the children marked on the wall, that sort of experience was nice and gave me an affinity to the place, but not an affinity that is—I wouldn't go and live there. But I have to think what's going on there now is absolutely—is excellent. Rebuilding Kreisau into a conference center, I think, is very good."

• • •

A question remains.

Why is Field Marshal von Moltke not lying in the empty mausoleum that he built to contain his coffin and that of the gentle Marie?

Freya von Moltke smiles and shakes her head. "I tell you the whole story," she says.

"You see, in the retreat, the German army had sort of set up house in Kreisau. They came to see me, and they said there was pressure from the east and they would have to leave, and they wanted to take the field marshal with them. I saw the future more realistically than they did and felt that if they took the coffin away, they would have to leave it somewhere in order to get away themselves, alive."

The army officers wanted to take not only the field marshal's coffin but also the ceremonial regalia that he had saved, including a saber that rested on top of his coffin, the black robe of a medieval knightly order, various clothes, portraits, and a pink porcelain wig stand for his wig. Though the countess refused to let them take his coffin, she allowed them this regalia. And to her annoyance, the saber did eventually turn up in Warsaw, where it was acquired by some diplomat. When the Moltke Foundation in Berlin heard of this, it requested the return of the saber for its collection of Moltke memorabilia. The diplomat put a rather high price on his acquisition, the foundation went to court, and bitter emotions were stirred.

So the coffins—"big, heavy, oak coffins, with no names on them"—remained in Kreisau. "But since there was the prospect of the Poles and the Russians coming, I suggested that they should put the coffins into the graves that had already been prepared, actually for my father-in-law [who had died in 1939]. Before my father-in-law's coffin arrived in Kreisau, our foreman had already started digging a grave. Then my husband said, 'This is not where I want my father to go. This is where I myself and my wife will go, in the future. And my father is to go next to my mother. So please make another grave there, and we will put my father there.' And they did.

"About the started hole, my husband said, 'Why don't you now get it ready so that it can be used later on?' So they put bricks into it and made a little brick chamber for our coffins to go in there in the future. And then they put wooden two-by-fours—the heavier ones, big wooden beams, right there and closed it up. So when the army wanted to hide the field marshal, I said, 'Why not put him into that grave for my husband and myself?' And they did. They had lots of sergeants and they carried the field marshal down there in that coffin. It was done quite ceremoniously. All the sergeants carried him down there, and they stood there at attention, and they put him quite ceremoniously into this grave of ours. There was room for two so they took his wife and put her next to him. And then there was still his sister. They tried to put that in there too, but she didn't fit in. She stuck out, you know, and they couldn't close the grave. So they took her up again and left her all alone in the chapel. Then they put the beams over the grave again. And that was it.

"Now when I came back to Kreisau thirty years later for the first time, there was a hole and no coffins in it anymore. The beams were there, and you could—but we had no tools, no nothing—and it was completely overgrown. You know what weeds do in one year in your garden, so you can imagine what weeds do in thirty years. Now it's all been cleared, but when we went there for the first time, it was a complete jungle, and we could hardly find the big stones over the graves.

"So now it was empty, and where were the remains? We don't

know. The stories are all different, and I think we still don't know the complete truth. But one Pole who lives there now, and who had come to live there while we were still there during the war, and who had been treated very well by the Germans there, and therefore took over in a very friendly way one of the farms and stayed there all his life—he told me this story about the Gypsies. He said that nobody from the village ever touched any graves, and he was very positive about it—that I should not have such a bad opinion of the people who lived there, the Poles. Nobody would touch the cemetery. But strangers came—that was the first version. I didn't know who the strangers were. When I saw him again, he gave me the version that Gypsies had come to stay on that hill for quite a while. . . ."

That any Gypsies should have survived the war in southern Poland seems something of a miracle. The Nazis pursued and exterminated them almost as relentlessly as they pursued the Jews. All this remains somewhat mysterious. Just as nobody knows exactly where the Gypsies came from, or why they spread over the whole world, nobody can explain the Nazis' lust to kill them. One theory is that they were somehow connected with the Jews, but Himmler seems to have adopted a quite different theory that they were descended from some ancient Germanic tribe that had preserved a unique racial "purity." Confined in concentration camps, the Gypsies were often treated with exceptional cruelty. At Buchenwald, for example, numbers of them had their hands tied and then were set upon by savage attack dogs, which tore them to pieces. At Auschwitz, they were kept in a relatively peaceful isolation, though subject, because of Himmler's morbid interest in their racial origins, to weird medical experiments. When Himmler lost interest, he simply ordered them all killed, and so, on the night of August 2, 1944, some 4,000 Gypsies in Auschwitz all went to the gas chambers. All in all, the total of massacred Gypsies has been estimated at more than 500,000, but nobody really knows. Nobody knows how many there once were or how many of them survived.

Perhaps there never was a family of Gypsies that turned up in Kreisau at the end of the war and took shelter in the brick-walled grave that contained the decaying skeletons of Field Marshal von Moltke and his wife, but that was the legend recounted by one Polish peasant who lived there throughout these years of turmoil. "And suddenly he—the story made some sense," says Freya von Moltke. "The Gypsies traditionally earn a living by repairing pots, and you need metal to repair pots. It's the old-fashioned way, which of course nobody does anymore in the West—they discard the pots and buy new ones. But in olden times, you used your pots as long as you lived. And if they had holes, you had them repaired with metal. And the Gypsies did it. For this they needed the kind of metal which was used for the inner part of very important coffins. Very important coffins had metal linings if you wanted to preserve the remains, and of course the field marshal had such metal in his coffin. This the Gypsies were looking for, so it's understandable that they opened the coffins. They were not very reverent to what they found inside, but we don't know what they did with what they found inside. Nothing is left. My Pole said that one of those modern machines, a bulldozer, came to push everything into the hill, but I have my doubts that such a machine worked on the hill. It didn't look to me as if such a machine ever went up there. So what has happened? I don't know. Nothing is left. That's the story."

We can only assume, as the Moltke family assumes, that the field marshal's bones ended, like the bones of so many of his soldiers in Austria and France, fertilizing the weeds that grow so abundantly on a quiet hillside in Poland.

A Note on Sources

Field Marshal Helmuth von Moltke was one of those people who wrote things down, published much of what he wrote, and saved much of what he did not publish. Eight volumes of his *Gesammelte Schriften and Denkwürdigkeiten* appeared in Berlin in 1891–1892. Thirteen volumes of *Militärische Werke* appeared in Berlin between 1892 and 1912.

Much of what was contained in his desk and files at the War Ministry in Berlin ended in the army archives in Potsdam. When the U.S. army arrived in 1945, it "liberated" these papers and carted them off to the National Archives in Washington. There they were eventually microfilmed, and copies of these microfilms may now be purchased for a modest $23 per reel. There are six reels of microfilm of Moltke papers as well as many more from such military leaders as Scharnhorst, Roon, and so on.

The discovery of unpublished Moltke papers in the military archives seems to promise a great treasure, but this large collection is unfortunately of limited interest. It contains large numbers of insignificant newspaper clippings, letters from distant admirers, anniversary messages from patriotic organizations, and so on. Most of the material is written in proudly illegible German script.

Since most Americans read German only with difficulty, if at all, I have preferred to cite German texts in English translations wherever they are available. Many of Moltke's writings were translated at about the time of his death. A valuable collection of his letters to his mother and brothers was published by Harper & Brothers in 1892 in a translation by Clara Bell and Henry W. Fischer. Harper also published in 1893 a two-volume collection entitled *Essays, Speeches, and Memoirs*. The first volume includes Moltke's long essays on Belgium, Poland, and France; the second contains his speeches to the Reichstag, the funeral service by Chaplain Richter, and memoirs of Moltke by various friends and relatives. A companion volume called *Moltke, His Life and Character, Sketched in Journals, Letters, Memoirs, A Novel, and Autobiographical Notes* was compiled and translated by Mary Herms and published by Harper in 1892. This contains Moltke's novel, *The Two Friends*, as well as a variety of biographical materials.

Many of Moltke's military writings have remained in print, presumably as texts for military students. Thus *Strategy: Its Theory and Application: The Wars for German Unification, 1866–1871* was published in London by His Majesty's Stationery Office in 1907 and again in 1971 by the Greenwood Press of Westport, Connecticut, which describes itself as a division of the Congressional Information Service, for the West Point Military Library. This is simply a collection of Moltke's plans, orders, and memoranda, what the German text calls *"Dienstschriften,"* literally service writings. His *Franco-German War of 1870–71* was published by Harper & Brothers in 1892, and republished by Howard Fertig Inc. in 1988. This account, which was written during Moltke's last years of retirement at Kreisau, purports to be "a popular history" but depends heavily on the general staff's official history of the war.

See also *Moltke on the Art of War, Selected Writings,* edited by Daniel J. Hughes (1993). For further analysis of these writings, see *Moltke, Schlieffen, and Prussian War Planning,* by Arden Bucholz (1991). And for one specific aspect of his work, see *The Rise of Rail-Power in War and Conquest,* by Edwin A. Pratt (1915).

The background and context for Moltke's military writings can be found in a number of interesting works. *The Makers of Modern Strategy, Military Thought from Machiavelli to Hitler* (1944), edited by Edward Mead Earle with the collaboration of Gordon A. Craig and Felix Gilbert, contains admirable studies of Frederick the Great and Clausewitz. The essay on Moltke and Schlieffen is by Hajo Holborn. *The Art of War, Waterloo to Mons* (1974), by William McElwee, contains valuable insights, as do *A History of Militarism* (1937), by Alfred Vagts, and *Strategy* (1954), by B. H. Liddell Hart. *The Sword and the Scepter, The Problem of Militarism in Germany* (1954–1968), by Gerhard Ritter, is an authoritative combination of deep scholarship and personal involvement. Walter Goerlitz's *History of the German General Staff, 1657–1945* (1953) is the definitive account of its subject. My favorites of all books in this field, though, are *The Nemesis of Power, The German Army in Politics, 1918–1945* (1964), by John W. Wheeler-Bennett, and *The Politics of the Prussian Army, 1640–1945* (1955), by Gordon A. Craig.

There exists also a useful and rather engaging collection of letters, *Moltkes Briefe an seine Braut und Frau,* edited by Max Horst (undated), published by the Deutsche Bibliothek Verlagsgesellschaft in Berlin.

Books about Moltke are numerous but often heavier than they need to be. Perhaps the most valuable, in German, is *Moltke,* by Eberhard Kessel, published in Stuttgart in 1957. See also *Moltke und der Staat,* by Rudolf Stadelmann, Krefeld, 1950. Among English biographies, the best is probably *Moltke,* by Lieutenant-Colonel F. E. Whitton (1921), though its emphasis is chiefly on refighting the great battles. The worst is probably *Moltke, A Biographical and Critical Study,* by William O'Connor Morris (1893, reprinted in 1971). Somewhere in between come *The Early Life of Moltke,* by Spencer Wilkinson (1913), which is really only a twenty-eight-page transcript of an Oxford lecture on Moltke's youthful trials as far as his trip to Asia Minor, and *Moltke in His Home,* by Friedrich August Dressler (1907), a memoir by a musician who enjoyed social visits with the field marshal.

Considerably more valuable are two detailed military studies, *The Battle of Königgrätz, Prussia's Victory over Austria, 1866,* by Gordon A. Craig (1964), and *The Franco-Prussian War,* by Michael Howard (1961). Professor Howard states in his preface that a bibliography on this war that was compiled in 1898 already listed 7,000 titles, but since the essence of all this may be found in Howard's own study, no attempt at omniscience needs to be made here. I will only mention that I have also been helped by *The Fall of Paris,* by Alistair Horne (1965), and *Napoleon III and His Carnival Empire,* by John Bierman (1988). For a detailed study of the preliminaries to Sedan, see *Gravelotte-St. Privat 1870,* by Philipp Elliot-Wright (1993).

On Clausewitz, the basic text is *On War,* edited and translated by Michael Howard and Peter Paret, with additional commentary by Bernard Brodie, handsomely published by the Princeton University Press in 1976. Clausewitz's account of his adventures in Russia may be found in his *Historical and Political Writings,* edited and translated by Peter Paret and Daniel Moran (1992). Paret has also written an admirable biography, *Clausewitz and the State: The Man, His Theories, and His Times* (1976), but this should not overshadow a much smaller but no less admirable biography by Michael Howard, simply entitled *Clausewitz* (1983).

The literature on Bismarck is of course enormous. I have been much impressed and much helped by the recent three-volume biography, *Bismarck and the Development of Germany,* by Otto Pflanze (1990). I have relied a lot, though, on earlier and simpler accounts, notably *Bismarck,* by Edward Crankshaw (1981), *Bismarck, The Man and the Statesman,* by A. J. P. Taylor (1955), and *Bismarck and the German Empire,* by Erich Eyck (1950). All of these, and particularly the first two, are marked by a rather patronizing hostility to Bismarck, but his achievements are nonetheless clear. The chancellor's fascinating memoirs were published as *Bismarck, The Man and the Statesman, Being the Reflections and Reminiscences of Otto, Prince von Bismarck, Written and Dictated by Himself After His Retirement from Office,* translated by A. J. Butler (1899).

Among the memoirs of the participants in 1870, Moltke's own account of his victory is *The Franco-German War of 1870–71 (Geschichte des deutsch-französischen Krieges von 1870–1871).* I have also used *The War Diary of Emperor Frederick III, 1870–1871* (1927), *Journals of Field-Marshal Count von Blumenthal for 1866 and 1870–71* (1903), and *Personal Memoirs of Philip Henry Sheridan* (1904).

Nietzsche's experiences during the crisis of 1870 turn up in several collections of his letters, such as *The Nietzsche-Wagner Correspondence* (1921), *Selected Letters of Friedrich Nietzsche* (1969), and *Nietzsche, A Self-Portrait from his Letters* (1971). See also *Nietzsche, A Critical Life* (1980), by Ronald Hayman, and *The Portable Nietzsche,* edited by Walter Kaufmann (1954).

For general background on German history during this period, I have relied chiefly on Hajo Holborn's three-volume *History of Modern Germany* (1969); *German History, 1770–1866,* by James J. Sheehan (1989) and *Ger-*

many 1866–1945 (1978), by Gordon A. Craig; both the latter are part of the Oxford History of Modern Europe. See also *The Origins of Modern Germany* (1984), by Geoffrey Barraclough; *Dreams and Delusions, the Drama of German History* (1987), by Fritz Stern, and, for a very Teutonic view, *History of Germany in the Nineteenth Century,* by Heinrich von Treitschke, edited by Gordon A. Craig (1975, originally published in German in 1879 and in English in 1914).

For more on the Napoleonic era, see *The Age of German Liberation* (1957), by Friedrich Meinecke; for more on 1848, see *1848: The Revolution of the Intellectuals* (1946), by Louis Namier, *The Revolutions of 1848* (1969), by William Langer, and *1848: The Revolutionary Tide in Europe* (1974), by Peter N. Stearns.

James Joll's *The Origins of the World War* (1984) is probably the best of the many versions of this complex event. Joll endeavors to separate military, diplomatic, economic, and psychological causes and finds that none accounts for everything. Winston Churchill's *The World Crisis* (1923–1931) provides a grandly dramatic account. For a more recent survey, see *The First World War, A Complete History,* by Martin Gilbert (1994).

Fritz Fischer caused an uproar some years ago by arguing, first in *Germany's Aims in the First World War* (1967) and then in *War of Illusions, German Policies from 1911 to 1914* (1975), that Germany deliberately provoked the war in order to win hegemony over Europe, and it has been widely said that Fischer's views are now generally accepted. At the risk of sounding eccentric, I venture to say that I find Fischer's thesis unconvincing. It seems to me based on the very debatable idea that everything said by Ludendorff (and, to some extent, Moltke) represented cast-iron German policy.

A related fallacy—that every nationalistic statement by a German is a forerunner of Nazism—underlies *From Bismarck to Hitler, The Problem of Continuity in German History,* a collection of tendentious statements amassed and edited by John C. G. Röhl (1970). For a broader survey see *The War Plans of the Great Powers, 1880–1914,* a collection of essays edited by Paul M. Kennedy, which includes valuable studies by L. C. F. Turner on the Schlieffen Plan and N. Stone on the prewar correspondence between Moltke and Conrad. The authoritative account of the Schlieffen Plan is *The Schlieffen Plan, Critique of a Myth,* by Gerhard Ritter (1958), which is notable for, among other things, including the full text of the plan. Also of interest on the origins of the war is *The Fateful Alliance: France, Russia, and the Coming of the First World War,* by George F. Kennan (1984).

General Moltke's own views on this and other matters have long been available in his *Erinnerungen, Briefe, Dokumente* (1922), a collection put together by his widow, Eliza von Moltke. Isabel Hull has complained, in *The Entourage of Kaiser Wilhelm II,* that "the brutal editing of these documents by his wife and Rudolf Steiner calls into question the reliability of these entries." The documents in the 1922 collection, as well as a good many more, were republished in 1994 by the Swiss firm of Perseus in a two-volume collection titled *Helmuth von Moltke, 1848–1916, Dokumente zu seinem Leben und Wirken.* A widely praised biography of the emperor, which I find somewhat too appreciative, is *The Kaiser and His Times,* by Michael Balfour (1964). More far-reaching studies are included in *Kaiser Wilhelm II: New Interpretations,* a collection edited by John C. G. Röhl and Nicolaus Sombart (1982).

A number of other participants have recorded their recollections of these great days. *My War Memories, 1914–1916,* by General Ludendorff (1919) describes the capture of Liège as only Ludendorff could have described it. Alexander von Kluck gives a rather unclear account of his maneuverings in *The March on Paris and the Battle of the Marne* (1920). Sir Edward Spears's *Liaison, 1914* (1930) provides an invaluable chronicle of the French defenders through the eyes of an admiring but often exasperated ally. Marc Bloch's characteristically lucid version is in *Memoirs of War, 1914–15* (1980). For a careful and detailed analysis of the military events, Robert Asprey has provided *The First Battle of the Marne* (1962) as well as *The German High Command at War, Hindenburg and Ludendorff Conduct World War I* (1991). See also *The Real War, 1914–1918,* by Captain B. H. Liddell Hart (1930). Many colorful details about the start of the war can be found in Frederic Morton's *Thunder at Twilight* (1989) and also in James Cameron's *1914* (1959). Alexander Solzhenitsyn covers the same ground in his *August 1914* (1989), but this is distinctly not one of the master's masterpieces.

There are good portraits of Moltke and his chief antagonists in *The Swordbearers, Supreme Command in the First World War* (1964) by Correlli Barnett. Trevor Ravenscroft's peculiar version of the origins of the war is *The Spear of Destiny, The Occult Power Behind the Spear Which Pierced the Side of Christ* (1973).

In a class by itself is Barbara Tuchman's *The Guns of August* (1962), which won prizes and popularity for its skillfully narrated story of the war's first months. Mrs. Tuchman's fervent admiration for Joffre and the Poilu is admirable, but her angry contempt for their adversaries is much less so. Rather similar is Rebecca West's lively but completely wrongheaded account of the assassination of Archduke Franz Ferdinand at Sarajevo in *Black Lamb and Grey Falcon, A Journey Through Yugoslavia* (1940).

The basic text on Helmuth James von Moltke is *Letters to Freya* (1990), originally published in 1988 as *Briefe an Freya, 1939–1945,* then skillfully edited and translated by Beate Ruhm von Oppen, who has subsequently edited a volume of letters by Moltke's mother to her family in South Africa. *Letters to Freya* is only a selection, but a comprehensive selection, about one-third of approximately 1,600 letters that Moltke wrote to his wife from 1929 until his death in 1945. Many of the later ones had to be smuggled out of prison, and she kept them hidden in the beehives at Kreisau.

An excellent biography of Moltke was written by Michael Balfour and Julian Frisby, *Helmuth von Moltke, a Leader Against Hitler* (1972). They both knew Moltke and have benefited from the cooperation of Freya von Moltke. Their book includes her own account of leaving Kreisau. The other main work on Moltke is *German Resistance to Hitler, Count von Moltke and the Kreisau Circle,* by Ger van Roon (1971). Roon, a Dutch scholar, includes many of the Kreisau documents, not available elsewhere.

The literature on the German opposition to Hitler is rather large and varies widely in focus since different authors have selected different figures (sometimes including themselves) as their central characters. See, for example, *The German Resistance: Carl Goerdeler's Struggle Against Tyranny*, by Gerhard Ritter (1958); *The Von Hassell Diaries, The Story of the Forces Against Hitler Inside Germany, 1938–1944*, by Ulrich von Hassell (1947); *To the Bitter End*, by Hans Bernd Gisevius (1947); *Canaris, Hitler's Master Spy*, by Heinz Höhne (1979); *Master Spy, The Incredible Story of Admiral Wilhelm Canaris, Who, While Hitler's Chief of Intelligence, Was a Secret Ally of the British*, by Ian Colvin (1951), and *The Secret War Against Hitler*, by Fabian von Schlabrendorff (1946); *Berlin Underground, 1938–1945*, by Ruth Andreas-Friedrich (1947); and *The White Rose, Munich 1942–1943*, by Inge Scholl. For a more eclectic attempt to include almost everyone, see *Conscience in Revolt, Sixty-four Stories of Resistance in Germany, 1933–45*, by Annedore Leber (1954). Some of these figures also appear in *The Restless Conscience*, a searching documentary on the resistance by Hava Bellers, shown on Public Television in 1992.

For a more general approach, I am indebted to *German Resistance to Hitler*, by Peter Hoffman (1988). See also *The Flame of Freedom, The German Struggle Against Hitler*, by Eberhard Zeller (1967); *The German Resistance to Hitler*, by Hermann Graml, Hans Mommsen, Hans-Joachim Reichardt, and Ernst Wolf (1970), and *An Honourable Defeat, A History of the German Resistance to Hitler, 1933–1945*, by Anton Gill (1994). On a more specialized track, there is useful material in *Target Hitler, The Plots to Kill Adolf Hitler*, by James P. Duffy and Vincent L. Ricci (1992). This becomes still more specialized in *Germans Against Hitler, July 20, 1944*, by Hans Royce, Erich Zimmermann, and Hans-Adolf Jacobsen (1969). For an interesting collection of resistance documents, including several from Kreisau, see *Deutscher Widerstand, 1938–1944*, edited by Bodo Scheurig (1969). The generals on both sides of the July 20 plot are ably presented in *Hitler's Generals*, a collection of short biographies edited by Correlli Barnett (1989). The best account of army machinations, though, is still Wheeler-Bennett's *Nemesis of Power*. See also *The German Generals Talk* (1948), by B. H. Liddell Hart. My version of Hitler's rise to power comes mainly from William Shirer's indispensable history, *The Rise and Fall of The Third Reich* (1960).

Although I interviewed Freya von Moltke several times myself, I have quoted briefly from the chapter on her in *Frauen, German Women Recall the Third Reich*, by Alison Owings (1993).

My account of the Jews of Denmark comes mainly from *Rescue in Denmark* by Harold Flender (1963). The Nazi version of the destruction of the Warsaw Ghetto is in *The Stroop Report, The Jewish Quarter of Warsaw Is No More!*, a collection of the official reports by General Jürgen Stroop (1960).

The story of the Manns' flight from Nazi Germany is well told in *The Brothers Mann*, by Nigel Hamilton (1978). That of Gropius may be found in *Gropius*, by Reginald Isaacs (1991), and that of Brecht in *Bertolt Brecht*,

His Life, His Art, His Times, by Frederic Ewen (1967). The latest appearance of the von Bülows in history is well told in *The Von Bülow Affair* (1983), by William Wright. Dorothy Thompson's brief encounter with Moltke is in *Dorothy Thompson, A Legend in Her Time* (1973), by Marion K. Sanders.

Like many who write about the German resistance to Hitler, I owe a debt of gratitude to Freya von Moltke, who gave generously of her time and energy, first in being repeatedly interviewed, then in reviewing the manuscript and correcting several errors. For similar efforts on a smaller scale, I owe thanks to Veronica Jochum von Moltke. Research assistance in Berlin was provided by Hannelore Wonschick.

I must also give thanks to Joan Fell and her staff at the Locust Valley Public Library for tracking down many of the books cited in this bibliography. And to Dorothy Marcinek for transcribing interviews and retyping the entire manuscript. And to Molly Friedrich for her enthusiastic work as agent.

Index